A Wetback in Reverse

Hunting for an American in the Wilds of Mexico

A Memoir by
Frederick Martin-Del-Campo

CCB Publishing
British Columbia, Canada

A Wetback in Reverse:
Hunting for an American in the Wilds of Mexico

Copyright © 2013 by Frederick Martin-Del-Campo
ISBN-13   978-1-77143-109-5
First Edition

Library and Archives Canada Cataloguing in Publication
Martin-Del-Campo, Frederick, 1965-, author
A wetback in reverse : hunting for an American in the wilds of Mexico
/ by Frederick Martin-Del-Campo. -- First edition.
Issued in print and electronic formats.
ISBN 978-1-77143-109-5 (pbk.).--ISBN 978-1-77143-110-1 (pdf)
Additional cataloguing data available from Library and Archives Canada

Contact Frederick Martin-Del-Campo at: snoobula@gmail.com

Cover artwork credit: Bryan Garcia Mitre, Randy Garcia Mitre, & Laura Mitre Rivera

Note: Elements within this memoir have been fictionalized in the interest of privacy and the author's creative license.

Extreme care has been taken by the author to ensure that all information presented in this book is accurate and up to date at the time of publishing. Neither the author nor the publisher can be held responsible for any errors or omissions. Additionally, neither is any liability assumed for damages resulting from the use of the information contained herein.

All rights reserved. No part of this publication may be reproduced, stored in a retrieval system or transmitted in any form or by any means, electronic, mechanical, photocopying, recording or otherwise without the express written permission of the publisher. Printed in the United States of America, the United Kingdom and Australia.

Publisher: CCB Publishing
              British Columbia, Canada
              www.ccbpublishing.com

This book is dedicated to

Bryan, Randy and Laura,

Thanks guys. Your story, your struggles, your suffering was the stuff of inspiration as well as compassion.

Live, rejoice, and suffer all that you can stand ... and then let me write about it!

Books by Frederick Martin-Del-Campo

On the Hill of Contemplation

*Bound for the Promised Land Part 1:
The Trials of Manhood*

*Bound for the Promised Land Part 2:
The Sentiments of a Woman*

The Island of Estasia

The Donation of Constantine

Chronicles of War and a Wanderer

The Meditations of Misery

A Wetback in Reverse

and his latest work in progress...

Children of Anger

Contents

The Journey Begins 1

To the Wilds of Hispanic America I Go 4

Learning about Mexico in the Movies 6

Biblical Plagues in the Land of Maiz 11

Getting in Touch with Long Lost Friends 18

The Pig Virus Strikes Again 23

A Wetback on the Move 29

Connecting with the Folks Back Home 34

Getting the Dirt First Hand 37

Jesus Christ, Save Us from the Pigs! 40

Thunder Rolls Over Aztlan 47

Across Borders, and Class Divisions 52

Getting *Wicked* in Veracruz 62

Knowing yet Not Knowing about Nothing 67

The Poblanos and the Pigs 76

The Unique Hell of A Mexican Mother 84

Dirty Little Secrets Betrayed 105

The Days Pass, and Life Goes On 121

Humor to be Found in the Porcine Flu 138

Stocking Up on Hope 145

The Vagaries of Wayward Vagabonds 155

Waiting Around for Something Nice to Happen 161

Beating A Dead Horse	170
Cry Damnation for the Pathetic	176
"I Want, I Deserve"	181
The Music of 'Good-bye'	194
Towards the Western Horizon	201
Under the Volcano of Fire	207
Domestic Troubles	213
Family Feuds	221
Drug Pushers and Dopers	228
Jews in Mexico	234
The Treaty of Hidalgo and the Trouble with Wetbacks	239
Drug Addiction in the Family	246
A Pirate's Life for All	252
Misconceptions about Mexico	260
Hijackings and Kidnappings ~ Mexican Style	264
Have It Your Way at McMexico	270
Pantyhose Wearing Terrorists and Other Weirdos	278
A Smoker's Delight	282
Getting My Moxy Back	288
A Multitude of Sins	293
Playing Cat and Mouse in the Streets	298
Indefensible ... Irresistible	303
A Season of Evil and Hate	308
Red-Light Livelihoods	313
Guns and Gangsters on the Run	320

The Pity Problem with Prostitutes 327
When the Lights Went Out at the Movies 332
Aftershock 337
The Storms that Bring Out the Stress 343
The Reason Why I Was Named What I Was Named 346
Forward Back to America 353
Epilogue 363

THE JOURNEY BEGINS ...

"*I have learned silence from the talkative, toleration from the intolerant, and kindness from the unkind; yet strange, I am not grateful to those teachers.*"

... I have no idea who spoke these words, but they form my guiding motto through this unique experience of traveling through a Tequila inspired "Lala-land!"

Or, as my father would say, "Asi me gusta, que se expresen como macho con huevotes!" ("That's how I like it, that you express yourself with the balls of a real man!")

... Well, so be it!

The beginning of any voyage, indeed of any adventure, is always laced with uncertainties, particularly about things which you may have seen or experienced in the past. You may be afraid they might return fraught with mysteries, especially about things which you likely have never seen or experienced before. They are strewn with many riddles, which are bound to crop up in the course of experience, and trouble your dreams thereafter.

It was such a beginning that greeted me when at last I'd made the decision to get up, shore up, pack up, cell-phone and lap-top specifically, and send everything else to Hell. Like the song in the musical *Sweet Charity* says, "There's gotta be something better out there," and so I headed for the border: I was bound to go Mexico Way, come Hell or high-water!

And, no sooner had I made the fateful decision when uncertainties, mysteries and riddles placed one obstacle after another before me on the road to nowhere, not to mention the Hell that greeted me upon arrival, and the high-water that nearly drowned me along the road of perdition. I was bound to realize a personal quest, and that's all!

Many Mexicans and other foreigners entering the United States arrive illegally, without proper documentation, are derided for their ignorance of the law and lack of consideration for the customs of the country they hope to adopt for their own. Mexicans, in particular, are regarded as *Wetbacks* because of the arduous journey they must undertake, which includes crossing the Rio Grande or enduring the awful heat of the South-West, drowning in their own sweat. Whatever route they chose for their exodus from their home country, they end up all wet. In my case, however, I would be known as the wetback in reverse ~ an American-born Mexican who was heading back for the homeland of my fathers because life in the USA was becoming more and more uncertain and expensive; because the global financial meltdown forced me to confront hard choices about the future, and job prospects were nil and void; because I suddenly felt the impulse to take off and search for my ancestral roots; and because life in the USA was unendurably boring in the extreme. Thus, I felt I needed some of the stimulating vulgarity, violence, vanity, vagaries, vexations, vituperation and vacuous venality that make up survival in most Mexican towns in order to get the old wheels and turbines of purpose and devotion cranking again. Also, just to get my jollies off, I'd thought to try my journalistic hand, and this country would be just the place to put myself through the investigative ringer, as it were. There is much to be said as well for the simple, unobtrusive, undemanding existence of Mexican village life, however, where-about, most often, you have to chase down and kill your own supper!

Well, here I am, here I am stuck, to live, experience, to suffer a year in the life of Great Mexico!

To begin with, Mexico is one of the worst (many Mexicans themselves believe) racist regimes in the world. The majority Mestizos frequently find ways to sideline minority Indians and even the privileged Criollos. The Mestizos are generously assisted by the Government, which fears their political backlash if they don't cater to their demands. They are given scholarships, loans, grants, business opportunities, even cash hand-outs just to placate their half-blood resentments. They even fix examination results so that minority groups, especially Amer-Indians of the South like Zapotecs of Oaxaca or Maya tribes in Chiapas, score lower to make the Mestizos from the Valley of Mexico and other densely populated areas appear smarter. However, well-to-do Criollos and some Indian communities have learned to prosper in spite of adversity by going overseas and making their money there on the one hand, or have found ways of undermining the local practices of corrupt officials working within their communities on the other.

The egotistical way of thinking, "I know and you don't," is dividing all Mexicans. We all know nothing! The "right," then, is no "right"... we all read from some book, most likely a religious book, the reason for our belief in the "right," but what we really want to believe in is that we alone are in the "right," for what it is worth. How do we know what we read today will not be proved wrong tomorrow? None of us will be there to even defend it, regardless of what that "it" might be, and few Mexicans will defend their rights.

DOES ANYONE REALLY KNOW ANYTHING!!!!

TO THE WILDS OF
HISPANIC AMERICA I GO

In the smug comfort of my California home, I realized I was deprived of my identity. Hence, I resolved to discover the reason for my name. It would be a quest to come to terms with my past, my heritage, and secure the future with identity in hand. I would visit old friends, beg them to help me with my quest, and discover in the process the wilds and wonders of the land, which had shaped the lives and legacy of my ancestors. I would go forth to find myself amidst the shadows of forgetfulness and obscurantism.

Upon crossing the border into Baja California from San Diego, California, I headed for the nearest Tijuana bus station and hopped on the first bus out of there regardless of the destination. Well, to my consternation, the first place I ended up in was Reynosa, located in the state of Tamaulipas, across the Rio Grande in Northern Mexico. Indeed, it is a strange place with a large population, and even larger poverty statistics, yet with a bustling economy. There isn't much around to recommend it, very few remarkable landmarks to boast about, but I found it typical of many a Mexican town I would traverse or visit in the course of this extended trip. It is located on the extreme north-east point of the country, and an unlikely place in which to begin my sojourn, but here I am to wonder what crap will be flung at me the minute I get off the rickety, air-polluting bus, which I somehow managed to survive. No sooner did I arrive in Reynosa when the wires were all burning up with news that there was a fire-fight between federal soldiers and narco-traffickers not far from the hotel-dump I'd just entered.

As I heard it, 30 masked soldiers in combat gear, and acting on a tip, busted down the door of a boarded-up house to find 55 terrified migrants; all hostages of the Gulf drug cartel. Amid screams and the smell of urine and sweat, they found a blood-spattered room and a nail-encrusted log used to beat the captives and extort money from their families; $3,000 each, or so the locals reported. I, for one, found it hard to sympathize since many of the victims were once perpetrators of the wicked trafficking, which, to boot, provides quite a decent living for many starved out and desperate natives. So, at once I don't sympathize, but at the same time I pity them and have to understand why they do it.

This is not quite what I was expecting by way of a welcome from the ever accommodating Mexicans, but it was the noise of gun-fire and reports of blood spillage that provided me with a cheap thrill.

Hence, as the events unfolded while I looked for another cheap hotel to stay at (the other one, to my unceasing horror, was full of roaches, human as well as the six-legged variety, and bed-bugs), many of the bystanders rumored about, like a bunch of haphazard reporters clawing each-other to be the first one at the scene, that five suspected kidnappers were hauled off in a military truck, including the alleged leader ~ the son of a local police officer. So be it for counting on the honesty of the police officials, and, or their relatives to uphold the law! Yet, this first run-in with the corruption inherent in Mexican Society was a tiny taste of what was to cross my way in the course of this already haphazard sojourn.

LEARNING ABOUT MEXICO IN THE MOVIES

Whilst I went about exploring the interesting (sometimes) sights, and irritated by the unpleasant sounds of the town center, I came across a heavy, mustachioed, more than 90 year old buzzard of a man sporting a wide-brimmed hat, resting his hands on an elegantly carved cedarwood cane who, allegedly, spent hours every day at the local tavern, "La Aguila Desnuda" (The Naked Eagle), recounting stories of his self-aggrandized life as a movie-maker throughout the golden age of the Mexican Cinema during the 1940s and 50s. He would be the first really weird character I would come across during my experiences in this country, and as my journey progressed, his weather-beaten old face would haunt me, especially during the wee hours of the morning when I'd be inside a crowded bus en route to the next destination.

He couldn't be bothered by reports of a shoot-out or a narco-trafficking drug-bust. He only talked about two things, according to a couple of drunks that would pace their drinking according to the length of his anecdotes: himself, and his fall from artistic grace.

Apparently, he had actually suffered the alleged downfall, and was persecuted by the semi-socialist PRI (Partido Revolucionario Institucional) regime of the time, because he was no longer thought of as a wild and crazy radical but had matured into a staid and dull reactionary while using his influence to turn the youth of Mexico against the by-then paternalistic and corrupt government.

His name, I later learned, was Fulgencio San Roman.

San Roman was a typical product of Criollo parentage: large, gray, robust and spoiled by inherited wealth. Soon I gathered sufficient dirt on this fellow to be able to relate that he flourished as a movie-maker until his own pride brought him to the gates of ruin. The younger generation, despite his very liberal attitudes, just did not click to his narrative style during the 1960s; they found his stories too intense, overly-dramatic, almost Wagnerian, that celebrated a revolutionary

Mexico that no longer appealed to their forward-looking imaginations. They were looking for something that would make them twist and shout along with every other member of that libertine 60s generation. Upon gathering more research about his singular achievements, I discovered that his most notable works were made between 1940 and 1960, and they included such classics as *Thunder Over Aztlan*, about the state of Mexican society after the 1910 Revolution; *The Eagle and the Serpent*, about the struggle to maintain an independent democracy under Benito Juarez following the invasion of France and the installation of the Archduke Maximilian of Austria as Emperor of Mexico; *Tonantzin, Our Lady of the Roses*, which took a biting look at the devotion of the common masses to their idol of Guadalupe; *The Return of Quetzalcoatl*, about the prophecy of the return of the Toltec God of the Wind, of civilization and the arts to liberate Mexico from the tyranny of the Aztecs; *The Wind that Swept Mexico*, a grandiose epic depicting the drama of the revolution against the Diaz regime; and finally, *Once Upon a Time in Old Mexico*, which took a hard, poignant look at the feudal conditions still existing, and the oppression of the Indian and Mestizo peasants by the landed gentry, in the haciendas just prior to the Revolution.

According to his own accounts, however, San Roman's downfall was due to his self absorption. His first movies, going back to the late 1930s, are more story or drama centered, and have some old-fashioned insight into characters. By the late 1950s they had become increasingly superficial, self indulgent and outlandish for no good purpose, though many would argue, including me, that those later films (once I had a chance to see a few of them) were, visually, among his very best.

Camera wizardry, outlandishness of plot, and weirdness of characters were not, according to his ardent critics, enough to carry a film. Of his earliest films I can't say much except that I hardly understood what they were about, whilst others placed more emphasis on plot and characters, but they were still devoid of the style and color that marked the later ones.

The self-admitted self-absorption reflects that of Mexico's society more than anything. It is a society not unlike America's, and there are few things on this planet that are more self-absorbed than a typical Mexican, particularly in regard to his culture and origins. This society is one where a vast majority of its people live in abject poverty, fighting always for water, space, and beliefs (the latter a courtesy of an idol-strewn Roman Catholicism with a uniquely Mexican flavor to it) that replace scanty food for the living flesh as sustenance for the soul.

As I learned more about this curious fellow, I came to realize that his glorious vision of a mad world, where an aristocracy of eccentrics abandon themselves to leisure and luxury, portrays in abstract terms the very character of *Mestizo Mexico*; bathing in an orgy of blood and copulation, violence and mirth, whilst making fun of death and misery, it is the combined inheritance of a soul half-European and half-Amer-Indian. Hence, San Roman, who I would never have come across under ordinary circumstances, turned out to be the cinematic circus-master of the Mexican people I had only heard about in legend; a player of jokes and angry tricks throwing the distorted mirror in our faces. It is as if *El Cucuy* (the Bogey-man of Mexican Lore) comes for its prey, which is what some would say of the intent of San Roman's "perverted" mind.

What then have I to understand of this early run-in with an eccentric figure of Mexican art? It would be an intriguing experience to delve into the heart and genius of this creature of mystery; a random set of chance occurrences that left me muddling over the workings of coincidence. To understand his movies, so I was convinced, is to understand the mind of Mexico. The whole idea behind some of San Roman's films involves what he remembered as a child, and it's really not the movie you are seeing, if you are trying to follow it. It's the mind of San Roman you are looking through, perhaps even at the subconscious level.

It's the soul of Mexico he was trying to release from the bondage of ignorance and superstition, which Mexico is still suffering from, by way of his Art.

Thus here, in the art of this mysterious cineast, a man who is dated by his special vision of his own culture, we learn that his own people are like a plague on the land, infecting even the dreams of the coming generation with doubts about the meaning of their survival in a world increasingly pre-occupied with transforming itself into a homogenized society of *haves* and *have-nots*. This is so eerily reminiscent of dilemmas faced by humanity before; dilemmas involving the future of modern nations increasingly inter-dependent by way of commerce, politics, and the welfare of their natural resources. This is so typical of the lessons coming out of history books, but no one, except perhaps a freak like San Roman, is smart enough to recognize the unfolding of events that will cause the Muse of History to visit Humankind once-more with old-time miseries and calamities.

At the human level, notwithstanding, all that San Roman could do was hold a mirror up to the society that forged his character and nurtured his prejudices; thus you have a man crying in the streets filled with mendicants unable to hear his complaints about their own filthy habits; thus you have a self-righteous artist condemning the sneaky beggars that make up a significant sector of Mexican society, and who have made of begging a going-concern. They profit from the misdirected compassion of superstitious, though sincere, people devoted to their idols, like *La Guadalupana* (a cognomen for the *Virgen of Guadalupe*, and don't get caught calling her an idol, lest you imperil your life for lack of discretion), and worried that, if they don't make gestures of charity, they might imperil the divine grace they hope will save them from from their own ignorance.

Yet, the beggars happily play on their fears and sense of charity by using their own children to do the begging for them, and if the latter are remiss in their daily tallies, they get beaten without need of justification. Others yet put their children to sell trashy wares while the adults thieve around, their barbarity against their own offspring is almost too incredible to abide. And yet, this is supposed to be the reality San Roman grew up with, and tried to express through his art? I wondered about him and his intentions, for even the dirty habits of the common masses are loudly revealed through his images; the sputum on the streets, the vomiting and urinating, the drunkenness, the demanding righteousness and violent outbursts of provincial wretches that insist you buy them a drink if you happen to cross their malodorous path; peasants who have no escape from the harsh elements and oppression of their social betters, except to seek consolation in liquid spirits, to imbibe without restraint. These revolting details are poetically projected on to the cinematic screen.

And yet, his movies are regarded as out-dated, obsolete, old-fashioned and reactionary just because he insisted, by way of message in his films, on self-determination and personal accountability, rather than finding new and modern ways of blaming your parents, the Church, and society at large for individual sins and disappointments.

Thus, Mexico's society, in spite of San Roman's unheeded protestations, continues to be plagued with congestion, overpopulation, hunger (30 million people, as of 2010, are without enough to eat, or a place to rest in), ignorance, lack of opportunity, disease, pestilence, social unrest, and social decay. All that San Roman could do for the society he ostensibly loved was to grouch about all these things he knew could never be fixed, especially in view of the fact that nothing was really broken that needed fixing (or so his compatriots complained)!

Now that I got an education, albeit cinematic, on the whys and wherefore of a Mexico lost in the Sea of Fate sans a compass, I go on to the next rendezvous, the next random occurrence, reaching out to random hearts with a faint understanding of what next to expect.

Into the stream of consciousness I plunge, ready to let the current take me to wherever perdition wishes me to go!

BIBLICAL PLAGUES
IN THE LAND OF MAIZ

Whilst ruminating, palliating the setbacks of, and digesting, most excruciatingly, the vomitable crap that passes for food in Reynosa (and don't you believe anybody that tells you that Mexican food is good wherever you go in the country), I would be exposed to more than a few odd, or downright bizarre characters. Speaking of the "beauties" of nature, if my mind didn't have enough to worry about, I just got wind that Mexico is being over-run with an epidemic of the Swine Flu!

That's all I need; to end up sneezing uncontrollably like a pig! (no pun intended ... that is, consciously)

Yes, I heard about it one fine Thursday morning on the TV news. I wrote to an old email correspondent, a certain Cecilia notable for her remarkable derrier; she wrote yesterday that there was very little mention of it beforehand, and on the Friday before the alert had been reported all over the news, people began wearing face masks, and all schools in the Distrito Federal and surrounding areas were closed ... gotta' watch out for everything these days.

Things weren't all that hot in Reynosa either, and soon I noticed many of the youngsters hauling off to school were wearing face-masks as well, and general car-traffic was down considerably ~ at least the awful virus did have that salutary effect. These initial days of my grand sojourn, it would appear, were already fraught with unseen dangers. I thought beforehand that I might catch some disease from something I ate, not from just breathing the air.

The next day, as I prepared to move on to my next stop, I learned that the danger was spreading throughout the land, and panic was beginning to set in, all of Mexico closed its schools, students across the land were asked to stay put on Friday after at least 16 otherwise healthy people were reported dead, and nearly a thousand others reportedly fell ill from what could be a totally undiagnosed strain of the strange swine flu. According now to the TV news-reporters, The World Health

Organization worried that it could mark the start of a flu pandemic. FANTASTIC! Just as I get to this country, now I have to worry about a pandemic?

No one can know, especially not the Mexicans who distrust anybody with an academic pedigree, if the scientists in the U.S. and Mexico were actually working overtime to make certain if the deaths were all due to the same new strain of the pig flu that sickened seven people just in Reynosa, never mind the rest of the country.

Furthermore, the same World Health Organization counted at least 57 deaths in Mexico City, although it wasn't yet clear if this larger number was due to pig flu. It might have been old-fashioned stabbings, love quarrels, or drunken binges that did the job of sending a few dozen more Mexicans to their *final* retirement locales.

"We are very, very concerned," the mayor of Reynosa announced on the radio, and said, "We have what appears to be a new sort of virus and it has spread from human to human."

First of all, *Really, you don't say?* to the mayor. Then, if international spread is confirmed, and with so many impoverished locals unaffectedly climbing over the border fences before *La Migra* (immigration officials) gets wind of their illegal crossings, and it will assuredly happen, then they will meet WHO's criteria for raising the pandemic alert level, and they will have Mexico to thank for it.

Other officials raised the internal alert system on a Friday, enabling the federal ministries to divert more money and personnel to dealing with the outbreak, which really puts a damper on all the money laundering and other corrupt activities going on within the halls of the federal government.

So, with Mexicans getting in a tiff over a pig flu pandemic, well then, "It's all hands on deck at the moment." as the local mayor said.

What is a dumb tourist like me supposed to do under the circumstances? Now, it would seem they won't let me go home because I might already be infected, and they don't want to risk annoying Uncle Sam lest the virus should spread to Main Street America. I scoured the newspapers for leads; the latest coming out of the capital was that Mexico's Health Secretary, Jose Cordova, said only 16 of the deaths were indeed caused by the new strain, through testing at government laboratories. Samples from 44 other people who'd died suddenly were still being tested, though the officials were loathe to admit to the flu as the principal cause. The public health ministry put the exact number of the unlucky ill at around 943 throughout the country. How they came up with the statistics so quickly I was left dumbfounded, especially in view of the fact that they never seem able to find out where so many public funds go to, once one of their clerks discovers they're missing.

But, what the hell does all of this have to do with me?

Hence, this fellow Cordova said samples were also sent to the U.S. Centers for Disease Control and Prevention (since Mexicans distrust their own agencies) to determine whether it was the same virus now infecting seven people in Texas and California. As of the moment, while I emptied my coffee cup, sitting here like an idiot in the "La Cocada" Cafe' and unable to go nowhere until the officials said it was safe to take one of the buses again, the health ministry pawns reported that tests show the flu is a "new, different strain that originally came from pigs."

Wow! Who would have thought that the Pig Flu actually comes from pigs! Personally, I thought the virus came from my brother Alberto's boyfriend, whom everyone refers to as *Juana la Cerda* (Johnny the Sow ~ and what a sow he is, right down to his feminine hygiene).

Yet, Cordova, media hog that he turned out to be, came back to the air-waves and announced, "We certainly have 60 deaths that we can't be sure are from the same virus, but it is probable."

Furthermore, Cordova described a scary new strain that had felled only people among the expectedly less-vulnerable youth, as well as the mid-adult age range. One suggestion was made that the most vulnerable sectors of the population, babies and the old, had been vaccinated against other strains, and that the normally reliable vaccines may be providing some protection. But, how the Hell does that help me, considering the fact that I had not been vaccinated hitherto hopping on the bus for this country?

Some local clerks I asked, once panic started to irritate me, tried to reassure me that, "at this point, we do not have any confirmations of swine influenza in Mexico," of the kind that sickened local residents, as well as the students in Mexico City.

All seven of the alleged U.S. victims did recover from a strain of the flu that combines pig, bird and human viruses in a way that researchers had not seen before. So, I was left to worry about the swine flu's symptoms, especially if they'd turned out like those of the regular flu, mostly involving fever, cough and sore throat. If it turned out the symptoms included vomiting and diarrhea, then I would be proverbially screwed, because the latter symptoms were already giving me a run for my money, actually and figuratively. And yet, they could've been due to the extraordinary cuisine of these parts.

Closing the schools in every city, particularly one with 20 million inhabitants like Mexico City, is at least containing this bizarre virus at the school level. Also, it was announced that they expected to keep 6.1 million students home from day care centers through high schools, and thousands more might be affected as colleges and universities gave their less than disappointed alumni an early Spring Break. Already it appeared that parents scrambled worriedly to juggle work and family concerns due to what the ever exaggerating news reporters decried was the first city-wide closure of schools since Mexico City's devastating 1985 earthquake. The latter left me a bit sad since I was just beginning to enjoy the sight of attractive youths romping about getting to and from their schools by hopping on public transportation, or otherwise.

Cecilia, a grade school teacher in her own right, e-mailed me that she and other teachers at the Cuitlahuac World preschool scrubbed down their empty classrooms with Clorox, acid and Lysol between fielding calls from parents scared right into committing diarrhea on themselves. While the school had had no known cases among its students, good, ol' trusty Cecilia actually applauded the Federal government's decision to shutter classes, especially in preschools.

"It's great they are taking these measures," she wrote me. "I think these dildo-headed officials are finally using their heads, no pun intended."

No pun taken, Cecilia (she certainly is good at describing people).

The less than overly-excited authorities of Reynosa advised local residents not to go to work if they felt sick, and to wear surgical masks if the moving crowds showed any of the symptoms. A wider shutdown including the shutting down of government agencies was being considered. If they had carried out the latter, needless to say, no one would have noticed!

Well, Cordova went back on the air-waves and announced cryptically, "It is very likely that classes will be suspended for several days. We will have to evaluate, and let's hope this doesn't happen, the need to restrict activity at workplaces."

Damn! I really could not give a crap, except for the fact that I would be stuck in this dump indefinitely.

Still, other authorities insisted, there weren't any reasons for alarm, unless more cases showed up in the United States. The five in California and two in Texas had all recovered, and their testing indicated some common antiviral medications seemed to work against the pig virus.

What was I to believe, therefore? The new strain could spread human-to-human, which is unusual for a pig flu virus, but the knowledge wasn't helping with my case of the *runs*, and I was running out of toilet paper very quickly. Now the local feds (federal officials with the help of the local police) began to check for people who could have been in contact with the seven confirmed U.S. cases, who all got sick between late February and mid-March. I felt this was the last straw. They were taking this far too seriously, but obviously they were afraid of losing all that good tourist and narco-trafficking cash to a case of the flu jitters. Therewithal, they had to check every human bodily orifice from the cantinas on the El Paso border, to the *Fayuqueros* (the stolen goods stalls of the black market) on the border with Belize. That's all I needed ~ to have some masked lab-rat of a technician snooping up my anus for any signs of the flu!

Frankly, it was obvious that the U.S. cases formed a growing medical mystery because it's damned strange how these hapless patients caught the virus. The U.S. center for disease control reported that none of the seven people---seven out of nearly 420 million people between the U.S. border with Canada and the Mexican border with Guatemala---were in contact with pigs, which is (surprise! surprise!) how people usually catch swine flu. And, only a few were in contact with each other ~ but how much *in contact* they were, if you know what I mean, they didn't say.

Hence, I went back to the Ayuntamiento (the city-government hall where all the agencies are located) to ask if they had learned anything relevant since the last fright they'd served us; these clerks could not honestly tell their olfactory orifice apart from their own anus, but they tried to describe the virus as having a unique mixture of gene segments not noticed in people or pigs before. The bug that I was supposed to be scared about contains human virus, avian virus from North America, and pig viruses from Europe, Asia, and North America as well. In other words, it just left me to wonder: where and when had this sick and twisted sort of orgy taken place that produced an illness, which could very well have been a sexually-transmitted disease, that affected all three species?

Forget it. I really don't want to know.

Anyway, these less than qualified officials described having seen mixes of bird, pig and human virus before, but never such an intercontinental mix with more than one pig virus in the fray.

With all this free time on my hands to play with myself, figuratively speaking, I pondered: how could I know that I would travel hundreds of miles on a voyage of adventure only to have to keep a discerning eye on flu viruses that emerge from pigs! The animals were only fit as pets (maybe), and for the kitchen, as far as I was concerned. Thence, I had to worry that they are very susceptible to both bird and human viruses, and a likely place where the kind of "genetic re-assortment" (a so-called expert said) can take place that could lead to a form of pandemic flu never seen before?

Time has at last caught up with science fiction ~ at least when it came to bizarre diseases threatening the future of mankind, that's for sure! Now I was beginning to feel like I could not tell apart my own nose from my butt-hole, with due respect to the government clerks, but this damned virus might have been something totally new. Or, it may have been lurking about for a spell and was only recently noticed because of all the people going around defecating in their pants without having had a taste of the local chili-beans, as well as improved lab testing and disease surveillance, or so I was informed.

When the virus was first detected, I had no idea what it meant, and never learned the facts, except that it may have actually started somewhere in America, most likely in California.

And, I never learned if anyone was getting sick from the virus right then, as I bumped a few heads in the Ayuntamiento to get some relevant answers to my fears. I also did not learn if the seasonal flu vaccine that

Mexicans as well as Americans suffer every autumn were taken early this year, or if they even protect against this type of virus. All I could say on the subject is that people should just wash their hands and take other customary precautions. But no! With the local bums (mostly a motley cross section of Mexican males) stumbling about in the local cantinas hiding from their spouses, and emerging from the rest-rooms without having washed their hands after handling their manhood, and then sticking them in the peanut or potato-chips platters reserved for paying drunks, there was no chance that people anywhere would quickly change their hygienic habits, even for the sake of their children.

For me, I would just have to spend another jolly day in beautiful, down-town Reynosa listening to Mr. San Roman's intriguing tales!

And so it was that I got a real-time fore-taste of all that would fill my "journalistic" diary until I got the hell out of Mexico for good.

GETTING IN TOUCH WITH LONG LOST FRIENDS

Finally, I made it out of Reynosa, God be praised! The smog and the stench of the local beans were really giving me cause for anxiety, and I don't think my nose would recover for a while.

I hopped on the first bus out of Reynosa, and headed straight for Chihuahua City, in the great state of Chihuahua. This would be the *de-facto* place where my hoped-for adventure would truly commence. It is the city of some of my maternal ancestors, and though dry, cold and windy, it is also filled with the exaggerated grandiosity of Spanish Baroque, and the clang of her cathedral bells awakened me each morning to a special kind of reality that hearkened back to another age. Things in any part of Mexico certainly still move to the pace of agriculture, the sowing or the harvest having to wait till the field-hands sober up after the previous night's binging.

The people are generally kind and friendly, and the mix of Spanish-Whites with the always half-naked Tarahumara Indians as they cavort about in the streets surrounding the *zocalo*, or town civic center, and the Mennonites from the Heartland of America ubiquitously selling their cheese products about the surrounding streets, made for an intriguing scenario that I would not have noticed had it existed back in California.

Yet, here I would have the opportunity to get in touch with an old friend who had settled in Chihuahua about 10 years before ~ my old buddy Billy: a Gringo from Central California, tall and lanky, though solidly built, he wore glasses, a beard, and was instantly self-righteous about his newly adopted liberal attitudes as they rolled off the pinko assembly-line for the mindless consumption of arm-chair-wanna-be revolutionaries, just like my blustering friend. He had migrated, or *wetbacked*, his way to Mexico trying to escape drug-traffickers to whom he was indebted for an undisclosed amount of Marijuana sales. I have no idea why he'd dealt with them since he grew some find stock of his own, but now they were after him, and he has successfully eluded them during all these years past. I was genuinely fond of him, and he does have his generous and compassionate side, which brought us together in the near and distant past for many a cultural repast. He knew I too had been persecuted by druggie-gang-bangers, but for very different reasons; I had grown up, and had been friends with, some of them during our childhood and adolescence. Once the age of decision dawned on us, they chose to abandon their lives to crime, whilst I decided on a life of artistic, though impoverished, expression and contemplation.

I had received numerous emails from Billy since coming here. Apparently he was "thrilled," that I'd made the decision to send the past to Hell, and undertake this so-called journey of discovery.

I thought it was very sweet of him to track me down, and he called me to find out how things were going once I rolled into Chihuahua. My guess is that the news of the pandemic hadn't reached his ears yet; he is rather slow to get wind of really important matters. His call was very unexpected yet most welcome, and it left me thinking about the purpose of my trip. Furthermore, he really had me thinking aloud ~ I did indeed have moments of doubt when I'd wonder if I would really be better off back in California. With my loved ones begging me to go back, not to mention my cousin Maribel's offer to find me a new job translating manuscripts, I really got nervous, and, though I had always avoided the subject with her, this time she had to talk to me directly about it.

But, the same old conclusion: I can't return ... I have to move forward, come hell or high water, for the sake of my soul. I have to realize this journey, even if it ends in disaster.

I felt very guilty afterwards, having rejected her offer. Her own life is hard enough. I had Billy to contend with for the time being. With him, it was the same old domestic troubles and shouting matches with his lovely Mestiza-Mexican wife, Juana Benita with the big black eyes and long eye-lashes, all the time. She was very warm and welcoming as well; I had promised myself I would not give a shit about their domestic squabbles any more, but I guess I missed interacting with this very lively couple, and that forced me to eat my words. Upon arriving in their charming suburban flat they treated me to a feast of *Carnitas*, and had been so nice about my woes, and free with the beer and Tequila, that they forgot to fight during the whole time I spent with them. They hadn't been so courteous to each-other since they were married, many years before! I couldn't believe it, the quiet and calm was too eerie even for me. I guess I needed my dose of watching them heap abuse and bitterness on each-other. While they acted sweet and tender towards one another for my sake, I just laughed out loud while holding my belly from the disgust!

Actually, it turned out, these lovely people hadn't really fought in 3 months. Oh, some of the same troubles about money and dividing up the house-hold chores between them, but the terrible fights that ended in violence and destruction of personal property all over suspicions of infidelity and jealousies seemed to be receding at last, and they were truly jealous of each-other to the point of mutual murder. For their sake, I hope this peaceful truce really lasts forever. I know I really needed some breathing space upon deciding to get out of California and all the conventional bull-shit I was trapped in. That is so important to understand when one undertakes such a journey, and Billy and wife were clearly so fed up that they made of their exile a permanent one. They empathized, and knew all too well that I felt like I was suffocating with things as they were: my family, my greedy parents, Los Angeles, and the pretense of trying to move up while everything around you seems to be decaying. I knew I was just too close to my problems, too close to the people that ruined my life, albeit my own loved ones. I badly needed breathing space.

Billy did his great part to convince me to send everything to Hell, and take my Fate into my own hands. He understood that I hesitated for psychological reasons; he wrote me once, "That is so poignant, and so revealing, when you tell me *I need my dose of abuse.* Forget it brother, time enough for abuse in the afterlife. And the worms will be busy on your body long enough!"

I did not know it until he opened my eyes to the fact, but I had become pathetically co-dependent, and sought affirmation from my very oppressors by exposing myself to their predictable abuse, and thus my identity was re-affirmed. Lord knows I had no idea I was so blind to my own sad situation. My guess is that we grow accustomed to the humiliation, and it either sharpens our wits, like it did with Billy---it keeps your fighting skills, which one needs, ready in case of that next challenge or battle against the world---or the abuse weakens us, as it did with me. I never could get anything done when I was constantly assaulted like that, with insults and derogatory reproaches, reluctant offers of help, and expressions of repugnance for having been born.

Well, *whatever*, Billy would assure me, I deserved my peace and quiet as well. Therefore, to Mexico I did trek, and would sweat, cry, scream, bleed, and defecate the misery and uncertainty of my former life out of my being, and learn, at last, what being a Mexican is all about.

I thought it great that Billy and wife found a new phone-calling plan just for me, so I would be able to reach them wherever I happened to be trapped in throughout Mexico. I would really have to depend on them, now that the precious hypocrites I once depended on had let me down so badly ~ especially my old associates from the university. And, if I should need help, then it will certainly make me think about California the more.

I do want to return, and I do love the old haunts I frequented. California, expensive though it may be to survive there, is a great place to live in. But, I tell my dear friends, as long as my enemies are there, selling toxic drugs to innocent teenagers like they have been, and terribly worried that I, an old acquaintance of theirs, know all about it and they worry that I will rat them out, my chances for conciliation are destroyed and further destroyed. Their continued existence is the key to all this. Their (eventual) murder, or assassination by whatever means, would solve so many troubles (or, at least, all of my troubles), especially since I'd found out they were intimately connected as well with the narco-trafficking syndicates of Mexico. I did not set out to find out about the activities of these drug-lords, but as long as I had troubles with them back home, I couldn't help myself but to find out more, and carefully document what I could in my trusty little journal.

We are, Billy described, all victims of circumstances, *children of bad-luck*, and he is absolutely right about the fact that victims of our type need that dose of adrenaline that comes from oppression, and, unfortunately, for some it impairs their basic survival skills, which is probably true in my case. The way I felt after years of living under those circumstances, first with my family, and then dealing with the local Chicano drug bosses in Los Angeles, left me with the belief in *Bad Luck*. Thank God I freed myself from that. All children of bad-luck should feel the freedom I am enjoying, and should try and do the same. I know it is not, and cannot be, easy, but it is not impossible. I lived it, survived it, and the long coveted liberty from such a dreadful, monotonous, yet dangerous, life was not impossible.

... I wonder what Maestro San Roman is doing just now ...

He did speak much of the transformation of Mexican Society due to the onslaught of these narco-syndicates while he elaborated his tales in front of the other admiring drunkards. He had me transfixed for hours, though I didn't really understand what he meant at the time. Now I found myself actually wishing I was back in Reynosa, at least long enough to ask him a few questions.

So, what could he have been doing just as I wrote in my journal? Probably imbibing that Cuervo Tequila he is so fond of, eh?

THE PIG VIRUS STRIKES AGAIN

No sooner did I pack up, salute Billy and wife, and prepare to ride to another part of Mexico, when there came more news out of the capital that, again, put a damper on my plans: A new pig flu bug had murdered more than 70 people, and laid low more than a thousand who, we were informed, just would not make it unless the Virgen de Guadalupe appreciated the tamales some of them had placed on her altar in exchange for a cure. The creepy officials were once again calling out the "pandemic potential," and the World Health Organization was getting involved, saying on a bleak Saturday morning that this newest outbreak might not be contained in time before it spread to other parts of the country---thanks, according to them, to a few irresponsible Gringoes who just couldn't "keep it indoors" while the epidemic scare was being touted from steeple to steeple.

The wicked sickness had actually reached Chihuahua by the time I'd arrived, and with dozens of new or supposed cases being reported even by the local street dogs, it left my plans in utter uncertainty. Once again, schools were closed, and public events postponed in the major cities until the same-said officials came out to announce the end of the alert. Sadly, more than five-hundred concerts and similar gatherings had been canceled, and, conveniently for the promoters, no refunds were being offered. So much for catching Placido Domingo singing at the bullfights!

I tried calling a health-hot-line, but they had fielded so many thousands of calls in their first few hours of operation, that no way in Hell could I get through to find out if they would restrict travel again. Too many frightened nellies suspected they had contracted the bug based on specious conditions, and hoped to get a few vaccinations. Soldiers, diverted from their bases, were obliged to hand out face-masks at all traffic stops; hospital workers, at least, dealt with panicky crowds seeking answers to their fears, and they also handed out disinfectant gels and rubber gloves to people who requested them.

A Wetback in Reverse

I got my share, of course, since I wasn't going to expose myself to the dirty habits of the locals ~ I would have taken precautions, virus or no virus.

I tried to make due with the free time this new scare, regrettably, afforded me. Even Billy informed himself of the situation, and advised me, "The crap is moving very quickly, and since the scientific nerds still don't know how to define a new disease, then you'd just better take every precaution against the cooties, my brother."

Very prescient advice on his part.

In either case, this sickness, this strange virus that is a mix of bird, pig and human cooties, had prompted the officials to get together to consider declaring an "international public health emergency."

Who could know if this measure would result in more travel advisories (which concerned me immensely), border restrictions or new trade barriers. In either case, the rest of us, all 110 million Mexicans, plus Billy, his wife and me, would just have to wait until the (ir)responsible officials enjoyed their last sip of champagne.

I had heard of these warnings for years, about their danger of causing a pandemic from viruses that mix genetic elements from humans and pigs. Causes for worry included, according to people who know better, the corroborated fact that susceptible children and the aged were not counted among the dead, only the once prime and healthy young and mature adults. The Spanish flu, which, following the end of World War I, killed more than 40 million people worldwide (if I remember my history) had initially attacked healthy young adults as well, so the weak and infirm were doubly screwed.

The different variants of the flu could have similar symptoms, like the vomiting I got after having those bad beans back in Reynosa, but the fever, cough and sore throat that accompany it were not yet manifest. The American victims who'd recovered, reputedly, also experienced vomiting and diarrhea, so, obviously, I would never know if I had indeed picked up the pig bug. Unlike with the common flu, however, regular people do not have a built-in defense against an awful virus that includes porcine and avian genes, much to my chagrin. The new vaccines, on which I had placed all of my bets, could very well take many weeks, even months to distribute, let alone prove effective.

The ever faithful officials and experts at the WHO and the U.S. Centers for Disease Control and Prevention insisted the nature of the outbreak could have made containment impossible. Well, fantastic! Billy and wife, at least, were very generous in assuring me that I would continue to have a home should travel restrictions be actively enforced. According to the Chihuahua papers, more than 1,000 people had been infected in as many as 14 of Mexico's 32 states, including Chihuahua.

After I had a chance to go to a local clinic to get tested, the lazy workers there casually reported that more than 20 people who had previously entered through their doors just up and died of the actual pig flu, and another four or five dozen sudden deaths were expected to follow ~ it sounded to me like the cure *was* worse than the sickness!

God! I thought, who even knows if these people bothered to wash their utensils, or if they re-used infected needles. Maybe I should count myself among the four dozen---I was feeling woozy by then.

Furthermore, I was warned that if I insisted on traveling, I might be screened or probed, with all the humiliating connotations attached thereto, as they had many other passengers traveling to and from Mexico. The symptoms were catching up with everybody it seemed, regardless of the simple fact that some of the symptoms might very well be due to something more obvious, like bad food or drink. In either case, now a quarantine around Chihuahua was being warned.

The same, not-too-overly concerned officials, however, dismissed the idea of trying a quarantine in the United States where the virus was spreading like wild-fire. Some less than brilliant expert said it was too late to try to contain the spread of the virus.

Well, what the Hell was I then supposed to do?

I was itching to get out, in spite of my friend's generosity.

They noted there had been no direct contact between the cases in the North Mexico and Southern Mexico areas, suggesting the pig virus had already found its way across divergent geographic areas, and had crawled up an undisclosed quantity of unprotected anuses.

My guess was that whatever they did right then to *contain* it would prove to be a political move, a measure to *contain* the fears of the masses. It was obvious that they did not know what they were doing. I had nothing to do but twiddle my thumbs until the next news report offered up some more frustration to my "journey of adventure," as I sipped the draughts of CORONA beer my good friend left for me. Well, the news reports finally did announce something new: Mexican President Felipe Calderon' announced that his administration barely discovered the sinister presence of the virus just a few days before, thanks to the warnings of international laboratories.

"We are doing everything necessary," he said in a brief statement.

Again, FANTASTIC! (so I said with a measure of cynicism).

Indeed and fact, I would be stuck again indefinitely. Why, oh why did this have to happen when I had just begun this grand voyage? And no, assurances that I was "living and experiencing a unique sort of history," that I could relate to my grand-children was no consolation at all. These growing flu caseloads were nothing unusual, or so the clinic receptionist assured me, so why all the fuss then? Everyone knew that containing the outbreak would be difficult, yet the turn-around angered many as suddenly as the virus got to them. Needless to say, it left me smoldering in my own righteousness.

Where did it break out? What's the prognosis on curing everybody before it gets worse? Why did it break out in the first place?, or so I asked myself again and again while pondering what to do with all the free time. I mean, I could not even visit a cinema, or a museum (where I could view more Fulgencio San Roman movies) without being harassed by some resentful police-youth, forced to beat the streets while the fat, older veterans stayed home to celebrate the latest feast day of some obscure Catholic saint.

Across Mexico's big cities, citizens reacted with confusion and fatalism, rage, and exasperating horror at the thought that their special town might be a breeding ground for the next viral outbreak. Meanwhile, goodbye for now to rich and juicy roast pork!

The Chihuahua big-wigs insisted that people should stay in their houses if they were feeling weary and woozy. Billy was assuredly disgusted to learn that they were discouraging people from kissing even their own wives, children, relatives, and/or concubines (in Billy's case, he had at least 3). Outside the Pancho Villa Clinic in the city's middle-class Centro district, a tired old doctor leaned against an ambulance and sipped coffee, one fine Monday morning on a break from an unusually busy shift. "The people are shitting in their pants, they are so scared," I overheard him say to his aids and workers. "A person gets the sniffles, or a child gets a fever and they think it is this people-pig-bird flu and rush to the hospital."

Apparently none of the cases thus far at his clinic had turned out to be the dreaded flu, but his patients gave him enough to worry about, especially if facial ugliness turned out to be viral as well.

I decided to relieve my boredom, and hopped on a city-bus that morning, fooling myself that I would be taking a city tour. But, after a dozen too many stops, I just felt I couldn't stand to suffer the germs of the locals getting on and off for even one more station. I got off, walked over to the street corner near the park, and decided to buy a news-paper. The old *boy* at the stall confided to me as he set up his rack for the newspapers on a busy thoroughfare, "We're really in danger of contagion, *hermano*. ... I'm worried. But, *Jesu-Cristo y la Virgen* save you from such a dread."

The same virus continued to sicken more and more people, Mexicans and Americans, even though the silly government spokesmen were now announcing that they felt additional vaccine production may not be necessary. In any case, the manufacturers' spokes-people retorted that they needed special "seed-stock" that was genetically matched to the pig virus to be able to make the touted vaccines. They wouldn't make any more vaccines than they felt were necessary in any case, particularly since no more deaths were being reported, so that put an end to that matter.

Good, old-fashioned Tami-flu and Relenza medications seemed effective against the new strain, and I was certainly relying on them en lieu of a vaccine. They were effective against most symptoms, though Billy's wife insisted they exacerbated her case of the "Aztec-two-step" (diarrhea). Meanwhile, we couldn't even find bacon for my breakfasts anymore, not that it bothered my hosts since they were practically vegetarians ~ though, in Billy's case, an avowed philanderer and connoisseur of female genitalia, he was an unrepentant self-described vagi-tarian. Yet, the wicked little virus would put a temporary halt even to his extra-marital "consultations," or so he referred to his adulteries as such.

Good, ol' Jose Angel Cordova (to reiterate, Mexico's Health Secretary), hungry for more media exposure, went back on television and assured that the country had enough Tami-flu to treat 1 million people, at least in the Mexico City area, but the rest of the country would be screwed. The effective over-the-counter medicine would be strictly controlled and handed out only by doctors, so hurray for me that I was able to horde a few bottles before the restrictions were enforced!

The next day I went to that park again to see if the old man was still selling his news-papers, and he was; I approached, inquired into the state of his health, and he cryptically replied that he was, "waiting to hear" whether his 18-year-old daughter had been infected by the frightful new virus. Apparently, she had been suffering from sneezing, dizzy-spells, coughing and fever for a week without her father ever knowing about it. "If they say that it is the virus, then we'll all fall together." He said. "We are Tarahumara, and have no defenses against European illnesses. Until it hits all of us, we don't want to think about it."

Think about it? Who would want to do a silly thing like that!

Oh Maestro San Roman, where are you to capture history in the Making?

There's plenty of celluloid still around to record it all.

Now what do you think of *your* Mexico?

A WETBACK ON THE MOVE

The days came and went in a hurry. People were beginning to settle down, and the pig-flu virus scare turned out to be more like a practical joke. I certainly had little to worry about, though, I admit, I was scared right down to my under-wear for a spell. Chihuahua didn't seem so awful to me anymore, and I looked forward to removing myself from the ever-ponderous sloth that had weighed me down throughout the so-called public emergency.

I packed up again early one morning, bade my adieus to Juana and Billy (who had just arrived, exhausted from the previous night's sexual deviancy), and called the bus station to reserve my seat on their hauler bound for Monterrey, in the state of Nuevo Leon.

It was a tender, somewhat morose farewell, for they had been very tolerant hosts, and I was beginning to like the quiet, hippie-like ambiance they'd established around their *colonia* (neighborhood).

Hence, Juana, a faithful Catholic like all good Mexicans, genuflected and gesticulated with the sign of the crucifix on me, and then Billy, philosophical as always, typically addressed me with an assurance that, *the kingdom of heaven is within you; free your mind, and your ass will follow.*

So, I left with their blessings in tow, free of doubts and negativity, and headed straight for the bus station, my unwilling ass dragging behind me.

Once boarded, the damned, obsolete vehicle trudged out and made straight for the periferico (highway). The unreliable bus schedule would afford me long hours of reflection on my expectations of this Mexican experience. Monterrey came upon us with a light fog and slight chill; "Sultana of the North," I found this industrial metropolis to be a most elegant town, and her populace to be most engaging. Her notable landmarks, like Cerro de la Silla, the baroque Episcopal palace, the elegant government palace, made for an afternoon of touristic fun, and the food, hot and spicy, was better than I'd expected given my bad bouts with beans recently. I particularly enjoyed roasted cabrito (kid-goat), the most popular of the traditional dishes in this region, and the tour of the brewery *Cerveceria Cuauhtemoc Moctezuma,* proved to be most jolly. Later I enjoyed a good soccer game at the Estadio Tecnologico; the host team, Rayados de Monterrey, defeating their visitor-rivals from Coahuila. Mostly though, I spent my time just thinking; I couldn't help but ponder all of my expectations of this country before having crossed the border vis-a-vis all the frustrations that accompanied me the minute I had arrived in Tamaulipas. Already I had imbibed enough of the attitudes, customs, curious idiosyncrasies, vulgar dialects, and downright bad habits of representative natives to make a few frank conclusions of my own regarding the meaning of what it is to be a "Mexican"; frankly, a few more months and, I feared, I just might go ape, or as much as the expression lends to the individual worry. So much of the country's history was still playing a less than healing role in the evolution of its society. So many of the native prejudices that have shielded the native Indians and their progeny of mixed blood from the humiliations of the Mexican-born European overlords, or *Criollos,* throughout the centuries, had now left them stagnant in superstition, isolated from making any sort of social, cultural, industrial and scientific progress.

Therewithal, I came across a book written about Fulgencio San Roman, which contained many of his quotations stretching back to the 1940s. They made as much sense today as they had many decades ago. In essence, he complained that there was too much cynicism, and parody, and gossiping about the future of Mexico.

It is to deride, his generation would say about the stagnation of Mexico, in spite of superficial *political* progress. It should be the reverse; it is to cry, and then to damn, since the most important cultural and historical region of Latin-America, and one of the most intriguing in the world, is being oppressed to death by this faith in a bigotry its people clings to, and cannot separate from its collective soul. At the same time, its people vomit their own values in the hope of achieving some kind of obscure modernity that promises much, but was not likely to deliver on anything.

His many experiences, unlike my few, in Mexico, working for a government that regulated even the arts and the content of movies, were both risible and lamentable. He certainly laughed and cried on many occasions upon reflecting on the puzzling course his country, as well as his career, was taking. Overall they are, just like my recent tribulations, sad, very sad, when looked at as being simply the unraveling of history's mysteries. And yet, he laughed at his own tears. I am sure most Mexicans find their traumas to be more than amusing given all the suffering this land has known.

I had no complaints to make about my Mexican hosts thus far. Everyone (mostly) had treated me with the utmost respect. And yet, pig flu or no pig flu, I sensed there was such an aura of fear cast around me, if only because I did not look weary and oppressed like many do here. According to San Roman, many of his contemporaries appeared afraid out of their wits about what next he might do, so unlike the feeling of sans-gene that people today have regarding freedom of expression. And, it wasn't that he decried the temper or attitudes of the times, or that he actively opposed an increasingly paternalistic government founded on one-party rule. It was that he might want to do something crazy, or in an anti-socialistic way that romanticized the pre-revolutionary past. They seemed affrighted by innovation, by reality as they really saw it, but were forced to interpret in contradictory terms ... The only two things that he seemed to approve of during that era of change were the reformist administration of President Lazaro Cardenas, and the promotion of tourism by the administration of President Miguel Aleman following World War II. Otherwise, according to his interpretation, everything else just stunk to high Heaven, giving little hope to Mexico and the future she faced.

When he set out to promote the Mexican Cinema, he insisted that he felt that Mexican moving pictures were the most promising in the world, but not because they were his, or Mexican in particular, or because he thought of himself as a unique genius among film-makers. It was simply because he and his Mexican peers attempted, in Mexico, to give their native cinema a special, inimitable flavor. They sought to educate youngsters as technicians, first of all, then as producers, directors, actors, et cetera. He believed that the wheel of change, as he put it, had constantly to be turning, exposing new ideas, new personalities, and plenty of pretty faces. He argued that neither the Germans (Expressionistic and Nazi-era films), Soviets, nor even

Americans could provide all that, and, in the latter's case, didn't even try to achieve any of it ~ it goes to show what he really felt about Hollywood!

Many people warned him about how difficult it would be to crash through the old attitudes and practices of his times, and how difficult it would be to measure up to expectations he'd set for himself. He realized, however, that he had erred in that respect. He went ahead, in any case, encouraging their scrutiny, inviting them to bring on the polemics no matter how *scarred* they'd leave him, or how *scared* he'd leave them.

He ultimately cared not if his defiance would end with a bed full of broken hearts, or a house full of angry resentments. Consoling himself was a talent he learned early on, and he told himself repeatedly that broken hearts make up a great art, and none more so than film-making. It was the broken hearts of myriad idealists who had failed as painters, or writers, or film-makers that have made those particular arts alive and surging, while and when they were!

Hence, I trudged on to the next destination, thinking not of what was to come, but pondering on the weird coincidence of having met this semi-legendary film-maker who may have broken many hearts besides his own. I trudged on to make sense of the Mexico he tried to describe, and the Mexico I was now trying to understand.

I tried to make sense of what the hell this pestilence that overtook the county was all about, but all that came to mind was that Mexico was still condemned to struggle against all odds for her own, basic, elemental survival; for her dignity among nations. Mexico was damned to strive against the shameful divisions existing between the social classes; between Europeans and native Indians, and between the iconoclasts and the superstitious. None could have elucidated these anomalies better than San Roman, but instead he chose to exacerbate them by his defiance of society.

To think, I learned all of this just by watching his nearly-forgotten movies. Perhaps I would have learned all that I wanted to learn about Mexico just by staying home and renting DVDs of his films. But, since I did not know who the hell he was prior to undertaking this quickly degenerating journey, the fact of our paths having crossed must be ascribed to Fate. All this, the extraordinary connection and sympathy I now have for the man, and having met him (sort of) personally on his own turf, took this unique experience of life far beyond the realm of coincidence.

And yet, who the hell knows? The bastards, both his contemporary nemeses and my present-day oppressors, could not have planned it that way, and would have and were doing everything in their power to make sure we never met again. If I had known my fascination with him would grow so much since leaving Reynosa, I never would have left the stinking place. But, now to get back, would it be worth it? Could I find him again? Would he still be there?

CONNECTING WITH
THE FOLKS BACK HOME

Well, the bus made good time, it was consistently cold outside, and we swung through Monterrey without a hitch. I decided to contact a long-lost cousin of mine since we had been *simpatico* with each other ever since we had first met back in the 1970s.

Her name is Angelina, or Cousin Nena to the rest of us. She was in the habit of writing exceedingly long letters, then, with the Internet revolution, annoyingly long emails. She was always thanking everyone for their support during every significant event in her life.

For the time being, I would be in need of her persuasive skills should I need somebody as a reference now that my two-week tourist visa had expired, and from thence I would be regarded as a roving *Wetback*! She would be pestering everyone, not to mention my long-suffering lap-top computer, however, and for the time being, about the swine flu epidemic. She wrote something personal about her brush with the illness, and things about her former husband who had actually been afflicted with the virus. So, she informed us, the bastard, revenging himself against what he saw as a personal slight to his ego, tried purposely to spread the contagion wherever he went.

Speaking of this fellow, Jose' *Pepe* Martin, when Angelina was a high-school senior years ago she went to Canada for a hasty vacation, met this guy at a beer-tavern, who turned out to be a fellow Mexican, hastily spread-eagle for him, then married him. Eventually, however, things didn't work out, and she returned to Mexico. She never filed for divorce, however, and neither did this "bozo" (her term of endearment). All this was in the past, and, as far as she was concerned, the boisterous and ponderous opera that was her marriage with him was over.

Now, back towards the future ... 15 years later, she had recently returned to Canada to file for divorce. Yet, upon reuniting for the first time in a long time, they mutually started hinting about the possibility of getting back together for no other reason than to renew their matrimonial vows ~ due to the fact being that they are still legally married, through the church and the state, and the whole she-bang. I don't know whether she was seriously considering going back to him, but she certainly made it clear to the rest of us that "the possibility was certainly plausible." More than anything else, I think she just wanted to get a feel for what everyone else thought regarding the pathetic possibility. Who knows, maybe she was seriously considering getting back with "bozo"? Anyhow, her emails have been a little graphic (and have afforded me some very needed amusement during this uncertain time of transit).

There was sex involved, which resulted in their being exposed by the hotel clerks who'd discovered them in *flagrante delicto* (Oh My God!), and there was a couple of "peace pipe" incidents (and that's all I know about the latter, no other details to report), which led to the involvement of the police. Consequently, they spent a couple of nights in a Canadian jail. Some of the other cousins, upon hearing the gory anecdotes from a couple of Nena's less than loyal siblings, began to email derogatory comments regarding all of this, but as these impertinent remonstrances were flying back and forth, and the bastards did forget to include me in the email discussions, I got a sense of Cousin Nena's justifiable contempt for the very cousins who had hitherto forgotten all about her. They'd contributed not a single moiety to her happiness, but were now heaping invectives on her situation, and making it seem far more pejorative than it actually was. Perhaps it was just as well that they blew things out of proportion, for then I could get a better perspective on the facts.

I learned about Cousin Nena's latest personal drama with the self-righteous and vindictive cousins by way of Cousin Rosa who had been always popular with the rumor-mongers. She did complain that she too had been "left out of the loop," as it were, thus she loudly complained that, "all this shit was being tossed back and forth without my having a clue as to what was going on, so I had to squeeze a few balls to let them know just how I felt about the fuck-heads for leaving me out of all the fun!"

Even she recognized, though, that everyone's proverbial cup was full of abominations (as she put it) and were hypocrites for having so hastily judged a cousin who'd always been sweet and nice to the rest of us: "Yeah, Freddy," she confided, "we're all fucked up with divorces, marriages, crummy jobs, crimes against bill-collectors, kids out of wedlock, drugs, life, death, stuff after death ... but who's gonna give a shit in a hundred years!"

GETTING THE DIRT FIRST HAND

Cousin Nena at last got in touch with me, and invited me to stay in her lovely, Victorian-style decorated suburban home for the length of my visit in Monterrey. She drove, and showed me about the leather-goods production district, where she had employment as some fancy bill-receiving secretary. We talked much about our lack of regular correspondence considering our sympathetic bond, and easy-going trust in one-another. Oddly enough, we both complained that perhaps the other one did not appreciate the long-letters, and later emails, we sent to each-other, which made the lack of communication all the more apparent: "You thought what you wrote was a lot?" I asked her. "Well, coming from a *writer's* point of view, that ain't shit."

Anyway, it was fascinating to learn what she really felt about what was being written about her. I only regretted not having communicated with her earlier.

Furthermore, her tale of getting back with "Bozo" after not having seen him in 15 years, I thought this was drama for the ages ~ Her own story proved more intriguing than I had supposed. I even considered writing a whole book centered around her unique experience of life. So, what could I relate about her life to my own? With all that was happening and her erratic behavior, did either she or her ex-husband feel the proverbial "cold weather" coming in, or what? Did my sentimental cousin feel the spark of love, of "Spring-time" again? Was his libido stimulated once more by the sight of her ample bosoms after years of consoling himself (according to Cousin Rosa) with "Rosie Palmer?" No one would dare answer!

In any case, I fully appreciated her righteous indignation against the other cousins. I was already under the false impression that they'd automatically included her in all of their threads, so for a subject as intriguing as this one about cousin Nena, I can imagine just how angry she must have felt.

I admit, I did get copies of the threads all the time from likes of

Rosa's brothers, and even Nena's sisters, like Theresa and Maribel. Since I received them too, I thought it alright for me to join them, supposing I had something witty to remark upon, much to my regret and consternation.

I had enough troubles right now, however, protecting myself from the local drunks and mendicants as they foisted their crippled children in front of me for a hand-out, spreading their porcine flu germs in the process, to care about my reputation among cousins I was not really familiar with, and today some inspector almost forcibly entered Nena's house to drop repellent-pellets against the mosquitoes that spread Dengue Fever ~ they were expecting a bad outbreak this coming Summer.

Funny, I thought; hitherto undertaking this trip and what route I would follow, and then coming to this damp and chilly *beer-cooler* of a region, Dengue Fever, Pig Flu, et cetera, were just names of musical bands that played alternative rock music (you know the type---"rock" music that is little more than screeching, boisterous cacophony, which drug-addicts and pot-smokers find to be mellow and soothing.) But, the house was found to be clean, and no one about was in any imminent danger of catching anything, much to my relief. It would have been something else for my diary had I succumbed to some greasy bug served up by some half-wit stupidity of a man who cared nothing of my plight and vulnerability to these foreign illnesses. As far as some of the intransigent natives were concerned, even if they did not fully understand what was going on within their precious country, *the more the merrier*! Now, back to the Nena drama, and yes, it was a drama. Her husband had engendered a child with some woman that wanted to marry him, but of course they couldn't because he was indeed still married to Nena. The latter gave cause to the "sudden" divorce (yeah right, 15 years later). Apparently they were both (sort of) having second thoughts after seeing each other again. You know, I truly believe in following your heart, but I also believe that in situations like this one a person needs to use their head and not let him/herself get carried away with day-dreams that, in Nena's case, pretty much went up in a puff of smoke (almost literally, considering the marijuana meditations upon which they had based their marital vows) many years ago. More than anything, observers were left to ask themselves: why did it take "Bozo" so many years to contact Nena? If he had always kept the flame burning for her, could one not think that he would have tried to get in touch with her sooner?

Well, that was my brush with "embarrassing relations" for the moment. Nena and her family were very courteous with, and made me feel like a true-blue Mexican whilst savoring the local delicacies and cultural activities, which included a couple of native dances performed by the local Indian tribe, and a parade sponsored by the Monterrey beer brewers in order to stimulate public pride in their sweetly palatable product. My relatives would always make me feel welcome in either case because that is how they felt about family relations. All that I had to do was contact my cousins and introduce myself as "hijo de Tio Pancho", and would be so sure that they would love to hear from me personally. In fact, because I was now traveling in Mexico for an indefinite term, there was always the possibility that they could even take advantage of where I happened to be stranded during any given time to rendezvous with me, as it were. That way I would establish my own special relationship with them, free of parental or avuncular interference. They really were all quite engaging and generous in their own way, and, with respect to anecdotes we exchanged regarding the traumas and disappointments served to us by our parents, we certainly had a lot in common!

JESUS CHRIST, SAVE US FROM THE PIGS!

Woe is me ... woe is pitiful me, or so goes a traditional song well remembered around and about these parts, appropriately titled POBRE DE MI (Poor Little Me). The bus operator played it on his ancient cassette player as the old vehicle trudged towards Queretaro. My goodbyes were brief, and my cousin was wistful about family reminiscences. I just wanted to move on to the next leg of the adventure, though I admit, I enjoyed Monterrey immensely.

Our arrival In Queretaro City was wet with unseasonable precipitation, but it gave me a fine impression anyway. Nonetheless, my enthusiasm for the place was ruined almost at once with the news from Mexico City: The Pig Flu was back! Churches stood empty, masses were precipitously postponed, other Roman Catholic services were deferred until a green light was given indicating that all was safe. Then, local officials advised that health-department flunkies would be screening people suspected of carrying the latest strain of the pig flu in bus stations and airports, and the so-called experts touted that they feared it could spread again, and grow to world-wide epidemic proportions.

The recriminations would begin once more. President Felipe Calderon, it was announced worriedly, had assumed "special" powers to separate the sad dolts infected with the fatal flu strain that Mexico's health minister said had felled almost ninety persons, and had likely attacked nearly 1500 throughout the 32 states by the time I arrived in Queretaro. I just couldn't describe to my own diary the attitude of *je ne sais quoi* that afflicted many Mexicans.

Mayors all over the surrounding states complained that the ministries of Health and Disease Control did not advise them in time about the confirmed cases, so now they were afraid the public school students were the most dangerous purveyors of the sickness.

Well fantastic! Now I had to guard myself from the pimple-ridden punks who were more guilty of noise pollution than anything else. Mexican officials previously had whined that there were dozens of "probable" cases amongst the high-school student bodies themselves, but tests later confirmed that it was swine flu. In Queretaro the Mayor's office stressed that the incidents were mild, and many of the young folks were recovering.

So, I informed my diary, whilst I was looking about for an easier way to sneak out of the state for my next stop, be it Zacatecas or Veracruz, hundreds of people just hanging around the *Auberge* (hostel) I was staying at had come down with the symptoms, and this would be the closest I would come to being overwhelmed by a mass infection. Later, I learned that many older students played it smart and took off for Cancun, or Acapulco with their friends for a protracted spring break romp. No one, as far as I know, had reported the pig germs in, or had reached the Caribbean coast, but I suspected the Flu Virus itself didn't want to compete for victims that rightly belonged to Dengue Fever. Yes, viruses are very jealous of their own turf!

In Mexico City itself, or so the news agencies reported, soldiers and health workers kept a vigilant watch on the capital's subway system throughout the week-end, giving out surgical masks and rooting out possible flu cases in the process. Citizens were asked to get medical help should they come down with multiple symptoms. Speaking of, there were moments when I thought, and felt, I had a fever of more than 100 degrees, a sore throat, body aches, respiratory congestion, the dreaded uncontrollable coughing, and, with due respect to the local cuisine, *puking and the squirts* (as Billy colorfully described *vomiting* and *diarrhea* in his weekly e-mail, and from which he now suffered).

Hundreds of public events, AGAIN, from concerts to sports matches, were postponed or canceled to keep the stinky masses from congregating, thus spreading the symptoms from within the irresponsible crowds. Zoos were closed, much to my irritation since I enjoy paying a visit to the local animal-park in any town I happen to be passing through, and even family visits to prisons were suspended; if I had been in California during this time, I certainly would have had cause for annoyance since so many of my one-time acquaintances now called jail their home.

A Wetback in Reverse

Whilst going out to find me some evening grub, I noticed that about a dozen state police in blue surgical masks stood in front of Queretaro's elegant Churrigueresque Cathedral, which had been emptied of its superstitious devotees after a measure calling off services had been enforced to discourage large concentrations of the faithful, tithes or no tithes. While I crossed the street to ask one of the policemen if he knew when they would open it again, a young woman in her twenties (I think) interrupted, and complained that she had arrived for her confirmation only to find a sign announcing that all Masses, baptisms, and confirmations were canceled until further notice. Her subsequent bawling was enough of an incentive for me to get the Hell out of there.

The last thing she cried before I re-crossed the street was, "We are all faithful Catholics ... this is an awful thing you do, closing the cathedral." She went on bawling while cradling her squirming brat in her arms, "This god-forsaken flu must be bad. But what will I do? I don't know if I can return any time soon?" ~ well deary, I thought to myself, the cooties are the cooties, and there wouldn't be any fiddling with even the local drunkard's health; actually, the town boozers were the least in danger since all of those alcoholic beverages they consumed actually protected them from infection. Huh! who would've known that cheap whiskey was the best defense against pig cooties. Live and learn, eh?

And so, as the hours ticked by, the markets and restaurants were left devoid of patrons; throngs of Mexicans, some with just a fever, rushed to the by-now congested hospitals, and I felt like I had the whole city to myself.

Queretaro, like most of Mexico's big cities by now, appeared to have lost valuable work days in discovering the, as of yet, newest flu strain, and humans may have no natural immunity to it. Health officials at the federal level had found cases in 16 Mexican states, including Queretaro. What a shame, and it is such a nice state too. But, just since I've been here, perhaps three dozen new suspected cases had been reported on that previous Saturday alone.

Regarding the state of the epidemic in other states, the first death was reported in southern Oaxaca State by late March, but the federal officials didn't do anything about it, or appeal to international agencies, like the Center for Disease Control and Prevention, until several days later, which was around the same time they'd sent trained teams to hospitals all over the country to root out victims with severe symptoms. Accordingly, they were said to have noticed something odd: the combined flu strain was knocking out mostly people under forty years of age. Flu victims, everybody knows, are usually either infants, the aged, or hard-core stoners, like Billy once had been. Yet, once again, one needs only to remind oneself of the Spanish flu pandemic after World War I: plenty of young adults had perished then, and now history was repeating itself, except that now pigs eaten by Spanish-speakers were getting the blame.

Once again I fiddled with my diary, and twiddled my thumbs while wondering what next could happen. The government health agency would soon ask all townships and cities to step up their spying and rat on suspicious sorts, as airports around the country were screening travelers from everywhere for any symptoms.

On Sunday, Mexico City radio broadcasts reported that a dozen students "likely" had the swine flu after a school trip to Guadalajara, though the Health Ministry reported that none of the youngsters was seriously ill, and there was no guarantee they had the damned flu. This was a surprise; I had always known that people from the Capital regarded people from Guadalajara as a bunch of pigs, but never figured they'd blame them for the disease!

As far as Guadalajara's Health agency was concerned, there was only one or two suspected cases in their region, and the rest of the state of Jalisco was checking out reports of five more possible cases.

With the police harassing me that I could not leave the immediate precincts, I insisted they let me talk to the person-in-charge of the growing quarantine, and she said that the outbreak of the never-before-seen virus had "pandemic potential." I asked her then to tell me something I *didn't* know. But, she said, it was still too early to give the alarm if it would become a pandemic.

Damn it! Now what? Where was I to turn? There was no Billy or Angelina around to bail me out, so what the Hell was I to do?

These people had already issued calls for isolating the sick, and blanketing anyone around them with anti-viral drugs such as the ever reliable Tami-Flu; I still had a neat supply I had brought with me from

Chihuahua. Too many of the afflicted had been identified in and around Queretaro for such a solution now. The pandemic flu experts, however, said it was also too late to contain the disease to Mexico and the United States.

Therefore, now I would be stuck here due to politics, and that is all it was, just stinking politics. The average crowds didn't betray any palpable signs of panic, so what the Hell was going on with these imbecilic experts? Why were they fanning the flames of alarm?

Regardless of their real motives, the local authorities ordered schools closed in their state clear through the first week of May.

Then, teams from the Center for Disease Control were in lurking about spying and ratting, but ostensibly to assist in setting up detection testing for the pig flu, something that the officials forgot to to do the first time around.

Nevertheless, the number of cases continued to grow, and the local big-wigs were scared over a reported threefold spike in the number of victims by the beginning of Spring, but then tried to convince themselves that it was a late rebound in the December-February flu season. And, testing at domestic labs did not warn doctors of the causes for the latest outbreak. Even though just about everybody had known about it, Mexican big-wigs continued to refer to the outbreak as a "late-season flu."

New virus or old, I was going to "outbreak" with rage. There was nothing I could do to avoid all the proverbial red-tape. By Thursday of that week, I was beginning to feel a serious case of "the blues."

I thought to reflect on all that was happening, and asked myself: why in the Hell were there so many deaths in Mexico, and, so far, none to be reported in America? Was it really a case for lack of immunity that felled the adults? Would I be next? I mean, I had already come into close contact with infected people, so when would the symptoms of complete infection be manifest? At least in America the cases mostly involved children, so they might have a chance to get over it. This strain that affected adults was something scary all-together. Frankly, I think that the fatalities were due to negligence on the part of the victims; each one just ignored the symptoms, and thought to cure themselves with traditional Mexican remedies ~ hot cinnamon tea, a ripe lemon to suck on, and a shot of tequila.

I finally got around to wearing the confounded blue surgical mask the health-worker gave me the previous weekend, especially since I could not be sure that I was secure against infection even with the Tami-flu. More and more signs that things were returning to normal were about; street-workers sweeping up garbage, public-transportation drivers giving the average folk a hard time as usual, and local merchants giving everybody some of their bad attitude was practically a cause for rejoicing.

The chill air must've been doing me harm, I thought. I should have just stayed in my hostel room, but I was restless, and had to go to an ATM in any case; I was hungry, and did not have pesos enough in my pocket for even a bean and cheese taco.

What most locals had been complaining about was the lack of access to a proper vaccination. If the government had decided that vaccine production was necessary ahead of time, manufacturers would have needed seed-stock to get started, but they didn't do it, and now every healthy adult was screwed, and just had to take their chances out in the open should they opt to return to work or school.

Worse yet, cases of tourists from Europe and Australia coming down with the flu were now being reported to the local authorities, so now they were really worried, not just pretending to care like they did when they were informed that their fellow country-men had been infected. And, of course, the foreigners were given top priority at the hospitals, courtesy of the Mexican tax-payers. Cases reported in and around the popular beach resorts were given sensitive treatment because officials feared any further outbreaks might adversely affect their precious tourism revenues, which they did in any case. Most cases, though, turned out to be negative, so, *hah! hah!* to the puerile pansies who were afraid they'd no longer be able to charge the hapless visitors nine-American dollars for a Coca-Cola!

Anybody and everybody was suspected of carrying the germs, hence, everybody would be observed with a cynical eye and treated as if one's neighbor had been suddenly turned into one's closest enemy. The wavering panic and citizen surveillance activities felt like some Stalinistic political purge was being carried out, and I'd be next on their hit list. Hence, for the rotten time being, Mexico's schools would remain closed; museums, libraries and theaters, in a measure to contain the outbreak after hundreds were sickened within their respective walls, would be barred to the public, and I'd be left to record it all in my diary before going back to play with myself ... figuratively speaking.

The next day, the reporters announced that more clueless persons had succumbed overnight to the flu in the local hospital, and four other fatal cases were blamed on the returning strain.

The officials also reported that nearly four-score had been hospitalized with the illness, but they just did not know if many of them, or any of them had been due to the actual pig flu.

Most of the recent or expected deaths involved victims who wanted and demanded medical help, but only after the disease was already well-advanced. Consequently, all would have to pay for everybody else's negligence. Even with the urging and the alerts and warnings, however, people will be people, and they just could not give a flying damn about someone else dying from the flu. They were all smug in their nests so long as it didn't touch them. As the clerk at the hostel said, "If you notice your neighbor's head has been sheared, get ready to be shorn!"

I wonder what San Roman was thinking just now ...

THUNDER ROLLS OVER AZTLAN

At last I could safely pack up again, and roll on out of Queretaro. I have to say, in spite of the newest pig flu scare, I enjoyed myself enormously; of the interesting sights and sounds to be had there, the most prominent feature of the city is its humongous aqueduct consisting of seventy five arches, each twenty meters wide, was built sometime in the 18th Century at the request of the nuns of the Santa Clara Convent to bring water to the residents of the city from La Caida.

Most of the remainder of Queretaro? fascinating landmarks are to be found near the historic center. It is friendly to pedestrian-traffic, and filled with lovely Spanish colonial-era buildings. I have to felicitate the local yokels for doing a fine job of up-keeping the area, if not for themselves at least for the sake of tourists. Cleaning crews keep the streets swept, and the police regulate the nasty vendors so that they do not bottle-neck the streets and sidewalks with their worthless junk. At every eventide, the town center fills with, mostly, young people; strolling the plazas and alamedas, patronizing the traditional restaurants, cafes and snack stalls, I could feel their joie de vivre.

One of the best ways to experience this part of the city is during the *Noche de Leyendas* (Night of Legends), which is a hybrid between readers' theater and live historical docu-drama. A group of actors would guide their audiences through the romantic streets of the old town narrating legends and fables about what was historically endemic about the respective place. The event begins at the Plaza de Armas in the center of the city with a reenactment of the legend of *Carambada*. The spectacle then meanders through the streets, all the while guides recount tales related to bandits, romantic trysts and myths. These tales require audience participation, providing verses and dialogue, and provoking debate amongst the hapless participants. This just shows some of the more pleasant aspects of Mexican life in given regions, and helps one to understand that, despite all the daily miseries that assault your average Mexican, there is much to experience, much to enjoy, much to remember with fondness and delight. I could do no worse, so I decided just to enjoy it all. I then got my gear, and hopped on the bus for another state.

As the bus rolled into the state of Hidalgo, *wandering* it felt like, through the *Llanos*, or plains, of Apam, scattered haciendas breaking the rolling fields of magueys, I suddenly became introspective; the images of San Roman movies certainly moved my thoughts, and my imagination felt free to soak it all in, the fleeting winds blowing dust through the bus windows as our attention was directed toward the monolithic Toltec sentinels standing in the ruins of Tula looming in the distance. By now it was obvious that this country is not a happy garden where primordial beings of virtue and innocence dwell in accord and abundance. Mexico is not the wonder-land of mystery and play that, many say, San Roman tried to create in his movies. Mexico may be colorful and exotic, Toltec temples adjacent to living Tule trees more ancient than the ruins themselves, but the impression is illusory. In this country, the peasantry have progressed little since the devastations caused by the 1910 Revolution; the peasantry continue to be excluded from the prosperity, are shamefully humiliated, allowed to wallow in their own ignorance and superstition for the sake of traditions, tribal loyalties, and the preservation of their indigenous cultures. Their present leaders are no more sensitive to their desperation than were the military dictatorships that ruled them prior to the great revolution. In the war against the narco-traffickers they have amassed a record of cold-blooded executions to match the sanguinary murders of the drug-pushers themselves, whilst exploiting the fears, and degrading the expectations, of the paranoid masses for the sake of national unity, or, better yet, "law and order." There is something definitely ruthless running in the veins of every-day Mexicans that leads them to justify, at least in their minds, the reprehensible repression that ranks with the worst of the cocaine overlords whom for decades made of Colombia a killing ground of innocents.

The wild and starkly contrasting beauty of Mexico can capture your breath, cause you to pause in astonishment, to sigh in bewilderment, and to remark self-righteously on the barbarous attitudes that pervade their feelings toward the society and culture that have borne them. I have tried to capture as many images with my faltering digital camera as with the descriptive powers of my pen, but none would fully understand the pictures I'd hoped to share, unless they come to see it all for themselves.

Nevertheless, average Mexicans are losing their right and title to their lands, slowly driven away by force of economic-industrial development, promoted not by their own entrepreneurs, but, once again, by foreigners; they are promoted by Americans whom love Mexico so much that they are all too willing to trade any amount of cash for the whole shebang. Many Mexicans, all too aware of the power of the *Green* (U.S. Dollar), are making it easy for them.

But, that is not the whole story. Vicious bands of mafioso officials, mixing socially with murderous narco-traffickers and using any excuse to pilfer public resources for their own enrichment, and nothing else, feel justified by the speculative activities of Americans. Whether legitimate or related to the drug-smuggling, the sale of human lives for cheap labor in sweat shops, as well as dangerous passage for illegal immigrants willing to lose their lives for a chance to creep into America, the narco-pushers have utterly plundered the natural treasures of their country. They have exterminated, or tried to, local opposition groups. Organized peasants, fighting for the legacy of Zapata's fight for their rights, have faced eviction from lands they and their ancestors have tendered for centuries. It is almost too sad, too maddening to face with an objective eye.

Thus I say to Maestro San Roman, or anybody else who has turned a blind eye to the dark side of Mexican culture and history, there is nothing beautiful or inspiring about these heinous deeds. There is nothing wonderful about the murder of honest police officials who tried to rise to the demands of their duty, and were brutally cut down for caring too much about their own people. There is nothing charming about rounding up teenagers and younger children for the purpose of turning them into criminal drug-addicts, destroying the institution of family in the process.

That is why I say that thunder rolls over *Aztlan*---the name of the traditional home of the Aztecs before they abandoned it to seek the land promised to them by their god of war, and ultimately arrived in the Valley of Mexico---presaging a new disaster, social, political as well as natural, that will consume the entire country in its explosive rage. That is why I say that to celebrate the boasts of their political leaders, that they have brought Mexico into the First World of economic progress, is adding insult to injury. No amount of poignant images, of moving dialogue, of disturbing messages or sub-text by San Roman or anybody else could convince me that Mexico's greatness is vindicated by the misery and useless sacrifices of its people. They all know that they are dealing with the on-going, ever-repeating, struggle of the Mexican masses for emancipation from the degradation of their own superstitions, enveloped beautifully and majestically in the trappings of church ceremonials; expressed in the profusion of idols, which the faithful insist are not idols but statues representing their favorite saints, they worship them as if the statues themselves could grant them their wishes just like old-fashioned pagan idols could. Mostly though, they struggle against the oppression and down-right tyranny of their elected officials, though they call themselves defenders of democracy and friends of the people. Little could Pancho Villa or Emiliano Zapata, still potent symbolic figures of resistance against reactionary dictatorship, have imagined the monstrous distortion that became of the Mexico they fought and died for, needlessly.

My observation is that Mexicans live, thrive, and connive at constructing a Mexico founded upon a distortion of reality ~ the reality they wish for themselves, but do not trust their fellow country-men to uphold, to protect and defend against all onslaughts of corruption and threats of recurring tyranny, even while clinging to their much-abused facade of democracy, which reassures them of the status quo.

Perhaps I am being unfair to Fulgencio San Roman. Perhaps it was the very beauty of his cinematic imagery that obfuscated the reality I was experiencing, and confused the meaning of his art. Perhaps he did in fact see right through the distorted reality fed to his people by their leaders and left-wing intellectuals, and he could distinguish between what was truly inspiring about Mexico, and that which provoked our mutual repugnance. His original conceptions ultimately did satirize or condemn rather than glorify the state of affairs. He never actually romanticized the reactionary practices of the Mexican regime, especially as it stood after President Plutarco Elias-Calles imposed one-party rule back in the late 1920s. On the contrary, through his masterful montages and tragic scenes we do in fact learn that his Mexico is a land of sorrow, of unrequited fears, and of chronic despair. Thus, the children are taught, as they have been for centuries, to mock death early on, and to invite it to preside over their most life-affirming rituals and festivities.

I would, if I could, call upon all faithful Mexicans (or, at least, fans of San Roman movies) to re-affirm, and to live out the motto that has sustained oppressed generations of the common herd: *Me Vale Madre*! ~ so says the motto, or "I don't give a shit!" And, like magic, everything is restored to a proper perspective. Reality may still be distorted but, they figure out for themselves, who is really qualified or wise enough to interpret what reality is supposed to be? Therefore, I would say as well, let their protests be heard wherever pretense and presumption are being plugged up their asses by their their pablum-puking politicians; May their own posterity allow their protests to echo in their own hearts before ignorance creeps around, and history repeats itself ... *Again*!

It is true (one can assert, now that I know more about the man) that San Roman had expressed the pious hope that his body of work should be imbibed by what he called the "pop-corn popping crowds," instead of by a relatively limited group of devoted fans and film-touting intellectuals, but the latter turned out to be the case. Even so, the silver screen no longer graces his compelling imagery, and most Mexicans have never even heard of their native-son, revered in other countries as one of the greatest artists of the 20th Century.

What does echo in my mind are the comments he included in one of his last films, *Once Upon A Time In Old Mexico*:

"If the lie returns to the mouth of the powerful, our voice, aflame with righteousness and truth, will cry unto the angel of Justice again ...

We are tired of years of oppression, lies, and hunger.

We have the right to fight for our lives and dignity!

Death does not scare us, though the tyrant invokes it to scare us.

The angel of death is, after all, our friend ..."

ACROSS BORDERS, AND CLASS DIVISIONS

The days passed slowly in Hidalgo, the dry fields and dusty rows of maiz seemed to delight in the quiet of sunny afternoons. I too felt a certain serenity, in spite of the abundant evidence of poverty and filth around me. I was permitted to stay at a traditional hacienda called Itzlayac, which belonged to the Quezada-Potrillo clan; an old Criollo family, which had been upholding traditions around these parts since the era of Emperor Agusto de Iturbide, right after Mexico had gained her independence from Spain. It was a fascinating stay, and our hosts were stiff, dignified, but forthcoming nonetheless. I left with no complaints, only indelible memories.

It was also about that time of week when I could expect an email from Billy in which he reports his activities, gossips about his adulteries, or shares some bit of poetry or lyrics he'd learned recently and wished to impart to me, if only to bolster my usually sour mood. The latest lyrics, I think, he heard from a modern Christmas song, but this time around they touched me for some reason, and resonated in my head for many days to come:

"A Birth Certificate shows that we were born;
A Death Certificate shows that we died;
Pictures show that we lived!
Have a seat. Relax ...
I Believe ... that just because two people argue, It doesn't mean they don't love each other. And, just because they don't argue, It doesn't mean they do love each other.
I Believe ... that we don't have to change friends if we understand that friends change.
I Believe ... that no matter how good a friend is, they're going to hurt you every once in a while, and you must forgive them for that.
I Believe ... that true friendship continues to grow, even over the longest distance. Same goes for true love.

I Believe ... that you can do something in an instant that will give you heartache for life.

I Believe ... that it's taking me a long time to become the person I want to be.

I Believe ... that you should always leave loved ones with loving words. It may be the last time you see them.

I Believe ... that you can keep going long after you think you can't.

I Believe ... that we are responsible for what we do, no matter how we feel.

I Believe ... that either you control your attitude or it controls you.

I Believe ... that heroes are the people who do what has to be done when it needs to be done, regardless of the consequences.

I Believe ... that my best friend and I can do anything or nothing and have the best time.

I Believe ... that sometimes the people you expect to kick you when you're down will be the ones to help you get back up.

I Believe ... that sometimes when I'm angry, I have the right to be angry, but that doesn't give me the right to be cruel.

I Believe ... that maturity has more to do with what types of experiences you've had, and what you've learned from them and less to do with how many birthdays you've celebrated.

I Believe ... that it isn't always enough, to be forgiven by others. Sometimes, you have to learn to forgive yourself.

I Believe ... that no matter how bad your heart is broken the world doesn't stop for your grief.

I Believe ... that our background and circumstances may have influenced who we are, but, we are responsible for who we become.

I Believe ... that you shouldn't be so eager to find out a secret. It could change your life Forever.

I Believe ... two people can look at the exact same thing and see something totally different.

I Believe ... that your life can be changed in a matter of hours by people who don't even know you.

I Believe ... that even when you think you have no more to give, When a friend cries out to you ~ you will find the strength to help.

I Believe ... that credentials on the wall do not make you a decent human being.

A Wetback in Reverse

I Believe ... that the people you care about most in life are taken from you too soon. The happiest of people don't necessarily have the best of everything;

They just make the most of everything they have.

... I Believe ... I Believe ... yes, I Believe!"

The sentiments are soporific, the message is mawkish, but Billy meant well, and the verses would serve me well to remember in the weeks ahead. Now Zacatecas beckoned: a stern and graceful old colonial city with steep and narrow streets, and a friendly, mostly White-European citizenry bearing a palpable pride in their traditions as well as their land. The minute I had a chance, I headed straight for the nearest inn and ordered a bowl of their famous Menudo stew, which was just what I needed to get over the beer-hangover that followed me the rest of the way. The hotel was not much to smile about, but it overlooked the stunning civic plaza, the stately cathedral to the right of my balcony, and the sumptuous governor's palace to the left. In spite of the quiet welcome, the empty streets, and the chill air rolling down from "La Bufa" (the cave-infested mountain land-mark), fear lurked about with the alert of the oncoming Swine flu, crossing new borders on its way further south. A number of confirmed cases of the damned malady led to the immediate closure of restaurants (which were allowed to serve take-out in order to curb unnecessary gatherings), and general service stores.

Meanwhile, I thought I'd get in touch with an old acquaintance, Jose "El Chepe" Antonio Salinas: tall, lanky, funny-looking with a long nose, he lived in a crummy house and didn't realize it, and, to date, he was most notorious amongst friends for his malodorous feet. I thought he might be able to help me out while I walked around his quaint town. Indeed, Zacatecas is relatively small, everyone seems to know each other, and neither secrets nor rumors are borne with much humor. This newest alert sent us all on edge, and the common folk were as worried as the responsible officials feigned concern that the damned virus appeared to be settling itself in smaller communities, like Zacatecas, and could spread therefrom, thus worsening the prospects for a pandemic.

I expressed my concern over the whole dirty mess to Chepe, and he responded, "Yes, I know ~ It's a frightening possibility, but don't get your panties into a tizzy just now. I think it would be wrong to think all this is inevitable."

So, what could I do but follow his calm example. He was always pretty reliable in a scrape, and as long as I enjoyed the Old World charms of his town, the last thing I wanted to think about was the odds of catching the damned flu.

In addition, he cited cases in which some local students had been exposed to the sickness but did not spread it around to their clueless classmates, most of whom were very susceptible to it. Unlike the real fear in the streets I experienced in Chihuahua and elsewhere, the people of Zacatecas, even with some of their neighbors stricken with the infectious germs, watched the unfolding events very carefully.

Little could he know, and I only found out about it through the newspapers, that this particular strain of the pig flu had spread to six other states, prompting the hapless officials to call for another alert, which would last till the next Monday. Fortunately, and much to my relief, they did not call for a ban on travel or inter-state border crossings. They did warn against non-essential travel in any case. The only ones to be affected by the latter warning, and Chepe would agree with me, were the ever restless drug-traffickers since their business lived and thrived by inter-state commerce.

I asked if he'd experienced these sorts of restrictions before, and he responded, "Well, yes, in a way. Border controls never have worked ~ Mexicans are just too restless, and will be damned if any *chota* (police), or low-grade official is going to tell them when and where they can move or not. Travel restrictions are definitely not respected, even if it's for the people's own good; even if it means saving lives, and helping the oppressed ... they just don't give a rat's ass!"

There would be much more economic frustration by the look of things, and that, more than anything, would provoke a public outcry. After all, people have to eat and earn money, and the safety measures were not to their benefit. The local ayuntamiento implored the surrounding communities to provide treatments and other assistance to sick people, should they come forth to seek help, and to stock up on medicines and food-stuffs in case of a greater outbreak. I had little to worry about because Chepe and his family were solicitous and forthcoming; the hotel was getting to be a little expensive, but I had my vista, the clang of the cathedral's bells wafted me to another reality, another experience of Time, and the local food was genuinely palatable ~ these people, in contrast to inhabitants of other states, kept the flies out of the soup!

A couple of days passed by, and things were genuinely calm around the town zocalo. Chepe complained that, "These local governments don't have any real power, or they just pass the buck. They don't think about larger-scale measures to prevent or treat illnesses, even in emergencies they manage to fumble everything, and then blame someone else for their loser attitudes."

Do they even have the infrastructure? Do they have the necessary provisions and equipment? Do they have the medicines?

These were questions that resonated in my head as I considered his complaints, but Chepe was always one to be prepared whether for an atomic war, a flash flood, or worse: being confronted with news that his latest girlfriend might be pregnant!

Even when news that Bird Flu and SARS had broken out in Asia a few years before, my intrepid and gung-ho friend was at the forefront preparing his fellow Zacatecos to guard against any uncalled for intimacy with their family chickens ~ and with sexual frustration rampant amongst teen-aged boys, not even poultry were safe during a full moon.

Well, Monday came and went, and the number of proven flu cases had risen to 64, but they expected the worst was over for the moment. To me, this was becoming frustratingly monotonous.

The Flu was nothing new to anyone, and this time around people were expressing annoyance more than anxiety. People die of the flu, that is a fact of daily life, and some people I overheard gabbing in the hotel lobby said that they'd rather die in bed from the flu than from a hail of drug-traffickers' bullets, or from the dysentery they might catch from the previous night's fly-infested taco-fest. Obviously it was more of that uniquely Mexican defiance of death that keep them psychologically healthy while they surrender their bodies to high-cholesterol foods and deliciously fattening beer.

One city ordinance that did irritate me was announced on Tuesday: the mayor "advised" that sports clubs, gyms, swimming pools and cantinas be closed, extending a growing quarantine of sorts that had already included schools, cinemas, and other public places.

Luckily, the order did not include restaurants since one has to eat when one has to eat. Chepe was not in agreement, however, but, I argued, they shouldn't be prohibited from serving since the latest alert proved to be rather feeble even if people gathering in close proximity may not always be the smartest thing to allow given the nature of the virus. Still, for my part, I had imbibed enough Tami-flu and *Presidente* Brandy to give me the courage to defy any virus that dared to nuzzle my lips and nostrils.

Mexico City would be one of my destinations, so news from Hidalgo and Nuevo Leon, both of which I had recently visited, that several of their respective residents who had recently returned from the capital had contracted the virus, and they turned out to be especially nasty cases, did distress me. The symptoms were unmistakable, but all cases reported from Mexico City were particularly vicious, how could this be? Why were the latter cases worse than those reported from the other states? The provincial Mexicans themselves, of course, regarded the riddle with a cynical eye because everything that comes out of Mexico City, they say, is nasty and degenerate even if comparing strains of the same disease.

Well, that certainly made me feel better about the whole mess!

I tried contacting Angelina in Monterrey, and one of the members of the Quezada family in Hidalgo, to find out how things were transpiring in their respective regions, and they confirmed that the disease was spreading, but, sadly, it was the poor who had the most to worry about since they had next to no protection, medical, financial, or otherwise. Angelina, who worked in a hospital on occasion, confided that some patients she had treated had recovered, but they would remain hospitalized until they received word from the Health Ministry, all the way in Mexico City, that it was safe to release them. It was really all this waiting and uncertainty that exacerbated the simmering anxiety.

And, a spokes-person from the hospital the Quezada family sponsored, located not far from the central town of Tula in Hidalgo, said that a 50 year-old Roman Catholic priest, who had just returned from a clerical conference in Mexico City three days before and had checked himself in when he had grievously soiled himself in public, had in fact contracted the virus and was being kept in less than spiritual isolation. But, thanks to the Virgen de Guadalupe, Santo Nino de Atocha, or, mostly likely, a couple of shots of good Tequila, the ol' closet-Protestant was expected to recover without further incidence; later, he was presented with a gift from one of his parishioners, which consisted of new under-wear.

Meanwhile, several more cases involving high-school and college-age students had been confirmed by early Wednesday ~ this could not be good. As many as 26 had taken ill and were under observation, but their individual conditions were not serious so everyone could breathe a sigh of relief ~ especially me because some sinister dope in the Mayor's office was advising in favor of imposing more travel restrictions just as I was preparing to wrap up my activities in their town.

There really wasn't anything to worry about, and the daily occurrences of city life were as evident as they ever had been. The coming days were, by now, sure to be filled with more warnings about this sickness, so why all the scandal? I never imagined these people could get so paranoid about nothing.

Good food and preventive drugs were really the best things anybody could take to avoid coming down with the sickness. Yet, once again, people will be people, and if they can find a way of screwing things up for everybody, they assuredly will, and once again they would have to deal with a growing outbreak-related panic.

Deaths or no deaths, I was beginning to feel blue all over. My original plans, to seek some companionship, were shot to Hell, and a lovely wench I was supposed to meet, an especially sensuous Latin lovely named Araceli, "stood me up," as they say, without apology or advance-warning. Now what the Hell was I supposed to do? My libido wasn't going to simmer down just because of these insensible outbreak warnings. So, what if 152 new cases were reported in Mexico city, would that make romance more desirable? So what if no one bothered to find out where the outbreak began, would that satisfy the flesh of its cravings? Ah, romance in times of war, pestilence and death is supposed to be intense and passionate. Instead, all I could think about was pigs, pigs, pigs, and more pigs. And to think, I got out of America to get away from the stifling sexual frustration that seems to have gripped everybody with its mocking talons, only to end up in this lustful land stricken with a pandemic that originated in America! Clearly, my demons had resurrected and had organized this entire folly just to go after me. Yes, I know it to be true ~ they'll go to any lengths just to see me stumble and fumble all over myself.

"I think it is stupid to say, or want to say, how it all began, or where it began, given that we had been hearing of some bad cases before," insisted Chepe after I'd called him to complain of my deteriorating mood. "Your lust will just have to find some other outlet of release, no pun intended. All of Mexico can't be concerned if you are deprived of some affection, mi amigo. So, just bite the bullet, and call on *Manuelita* (Mexican version of "rosy palmer" = masturbate) again."

Fine and dandy, I thought, so it was back to lonely fantasies, and damning Araceli in private and every other coquettish hussy who'd left me stranded as of late.

At the local hospital the next day, lines of people had formed in order to take advantage of some free government-sponsored vaccinations, only to discover that amid their ranks 29 hapless souls had succumbed to the virus ~ I certainly am glad I decided against going there at the last minute. Amongst them, however, was a sad little 5-year-old boy who'd tested positive for a particularly nasty strain of the swine flu, and the fact that he'd arrived there unaccompanied raised the question as to where he'd come from; it seems the pathetic ass-monkey had been abandoned there without papers, without money ... nothing but the infection flicking in and out of his facial orifices. Some passersby commented that he had the look and manners of a Veracruzano, which raised further questions about *how* he got to Zacatecas. I couldn't help but to feel like he must have felt: alone, abandoned, scared and rotten, though I, at least, could call on my friends for some aid, and just gather my duds and get the Hell out of there.

Finding solace in a bottle of *Viejo Vergel* and consoling my ruined hopes for romance by damning the very word "woman" whilst playing out my titties-fetish fantasies in my head, I then gathered my things, sent Araceli a nasty note of repudiation---flowing red-hair, hypnotizing jewel-like eyes, and scrumptiously perky breasts and all---and called to reserve a seat for the first bus to Plateros where I'd visit the shrine of Santo Nino de Atocha just for the Hell of it. I had sampled the local Pozole stew, and mingled with Spanish Criollo folks before heading off to mingle with the Morenos and Mulatto folks of Veracruz, which beckoned ever so seductively.

At least the local cultural society put on a show before I'd left in the sunken plaza in front of the governor's palace whereby the philharmonic orchestra played some Mariachi classics, as well as the *Marcha Zacatecas* again and again, and so loudly in fact that the hotel windows vibrated. But, it was a pleasant interlude amidst all the festering resentment and inquietude. Hence, who cared that the health ministry reported a Phase 4 and 5 alert that the sneaky virus was becoming adept at infecting humans despite preventive measures as well as treatments? The full-blown Phase 6 pandemic alert was just around the corner, and Mexico would assuredly get the full brunt of it. So, it was to back to singing, dancing and invoking the demons of "I don't give a damn" for the festive yokels, to fiddle away the night with her misfortunes and sinister tricks, as well as egging their compeers on," Let us eat and drink, for tomorrow we are to die." (Corinthians, chapter 15: verse 32). Such an attitude often leads my friendly Mexican hosts towards overeating, heavy drinking and anxiety, not to genuine peace of mind. And yet, who the Hell cares, eh?

I must admit, I thought I was beginning to come down with a fever of more than 100, and during those early hours of sobriety I awoke to find myself coughing, whining about joint aches, swooning about with a severe headache and, for all practical purposes, vomiting and holding in *the Squirts*. Meanwhile, the locals were distressed to learn that it could take months before they could receive their fair share of vaccines. For the present, they could rest assured that some anti-flu drugs could alleviate them once they were infected. Much to my romantic consternation, the best way to keep the virus from spreading, obviously, is to avoid intimate contact with others, peculiarly their private parts, and taking obvious precautions like frequent hand-washing, staying away from public places if not feeling up to the occasion, and, what seems most difficult to do for these provincial cro-magnons, just covering up their mouths while coughing and sneezing. I certainly don't look forward to the prospect of being quarantined just because somebody rudely coughs without a hanky.

It was further to be expected that the recent developments would have a deleterious effect on commerce. I am sure the local bakeries, tortilla-makers, beer-peddlers, what-have-you, felt derailed by the needless curfews imposed on the surrounding communities, but they'd soon recover. Now, to travel and tourism, and how the latest flu-scare had hurt the latter ~ It was my concern, and the negative effects would be needlessly prolonged. What would I do now? Chepe wasn't exactly encouraging, so I thought to creep out of his town without a peep. The bodily parts that were "blue" begged me to get out, and head for the swarthy sensuality of Veracruz.

Hence, to Veracruz I went, boarding the bus without even waving good-bye.

GETTING WICKED IN VERACRUZ

There must be something really special about Veracruz, this state on the Eastern-Gulf Coast of Mexico! The atmosphere is scintillating, and the people, a mix of Spanish, Negroid, and Indigenous peoples, are among the most sensual, virile and healthy, not to mention desirable, people in the whole of Mexico. I must admit though, as the bus pulled in to a border stop around midnight of that same Friday when I had departed Zacatecas, it was very humid and stifling, the waitresses weren't particularly pleasant at the local cafe' and, since it was an open-outdoor place, flies and mosquitoes abounded, much to my chagrin; but, there were plenty of insect-eating bats flapping about, much to my delight. The town was La Gloria, a foot-hill settlement near Mount Orizaba, the largest mountain in the state. The residents in this community of about 3,000 would all be rather hostile since, I later found out, they believed all outsiders were infected, and were afraid their town might be ground zero for the next pig flu outbreak even if their local health officials wouldn't admit to it.

It didn't help either that more than 470 residents are involved in the hog-raising industry, many of whom admitted that they had suffered from respiratory problems for quite some time, and the latter could be due to contamination spread by pig waste at the nearby breeding farms ~ conveniently co-owned by a U.S. company. Well, here we have more evidence that this terrible pandemic everybody was blaming Mexico for actually emanated from the United States, or at least from Americans working in this country. Naturally, when pressed with accusations, the company lackeys insisted they had found no sign of the dreaded flu on its farms, and Mexican lackeys hadn't determined the outbreak's origin as of yet.

The flu strain was blamed for more than 150 deaths in and around Veracruz alone, and cases had been confirmed in at least three other surrounding states, especially Tabasco.

I thought I had some maternal relatives I could contact in this delightfully tropical state, but there was no one to track down, so I'd be chasing plump buttocks without a compass (in a manner of speaking). I had tried to make it for this state alone as far back as late February, but it is just as well that I did not; roughly one-sixth of all Veracruzanos near the western border with Puebla had been complaining of respiratory infections that some whistle-blowers reported could be traced to a farm that lay upwind some 8.5 kilometers to the north-west, in the town of Xaltepec. Luis the Lout, a gregarious drunkard I'd met on the bus and native of those parts, whined that he understood the second he'd heard about the latest alert by way of his relatives and their confused description of the symptoms, particularly the coughing, headaches, and joint pains, that it was the dreaded flu, and everyone he knew in the locality had come down with it.

"When we saw it on the television," he loudly said to the other passengers, "and my loved ones cried, 'This is what we had.'"

He went on to say, "It all came from that dirty place. ... The symptoms they are suffering are the same that we are suffering from here."

San Juan de Dios and San Juan del Diablo, two very quaint brother towns in which I had a chance to look up my distant cousins, turned out to be infected as well; the local chamber of commerce informed me that about half of the residents in each town live and work in and around the centers of the Veracruz outbreak. They could easily have infected others as they commuted between other Veracruz towns, especially the Port of Veracruz where the largest number of infections were now being reported.

Later I learned that Granjas Baltimore de Mexico, mostly owned by a Maryland-based Foods company, has nine farms in the area. Curiously though, none of their American employees working at the Veracruz ventures, or anywhere in Mexico for that matter, had any clinical signs of the flu strain or even of its presence in its pig herd. Consequently, some began to entertain conspiracy theories, whilst others considered the obvious; Mexicans were far more susceptible to this particular strain than Anglo-Saxon Americans, which is all the more remarkable considering the amount of pork products consumed by your average Mexicans.

A Wetback in Reverse

I have always been bothered as much as the next guy by the fetid smell of those sorts of farms, and they always seem to have been founded down-wind of any given community; I am sure, while others just suspect, that Veracruzanos have had their water and air contaminated by the said waste.

A couple of days later, I jumped at an opportunity to visit one of those farms just to satisfy my festering curiosity. When I entered the premises the morning of the following Monday, everything and everybody was sprayed with some chemically-treated water and handed white overalls, rubber boots, and masks before entering any of their odorous warehouses where the delightful pigs were housed. Only after we'd all been humiliated by this unannounced precaution, the farm fore-man informed us that, after we had been through their grounds, we'd be pressed to shower if we were to avoid carrying any undesirable germs to other parts of the state.

During the grand tour, the fore-man showed us a gray plastic lid that covered a swimming pool-size cement container of pig feces to prevent exposure to the outside air; without a doubt and without a second thought, pig feces has to be the foulest smelling of all forms of feces ever conceived by Mother Nature.

"Our pigs have been responsibly vaccinated, and they are all nurtured according to current sanitation regulations In Mexico," (small comfort, I thought), and he went on to complain, "What happened in San Juan de Dios and San Juan del Diablo was an inevitable coincidence with an awful dilemma that is happening now with this new flu alarm."

Murmurs of resentment felt by the residents of said towns filtered though the small talk; apparently the poor folk had been fighting the said company for more than a decade to force them to clean-up their pig-waste management, in more ways than one. Later, it was discovered that the source of the disease was traced back to La Gloria to a type of fly that reproduces in pig shit ~ Surprise! Surprise! Who would have thought it was all due to the filthy flies?

Naturally, the accountable officials, stinking in the perfidy of their own cowardice, downplayed the revelations or any claims that the epidemic could have started in this or that town, or anywhere else for that matter. All that anyone knew for certain is that mucous was

Frederick Martin-Del-Campo

pouring out of an increasing quantity of victims' noses, infants as well as the aged, and the number of cases was likely to increase exponentially unless Mexicans themselves finally looked up the meaning of *Hygiene* in a dictionary (assuming they can read, of course ~ this is no joke, and illiteracy abounds).

A couple of days came and went, and I found my way to Puerto Alvarado, a lovely, colonial-style town that nearly charmed the pants off of me, literally. I mean, with the warmth, the refreshing Caribbean winds, the tropical atmosphere, the palm trees, the cloistered hostels, the balconied restaurants, one is left helpless before overpowering sensuousness, and it made for a picture-perfect escape from the impending reality of pestilence, which had pervaded every facet of Mexican society. As far as I could gather, or was concerned, there were no signs of pig flu amongst the pigs, actual or of the human variety, anywhere in Veracruz, just the normal maladies associated with lazy living and an indolent indifference to misery. People will be sneaky though, and the common folk weren't going to step forward with their problems, only ignore them and hope they would just go away ~ you know, the typical Mexican solution to all of Life's troubles.

With a mix of the lecherous with the lugubrious, the Mexican character asserts itself against all onslaughts. With no evidence of sick or dying swine, on the farms or in the cantinas, the average person's *etre sans espoir et sans gene* attitude would bear all sins, particularly those suffered from their own leaders. The whole pig situation was under control, though the actual virus was still out there, still waiting to find *my* weak spot, and my unrequited longing just might prove to be the opening it was looking for and would exploit. More worrisome though were the rumors that people, especially visitors like me, were being spied upon, surveillance systems hastily placed in public stations, specifically transportation depots. The state's commercial pig population wasn't safe from the espionage, but most people agreed that it was a good way to eliminate related or unrelated diseases, which are indications that they, the responsible authorities, were on the job conducting adequate reviews of people with pig flu, as well as pigs for bird flu, and maybe even birds for people flu (?) ...

I don't know! To me these bird-brained excuses for people are a bunch of pigs with no real concern for social health issues, or the spread of viral illnesses. The recalcitrant epidemic in and around these quaint towns was more like a viral and bacterial combination of sicknesses, made worse by the heavy, dry atmosphere and Spring-time heat. Since it was the dry season in Veracruz, as in elsewhere, dust dries up the mucous membranes and eases environmental conditions for the transmission of viruses of this type. At this point, I would have been grateful for a very wet nose.

KNOWING YET NOT KNOWING ABOUT NOTHING

Traipsing about the colonial-era charms of Veracruz gave me more than cause to abandon myself to the sultriness and salacity that the sensual atmosphere afforded me. Here, small things take on a greater importance than I could have imagined; here, small things are regarded with great concern, whilst greater matters are defied as merely impediments to innate human happiness.

At this juncture of my aimless vagabonding, I had many an occasion for pause and introspection. While gazing at the faces of Veracruz natives, I recalled many of the people I had met while growing up, including some Veracruz cousins I'd once met and never saw again, and all the dumb questions I'd asked them about life, fairness, justice, the cruelties of Fate, and the positive examples ~ the role-models I'd sought to emulate in order to make of my life something besides a mass of trivialities and anxieties.

I grew up restless and frustrated after experiencing more than my fair share of the injustices of life, and the fact of my being the introspective, philosophical type, impelled me to share my feelings, my complaints about the unkindness and violence I had witnessed and suffered over the years with potential sympathizers. I was, however, always disappointed with the puerile, self-satisfied answers they would give me, and one could sense the self-importance that drove their persnickety little egos. Whether invocations of the Bible, specifically Old Testament condemnations of human weaknesses caused by the very deity that created humanity, or invocations to the memory of their bigoted, religiously intolerant forebears, these people I had confided in always had some smug, narrow-minded reply that revealed their ignorance more than showed up my confusion, which was their real objective when answering my questions. They were quick to reply, "Oh, grow up, that's Life!"

Or, they'd say, "God willed it, so just accept it."

I wouldn't, and shall never accept it, however, because the problems I'd discuss with them had nothing to do with God or Nature, or Life in general ~ I'd talk about apples, and they'd insist on anuses. The problems most of us suffer, strive against, and sometimes survive, were, and are due to the failure of Society to take care of its own; the failure of people to uphold their promises to each-other. Therefore, I shall always defy their timid resignation to ignoramuses who think they have all the answers, and their habit of scape-goating everyone ~ including God himself!

In begging their word, I had lent myself as a pawn of their stupidity. In begging their indulgence, I played the fool.

Part of my motivation for traveling through Mexico included the desire to find some sincerity in these droll and practical people. Boy, was I misinformed! Not only did they wallow in their own ignorance and superstitions, but are as narrow-minded as the presumptuous, yet ever so pious, morons I'd known back in America. None were up to the challenge of answering my questions about life, love, and the liberties we mostly take for granted. None were forthcoming about their own experiences, or weaknesses. All were content to be brainwashed, content to find security in their religious prejudices ... all content to spew out their superciliousness, vomit their vindictiveness, ejaculate their execrable exhortations upon me with the false notion that I actually respected them so much that I'd follow their stupid sermons or asinine advice without question, thus making them feel superior to me. Ah humanity, how base is your ego that I should suffer your pusillanimous pussyfooting, or tolerate your preposterous pablum-puking for the sake of discovering the truth about Life? Forget about it! It took me many years, but I finally awoke to the inscrutable fact that all they had to offer was more ridicule. My complaints and cries unto heaven were carried away by the wind breaking out of the anus of ignorance.

Thus, I wondered, what would come of asking Fulgencio San Roman the same questions, posing the same riddles for his singular, puzzle-loving conceit? He seemed to hold all of the answers to the muddles and bizarre apparitions that greeted me every step of this Mexican way. What could he tell me about the significance of such lowly objects of Mexican lore, like *huarache* sandals, the large-brimmed *Charro* hats, or the *rebozo* shawls of the native women? Probably nothing. Possibly the most obvious, which I'd ignored.

So, how could I know that I didn't know anything about nothing of no importance? For example: Is one supposed to know inherently what a *"Sarape"* is? I didn't before coming to Mexico, and never suspected it held some deep significance for the natives. A Sarape, I found out, is the striped blanket that the Mexican Indio, the Mexican Charro ... just about every Mexican is familiar with, but has no idea it contains some historic or cultural clues to their ancestral origins. A Sarape could be the metaphor of Mexico, or at least of her culture; so striped and violently contrasting are the cultural hues in Mexico today, living next to each other, and, at the same time, separated by centuries of human wretchedness. No mystery, no riddle, conundrum or enigma could run through their historical Sarape without being false or contrived. And, a riddler like San Roman could take the contrasting, yet integrated links of its violent colors as the collective symbology for constructing his films. For similar reasons, I thought, I wished to experience Mexico as though *living* one of his films. As each destination offered its own set of experiences, the temporary periods I'd spend in each place would be like episodes in the true-to-life film, following each other as the strange, as-yet unwritten plot unfolded. I was, and would be, a different character in each chapter, and different people, different fauna, even flora and seasons would flavor my expectations in each region. And still, by the very character of the Mexican people, the raison d'etre of my story held the unity of the weave. It would be, just like one of his films, a lyrical and musical composition, and an unraveling of the meaning of Mexico.

And what of San Roman himself? Death ... skulls of people, and skulls of stone, these would be the metaphors of his legacy ~ the same symbols, the same conclusions; the same ingredients that contain the possibilities of things to come. He knew what he was doing, and he knew what they meant in the scheme of a Mexican's life. The frightful Aztec gods, and the truly bizarre Mayan deities near the mysterious ruins and pyramids, what could they all mean to the modern Mexican who has no inkling about the origins of his/her own culture ... no inkling to find out the reason for his/her being? A world that was, and is nothing more than an endless becoming? The great Olmec heads of

A Wetback in Reverse

Veracruz, just faces of stone, but they reflect living faces of flesh; rows and rows of carved volcanic rocks, carefully set by the Mayans or the Toltecs to reverberate to the rhythm of the cosmos, they seem to reproach the ignorance of today's inhabitants. The typical Mexican of today is the same man who lived thousands of years ago, but now the wisdom of his ancestors has been replaced with the confusion of modernity. And yet, that character that has endured the endless siege of Time itself remains unchanging, intractable, perhaps even eternal. The great wisdom of his ancestors guards him against death, yet befriends death for the next becoming. Therefore, San Roman reminds me to focus on that unity of life and death, the birth of one proceeding the passing of another, and nothing changes, nothing moves. It is an endless cycle Americans could never really comprehend, and yet Mexicans are ignorant of that very wisdom, which has supported Mexico throughout the centuries; the wisdom to celebrate the endless cycle.

November was still far off on my travel schedule, but on the first of November the whole country celebrates the Day of the Dead, "Dia de los Muertos." It is a day of mirth and merriment, and a day when the living mercilessly mock and defy death, and yet honor the dead. Death is but a door-way to another plane of being, a passage to a new beginning. Hence, fear of it is quelled, fear of the unknown is laughed at, fear of themselves is rejected for a new meaning of love.

All types of stores display skulls wearing straw, Charro or top hats; candy takes the shape of skeletons in chocolate or vanilla, and coffins in confectionery. Family groups wander solemnly to the local cemetery, taking food to their buried; parties romp about and sing on the graves, and the food brought for the dead is then eaten by the living. The drinking and the singing grow louder. Next comes the Night of the Dead, and all ghosts and ghouls take the field.

The food of Veracruz and other parts of this region was quite good, I cannot complain; peppered with exotic ingredients and enlivened by many spices, no wonder so much beer is consumed around here.

The Day of the Dead is, at the same time, the actual birthday for new lives. This reality is ironically manifested when the brimming face of a new-born peeps beneath the striking skull of the masquerade of death, hence affirming the immutable law of existence that death follows life as life circles around death.

Life ... in Veracruz as in Oaxaca, or the rest of the sultry south, it emerges from the moist, muddy, sleepy sumptuousness of the tropics. The branches of trees heavily laden with fruit, dreamy waters emptying into placid lagoons, and the dreamy eyelids of the indigenous folk are barely lifted to allow their eyes to drink in all the light and color that waft in from Caribbean horizons. Dreams of love-making, of lovely youths, of future pregnancies (no one's right to reject them is recognized), and of future strife, all part of the rhythm of the Cosmos reverberating in each one of their lives. The Mexican mother, representative of the fore-mother of all, rules in these regions, from the ruins of El Tajin along the Costa Esmeralda, to the ruins of Monte Alban in the foothills of Tehuantepec.

It came as a fascinating lesson, in this land of male-chauvinistic bluster, that the matriarchal hierarchy has been upheld and honored for centuries, and still holds sway in the 21st Century. The people seem to meld harmoniously and imperceptibly into the surrounding eco-system. The indigenous folk are like branches on the patriarchal trees, and like serpents are the branches of the strangest trees I've ever seen; their respective blossoms serve as food as well as aphrodisiacs. Like insinuating serpents are the braids of raven-black hair framing the dreamy, almond-shaped eyes of maids waiting for their men ~ toilers of the sea, field or forest. In the ancestral towns, toil is the lot of women, and from girlhood the individual woman begins nurturing the cradle of a new family. Hours and hours wasted at the market-place, food preparation, butchering animals, fruit-picking, hawking house-hold wares, weaving, and simple idleness ~ thus are the slowly moving, yet crowded, typical *mercados* (market-squares) of Southern Mexico. Day in and day out, the joyful toil is undertaken, but it does take its toll as seen on the shriveled faces of the grandmothers. A golden chain with hanging gold coins is regarded as the reward of a life-time of sacrifice ~ coins with the Mexican eagle, and coins with the Spanish Imperial Coat-of-Arms are the most highly prized.

According to tradition, a Wedding is called "Casamiento" in Spanish in recognition of its natural meaning ~ foundation of a new *casa* (house). A new home spells a new family, hence the understanding is clear. But how do these simple, often illiterate, folk pay for these considerations? All with grandmother's coins, and all displayed around her neck and wrists; all can rely on their doting matriarch to provide fortune and liberty, bank and dowry. All may have a new home to rejoice in with their own family. Through loud and colorful fiestas, with vestiges of their most ancient customs like scarring the face with red colonial irons in memory of the Spanish invaders who branded cattle and Indians, their dances illustrate the destiny of a human life. They are performed in traditionally fashioned robes of silk, embroidery, and gold, and some of grand-mother's borrowed coins.

Dances follow love stories, and stories of adventure, or of the sowing and harvest, so important to the soul of their culture. Their customs and rites move their collective myths from the harvest, to love and coupling. The "Sandunga"(dance) of Oaxaca, in particular, hails the casamiento, though is overshadowed by the snowy white and embroidered "huipil," or native dress, and the mountain-like headdress of the triumphant mother and wife. Life is affirmed, and the new couples head off for the lucky palm-shaded new home. These simple rituals of society respond to the rhythm of all existence.

Gazing at the peak of Orizaba from my balconied room gave me cause to reflect on its snowy serenity ... snowy like the gray-mantled Popocatepetl, one of two mountains sacred to the Toltecs and Aztecs, but thorny and harsh, rough and unyielding is the vegetation at its base. The harshness, roughness and cruelty is inherited by the male tribe of "Charros," or Mexican cowboys, campesinos, and hacendados who dwell within the intractable environment. The endless fields of magueys, or "green gold" to the enterprising few who have made tremendous fortunes by its products of pulque and mezcal, or henequen fibres and sisal; but it is the wretched Indios who must cut the prickling, sharp leaved cactus, or have to suck, through exhausting labor, the sap of the Agave's heart in order to extract the sweet honey-like "aguamiel," which when treated becomes the much reviled "Pulque." To the sad and ever-struggling natives, it is their uniquely Mexican brandy, a relief of sorrows, and sorrows are forever recurring. There is little to be found of the aguamiel's sweetness in the Criollo entrepreneurs who still command the commerce and industry of provincial Mexico; their agents and henchmen crack his whip and roar his orders, and lower bend the backs of the native Indios, even in this day and age.

Today the drug-traffickers are the cruel overlords, and the daily news reports about their crimes are nothing like the tales told of the feudal social structure that existed before *La Revolucion*. There is nothing romantic about the insensible tribulations and barbarity they endure for the marijuana harvest; nothing romantic about the bloody tortures and shocking murders perpetrated by provincial drug barons.

As I hiked along the foothills surrounding Xalapa, the capital of Veracruz, I noticed a tired, middle-aged Indio down the road trudging along with his little burro, which all day must drag the delectable load of aguamiel from the boundless fields to the fortress-like bodegas, or ware-houses. His ancestors must have been doing the same for centuries, which goes to show that, despite all the developments and shows of technological progress, not much has really changed for the jaded masses. Their living conditions have not improved in decades, and their standard of living is lowered with every generation, or so it seemed to me. Democracy might reign throughout the land, but the average person is still, thanks to the demands of trade and commerce, trapped in a state of pure slavery to the peso (like we all are, actually). Socio-economic troubles abound, even in these festive and easy-going lands where life is taken one day at a time. Living in the Twenty-first Century may have its advantages, but the jaded masses' state of mind is still medieval, and their life-style is still primitive in ways and habits. Females today do not seem to have any more rights than their grandmothers did, since they still cry the same complaints about their insensitive men ~ thanks to their religion and tribal superstitions, the right of the men to their women is, in practice if no longer sanctified by Time and Tradition, absolute. Nevertheless, they both must work in the fields, in the factories, or in commerce like equals. Conflicts abound between the males for their women, honor, money and business, or for no reason at all, and they all go back to their tribes, to reassert ancient customs in spite of the age they live in.

The right of the people, their occasional outbursts of protest, and the cruelty of social repression carried out by individuals against their own laws, if it is not one thing, it is another that defiles the dignity of the Mexican character. And then the shadows of traditions and beliefs, of holidays and rituals guarantee the perpetual suffering of the Indios, though they are meant to affirm their bond with the Earth. Whilst worshiping their land as sacred, they weep and pray, waiting for better days... days of serenity before dying.

Masking their hatred for their betters, usually the Criollos and foreigners, under grim smiles, these "Christian" faces reflect the pagan masks of stone tigers and serpents worshiped by their ancestors, the Olmecs, Aztecs, and Zapotecs. But, the grotesque laughing of the living becomes risible in itself as they delight in the violence of their customs: cock-fights, dog-fights, bullfights, and the teaching of youngsters to mercilessly beat the card-board "pinata" faces for candy, thus imparting the lesson that by violence you get what you want in Life. Christmas dolls bring smiles to the innocent, until they are exchanged for the suffering expressions of polychrome Roman Catholic saints ~ Catholic idols of saints that were mounted on the sites of ancient pagan altars. Here, like exotic yet poisonous flowers, continue to bloom the iron and fire of the Catholicism that Hernan Cortez brought, even with all the shows of social progress. Catholicism and paganism, the Virgin of Guadalupe, all worshiped by wild dances, degrading prostrations, and bloody self-flagellation. Bleeding and mutilated, like the human sacrifices that were made atop pagan pyramids, the people uphold these awful traditions, ever waiting for better days ... days of serenity before dying.

They express their cultural identity by feathered costumes, disturbing percussion, dangerous acrobatic feats, like the *Voladores* (flying men) *de Papantla,* tower-high Indian hair-dresses, and sorry rituals like leading a procession of mendicant-pilgrims on their knees to the chosen site of adoration. Then the Spanish blood asserts itself in the Mestizos, and they emerge wearing either traditional mantillas, or Mariachi and Charro outfits, broad sombreros, leather boots, and, of course, Sarapes.

Hence, by exhausting hours-long dances in sunshine and dust, by the sprinkling of consecrated water done by arrogant bishops and priests in their fanciful canonical robes, by miles of knee-creeping penitence, by the blessing and display of favored farm animals, by the regalement of idols with unique flower decorations, and the resplendent ballets of bull-fighting *cuadrillas* ... the soul of Mexico lives on, and on to fight for a reason to go on existing.

All this is the legacy inherited by Mestizos as well. They know they are the dominant majority in Mexico, yet have lost their identity. They anxiously bear an inferiority complex, which burns in their hearts with respect to their still over-bearing White-European *Criollo* sires. It is as though they all had a bug up their asses with respect to what they think others think of them. Most of the time, though, they just go about their business asserting their place in the scheme of things, while bearing with a grudge their typically Mexican *Me vale una chingada* (I don't give a shit) attitude. Something always comes up, nonetheless, like an economic or political issue that reminds them exactly of the place they occupy on the social ladder, and the resentments are once again stirred, and the old hatreds simmer in the bile of slander, loathing, prejudice, and a violent anger explodes over the status quo they'd helped in great part to construct.

Still, they do not make any attempt to mask their contempt for their Indio relations. At once they lay claim to the country as the true inheritors of Mexico's bounty, and at the same time suffer the same doubts, the same insecurities all half-bloods anywhere have about belonging, about what they represent, and what their true place is in the society that bore, and supports their insolence and non-conformity. It is up to them, notwithstanding, to build the truly free Mexico that eluded their ancestors. It is up to them to bury the hatreds and ancient feuds that have made of this land a purgatory of oppression and brutality. They inherited their hatreds from their be-knighted ancestors. They just cannot bring themselves to abandon those medieval rancors, regardless of the social or spiritual catastrophe they invite as a consequence thereof, lest the saints and the spirits of their antecedents condemn their souls for faithlessness and blasphemous disloyalty. Oh, but such are the mocking reproaches of Time!

So, in spite of the revelations that have shocked my conscience out of the insulated intransigence that guarded my feelings against the unpleasant facts about humanity's evils, I am forced to ask myself once more: how could I know that I didn't know anything about nothing of no importance?

THE POBLANOS AND THE PIGS

As much as I hated to do it, I had to leave Veracruz for a spell because my *wetback* status was catching up to me; my tourist visa had long since expired, so it behooved me to keep on the move in order to dissuade the *federales* from overtaking me in any given part of the republic. It wasn't all together hard to do, and the constant traveling kept me light on my toes. All I had to do was cross the border into Puebla, and I'd be safe. Well, I wasn't safe for very long since I had disembarked at a stop not far from the capital city Puebla where I just had to try some *Mole Poblano* ~ the rich, dark local recipe for the well-known gravy. I was not disappointed with the taste. I was disappointed, however, to find out that the kitchen was infested with flies, and the cooks failed to wash their hands every time they used their urine-soaked excuses for public restrooms, and not 24 hours passed before I started with the wrenching stomach pains again. I rushed to procure more American Pepto-Bismal to allay the mounting agony, which had firmly gripped my belly, but the local beer did a better job of curing me. This would not be the end of my frustrations, for no sooner had I crossed the border into the lovely state (though her people surely were wanting in courtesy and friendliness) when the flu scare showed up again.

Mexico was again telling its weary citizens to stay home, urged commerce to limit operations, and government business would be curbed for a few days while they waited for word from the world health organizations to give the green-light that it was safe to emerge from their hovels once more.

In Puebla alone the local officials announced on TV and radio that the number of cases within their state had risen to over 100. The presidente municipal, Bartolome Obrador, told his fellow citizens, by printed fliers and other means since he was loathe to mix with the unwashed populace, that his local government was "taking the necessary precautions and procuring the necessary medicines" to stop the virus ~ I think he sought to solve the problem with good, old-fashioned Quinine.

Things at the national level weren't all that encouraging either, so people were advised to carry out only indispensable tasks, and that only "essential" places like markets, pharmacies and hospitals be permitted to operate; and some witty fellow suggested that non-essential agencies, like the government, close down for a spell, leaving critical services, like the police and military, to keep an eye on the common folk lest anyone should sneeze on someone else just for the sake of malice. They would indeed remain on duty, by the look of things in Puebla, guaranteeing the safety of the local yokels for the time being. Schools, fortunately for the grade-school children, had already been locked up, and the parents of said students were exhorted to take their progeny to centers of examination and vaccination. At least in this operation I was impressed with their resolve and activity.

Hence, now that I worried that I would be deported for remaining illegally in the country, and all too conscious of the irony of my situation, it did not take me long to recognize that the steps being taken to stop the further dispersion of the implacable cooties might be the very means by which the *federales* would nab me in the end. Frankly, I had no desire to be fustigated by the Mexican police, regardless of any individual background. They all had a well-deserved reputation for sexual sadism, and I was not going to give them any reasons to probe me for evidence that might lead to my incarceration, penetration, and eventual expulsion. Blamed already for many deaths, the virus changed their minds, so officials focused instead on minimizing its effects rather than containing its spread.

Upon settling down in a local *pensione*, or boarding house (very inexpensive and rather pleasant, with good, home-made cooking, I would be alright for the length of my stay), I just had to ask if I'd be alright there given the epidemic scare, and the concierge assured that "There is no safer place to protect yourself against catching swine flu, except perhaps for your own house."

I supposed he was being forthright, despite the presence of many strangers. Yet, he defended the actions of the people in charge against derision, or typically Mexican excoriation ~ that they'd been slow to move their arses, and arrest the dangerous illness.

A Wetback in Reverse

Though Puebla has no coastline, it is a state of special beauty. The low-lands of the state typically enjoy dry or semi-dry conditions, while the valleys of the south present a hot and sub-humid climate. This would be fine with me since I had already acclimatized myself in Veracruz to such weather differences.

I found the state to be particularly startling because of its mountains, and those it shares with other states. The Pico de Orizaba, the highest peak in all of Mexico, is shared with Veracruz, its neighbor state to the East. Other major elevations in Puebla include the famous, and, regarded by natives, sacred mountains of Popocatepetl and Iztaccihuatl, the warrior and sleeping maiden of Toltec and Aztec mythology. Thus, I had some pretty stunning scenery to accompany my thoughts as I suffered my latest bout of wanderlust. It was actually fun just exploring around by foot, and the *pueblerinos* were quite friendly and accommodating for the most part, and making up for the initial rudeness and hostility, which had greeted my arrival.

I had little to complain about while the flies stayed out of my food.

Further on I learned that officials in Mexico City were advising families everywhere to stay off subways and commercial airlines again because of the obvious, and made a special effort to dissuade people from traveling to America now that it was apparent to the rest of the world that the virus did in fact come from there. I thought I might cut short my stay in Puebla and backtrack to Veracruz where the sensuality available left me with a desire for more, but I weaseled out at the last minute. The recommended precautionary measures went beyond what most people expected from the latest outbreak ~ everyone, naturally, just wanted the damn thing to go away. In retrospect, it didn't hinder me so much since that day I'd left Billy and wife back in Chihuahua. Mostly though, people were being urged to wash their hands, cover their coughs, and stay away from public gathering places, especially if they felt sick. Simple, logical advice? Not to the average Mexican. Unless it is a direct order given under the threat of death, he/she would likely ignore such advisories.

Fortunate as well was the report that they would not be closing the U.S.-Mexican border to stop the flu because I certainly would not like to be corralled along with other foreigners should I be faced with an emergency that forced me to cut short my sojourn.

The Health Ministry did in fact raise the alert to a Phase 5, the second highest, which meant that the spread of the virus was imminent. I did not let that limit my activities, however, and went about interviewing people about what they most liked about their state. Many of them replied that it was the very centrality of their home-state that afforded much trade and traffic with the surrounding states, that it was historically significant, and that their mountains protected them from their neighbors as well. The local culture, I agree, is most quaint, and the sight of *China Poblana* maids promenading with their Charro outfitted gentlemen on Sundays made for a mental postcard that I would not soon forget.

There was nothing, to my knowledge, in their state's past that should make them ashamed of their own history. On the contrary, the placidity of their surroundings reflected on their faces, and the unique dishes of Poblano cuisine kept me experimenting and snack-ing while I could. The alerts had been subdued, so there'd be nothing to prompt me to get the Hell out all of a sudden.

At this time, again, they repeated that there was nothing around; nothing which suggested that things would get immunologically worse. Therefore, everyone breathed a sigh of relief and went about their business. The country was entering a "period of stabilization," according to the Health Minister ~ the very source the people wanted to hear from, not their conniving political leaders. They expected a downturn, and would liked to have seen the trend continue indefinitely, but that was too much to hope for at this point of the emergency. At the same time, the same officials offered hope that deaths and new cases were leveling off.

It behooved the banks and currency exchange offices to insist that, so it appeared, things had been getting much better in just the last forty-eight hours. I didn't need money just then, anyway.

As for Poblano commerce itself, Puebla stands out nationally in the production of flowers, eggs, coffee, beer and beans in open uncovered environments, and the restless natives would remain as busy as they ever were. Even the traditional production of marble and onyx and related products was kept open, regardless of the warnings against it.

During this whole time I sought to take it all in stride. Happily, the dogs ceased to bark just for the sake of restoring quiet to the beleaguered town. Everybody seemed to be twiddling their thumbs as rumors passed among the commons that patients were being mistakenly released from the hospital after a check-up, then hastily readmitted on the grounds of a sneeze or a mild cough. Most of the commons were out and about crowding the streets, fighting over merchandise, or dirtying up the markets while they shopped, or conducted other business or banking, or eating. Other folk, mostly visitors from other parts of the country it turned out, had contracted symptoms of the Porcine flu and were being treated, and even recovering well enough. I honestly couldn't say if they were coordinating efforts even at a local level in preventing the spread of the disease, but it certainly didn't look like it. Just more of the same, more of the waiting game that was making of my purpose more than an adventure.

So the responsible officials raised the tally to more than 250 of confirmed cases in Mexico, up from 148 or so, but that still did not seem like such a big deal in a country of over 100 million. This bit of history in the making will rank highly in the annals of human stupidity for damned certain!

The Mexican Red Cross had gotten in to the picture, boasting of the readying of millions of volunteers who could be sent anywhere, at any time to help slow down the spread of the virus, including by educating people about hygiene. Oh, how shameful, to have to be taught about hygiene as an adult. No wonder Gringoes, for all of their arrogance and presumptuousness, return from Mexico complaining that, "it's so dirty."

I honestly cannot blame them ~ they actually have a point, even though they aren't the most sanitary people in the world either.

But, the actual caring for the sick was another story, and there weren't too many volunteers willing to sign up for that.

Thus, the local newspapers went on reporting the deaths of this toddler, or that grandmother who had gone to Texas or California, contracted the flu, and then promptly passed away. It would seem that young adults weren't the only ones being affected by now; the damned disease had effectively over-taken all age groups.

Even the stolid members of the Military weren't immune from its threat; a notice was soon posted that over 40 Mexican Marines had been confined to barracks near Acapulco, on the Pacific Coast, after a couple of them (reputedly having just returned from a brothel no less) had come down with the virus, but it wasn't certain if it was a human or a pig virus. Since they admitted to having patronized a brothel thereabout, it could be they had come down with the *Bird flu,* but we'll leave the satirical details to the individual imagination.

Waiting for waitresses to make up their minds to serve me coffee, or the fat cooks to re-heat the stale rice, or the loud-mouth *viejas tamaleras* to finish up with the quesadillas, I paused to consider: if this mix of pig, bird and human flu is something to which humans have limited natural immunity, then what real chance did we all have to really combat it? How do we know it is the dangerous variant if it has symptoms of fever, cough and sore throat practically identical to the flu most people are accustomed to? Just to think that these local Mestizos, selling their execrable recipes in the streets or in unhygienic bistros, engaged in food preparation while picking their noses and scratching their uniquely sculpted asses, were spreading tiny particles of their mucous and other noxious germs through the air, especially after they'd coughed or sneezed, which easily could contain the virus! The mere thought of it, never mind the reality, just gave me the shivers.

A couple of weekend holidays were coming up, Labor Day and Cinco de Mayo, and word was spread that the authorities were considering using the five-day period for a partial shut-down of government services in the event emergency measures would be extended, or if they'd ease some restrictions. I couldn't figure out if it minimized the added disruption, but it sure as Hell was annoying.

People around must have learned of these latest announcements because traffic was unusually light by the end of the week, which was nice for a change, and this was before the shutdown went in to full effect. It was a humorous sight though, to see dressed up businessmen walking the streets wearing surgical masks, passing beggars who kept their masks on too while asking for alms. I think I was most happy that the air was relieved of so much automobile exhausts ~ one could actually breathe again in the middle of the day without choking from the foul fumes.

I asked one sympathetic bartender named Miguel, who fancied himself as good a singer as the legendary Pedro Infante, what he thought of the whole mess: he feigned indifference, then casually

A Wetback in Reverse

pronounced that, "I think ... well, in my opinion, (he then sucked on a lemon as he cleaned beer glasses) the solution to all this crap is to just keep vigilant, that all people act like they should when more of this illness is flaring up. It's mostly up to the families to take care of their brats, so they should take more preventive actions. This could make all the difference in the world. But will they? You can be sure that they won't, and that's why we are in this mess to begin with, DAMN IT!"

For a bartender who did not seem to possess much of a brain, he certainly made a lot of sense ~ common sense, the very thing that was lacking throughout this entire medical-hygienic fiasco.

Even while the populace was trying to celebrate Cinco De Mayo, scientists were announcing that somewhere in the world, perhaps a year before, the pig virus had hopped on to a unsuspecting person, though not before lapping up some bird poop, thus spreading amongst humans since then.

Now, why didn't they think of that before? It seems so complicated a matter, and yet so freaking obvious that it escaped half the brains of the world ~ not that half of them were functioning anyway.

As far as the blame game goes, Mexican scientists were blaming the Chinese for the mess way back when Bird Flu was found in their Bird's Nests soup, thus provoking world-wide hoopla. Conversely, the Chinese fired back and blamed the flu on Mexican food, since everyone "knows" that it causes people to dance the *Aztec Two-Step*.

So, just to patch things up between Mexican cooks, who chided the Chinese for eating dogs, and Chinese cooks, who accused the Mexicans of serving cockroaches in their tacos, all decided to hinder the Hindus, who do nothing but harp on everything, anyway.

To my great dismay, I learned that the dreaded symptoms were showing up in greater proportion back in Veracruz. This could be a problem, since I had every intention of returning there as soon as I had an opportunity. It seems they were blaming the pig farms again, and the small local clinics providing emergency health care were resentful of the fact that the said farms were not being very helpful or forthcoming with donations, so they went ahead and raised a stink (no pun intended) in the press about the nasty nature of hog-raising.

The earliest case that filtered out of Veracruz was that of a 5 year old boy, who had probably gotten dirty with something he shouldn't have touched, and came down with all of the symptoms. By week's end, unfortunately, hundreds of people had come down with it. The epicenter of the fracas was La Gloria, that same, less than happy town I had first stayed in. And, the people of La Gloria, even while struggling to breathe, kept commuting to jobs waiting for them in Mexico City, thus infecting untold masses in the old capital.

What some people will do to earn a buck nowadays!

A few days later, and much to my consternation, a door-to-door health inspector went about the local streets snooping into the private business of the locals. This could have been a disaster for me since, in seeking to root out sick people, he could have discovered my wetback status, and could have called *La Migra* to have them deport me. Much to my evil delight, I later learned that he had been hospitalized with "acute respiratory problems" not far from the boarding house ~ and he went ahead and infected 18 hospital employees as he settled into his sick bed.

Needless to conclude, I found that Mexico's health care system has become the object of widespread, and well-deserved, anger and distrust. In case after case, patients have complained of being misdiagnosed, were rudely sent away by the incompetent doctors or their nurses, and were especially denied access to salutary drugs ~ like that is going to hinder any self-respecting, drug-fancying Mexican?

The more you provoke a Mexican, the more he/she is going to turn around and bite you... literally.

THE UNIQUE HELL
OF A MEXICAN MOTHER

Time now for a provocative word to the mind: being a *Huara*, that is an illegal alien, in Mexico just ain't what it's cracked up to be! Specifically, I had it in mind for some time to open a checking account at a local Banamex locale in order to facilitate the transfer of funds from my American savings account since I was very limited as to the amount I could withdraw on a given day at any ATM location. Well, these obviously frustrated bank-workers gave me a rotten time, demanded all sorts of proofs to my identity, and then insisted I wait till it was all verified. I did just as they asked of me, and all seemed to go well for 24 hours, until I received a call from the silly clerk who told me that she had to cancel the paper-work after all, that my identifications did not check out, and that the office of *Gobernacion* would be informed of my questionable, possibly illegal status. Well, it was exactly what I wanted to hear from them, cynically speaking. Consequently, I trudged back to her office to verify all the poop she had alluded to over the telephone. Just as she was about to formally cancel the already signed contract, she was informed by a bank-dick (and he was truly a *dick*) from the managing office that the identification provided was legal, it did check out, and that there should be no more hindrances placed against my opening the damned account.

For her part, the timid *Jarocha* woman lukewarmly apologized, insisted she was new to that bank and was not totally familiar with their rules and regulations, never mind the fact that I had been humiliated, my time had been wasted, needless expenditures were made, and I was left to worry about getting caught as an illegal, and what-have-you.

One curious thing that came out of the whole process was being asked to provide a couple of valid references who could attest to my identity. One of the more significant ones was my old college-era friend, Rebecca (Becky) Ange-Ingel; in fact, I'd known her since childhood. In any case, the bank monkeys had contacted her, and

Becky, gracious to the end, gave me glowing reviews. At this juncture of the adventure, I resolved to personally contact her. Significantly, she lived near Puerto Alvarado, Veracruz, on a beautiful *Finca*, or cultivated plantation (sugar, I believe). It overlooked the Caribbean to the South. She had always called me *Primo*, or cousin, with affection, and I regretted not having first visited her, but my extra-legal status, to reiterate, forced me to side-step surreptitiously to Puebla before the Federales did.

It took me some time to track her down, but she finally received my call ~ in it I had forwarded a song from our youth, which I knew she really loved: Abba's *I have a dream*.

"I have to say that just today for the first time," she replied, effusively, "I really, REALLY listened to the lyrics *Estoy Soñando*. This song is precious ~ it answers, and it consoles my dilemma" (which hitherto I knew nothing about). "I do believe in angels and fairies that do good out there, and help us realize our dreams.

The lyrics say what I have always felt for a long time, yet have foolishly allowed, on occasions, negative people to have their say about the contrary, that they do not believe in the good there is to do, and have in this world. Why? I don't know, it just happened that way.
I have always thought that bad or dangerous things, which happened to me, are not so serious because in one way or another my guardian angels have looked out for me, although I have to confess that lately, I think, they have been taking time off." (she then laughed)

"Gracias primo, for all the intelligent conversations we've had in the past, and the future ones we shall have, and my faith in life is restored."

So ended our first conversation. I figured there was a lot more to her sentimental response but couldn't figure it out. I remembered she would get like that when faced with personal disappointments or impending disasters, or probable traumas that involved her loved ones. She was particularly secretive, and sensitive with respect to her children. *What could it be* was the question, but I'd have to wait a couple of days before I could contact her again.

I called her one Thursday morning, complained about my "Wetback" status, and thought to mention her children: "Saludos to the familia, Becky. I hope that Gamaliel (her eldest son, 18 years old) is doing especially well. Have you heard from him lately?"

At this point she dropped a hint that things were not especially well with them.

"Hola Primo. Gamaliel is well, but he has been caught up in some trouble with the local police. The charges were preposterous, but these people are so mean that they tear your life apart over the most spurious of accusations. We will find our way, we just need to keep our eyes open. As for your troubles about your illegality, don't give up. The good thing is that they aren't even looking for you."

... It did feel good to be reminded of that.

"Gamaliel is alright," she continued. "I saw him last Sunday, but he was upset, sad, and he cried constantly, and that just broke my heart. He was always my 'man,' never emotional about anything, so his tears felt like daggers to my soul. He usually visited me, here at the Finca from the Boy's College, every Saturday, but now it was my turn to visit him; as a matter of fact, I only visited him after suffering through numerous sleepless nights due in part to my youngest daughter Campanita's illness" (probably the flu, but she made no mention of it). "I had left for the prison-compound later than usual, conscious of the fact that it takes me more than 30 minutes by automobile to get there. This time, much to my angry frustration, there was much more traffic than usual, and so it took me more than one and a half hours to get there. I arrived fully ten minutes after closing time, and I did not get in."

Then, poor Becky started to get a bit too morose for my taste.

"I came home feeling sad and pessimistic about the prospects for an early release" she continued, "but went back on Sunday, I guess, because of the holiday weekend traffic. It was crazy, and again it took me an hour or more to get there. This time, however, I was there 20 minutes before closing time, and they did, finally, let me in. He wasn't expecting anybody, he said. When he did see me, tears started pouring out of his eyes. I've been thinking about that moment, and I keep asking myself, why did he cry? I think he is just a frightened little boy who is afraid that even his mother will abandon him; he has lost about thirty pounds, he looks really pale, but not 'sick pale.' I guess because he hasn't gotten any sun-light in a month, which, for a sun worshiper, must've been devastating, and he has not been eating properly.

I told him what had happened the day before, and why I didn't make it the previous Saturday. I went on to promise him, and myself, I would NEVER abandon him no matter what happens."

Her last comments left me a bit pensive: why had her son to spend so much time in jail? What were the circumstances surrounding his incarceration? Surely, she was leading me towards some dreadful revelation, but for the time being she was eliciting all the sympathy for her beleaguered son that she could draw out of me. She then went on to reflect, "Sometimes, primo, it gets really weary, this whole miserable business with the Law, but I won't complain ~ he is alive, and I know in my heart he did not hurt anyone. I am hopeful he will be deemed to be another victim of the system now that I am in this situation, and know what to strive for at last. I talk to people in jail: mothers, brothers, wives, and I find so many cases where the charges and the punishments are totally ridiculous as well as cruel. There is no cruelty like the sort of cruelty that one Mexican can inflict on another. When he comes out, I hope he doesn't have to do probation. Then, and only then can we get the hell out of here, even abandoning the Finca if we have to, if I find an opportunity."

Well, that was the end of it for now. She did not divulge any details, and I could not press her for any. I bade my goodbyes for the moment, but her situation really depressed me. I thought I was in a terrible fix, but now my dear old friend was going through a unique Hell of her own, endemic to the Mexican Mother ~ that of watching her children suffer at the hands of the sons of other Mexican Mothers, for reasons of revenge, repression, retribution of a sort that borders on the ridiculous yet repugnant, is remorseless and offers no chances for resistance. My heart goes out to her, as she would say of her son the next time she called me to confide the anguished compassion she suffered for her traumatized son.

I remembered an awful episode in my own life when I ended up in prison defending myself against a delinquent Mexican back in California, and could truly empathize with Gamaliel. I told her, with candor and genuine sincerity, "My heart so goes out to him." I admitted, almost tearfully. "I remember the 4 rotten days I was in prison, and I was totally abandoned by everyone, after my fight against that son of a bitch (I think his name was Jorge, and had caused trouble around the neighborhood for a long time; I think he's dead by now) who had tried to steal my wallet, and then tried, in a drunken rage, to rape me. That miserable drug-pushing piece of shit!

The memory of all that is still almost too burdensome on my conscience. I ended up, nonetheless, having to spend time in jail for defending myself against him, can you believe it?"

She was incredulous when hearing for the first time of this affair. Now the personal secrets would flow.

I went on to mention another incident, which involved an old neighborhood chum-turned drug addict who had screwed me out of my car, and then robbed my identity, which got me in trouble with the police: "Yes, Becky, and then there was Louie, who I had grown up with. That fool got me in so much trouble, and it took years to clear things up. Several years later, after the prison episode, the police came looking for me after that god-damned Louie had stolen the Mazda, which was still in my name, and ripped off my California identification card, then proceeded to commit crimes in Beverley Hills. That was not the worst of it, however, for no sooner had they caught up with him when he told the police that he was me, so I almost went to jail again because of that evil, dope-pushing ex-friend of mine ~ how do you like them apples?

So, if anyone knows about and feels Gamaliel's tears, it is me.

If there is some great deity looking out for us, I beg him to take special care of your boy. I hope some genuine, righteous anger finds its way inside of Gamaliel, that he stands up to these pieces of shit who have indeed victimized him (and you, in the process)."

I suppose I had surprised her and jarred all doubts, and she then felt she could confide more secrets to me: Gamaliel had been actually charged with driving a stolen vehicle, possession of stolen fire-arms, possession of illegal drugs and trafficking, transporting minors across state lines for illicit purposes. All these were very serious charges that could land him in prison for many years. There was nothing I could say in response, this was all truly shocking. She complained that she felt too weak to face reality; this new, unfamiliar world of harsh attitudes and vicious treatment. The last thing I said to her was, "Much strength and endurance go with you and Gamaliel."

At this point our telephone correspondence ceased ~ she had to go to the prison again to sign some papers on behalf of her son, and I had to trek on to the state of Guerrero. The bus stopped in the capital in fact, Chilpancingo, and more of that hot and humid weather greeted us along with unseasonable rains. But it was tolerable enough, and I could muck around there before heading back to Puebla, or even Veracruz; with a people comprised of a varied mix of Mexican types, mostly Criollos, along with some of the best-looking, physically attractive (and desirable) Mestizos I had yet seen, Guerrero is a state of low valleys, green hills, lush tropical coasts, typical-Mediterranean type architecture with red tiled roofs, along with many a modern hotel or government building. There existed a calm that certainly soothed my nerves during my stay. I thought to go on straight for the sensuous beaches of Acapulco or Zihuatanejo and give myself a much needed rest in their enchanting resorts, but time was against me, and I had to wait around in Chilpancingo till I had recovered from the brutal bus-ride. Emails between Becky and me resumed, which is just as well because our telephone conversations were growing a bit awkward. We both express ourselves better with the written word. Apparently, I had provoked her usually phlegmatic curiosity, for no sooner had I informed her of my experience in jail when she sent me the following note:

~ Forgive me for making a stink about this, Freddy, but when you were in jail, where were you, in San Fernando? Did anyone come to see you? Did you have to go to court? And about the other bullshit that Louis caused, how did you convince the cops it wasn't you?
Becky ~

I suppose she struck the right chord (or perhaps the wrong one), but I had to divulge all the ugly facts surrounding my clouded past, if only to re-affirm that empathetic connection with her. After all, I might need her help a lot more than I figured, and getting by in this land of suspicion and distrust might require me to trust in someone who has the means to get me out of trouble; Billy and wife weren't exactly in a position to get involved, and other relatives and friends weren't exactly forthcoming. Hence, in a spat of eloquence and passion atypical of our friendship, I replied:

~ You know, Becky, even after all these years (23 years since I went to jail due to that delinquent Jorge, and about 13 or so years since Louie pulled the fast one on me), it still feels expiatory to talk about such awful memories. Weighing things in retrospect truly reveals the relativity of all things, forcing me to realize that I'm all grown up. So, don't worry about my feelings, my dear friend, I honestly appreciate your inquiry because no one else in the world gave a shit about my pain ~ a pain that has never been cured, only repressed. There are moments, especially during a full moon, when it threatens to break its boundaries in a torrent of rage, violence and destruction. Only my intellect, my greater sense of reason, holds me back during which times I realized I still have it and am grateful I do, whilst others I could name clearly do not, and has thus far held me back from giving in to the anger and violence during all these years past.

But, strangely enough, even though I am far from the place where it happened, and am free of the negative presence and influence of the people who perpetrated these crimes against me, I am all alone, without one person I may need to help me. I didn't know what to do, and others I trusted ended up betraying me for no good purpose. Hence, even after all these years, here in the quiet of Chilpancingo and other Mexican towns, all those repressed memories and feelings are haunting my dreams. I wake up in the morning sweating, not from the heat, but from the terror of those dreams, and feel the anger surging within me. Then, suddenly, I get a rush of the images of those incidents, and I end up screaming something insulting.

Most of the time I think my feelings will overtake my reason, and it scares me. I try to ignore the sensations, which suddenly grip me. During other times, the whole trap of memory scares or irritates me enough that I have to question the very purpose of my quest, of reconciling myself with my past, my origins, and the prospects for the future. Why didn't I just die that day they hauled me off to prison, I ask myself during those moments of unintended introspection. Then I just succumbed to the feeling of helplessness, and exclaimed, 'Damned be the day when I was born into that miserable environment! Damned be the hour!'

Of course, I am just fooling myself because I know very well that the sullied past will never be requited to the confusion of the present. But, it all stems from those terrible memories. With my coming here, remaining indefinitely against my will, and dealing with the results of the latest betrayal I've endured from my colleagues, well, as you can imagine, I feel so lost ~ worse than if I were in prison, abandoned, hating myself more than I hate my enemies because I feel that I have lost control over my life.

These are feelings, of course, and must use every ounce of my lingering reason to control them ... sometimes I feel it is a losing battle.

Your Primo ~

Oddly enough, I felt like I was being manipulated with my own past. Becky's precipitous concern for my background caused me to unleash the store of hoary ghosts, which have been troubling my half-forgotten memory during all these years past. What could I do? Suddenly I felt like ripping my heart out and presenting it to her, if only to effectuate that catharsis I have been praying for, but was afraid to realize. I went ahead and sent her another e-mail without waiting for her to reply:

~ In any case, Becky, to answer your questions now: First, it was not San Fernando, but was all the way in the L.A County Jail because the crimes they accused the assailant and me of involved "attempted manslaughter." They were deemed as felonies of the worst kind. Second: No one went to see me, and when my father finally bailed me out 5 days later, it was not to reproach the bigoted police for doing this to me and giving the aggressor equal justice, since he had a police record of more than 15 years; various felonies and misdemeanors, was on probation, and had just been let out for an attempted rape charge. No! My darling dad, Fernando, instead screamed at me, demanding to know what demon had possessed ME. What had possessed me to be so sanguinary, such a "criminal!"

I tried to call home in the hope my own mother, Maribel, would understand and help, but the damned old hag just answered, "This is what you deserve for being so wicked, a violent son of a bitch!"

... Truly, it was a moment when I'd NEVER felt so alone in my life.

take care, Freddy ~

A few days passed before she replied, which caused me some worry; it turned out that she had been going repeatedly to the courthouse to plead her son's case, and was thus embroiled up to her tear-ducts with the festering situation. Thus, how could I insist upon anything given her personal grief? When she finally replied, I was actually surprised at the tone of her cry for comprehension, for now she felt unleashed of the chain of mistrust, and had to confide intimate secrets about her own past in someone. Little could I surmise from the pleasantries that surrounded our friendship that she had suffered and sacrificed so much to achieve what she has, and, more revealingly, the degradation she'd survived at the hands of her own family before achieving both financial and moral independence from them. Always, though, they blame Mexico for what they are.

In response to my own candor about my nightmarish memories and psychological burden, she confided most forthrightly:

~ You know, Primo, I know where you're coming from. I know those feelings you described, and don't feel I am the better for it. I know such experiences are supposed to make of you a better person, and I believe in strengthening the character by challenge and difficulty, but these demeaning traumas we've endured just don't make any sense to me ~ nothing about Mexico makes much sense to me, anymore. My own shame stems from my relationship with my mother, your sweet "auntie" Lydia, who I miss terribly since I moved away. God damn it! she really seemed to despise the very idea of my existence, no matter how much I sacrificed and tried to please her. She was all too glad to think the worst about me, instead of figuring that, because of HER terrible parenting skills, this violence between my brothers and me was an inevitable outcome. I mean, I realize this must be shocking to you upon reading this for the first time, but the warm relations that seem to exist between us now weren't always so.

It had first happened, in a way, between myself and Lorenzo (you remember Lorenzo, right?, the second to youngest in our family). He had broken into everybody's bank account, including mine needless to say, and made out like a bat out of Hell. We found out about it soon enough, and marched over to his apartment to knock some sense into him. But, because Lorenzo turned out to be a closet *puto* (homosexual), which fact nobody knew about, he wouldn't or couldn't defend himself. He just ran away *como mariquita sin calzones* (like a silly pansy), stayed at his boy-friend's house, known locally as *Eric the Tongue,* and no one cared. But, when that shameless Lorenzo tried to do it to Eric, he, after all the years of taking his abuse, was not going to take it from him anymore and unleashed a torrent of anger on him. He did nearly kill him.

Next, we would eventually have to go to court to try and recover our money. Lorenzo played the crazy druggie and even tried to joke with the judge, who'd recognized him from having arraigned him for previous charges and court appointments. Eric, due to the defender's advice, had to plead to NO LO CONTENDERE, or NO CONTEST, to the charge of assault and battery since, even though he did commit the act of beating the shit out of Lorenzo, he did not actually INTEND or CONSPIRE to kill him. Because his record was mostly clean, they let him off with a warning. But, the damage had been done, my parents betrayed me in a moment of constitutional crisis when, after after all the abuse, the obedience, trying to be the perfect daughter, doing everything they demanded of me, and all the guilt trips they laid on me that "I should not be like Lorenzo," I have to sacrifice my happiness for the sake of being a good daughter, they just turned around and betrayed me. They accused me of having encouraged Lorenzo's dissolute comportment, thus proving they were false all along, and their piety was nothing but hypocrisy (and till the day she expired, *la pinche vieja*--damned old hag-- acted as though it never happened, and it was not a big deal).

They easily forgave Lorenzo's, and my other siblings' countless crimes, but when I defended myself against his drugged-out violence then I was suddenly the worst daughter that ever lived.

It is funny, but for the longest time I forgave everything that my sisters and brothers did to me, and they did a lot of shit to me going back many years. I forgave them only because during that most painful, most difficult time in my whole life, they were actually on my side. They even cheered me on for kicking the fuck out of Lorenzo once when he had destroyed my precious imported dolls, and all because he was jealous of my having them. But, alas, those are distant memories, and my brothers and sisters continued to do shit to me. We are no longer friends, but they did help me endure a most risible crisis in my life.

In Lorenzo's case, just the fact that I never set foot in San Miguel Allende, where he had been stopped by the police in my car, helped my argument because it was only the San Miguel police that were after me, or rather the legal owner of the vehicle, which had not been reported as stolen. And, I failed to mention to you, Lorenzo fucked himself after all because he did go back to San Miguel on several occasions, and yes, he got caught by the chota (police). Then, when they thought he was me because he somehow managed to convince them that my name was his girlie pseudonym, he said "No, no, I am Lorenzo, the chota in your station will recognize me." So, they took him down to the station where he recognized one cop and started crying, "Hey, you remember me, you can clear this up, right?"

But, the cop, who DID recognize him, remembered him too well, and looked him straight in the face and said, "yes, I remember you, but back then you insisted that you were 'Miss Becky, the transvestite dancer,' not this Lorenzo you are now saying you are. Does that mean that you lied about your identity the last time?"

¡*Pues, que esperas!* Poor little Lorenzo *se quedo con el chili pelado* and burst into tears, realizing he had just BETRAYED HIMSELF, y acabo chingado ~ he had to go to jail for a few days. He made friends with a lot of gay criminals, and even boasted that most of his time in jail was a big laugh-filled orgy with his fellow SISTERS. I learned of these details while over-hearing his conversations with his friends, especially a certain Regina, who is a terrible loud-mouth of a bitch. But, she had the sweetest and most patient mother who'd actually helped to bail out Lorenzo from prison; and he never paid her back (something like $55,000 Pesos).

The warrant for the owner of the Ford Escort, my car, was still out for a few more years until the statute of limitations ran out, and by then the car had long been gone. I was broke by that time as well, and I never set foot in San Miguel Allende except to clarify the damned legal matter, so that is that.

As I remember, when we finally threw Lorenzo out of the *quinta* (family manor) back in 2002, he tried to get me in trouble and told the Veracruz chota, who had come over at the behest of our madre, about the warrant for the arrest. I used the occasion to tell them my side of the story, and both my siblings and our madre, who were not my enemies yet back then, swore to the fact that Lorenzo was the criminal all along and had lied to the police. Hence, the chota finally believed us, and told Lorenzo to clear the premises within 24 hours.

So, that is how Lorenzo lost the fight, and had to get the fuck out of the house for good.

But, instead of a victory, it left me alone with our madre, the household problems, and a lot more emotional baggage until 2005, when I moved out with my children and on to the Finca for good.

I had been at the mercy of their plots and scheming, and ultimately I lost the fight and had to accept exile (though a very pleasant one at that). I regret now not having killed a few of them back then like I had dreamed of doing for years ~ and it was all due to my crushing poverty. Things are different now, I am prosperous, relatively, you are among the precious few who have shown me again what hope is, for better or worse, and your suffering, the tears you've shed for unrequited justice as well as for my sons, have also helped me to mature, in an odd sort of way. I came to feel for the first time that we are both, along with all the other children of misery, nailed to this wheel of pain called life, charged to pay for the sins of others. I realize this sounds weird, like I have a "Christ-complex," paying for the sins of the world. However, I deeply feel that there are individuals charged by life to suffer for what others have committed, and yet others expect us to come out of the experience without complaining, resigned to our fate.

Hell No!

Knowing all of this does not, contrary to what others have said, help to deal with the pain, and you have not completely convinced me that killing my own family would be wrong, but you have helped me to forget about that for awhile. Your own suffering does put things into perspective. And now, especially, with Doña Chata, my revered grandmother, passing away, the repercussions have been felt by all; one who has most felt the Tsunami effect has been our madre, who ultimately faced her own mortality FOR THE FIRST TIME in her life (I think). She had actually been in danger in the past (after she had given birth to Lorenzo and me; her 2 car-crashes; and her two heart-attacks), but those things never seemed to bother her. It was only after Doña Chata died that she did finally face the fact of the way of all things.

So, now you know how the plot to the children of misery started, and now this tragic story has, at last, come to an end.

Take care Primo, and hope this answers any questions you may have had lingering in the back of your mind.

Becky ~

A Wetback in Reverse

Extraordinary! That was certainly some confession she served me. I honestly had no inkling as to the circumstances supporting her family and her personal life. She truly and sincerely divulged the bare facts, and confided her trust in me in the process. Obviously her pain was so deep that she needed to reveal the ugliness undermining her happiness to someone, and I turned out to be the sympathetic ear she needed to requite the wrongs she'd resentfully endured for so many years. Now that I had struck a sympathetic chord with her, I could not contain my curiosity for very long, and answered her as soon as I could drag myself from the Cafe' Nopal, and the delicious Kahlua laced iced-coffees to which I'd quickly grown addicted.

Hereinafter, I began, as tactful and understanding as I could be under the circumstances:

~ Becky, little by little I understand more and more why you have the feelings you have towards the whole family. It is awful because if I still love them the way I do, it is because I never knew this tragic side to the story. I found the support in your family that I hardly got from my family about anything. I am aware that when my mother trashed me, your mother supported her and helped light the fire. I could not blame her because my mother, on the other hand, did the same to me all the time with everyone.

What you wrote actually made me cry. Honestly, I don't know what I would have done. I even feel some anger for what they did to you. This is a typical trait of our mothers: we can be saints, and even though they see it, they will never give us the love and protection we deserve. I hear other mothers (especially Mexican mothers) will tell their kids that they will love them even if they were murderers. This is how, I am sure, you feel for your own sons, and I have seen mothers of real murderers defend their children with their claws and fangs.

I am sorry if I caused you to summon up some dreadful memories that had better remained repressed or forgotten. Therewithal, I can understand you so much better now, and I am glad that, at least a little bit, I have been of some help to you. I really don't think I have done anything, but if you think so, thank you for seeing it.

You take care for now. Hope to see you soon in Veracruz.

Your Primo,

Freddy ~

It did not take her long to respond, and she was anxious to gather what I really felt about her problems with her son, Gamaliel. Yes, I did try and include as much as I could about my own experiences in relating my sorrows and traumas. I am sure I left a lot out, but it was a daunting, monumental task trying to encapsulate so many years of bullshit, of putting it all into perspective, and yet keep it relevant to her own troubles. Towards the end of our conversations, I reflected on my prison experiences in greater detail, and exactly how it all came about. She was very open and solicitous about it all, and expressed a desire that I personally share my anecdotes with Gamaliel, if only to comfort and assure him that he was not alone in his sorrow. I had my doubts though:

~ Well, Primo, I wonder if you should share this with Gamaliel so that he could know, deep in his soul, that he is not alone, even though he hardly knows you. I can't have any idea what he thinks or knows about you though since you are generally known to be a peaceful, modest person (or at least that is the impression you give to most people). I think it would affect him positively to know how someone like you also suffered in jail; this could help to free him from any doubts by showing that we deeply know, and share his pain and humiliation. Indeed, even one like you has a closet full of traumas and abominations.

"Just Understand," is what some famous person said about the suffering of his people to his oppressor. That is what I ask of certain people, so the fact that I am coming to understand the reasons for the way you and others turned out as human beings is very important to me, and the understanding goes a long way towards ameliorating our common lot.

Again, I must insist that you not apologize for "making you remember these things." I tell you, these memories have never left me, they haunt my dreams all the time.

What you did was to lighten the burden of the isolation that has made me a prisoner of my own resentments for all of these past years. The fact that you are the first and only person that had bothered to ask, that had tried to understand, has helped to lift me, AT LONG LAST, from this sea of darkness and menace that has left me drowning, little by little, in despair for more than two decades. At last there is a sympathetic soul that will listen to, or read MY SIDE of the story. At last, I am expunged of the silence that threatened to follow me to my grave, and prevented me from reaching out to the truth; from reaching out to others who will share the light of vindication with others willing, and wanting to understand the meaning of the why-fore of our shared suffering.

Yes, others have been very sympathetic, bless their souls, and of course I owe it to them for having opened my heart to therapy and other help. Nonetheless, they could never quite see things from the perspective of an insider, a member of the family. Of that group, again I say, only you who, once upon a time, I thought would NEVER see things from my point of view, have been chastened by life; enough to be able to see things from the perspective of a person who has truly been wronged by Life. Only you have shown that your heart has survived the fires of compassion and enduring sadness, and can see things clearly without the bullshit that blinds the eyes of our vain and more selfish family members.

On another occasion you wrote: "I really don't think I have done anything." But, as the Hindus say: we are all like diamonds in the rough, but when the divine light is shed on us, the light of knowledge and understanding, it reflects on the facets of the other diamonds. In turn, the light keeps traveling, bouncing and reflecting from one diamond to another, towards infinity...

Well, you may feel you have done nothing, but your light has truly reflected on me, illuminating my existence. The reflected light travels on, bouncing off of others.

Your being able to understand sheds that divine light, that we may be able to see and follow the path that leads towards whatever Life has waiting for us; yes, us, the survivors of the horror, of the anger and sorrow we inherited from children of ignorance ~ children of the darkness who had little of the divine light fall on them. They all ended up giving nothing but the evil and barbarity that are inherent in the darkness.

As for my family, because you have it in your heart to love them still, that is why I entrust them to you, especially my mother, even though it is a burden I would rather not trouble you with, in pride or in shame.

Without you there is no one. Already all of my other brothers and sisters have totally abandoned her now that she is ailing and exhausted with Life. She now even begs help from me, the only one left who will speak to her. If she dies tomorrow or in 20 years, I have sworn not to tell anyone ~ assuming it is my terrible misfortune to have to watch out for her still after all those years.

I am beyond the hypocrisy, however, and the pusillanimous piety that makes others---pious hypocrites every one of them---feel good about themselves. I will not play into their hands so that they can feel sorry for themselves once their sweet mother Maribel dies. NO! Not anymore. They didn't give a shit about her while she was alive, I will not make it easy for them, like I have said many times.

Only you will know, only you I will inform, assuming that, if her death does take place years from now, we are still communicating as we are, or if I am still alive (I don't joke, or take the subject lightly considering the awful challenges we have survived just by living near a diseased riddled swamp---which spoils the serenity of our beloved Finca, and the damned local municipal government is slow to do anything about it---or this darkness that threatens to overtake my soul again, leading me towards my own, self-inflicted doom).

I would prefer you not tell anyone else outside of your immediate family, but that would be your choice whether to inform my remaining brothers and sisters.

I know my mother would rather I only inform Alicia, my third eldest sister, because she is still her darling daughter, but does not care if I inform any one of her other children.

If you still care, then you will be informed, and know that you are truly her son now, the only one who really seems to care.

In my case, again, she never showed that she would still love me if I turned out to be a murderer. On the contrary, she just might love you in spite of any faults you might have.

Oh well, I apologize now for this email. I did not mean to depress you, or harp on with my guilt and shame over the horrors we live with sans-resignation. You have enough to worry about.

I did not intend to cause you any embarrassment or discomfort. I feel that knowing is much better, even it did leave you feeling a bit embarrassed, than keeping you in ignorance, leaving you to wonder if anyone cares, or has even noticed your quiet suffering throughout all of these past years.

Yes, Freddy, someone does care, and has noticed your suffering ...

So, let's sing along again, and try to believe in angels.

Amor y besos,

Becky ~

This last reply really got me to think about my own situation again. The catharsis I was attempting to achieve by traveling, she was undergoing by way of her sacrifices on behalf of her children. She truly is a changed person, far different from the mischievous rapscallion of a tom-boy I grew up with, and never really liked at the time now that I think about it. Today, however, our mutual Fate was joined by our souls and common misery, and more and more I would come to rely on her counsel. Hence, to reassure her of my sincerity, I replied:

~ Becky, my prayers for now, and as always, are focused on Gamaliel. He shall over come, and you shall overcome ... some day!

I do hope that when your mother passes you will let me know, and of course, as for the others, I will not take the time of my day to tell them a single thing, especially after what happened with your sister Margara lately (when she angrily yelled at me over the phone after I'd called her to inquire about your mother's health). I have thought about that moment many times, and wonder what will happen to you when it does happen. For me, I want you to be safe first of all, that you have access to the assets that you handle of hers so that you keep them for yourself ~ I know you are well off now and don't need the money, but fair is fair, and even your nemeses would agree that you are entitled to every red cent. You, more than anyone else, deserve them, and I know that the first thing they will do when they learn of her passing is try to take away *hasta los calzones* (even your under-wear) from you. So, especially now that I know, I will not tell anyone if that is your wish. I would like however that you have a plan, move back to the States, go to Peru with your long-lost lover, Roberto (I know that you are still carrying a torch for him, so don't bother to deny it), to China as a teacher, like you always dreamed of doing, or wherever.

As for feeling embarrassment, please believe me I do feel shame for how fucked up this world can be, but not for what you did or failed to do. You were there, I remember that day, and I remember how you tried to shut up my stupid sister when I was holding the base-ball bat, and the sight of the bloody head of that delinquent Jorge who'd broken into the house and attacked us. You missed what happened next because no one would tell you. It comes as a surprise that only recently you learned that I had gone to jail.

I knew how you were back then, and you knew my family well; that bum Jorge deserved what he got, he had bothered others in the nearby streets, including yourself, many times. I remember also that on one occasion he got violent and abusive in the Pizzeria you worked at (remember that incident?), but luckily Sam, your boss, stopped him. It happened at one of the dinner tables, others were eating, and he had just been released from jail a few days before. It also must have been some time before the incident with me, all because he offered you drugs over the counter, and you refused. This surely must bring back many horrible details to mind.

So, my sweet Becky, I always knew we had a special connection since we were little, despite all of our fights for territory---you defending Mexico, and me defending my sweet America---but somehow, while my brother Fabian was hovering over you with incest on his mind, I felt that you started seeing me differently, just like Margara and every one else, and there were times when you even avoided saying hello when I visited, which is something we clarified a while back. I am so glad now that I can show my true colors, my actual face, as well, and most importantly that you can see it.

Cuidate prima y cuenta conmigo (take care cousin, and you can count on me) for anything that requires my support, which during these times isn't much. But, I believe that God will provide for both of us! We are survivors. I want you to know that I enjoy even what you write, although bad experiences as they are, they are somehow poetic and touching.

Yours truly,

Freddy ~

A whole new can of worms had been opened; memories long suppressed had emerged from my memory, and now would be her turn to stir the pot of nostalgia and trauma. What would come of it, neither of us could say, but we both felt that we were at a cross-roads in life, and the slightest misunderstanding might cause us to take divergent paths, even with all the sympathetic reassurances and vows to see to each-other's welfare.

Thus she stirred the murky pot some more:

~ Oh Primo, you were there when I fought against that nasty brother of yours? Damn that Fabian, he really disgusted me! Yet everyone, thinking the worst about me, thought that I had seduced him! Yes, that's right ~ I had just been with your family a few months or more. My God, I wasn't even 20 years old yet, right?

Whenever you get a free moment, please write me about what you personally remember. I do recall the terrible circumstances that followed so well, but the actual event at the house is now hazy in my memory. I only remember swinging that damned base-ball bat (probably the same one you used on Jorge), and stupid Helena panicking and crying her eyes out, *Why! Why!*, como mariquita sin calzones (like a silly pansy).

Wow! we really did participate in some history making, didn't we? Y, pa que veas (and, it just goes to show), I truly had no idea that you had gone to jail. This was a real surprise. I can't believe I did not know until recently.

And, even more surprisingly, I did not know that you knew about the incident in the Pizzeria when that stupid drug-pusher had harassed and threatened me. And, thanks for saying that ~ that he deserved what he got. Bless you truly, even after all these years since it happened, the fact that you are on my side really helps my self-esteem.

Yes, I remember the whole episode you suffered through, when you'd had occasion to beat the crap out of him, lasted almost 6 days --- 3 in the hospital, then actual prison, then the processing and then being let go---but to what purpose? I later learned they'd let him out soon after you'd been released.

With respect to Fabian's nasty amorous advances, did you lose all respect for me at the time?

Anyway, I am so glad that you understand those times now, and even why I may have stopped saying Hello to you. I am so relieved!

Becky ~

A couple of days passed, and not much went on between us. Gamaliel was still in jail, and I was still in Guerrero, but by now I had found my way to Zihuatanejo. It is a most enjoyable spot with languorous beaches, gentle Pacific breezes, lanky palm trees swaying to the rising tide, mouth-watering shell-fish cock-tails to be had at the palm-covered *coktelerias* (cock-tail huts), enervating Tequila Sunrises and Rum-Cocos offered gratis at the hotel bar, and gorgeous bodies, of both genders, sauntering about provocatively, enticing other less gorgeous types to abandon all cares to the sands. I followed suit, and slept on a hammock through entire afternoons without a care in the world. Then, on the second day, I awoke and discovered Becky's reply had arrived four hours before.

I prepared then to answer her without hesitation:

~ Becky, you know my stupid family could never understand. They only know that I was *soberbio* (proud), but that's how it was in those days. They forget that not saying hello is nothing. I mean, how can they reproach you for not saying *Hello* when I lasted almost 4 years without saying a word to my own father, even while living under his roof and eating his food? It was the same with my other brothers, and the last one I refused to speak to anymore was Fabian. Instead of going crazy with violence, like I had with the dope-pusher, I found it much safer to stop talking to my new enemies. Many times I would stop talking to my mother, but she always caved in and ended up talking to me, imploring me to be forgiving and let bygones be bygones.

It is too bad you are learning these bare facts the hard way, but it was inevitable. The evil was bound to slither out of dark oblivion.

Even your sister Margara's terrible attitude towards me, if you haven't learned of this already, is not really due to any personal animosity she harbors against me. I know that for a fact, since she has no reason to dislike me. No, just like when you stopped saying hello to me, I knew I had nothing at all to do with it; if something did involve us, it was all Fabian's and our own mothers' fault because of their rumormongering and accusations against us. He would act like a total asshole towards us, then blame us for turning him against us ~ blame everyone except himself, the obvious culprit.

It was also my mother's fault because she would repeat the slanders both Fabian and your mother, sweet "auntie" Lydia, had hurled against you. Fabian and your mother can be blamed because they actually started with the wickedly slanderous remarks against you, and someone as dumb as Margara or Alicia believed it all. But, as you yourself observed, my mother cannot be totally blamed since she was just stupid enough to believe what she was told. Like a cantankerous macaw, she just started to repeat everything she overheard without understanding the implications of the slander.

As for your attitude today, I thank you again for understanding, and for caring about my future. Maybe the fact that we are so close by way of email now, after all these years, is a vindication of that feeling you described about being connected since we were little kids. Funny we should both recall those days when we would argue about defending our territories as children ~ now that you are all pro-American and had lived happily in the U.S. while attending college, while I took many Chicano Studies courses, and now am experiencing Mexico like few others ever do. What an extraordinary irony Life has served us!

Yes, you do need a plan, and I would so much like to experience Peru with you, or even China some day. But, heading back to good ol' America has to be my goal. I may be an idiot, but I am already dreaming of buying, sleeping and taking it easy in that house that your old sorority sister, Corazon, is selling. I can see me now, lolling in an easy-chair, watching old sitcom re-runs, and having chicken-pot pie for lunch in between writing articles about tourism for the E-Travel blogger. What a nice, quiet, serene little life that would be!

Freddy ~

... As I proof-read my email looking for any typos and punctuation errors, I started wondering what old Fulgencio San Roman was doing back at that decaying old cantina where I'd first seen him. I wondered what he'd make out of all my tortured correspondence with Becky. Would he think it fodder for one of his movie plots? Perhaps not, even as I try to wrench some sense out of it. The past, nonetheless, is being resurrected for purposes of conciliation, and that's something neither Becky nor me intended. Old Fulgencio would likely find it all too humorous to think about.

DIRTY LITTLE SECRETS BETRAYED

Well, Zihuatanejo worked splendidly on my nerves, and I relaxed more than I thought I could. So far the food was decent, and the people overtly friendly, perhaps too friendly in the case of some beach-boys looking for *chamba* (work) by offering themselves for an easy exchange, so to speak. There was much to consider regarding Becky's correspondence, and during this phase of our long-distance relationship, some unhappy, even dirty, little secrets would escape that clandestine mental archive that guards them from impudent attention. Hence, I gratefully replied:

~ Well, my sweet friend, I must give you thanks again for all of your gentle reassurances. I was sincere by qualifying your writing as poetic and touching. It means a lot to me to learn these things, and just like you feel, it means a great deal coming from intelligent, educated people, like you, not from fucking *pendejos analfabetos ignorantes* (idiots, illiterates, ignorants), like a certain old woman I could name.

By the way, what else do you remember of that night when that slimy Jorge broke into our house and fought with me?

Hope you remember,

Freddy ~

Surprisingly, she replied forthwith, and supplied details even I had forgotten about:

~ Yes, Primo, I would be glad to ~ Well, it was such a long time ago, it is all hazy now. But, wait a minute ... That's right, I was only 18 when I lived with you guys, or your sister Clara, whatever was the case. What I do remember with some clarity is that your parents had gone out to a dance, they were all dressed up, and even invited me, but I was too tired from work. I used to get along with your younger sister, Helena, really well and I remember she used to come over on weekends from West Los Angeles where she lived. I remember I was there because we were going to do something special for the holiday, though I am not sure if it was for Thanksgiving or for the 1st of December, and we had to watch the grandchildren because your parents went out. Your friend Louie was there, and we were in the living room when that creep Jorge came in all bloody, and you behind him with the baseball bat; you looked so angry and scared at the same time.

Of course, I did not lose all respect for you: on the contrary, I knew that fool Jorge was something else, had suffered with him at the Pizzeria, and knew you were not so psychotic that you did not know what you were doing. Like I said, I knew that guy deserved it. I remember Fabian was on your side back then too.

I remember seeing him laughing at the issue, and then got serious because stupid Helena was going nuts with terror. I think Clara was on your side too because, back then, she was really bitter that Jorge, who had known Clara well from high school or some place of mutual acquaintance, and he happened to live up the street, accused her and Helena of being lesbians, and assured your father that he had seen them. He ranted and raved about what "sinners" they were.

And, your father was just stupid enough to believe a criminal street thug rather than in the sanctity of his own daughters.

Just out of curiosity, what exactly did Fabian say about me? Not that I really care; honestly, it was so long ago, and as you know me by now, I do not hold grudges against people that don't deserve anything from me, not even a second thought. I wonder, just like with you and your unfortunate encounter with Margara, I didn't do anything consciously to hurt them at all. I really wonder (as I am so innocent) what I did to him? What did I say?

tu prima,

Becky ~

My dear friend had obviously treaded on the cemetery of forgetfulness, and I was loathe to summon up painful recollections of people and events, which added nothing to our collective existence but rancor and palpable resentment. Despite my hesitation, I lifted myself from the lethargy the Pacific currents had imposed on me by now as I lolly-gagged on the warm sands, but I managed to reply to her questions as well as I could:

~ Hey babe, good to hear from you again. Frankly, I am surprised. You do remember details well, right down to the point about my parents having gone out for a dance that dreadful night so many years ago when all Hell broke loose and I ended up in jail with a genuine asshole! What I had totally forgotten about was this stuff about Jorge saying that Helena and Clara were Lesbians. Remarkable! How could you remember such a thing?

But, then again, life dealt me such a deadly blow by giving me epilepsy. So, for one such as I who lives for the contemplation of the mind, I have lost so much of my memory banks thanks to the damned epileptic seizures, and yes, they plague me still, but in a different way; instead of losing consciousness and shaking all over, now I get this horrible, head-ache like pain that runs from the top nerve of my brain, all the way down to my testicles. It feels like (I imagine) someone has cut into me from top to bottom with a razor blade, then I stiffen up, like I am suffering through a full-body cramp. It is so painful, my heart starts pumping fast, and I get dizzy but don't entirely lose consciousness. This sort of epilepsy only happens to people after a certain age, and though these seizures occur infrequently, they can lead to something deadly, like a stroke.

Stress triggers these attacks, and, since before I had taken off for this Mexican adventure, they have occurred more frequently, and yes, thanks to you-know-who (my own selfish and stupid family).

In fact, I had suffered a couple of seizures in the hospital after the police took me and that idiot Jorge after the terrible fight. But that fuck-head acted like he was fine and nothing had happened. I guess he was used to getting his ass whooped, so it was no big deal.

As for Fabian, well, again the epilepsy has done its part to wipe out many memories (some of which are strangely coming back in my dreams, as I'd mentioned earlier), and I have survived so many horrors from these *pinche hijos de la chingada* (dirty, rotten bastards) called my family, that it has become a blur.

But, of what I do remember, he basically would start out by mentioning certain times he would take you places (oh, and all those passes I gave him for the movies? Now he says he paid for all those just to take you out ~ what a rotten crud he is, eh!).

He would say then that you would order the most expensive things all the time, like at a restaurant, then you would act all "despota" ("miss high and mighty"), and that you would "tease him" about giving him some "pink taco."

During other times he would make fun of you, claiming that you were so picara and picuda (coquettish and horny) that you could not get enough of his chorizo (sausage). Nonetheless, he would end up disgusted because, according to his slander, you "were not a clean woman," that you had some dirty habits down there, which left him "afraid of getting a disease."

Then, he would complain about your "dirty mouth," that YOU would criticize and make fun of everybody and everything, and all that would leave him feeling like he had made a mistake about going out with you. In other words, he described himself and all the things HE did, and does, but then blamed you for it ~ just like other drug addicts would do, like Jorge or your brother Lorenzo.

Finally, of the little I remember, he would especially complain to my mother or yours, or to your sister Margara, that you were using him, that you were manipulative and trying to find some way of getting at his property, trying to get at his money. He accused you also that you were a habitual liar. According to him, during times he suspected that you were "cheating" on him, and after you had just been willingly defiled by some other guy, you would not even clean up before seeing Fabian. Then, to show up your alleged shamelessness, you'd beg for his mondongo (genital bulge), and have him "ravage" you either orally or anally, which caused him to "lose respect for her," which, again, just makes me wonder about his shameless hypocrisy.

Also, he would allude to your alleged dependence on marijuana, and that you loved cocaine and tried crack-cocaine. According to Fabian, most of these stories were due to the rumors spread by your own mother, who supposedly confided to Fabian that you were a pot-smoking libertine, and had tried everything, including "cow-pies and golden showers" (feces and being urinated upon), when you were especially drugged out on LSD, heroin, or some other awful drug.

¿Como lo ves? (how do you see it?) And this is considering the fact that my memory is fucked up due to the epilepsy!

Take care babe, and believe me, I DO NOT BELIEVE ANY OF IT ... unless it was actually Fabian who had done all these things himself, then I would believe it!

Your Primo,
Freddy ~

I am sure I left her aghast with these confessions; so much so that she forgot momentarily the suffering of Gamaliel in order to fire back a reply within hours:

~ Thanks for the trust you've placed in me, Primo, but what can I say about Fabian? *Hijo de la fregada!* (Son of a Bitch!) I didn't think he was such a marica (pussy). I really have just lost the little respect I had for him ~ yes, I actually still had some respect for him. Obviously he was, or still is so bitter because I never fell for his fucking desires.

I knew, and could understand how he would think I was using him when he kept on taking me places without my having to give it up. Once again, how could I cheat on him when we were cousins and nothing else? You all knew I had a boyfriend who even came to visit me from Arizona, right? Don't I have the right to my own life?

I can see now why all of you changed with me after I'd gone out with him, before finally putting a stop to his persistence. He trashed me with all of you, and, like usual, only the most stupid ones believed him. I thank you for trusting me, and for not believing it all; none of it, in fact, was true. The thought of sleeping with him always made me puke, now I am glad I never even tongue-kissed him.

Like they say, only time can tell and sin querer queriendo (without expecting anything), life has given me the opportunity to prove myself. Time shows who is who in this life. You are so right when you say you suspected that all he accused me of are things that he probably did when he was high on drugs. I do remember he was a heavy cerveza (beer) drinker and pot smoker back then. Some of the things that used to bother me about him I ignored, and yet I always tried and pushed him to stop abusing drugs because I did care for him and because he is my blood kin-folk, not as nothing else.

Thanks for sharing this with me. I really had no idea how much he had said, I would never have guessed it, or believed it if someone else told me.

Que hijo de la chingada! And your mother believed all of this crap? By the way, what is "pink taco"?

Tu prima, Becky ~

My delightful fall by the wayside in Zihuatanejo assuredly gave me much to reflect upon. I despised having to gather my things and leave all the soothing sensuality and physical beauty behind, but I would have Acapulco to garnish my expectations. It took a few hours to get there, but the bus-ride was peaceful enough, except for a corpulent swine of a bearish man who'd snored the entire way. Checking in at the EL CID hotel proved to be an unexpected hassle, but it was high season for visitors, and the demand for rooms brought out the bloodthirstiness in both tourists and the hoteliers.

Ah, lovely Acapulco with her rocky cliffs, looming beach-side hotels, fiery white sands, flying sails of wind-surfers, flying divers with their rich copper-hued skin risking limb and life for a tourist's loose change, the enchanting fair-skinned pretties giggling at every passerby, it almost made me forget about my stay in Zihuatanejo! In between swishing the gin of my authentically prepared mint-juleps, I just had to reply to Becky's inquiry:

~ Hey, babe, Looks like I really gave you much to think about ... sorry about that. Imagine if I had a better memory, and really told you all the things Fabian had actually said about you, especially all that he confided to both of our mothers.

First of all, in answer to your last question: "pink taco" is one of those metaphors for *panocha* (vagina).

Second, yes, my mother, like I mentioned before, is very gullible, especially when it comes to things about her precious "Fabiancito." You can only imagine the Hell I have been through having to live with both of them. I have sacrificed so much for that damned *pinche vieja*, and when Fabiancito came running after our parents had put all of their assets and property into a trust, to make his demands, *ella me manda a la chingada* (she sent me to Hell), and made it possible for Fabiancito to take everything I had worked so hard for; my rights to the house to begin with, and then so much more.

So, yes, she believed every little thing that he slandered against you, everything. And then, with your own mother trashing you, *pues mas iba creer lo peor de ti* (well, the more she was going to believe the worst about you). I tell you, she is a stupid, easily malleable, reactionary, narrow-minded, super-egotistical, provincial, superstitious, obscurantist, intolerant and racist bigot ~ and THOSE ARE HER GOOD POINTS!

Third, I disagree that he is, or was bitter for having said all those things about you. He is a bastard, a *canalla, hijo de la chingada* (a ratfink son of a bitch). No warm, human feelings for anybody, not even for his own mother who has helped him in everything, *y listo para chingar a todos los demas'* (and ready to screw everybody else).

Like all those exploitative drug-abusers, he just uses people to get what he wants, and when they are no longer useful, he trashes them to the ultimate degree. You were no longer useful to him, so he spread the slander wherever he could, achieving what this type of bastard wants: convincing idiots, like my mother and your sister Margara, that you were the trash and he is the wounded saint.

Again, this was a show of the egotistical, mean-spirited self-pity that drives his type of warped, drug damaged personality.

Anyway, I have to admit that my respect for you during those awful days was compromised, but not for the reasons you think; I never thought you were capable of incest, as he alleged or some such shit, and I never believed Fabian, having grown up knowing about his lies and twisting of the truth. Yes, even though we were not enemies at the time, I still had already learned to hate and distrust him since much earlier on.

When you started accompanying him, and I stopped being overtly friendly to you, it was not because I thought you were trash ~ instead I thought: "God, how can Becky lower herself to the level of that piece of garbage Fabian? I thought she was so much finer than that! ¿Que le pasa? (what's wrong with her?) Has she lost all hope for the future? Has she lost all respect for HERSELF? Why, oh why is she dating that scum-bag?"

But, alas, being *timido y aislado* (timid and isolated), I could not approach you with the question. I figured, well, it is her life; as long as she dates Fabian I have lost her as a friend, so what can I do? And, believe it or not, he is such a *perro mierdero, miandose por todos lados para marcar su territorio* (stray, crap-eating dog, urinating everywhere to mark his territory), if I had continued to be friendly with you, he would have taken that as a threat to his manhood, and he would have accused me of trying to "take his bitch away from him."

And, that would have led to a big fight with him!

Time heals all wounds, nevertheless, and rectifies the wrongs and injustices that Life itself presents us. Over the years you have justified my faith in you, and have shown that you were, and are the remarkable person I always thought you were.

Fabian was just a bad dream, and it is true that, because of our ignorance and blindness to the things Life throws at us, we end up having to put up with certain rotten people for a while until we can be freed from their stinking, rotten influence. Look at me, I am stuck with the rotten, stinking influence of my family, and am suffering still from the shit I got from Fabian, whilst you've been rid of the stench of his influence for a long time!

Tu primo,

Freddy ~

I suppose the last email soothed her troubled brow because she did not insist on clarifying any other issues. Things were probably intensifying with regard to Gamaliel, but she would not tell me as of yet. I was too busy enjoying myself by the Acapulco coast, and even inquired around about investing in an apartment or condominium which were selling cheaply at the time, to feel any guilt about her own domestic woes.

About three days had passed when she answered:

~ Well, Primo, thanks again for clarifying the reason why you'd distanced yourself from me. I just did not know the bastard, and I thought he was my caring, though kissing, cousin who just wanted to show me around town and treat me the way I would have treated him if he had gone to Mexico.

"Pink taco"? Ha! I learned something new today!

Pues una ultima palabra sobre esta tema (Well, one last word about this subject): As for Fabian, as much as I hate him now, I cannot judge what his actual motives were back then. Maybe he started out really liking me, so, as you observed, maybe there is some bitterness attached to his invective.

On the other hand, he did end up trashing me to the third degree, and it is the final result that counts. Thanks to him, I learned without a teacher to really hate, unless his was the subtle hand that guided me to the edge of the abyss. Rather than being decent about the whole thing, he just succumbed before his beastly passions, and did what he always does when he is defeated: he lies and slanders the person, and attaches his own crimes to them. Since I had lived with him more than 20 years ago, believe me, he is the one with the filthy habits, and I thought I would catch a disease from him just by using the same bathroom. He has a filthy mouth, is capable of fucking over anyone for their money, he stinks big time, and cheats on people while abusing drugs. Fear of him forced me to suffer his caprices time and time again, but I finally awakened to the truth that the thing you fear has no power over you; it is the fear itself that has the power. Until then, I was a helpless little "pink taco" to him.

That's all I'll say about that piece of fetid feces that is your brother.
Love,
Becky ~

I surely am glad my dear friend was no longer pulling any punches about a much reviled past and persons. I thought I would change the subject, since I despised having to think of Fabian in any case, and was morbid about an email I had just received from my own, nagging mother, so I again inquired about her pathetic son:

~ Becky, my dear, about Gamaliel, how the Hell is he doing?

Your beloved aunt showed signs of some spirit with the last email she sent; she actually just took off when her friend, who manages excursions, just up and invited her to go to Izamal, in Yucatan ~ like I really care. According to her, it was alright, and it felt like the real Mexico, not like our shitty barrio. It's just the authentic Mexico I've been searching for, and wanting to experience all along. Perhaps, though, I may just be chasing stereo-types not realizing they are not to be had, anymore.

Acapulco is fabulous; recently I went to some strange, abandoned beach called, of all names, Santa Clara ~ they assuredly weren't referring to my sister!

I am genuinely glad I've had this opportunity to see some of the beauty of Mexico, never mind my mother's "authentic" experience.

I pray that by next week you will be calling me, or writing to tell me that your son is FREEEEEE! Again, at this point, I feel like I am the one doing the time. You must be beside yourself with grief. I'm sorry you have gone through so much, and for what? Incompetent police!

As for Gamaliel, I feel it; and I don't have many premonitions of this sort in either case. Fortune, I think, will at last smile on both of you. I dedicate your favorite song again to both of you: *I have a dream.*

Yours, Freddy ~

The message of the song seemed to have worked its magic on her again, for she was quick to reply in thanks, and expressed the feeling of comfort she gets from it, as well as her gratitude for the moral support she was getting from me:

~ Thank you again, Primo, for sharing this beautiful song and for the positive vibe. I need all the positivity I can get while we are undergoing this traumatic episode, and so resolution to it all is in sight. I will go see Gamaliel today, and every time I go there I pray to God that some miracle will happen, that this will be the last day I have to step foot in that horrible place. He has a court appointment next Thursday, we have talked about it, and he even told me that I don't have to show up because it would be a waste of my time (which is true). I can't help it, nevertheless, it's like not being there when he fell off his bike and scraped his knee when he was four. I do have a conflict of filial interest: Campanita's (her young daughter, Campanita, or "Tinkerbell," and half-sister of Gamaliel) Winter Festival is on that same day, so I am torn between two loves. I made up my mind, nonetheless, that I will go see Gamaliel. My hope is that he will be the first, or one of the first to go in front of the judge like he had the last time. I was out of there by 10am. But, during other times I'd been there from 8am to 4pm. If my wish is granted by the forces of the universe (that I get out of there by 10am), I will definitely have time to see Campanita; she will be the presenter, and I am relying on my ex, Enrique Alvarez, to film the event. If Enrique finds out that I went to see Gamaliel, for whom he has no love, instead of Campanita, he will freak out. At least Campanita has him; Gamaliel has no one else, especially since his own father, Roberto, wouldn't take the time of day to inquire about his own son.

Como ves, primo?

Take care,

Becky ~

At this point, however, my mood had been spoiled by my darling old mother: it seems she had been sending me several emails trying to get me to do her dirty correspondence, to write missives and apologies of regret because both her relatives in Mexico City and Becky's family (who have fond memories of her friendship with their mother) have been begging her to spend a week with them upon her return from Yucatan. They have implored her, begged and cried for her, but, for some damned reason, she was adamant about not going. She complained that she could no longer stand her friends and relatives, even if they treated her with the utmost respect and affection. It was almost unconscionable to me that, after listening to her complaints for so long about her abandonment by her own children, the progeny of her sisters should guard such affection and compassion for her. I had no recourse but to go off on a tangent, and cry to Becky about this silly, ungrateful old woman, if only because my friend's own brothers and sisters were doing most of the insisting, particularly her elder brother, Santiago:

~ *Querida Becky*, I have received no less than three emails from your brother Santiago about getting my mother, who never informed me that she was taking a holiday in Mexico, to go visit them in Mexico City or Veracruz and see your ailing mother. He was brief and straight to the point, which makes it all the more difficult for me to rat on my own mother, who clearly is ungrateful and insensitive to their entreaties.

It breaks my heart, in a way, that he is going out of his way, and yet my confounded mother is willing to lose your love and that of your brothers by just not going, and making fucking, useless excuses for not being able to go, which is bullshit, bullshit, bullshit!!!

She even suggested, "Mejor nos quedamos quietos, y no les contestamos. Haber si asi paran de chingar." (It's better we just keep quiet, and don't answer them. Maybe this way they'll stop pestering me) ~ *YES, IN SO MANY WORDS, SHE SAID THAT!*

¿Que hago, prima? (What shall I do, cousin?)

Would you be willing to inform them all that my ornery, old mother is a vieja, egoista, sangrona, cabrona, vengativa, estupida, tacaña, falsa, desgraciada, y miente que no puede ir? (an old, egotistical, supercilious, haughty, mean-spirited, vengeful, stupid, tight-fisted, false, god-damned hag, and lies about not going?)

I just can't face it.

Oh well, maybe as we approach the actual date I might send my apologies. They deserve that much, if not more.

But I feel so low, so ashamed, so embarrassed, and humiliated that you and your family are so willing to make us part of your family, and this damned old hag doesn't care if she offends, and sends them all to Hell just because she feels like it. She acts like it would be a disaster to spend two or three hundred dollars to go, even though Santiago had promised to be her host, to feed and house her, take her on tours, and even throw a big barbecue feast for her!

Why did I have to have such a screwy mother like her?

I hate to say it, but maybe my father, himself an insufferable, evil old bigot, was truly right about her; she has been as much of an evil witch as he was an asshole.

Oh Lord, I am getting depressed again.

take care!

Primo ~

Apparently my frontal attack on my own mother, whom she had always respected, though she knew, by now at least, about her treachery and calumnies with Fabian, took her aback. She did not know as well that her brothers and sisters had tried to organize this reunion between somewhat distant relatives; to reiterate, I had met Becky back in childhood, but only recently did I learn that my mother was related to their mother twice removed, and my father had worked with theirs in the Ministerio de Gobernacion (Secretariat of State) back in the 1960s. Thereabout, she responded somewhat confusedly:

~ Primo, It really hurt me to learn about what she supposedly said. What part of her is a fake, I don't understand?

One thing for sure is that she is not like my mother; she would have not hesitated a bit, and even last year when she was so sick, she was just looking for the opportunity to go where the fun was. If I were you, I would be honest and tell them, Santiago in particular, that she is just making up excuses. I know they love her, even more now because we see her as a sort of surrogate mother. Since our own doesn't seem to give a crap about us, she reminds us to a great extent of our revered grandmother, Doña Chata. They will understand, and you can also say that YOU are interested in going. As for the money for the trip, Santiago is the one who is better off and might find a way for you to make it to Mexico City through PeMex (the national oil producing conglomerate he works for), who knows? Sometimes he is pretty resourceful, and if it happens for you to go, don't hesitate.

As for your mother, never, ever cover for her. When I talk to them I will tell them my way. I would say that she is probably too tired and old to do anything.

Thanks for letting me know.

Amor,

Becky ~

Since I worried about finances, and was getting to be a "pretty-boy spendthrift" in these stupefying resorts, an offer to travel and have a good time with old friends and perhaps some longtime-no-see relatives was very tempting. Hence, I replied with unaccustomed enthusiasm as I prepared for bed on an enchanting Acapulco night:

~ Prima, what's this you write? Really, really, really? Santiago might actually find a way to get us there courtesy of PeMex?

Did you find out about this just now, or have you known all along?

If you have, *ay chica*, then I wonder why Santiago hadn't offered this in the first place? I don't know, I guess I am overly excited now. I should not question why, and should hope for the best.

If you get a chance to talk to Santiago about the PeMex option, by all means, I certainly would love to go ~ even if I arrive as a pinche pediche, muerto-de-hambre, pidiendo limosna (a damned leech, starving vagabond, begging for alms).

... Oh God, I am all that in any case!

But, even with the sadness and the reproaches of last year (when her grandmother had died, and there were those who insinuated that she had been forcibly helped along to her grave), I had fun, and it was nice experiencing it all again for the first time since adolescence. It actually left me with a desire to see them all again, now that I don't have to be afraid about returning or facing their disapproval like I was last time. I felt that everyone, especially your family, still affirmed me. I was genuinely worried last year that they would not appreciate my presence for whatever reason, and, after I had overheard my mother tell your mother, "Ay que feo comparandolo a Fernando, ¿quien se va a fijar en el con esa figura?" (Oh, how ugly he is comparing him to Fernando---my father---who is going to notice him with that figure of his?)

Naturally, I felt hurt and dismayed that maybe others would not like me. But, everyone accepted me well enough, and Santiago and family, if I haven't mentioned it before, were the best.

If only you could make it there too, This would be a great get-together-family-and-friends reunion, don't you think?

Pero, haber que pasa. Mejor no me vuelo (But, we'll see what happens. It's better I don't get carried away).

Anyway, I fully agree with, and affirm your advice; as a matter of fact, I had already, just before I received your reply, communicated with Alejandro, your nephew, and told him straight that "auntie" Maribel was being a tranca-tacaña? (tight-fisted cheapskate), did not want to spend money, and lied about her reasons for not going. So, I guess I will do the same with the others, especially Santiago.

About your question about being a fake (falsa); it is simply that she lies, and pretends to love and appreciate all of you guys, but it simply is not so. She is a bitter, angry, resentful old woman, and because she spent 51 horrible years with Don Fernando, and she did a terrible job of raising her own children, she now blames us for *HER MISTAKES*. She has now reached her 80th year without the capacity anymore to appreciate what is good in others, to give them the benefit of the doubt, or to take some sincerity for granted.

But, now with all the scandal related to la Hyena Sandra, your "beloved" sister-in-law, and the unexpected calls she received from your sister Margara about it all, as well as your niece Sandy's rather hypocritical emails, which her mother, it turned out, made her send us to appear friendly, well, now Doña Maribel really suspects everyones' motives. She now thinks everyone is out to screw her somehow, to get her to part with her money, or whatever means to use, abuse and exploit her. In other words, she expects to get from others all that she has given to them, figuratively speaking.

I tell you, she is suspicious, and is a rancorous witch who never forgives ~ she does not forgive anything. Take your mother as an example: my mother never forgave Doña Lydia for the problems related to the purchase of a damned property in Mexico City.

Therefore, she is a fake lying to you about everything, about not calling you, about why she cannot go to Veracruz for Summer holidays ~ a fake about everything!

When you do get in touch with la familia, lay it on heavy, have no mercy. Stick it to old Maribel! They must know that she is not the sweet-heart they might think she is. She is a total, hateful phony!

Take care, and hope I, at least, can make it to the reunion!

Freddy ~

Unfortunately for me, Becky did not offer much reassurance about getting me some free transportation, though she had been the one to bring up the subject. Acapulco was getting to be a bit expensive anyway, and I thought about heading for Jalisco, or southward to Oaxaca. My mood wasn't improving, my mother's abrupt intervention had soured matters, and I couldn't focus on my mission, ill-defined as it remained, for the time being. But, she finally replied, and clarified, not especially to my satisfaction, the whole thing about Santiago and PeMex:

~ About Santiago and PeMex, Primo: I know that PeMex offers some kind of transportation that its employees can use for free, and I know that a while back they could transport relatives for any reason, but I am not sure how it works. I just know how my brother is, and if you tell him that you really want to go but don't have the means, he will sympathize. If he knows of a way to help you, he will.

On to other matters: so, your mother is really paranoid, huh? Most old folks get like that, and it doesn't surprise or trouble me in the least. Has anybody given her a true reason to think that way? What can they do to push her to give up something? Is it easier to refuse invitations and blame others for her failures, and suspect mal-intentioned plots fabricated in her own mind to justify her suspicion, groundless though it may be, so that she can be ready to say no? What is it with these people?

Good luck with all you do to keep her in check! Can you even talk to her about being honest and tell her that if she suspects we have evil intentions, she can be a mature adult and say, "sorry, no can do"?

Oh, I neglected to mention: Tomorrow is the Big Day!

I received word yesterday evening that my precious Gamaliel will be released! Too bad you aren't here in Puerto Alvarado to share in our joy. Good luck to you in Guerrero, and have a fabulous time.

I cannot tell you enough how much your empathy and support means to me. Thank You!

My sweet, precious son is as good as free!

Too bad we couldn't reunite for Christmas to celebrate Gamaliel's freedom and new lease on life.

But, better days ahead, that is for sure.
If you ask me, they couldn't get any worse!
Becky ~
So, the ways of simpletons make up the facts of life for most of us, and this is especially true of Mexico's inhabitants. The seeds of hate are transplanted from one loving heart into another, and no one in Mexico seems notices the irony ... no one, I think, except Mr. San Roman!

THE DAYS PASS, AND LIFE GOES ON

The hours passed slowly, and I heartily refused to face the moment when I had to vacate my hotel-room. But, I must, and had to, carry on, and would have to reunite with Becky eventually. I had involved myself too deeply in her domestic trauma to just up and disappear without a word. In either case, I honestly cared for their welfare, and was fond of both Becky and young Gamaliel; I always regarded him as a little brother, or at least a nephew. I hated to think about what he was going through given my own horror in jail, as well as the unique psychological and physical torments he was enduring for the present. How quaint the ways of paradox, though, and how gaily we mock common sense! I was presently dealing with a bitch of a mother, and imploring an angel accused of wickedness.

Perhaps Becky would be the first to negate her celestial qualities, but her suffering and sacrifices had gained my admiration. Nevertheless, her faith would be put to the test, and faced with circumstances that went against general belief. She had to dissect a difficult puzzle that led to a deeper truth; one which forced her to make amends with a contradictory life, which could only be false if it were true, and she was constantly having to deal with counter-intuitive people, including me. For the moment, she responded with much glee:

~ Primo, at last I can exclaim "Finally!" I am picking Gamaliel up from the Orizaba Carcel at 4pm.

I will fill you in with the details later on!!

Take care,

B ~

That was short and sweet, but she would soon have a disappointment: her beloved eldest son was not released like expected. As I traversed the winding, fecund hills of Oaxaca on my way to Puerto Escondido, I timorously scribbled my condolences for her big let-down:

~ Dear Becky, I am so, so sorry for your pain and disappointment. There are just no words to console you at this time, except to say that tomorrow is another day, and this legal processing bullshit is just a waste of time, so I hope you find the strength within you to keep going, put the disappointment behind you, and look forward to that better day.

Gamaliel is now possessed by Christ himself, crucified by injustice, but he will resurrect. He will be born again to a happier existence, and you all will come closer together a better and more unified family.

I am probably the worst person to give such advice considering what a melancholy fellow I am, but even I feel, and want to believe, that no matter what shit happens to you, this time, Springtime, and a time for new resolve and returning hope, you should be able to put all the crap aside and be happy, to celebrate, to rejoice with your loved ones along with the rest of society at least for a few days, and renew your bonds with, and to each other.

It is a time for tradition, favorite customs, parties, and fond memories, as you well know.

Since we both shall be missing out on many of these festivities, the native *Gelaguetza* festival of these aboriginals especially, because of mean and selfish people who don't care whose lives they ruin so long as their hatred is satisfied, I want to dedicate this music to you and your children since you, especially, have known and participated in such a tradition and understand the meaning of the songs. Enjoy, and our prayers and best wishes are with Gamaliel, as always.

(and so e-mailed her a couple of different songs)

Take care my good friend,

F ~

Frustration: Mexico be thy name! While I squirmed trying to find a hotel room in a town that did not match its reputation for colonial beauty or tropical delight, ingesting food that could hardly be digested, and dealing with local folk whom sadistically engaged in surreptitious transactions intended to dumbfound the honest visitor, my old friend was tearfully preparing to use legal force she never intended to use, while salvaging what semblance remained of her family, utterly devastated by this confrontation with justice. She responded, obviously quite disappointed with the situation:

~ Well, Primo, here I am, and here we go again. After waiting for three hours outside of the Orizaba Court, I get a phone call from Gamaliel, and he tells me that he did not get released today because they needed to clarify a warrant that he had, so he has to go to court again. I came back with all of my emotions destroyed, again. What the fuck is this? I pray it is only for a few more days that they hold him. The waiting game is wreaking havoc with my nerves.

In any case, thank you again for all of your support. I guess we continue to be prisoners of *Demon Fate*, and God knows for how long. It's a good thing I did not tell anyone, neither Campanita nor Emanuel (Gamaliel's younger, natural brother), a damn single thing. I wanted so to surprise them, and Emanuel missed his favorite dance lessons in order to be present for his brother's release. Here we are, here we stay, and no one gives a rat's ass for justice, let alone for my poor, frightened son.

Becky ~

All that I could add to her lament was to say, *poor, poor Becky!* Now she was imprisoned by the trauma as much as her son was behind bars, and she knew it, thus the source of her deepening grief.

I went ahead and jotted down my feelings about her admission, wishing to share in her grief, while expressing my own genuine feelings of distress for that unfortunate son of hers:

~ Oh shit ... Oh shit ... Why, oh God, why?

What is the meaning of these demonic pranks?

Why do you allow others to fuck around and get away with it, whilst the rest of us must bear and grin it as though "That's life, too bad?"

You know my hopes, feelings, and best wishes are with you, Becky, and with Gamaliel. It is just bullshit! It has to pass. It just has to pass. And Poor Emanuel too, who missed school for his big brother, that was really touching considering their contentious fraternal relationship. God, you really were a great mother if brothers love one another, unlike my rotten parents who fostered the hatred between my dirty brothers and me.

You have great children, remember that. Your love will keep you together.

May the force be with you, Becky ... always!

F ~

Poor Becky would remain sad and disgusted for a time. The uncertainty of unfolding events really stressed her out, and she is normally a very calm person. For my part, I had plenty of Rum at my disposal to keep me on an even keel, and the wicked waves of Puerto Escondido's coastline kept me on the beach as I reflected on the ramifications of my friend's apparent dilemma. I would have an occasion to take a launch to the secret coves and isolated beaches near Huatulco---a most enchanting nearby port and resort town---where the breakers were mild, the crystalline waters were relaxingly warm, and the shrimp-kebabs were dripping with melted butter and roasted garlic; it sure made washing it all down with Corona-label beer a joy I hadn't counted on. Once I had absorbed all the iodine-soaked atmosphere of the oceanside terrain, I anxiously returned to the lap-top to inquire about the latest developments:

~ Dear F, thanks, as always, for your unfailing support.

Yes, it was all fucked up. We all lost a lot yesterday; I missed time with Campanita and Emanuel, and missed important events at school. He was supposed to go to his Art Class which he takes after school from 3:30 to 5:30pm, and he really wanted to go. In the end, regrettably, he decided that he would come with me instead, but all for nothing. We waited out there for three freaking hours for nothing! That poor boy had an art project due this day, and he stayed up until midnight to finish it. It sucks, big time! And I missed my dear friend Gloria's wedding (she will be so disappointed in me, but I think she understands my situation).

Tu prima,

Rebecca ~

It always struck me that her mother, Lydia, was pessimistic about life, though she enjoyed it to the fullest. She always kept an inscribed jewelry box with a curious motto, the words of which she often repeated when her children expressed a gripe about something: "What we gave, we have; What we spent, we had; What we left, we lost ~ we lose much to the wayward fortune that falls upon us."

Yet, "Auntie" Lydia, Becky, and the rest of their clan, the Ange-Ingel's, still retained the plaintive motto, which asserted the dignity, and deplored the perdition, of their gradually disintegrating house. While they might sigh for past laughter and rejoicing, they are probably sensible of their many, tangible blessings. In the long series of the Ange and Ingel annals, the most splendid period is likewise the saddest; nor can any of their wealthy relations, either in Mexico or France, be inclined to envy the individual members who wandered over Mexico after their swashbuckling father, Pedro, had succumbed to cancer of the esophagus, to solicit alms for the support of their dignity and the defense of their properties ~ quite extensive according to whispering voices, and I had occasion in the past to partake of their plenty.

Things were not so happy with respect to the rest of the family, and she cried that her mother and siblings were giving her further grief over Gamaliel's alleged comportment, which led to the incarceration. Her mother, in particular, was suspicious of the circumstances. She took the side of the Law against her own grand-son, whom everyone thought she loved and favored. Instead, however, she demonstrated a vituperation that was assuredly unworthy of a grand-mother ... anyone's grandmother. I offered thus my regrets, and tried to reassure her, ineffectively, of my sincerity:

~ Of course, my dear Becky, your madre will go on suspecting till the day she croaks. Things here are never better or even good, only bad or worse. Right now it is between the two ~ just plain shitty.

As for your inquiry about my plans to make the reunion in Veracruz? Well, all that I know is that, without word from Santiago about the PeMex option, I won't be going unless I accomplish my purpose beforehand. Right now, everything is up to chance.

In other words, I am fucked, as always.

One nice thing that emerged from the correspondence with your siblings was that Lazaro (Becky's oldest brother), and even Lorenzo assured us that we'd always have a home to visit if we were to go to Mexico City or Veracruz ~ that your house, which still belongs to Doña Lydia, is always at Doña Maribel's disposal, which actually made the old hag of my mother feel better. When she was considering going, after Santiago had come to invite her a few weeks back, she wondered about staying in the main house because, for some god-damned reason, she really did not want to stay with Santiago and his familia at his ranch in the state of Hidalgo. She is always trying to bullshit me that she "loves it" because it is so peaceful and quiet---BULLSHIT! She is always complaining that she would hate to stay in Hidalgo with them because she would "not stand all that peace and quiet!"

Pa que veas, lo pinche rezongona, vieja que nomas le gusta dar te la contra para todo! (So you see the damned whining bitch, old hag who just enjoys contradicting everyone about everything!)

But, wish me luck: I got me my ticket for EL GORDO Loteria Nacional, the BIG year end Lottery prize. It is no big shit, but it gives me hope, at least until December.24 when they choose the numbers. It is then back to my hum-drum life, dreaming of better days ahead.

Well, for the moment, it's back to watching the bullfights on the Univision channel before heading back to the beach-side cokteleria for an enormous shrimp and oyster cocktail, and a couple of liters of refreshing, ever so nourishing beer.

Have you ever been to a genuine bullfight?

Take care,

Freddy ~

Now the email exchanges would be mundane and frivolous for the time being since no one had received word about Gamaliel's legal status. It was far from certain if her son would beat the rap, serious as the charges are, but she had boundless courage and patience ~ the very qualities a mother needs to support the problems and perils facing her own children. As for me, I was just battling pesky beach flies and a growing number of tourists, each vying for the best, well-shaded spot on the sands:

~ Primo, I wish with all my heart that you win the prize, and it helps you to come back, to realize your goals, to free you of these financial worries that you feel are crushing you. You truly deserve much better, and you are a great human being with so much potential for yourself and the world, I hate to see it go to waste. You have so much heart and wisdom to share, it is about time you stop keeping it to yourself. The people around you who don't appreciate it, or even see it, should be made to see that it is they who are fools and will suffer depravation once you've sent them to Hell.

As for going to bullfights, yes! When I was little, my father, Don Pedro, was a fanatic of Corridas de Toros. We used to go to the bull-ring every Sunday, and he'd also take us to see the wrestling fights, Lucha Libre, at the Mexico City forum.

Take care,

R ~

Her unexpected praise left me a bit discombobulated, but I accepted it in stride. For the time being I was far from the source of my misery, and the exigencies of this "voyage of adventure and discovery" were forcing me to worry more about money than about seeking "the truth of my soul," pretentious as that sounds. Just to continue in the main of our correspondence, I thought to restrict myself to lightness and trivialities until I'd left Huatulco:

~ Dearest Becky, you lucky creep you! I have visited Mexico many times over the years, and have been here for a couple of months now, and all I have been to was this idiotic comic corrida with dwarves, but it was no real bullfight, it was just ... Stupid!

You actually went almost every Sunday? God, I can't imagine it, except that I watch some of the delayed broadcasts on TV on every Saturday---big deal.

I bet you have had your fill of it, eh?

As for the personal things you wrote, thanks for that wonderful, flattering encouragement. My eyes are welling up with tears.

But, they will dry up the second I get word from my family again, or I have a run-in with the Federales. Just knowing that they are around rooting out wetbacks, like me, while totally ignoring those country-men of theirs who wetback their way into the U.S.A, makes me feel like mierda podrida (rotten shit). And so, my life is "just a waste."

So, I say, bless you babe. It is almost too incredible for me that it is actually you, my "Prima hermana," who is actually giving me this support and affirmation.

All I can keep saying is, "God bless you and thanks again." The same goes for your children, especially Gamaliel, as always.

Freddy ~

Since bullfighting is still an important sport in Mexico, albeit bloody and sickening, it is imperative for a visitor to accept the cultural mores of the country he/she is visiting. Since I am of Mexican ancestry myself, I did not have any real qualms about this traditional experience, and feel that it is likely to survive the present age, regardless of the changing attitudes worldwide. Hence, I pressed my friend for more anecdotes about this esoteric sport, if only to give fodder to my journalistic quest, and nothing more:

~ Yes, Primo, We actually went to the bullfights every Sunday. We, my crazy brothers and me, used to get all kinds of souvenirs each time we'd go; they sell clay bulls of all sizes with fur and "banderillas" on them, and my father bought me a couple of them.

My dad dearly loved bull fights; we used to have a big bull-head, dedicated to him by an old bull-fighter friend of his from the days of yore when my father had tried out as a "picador," or lancer-man, mounted on the wall of our living room. When we were little we would tease Santiago all the time because when he was about five or so, he looked at the bull's head on the wall, and then would stretch his hand towards it as if he was begging, and plead, *Papa Dios, dar me pan* ("Lord Father, give me bread").

Why he'd say such a thing at that age, no one ever knew. Neither my father nor the rest of us would let Santiago live it down for a long, long time. For that very reason, I think, he has avoided taking his own boys to see a bull-fight, though he was a bigger fan of them than the rest of us put together.

Look, primo, I will make a promise to you: when we meet in Mexico City (which I hope will be soon), I will take you to the bull fights, and when we start traveling to Europe to attend conferences on academic issues like we'd always dreamed of doing, we will go to the Pamplona "running of the bulls," how is that?

yours always,
Becky ~

As I pondered Becky's offer, I overheard someone say that Huatulco is a "Gay Paradise." If this were true, it certainly came as a surprise because there was no sign of it anywhere. There were only average, every-day families and old folks enjoying the loveliness of nature unspoiled by tourism; no ugly, Bauhausian high-rise hotel monstrosities to be had anywhere. I noticed a lot more gay activity going on in Zihuatanejo than in these swarthy and lurid parts.

Meanwhile, I wondered what to do, and I thought to move on to Oaxaca City to partake of the *Gelaguetza* Festival. I didn't want a chance to climb the ruins of Monte Alban, if I could, pass me by. Though I did accomplish the latter, with much difficulty that led to a spraining of my right leg, and the vistas of Oaxaca City were quite pleasant in my estimation, I was very disappointed in my plans to enjoy the town. Because of the actual, proto-religious aspect of the festival, most commerce was shut down, and things were spoiled for everybody with an alert about the resurgent porcine influenza. Therewithal, I expressed my disappointment and downright disgust to my friend after she'd inquired about my well-being:

~ Greetings, Becky! I know you people are going through some unseasonable chills due to what seems like an early Hurricane season, but as for us, well I've grown so accustomed to 90 degrees weather while vagabonding about these parts that, when it tumbles to 79 degrees Fahrenheit, I actually feel that it is quite chilly!

But, true to form, my rotten luck would bring me to this place only to waste my damned time. Furthermore, the damned Porcine Cooties everyone is so worried about destroyed even this excuse to celebrate the traditional holidays ~ there wasn't even a Big Mac waiting for me. Everyone, it seemed, neglected to recall, and I honestly did not know since I have been here for only a few months, that in these provincial regions everything shuts down for the religious festivals, in this case a pagan-Zapotec one, including McDonald's and the town Mercado. So, with the festival on the one hand, and the virus scare on the other, I was doubly screwed.

There were no taxi's or buses operating, so I could not even go to some restaurant that might be operating down-town. All this because I was stupid enough to divert my itinerary, am too paranoid about the Federales, was too curious about the damned *Gelaguetza* Festival, I just had to climb the confounded pyramids of Monte Alban, much to my disappointment, and because I didn't bother to ask ahead of time about what to expect in these parts. The people of Oaxaca appear to deserve their reputation for being mistrustful of outsiders, and they don't come more from the outside than I do. I tried going out of the main town, to some remote pueblo to see if they had restaurants or taverns operating, that I might better feast at some greasy pit rather than starve. But, in the end, there was nothing.

NOTHING!!!

So, with no apologies from anybody, only a casual dismissal, *Ay, pos ya te chingaste, joven!* (Oh, well, you you're screwed, young man!), I boiled in my own anger and nearly starved until I just broke down and feasted on a bag of potato chips and a bottle of Coca-Cola I'd bought at a small tendejon' (convenience store) that, miraculously and much to my relief, was still open.

Later, around 11pm, some tipsy celebrants and well-wishers, singing and stumbling for the sheer fun of it down the street from the hotel, invited me to share a shot of tequila with them; we engaged in some trifling conversation, and I was half-asleep by the time they'd gathered themselves up and left. I met the rest of the primordial apes they called the immediate family, and that was it.

Lord, this now ranks as the worst, loneliest, most infuriating experience thus far on this crazy trip! I don't know why, I can't put the proverbial finger on the riddle, but it must be a psychosomatic condition, stemming from a childhood trauma, that causes me to react with such exasperation when I feel I've been excluded from all the fun. It really is stuff like this that knocks the wind out of me, and I just want to chuck it all to Hell.

Oh well, Becky, take care, Blessings to your children.

Oh, and what about Gamaliel, is he out?

With the Summer coming on, I wish all of your hopes for the season come true, and that we reunite sooner rather than later.

Freddy ~

Things would not be quite so predictable for my friend as they seemed at first: on the one hand, she awaited desperately for word about her son (having learned this from Santiago in a separate email he'd sent concurrently with Becky's); on the other, things were transpiring between her greedy mother and her rapacious sister Margara about some small fortune Don Pedro had left to his youngest offspring, namely Santiago, Lorenzo and, most especially, Becky, which had recently been discovered. The legacy was the only thing that spoke to Becky about how much her father truly did love his youngest child, and she was not about to forsake his beloved memory to the living, for whom she had no regard. Now it would be in probate, and the former two would contest it for its entire value. The ramifications of this legal challenge she would have to face revealed just how tortured my friend's conscience was, and would be for the foreseeable future. Despite my good wishes, her hopes for the season would not be realized without some disillusions, and anxiety caused by events beyond her control. With her business poised for bankruptcy, and the

Finca not paying for its own costs, she was facing, all of a sudden, financial ruin, despite the fleeting promise of the hitherto unknown paternal legacy.

What can be said about her and her family? That the challenges they vanquished exercised a base and impotent revenge; and ignorance, mixed with base desire, has long repeated the tale of calumny, which had disfigured the births and characters, the persons, and even the individual names, of the Ange-Ingels. Becky scrambled to salvage what remained of her sanity, yet fear is still more rapid in its course. With forbearance exhausted, according to Santiago, she fired back at their mother: "Damn you all! The *decree of Fate*, as you put it, is now accomplished by your own fault; it is the web which you have woven, the thorns of the tree which yourself have planted. I don't give a rat's ass about it, but I will fight you for that legacy until I see you dead and buried, and I will cover your corpses with maggots myself to make sure you all rot in hell!"

Their pride, however, was fallen, and their tone was modest, thus the anger was not felt, nor was a reaction expected. Following the mischievous discovery of Don Pedro's bequest, if we contrast the rapid progress of her mother and her evil genius in securing legal title to it, with the slow and laborious advances of Becky and her siblings to make a place in the world for their own, my old friend, according to the temper she might be feeling at any given moment, will laugh or weep at the folly of her decadent family. Evidently she did find time to reply to me, for no sooner had she cursed her mother (knowledge thereof courtesy of Santiago), when she forwarded the following missive:

~ Dear F: I appreciate your situation, and thank you for sharing your experiences with me. That is just awful, I hope you weren't too disappointed. In any case, I am sorry for not warning you about customs around these parts, but it never occurred to me, what with all that is going on with my family.

I suppose one of my brothers already told you about what is going on regarding the discovery of a legacy my dear father left his three youngest, eh? I honestly don't know how to handle myself. At this point I could use the inheritance, but I may get nothing after all the trouble with my mother, who honestly does not need it, and that vicious sister of mine just wants to annoy us, and is clearly showing her jealousy. I asked my silly mother, "if you were to get the money, what is going to happen to all of it when you leave this earth?"

But, I know she has been ill-advised by Margara herself. I hate to sound egotistical, but my brothers and I, at least, might be able to enjoy some of it as a compensation for all that we went, and are going, through, and for the honor of our father's name. It is an incentive for us, furthermore, to stay together, to uphold the family name, even though the eldest have done a rotten job of preserving our dignity. I just don't know anymore, but I am also thinking of my own children, the grandchildren of Don Pedro ~ I think he would have been so proud of Gamaliel and Emanuel, and would have adored Campanita.

Take good care of your-self,

Becky ~

With the shock of the revelation, and all of this new trouble she was handling, I momentarily forgot about my own concerns, and replied:

~ Thanks my friend, and blessings to all of you guys. But, you know, I very, very much doubt you will get anything from anyone, forget about your mother. I think she was indeed a victim of evil counsel. I know how you feel, that she has back-stabbed you so many times. I don't blame you for wanting to cut her off. You want to get out of there, far from her presence and from Margara, and never see them again. I will pray for you, for what it is worth prima, that you don't allow hate to poison your heart, though you are fully justified in having it. I had those very feelings for my own brothers, of rage and resentment, and it hurts the bearer more than it does the reviled.

Well, did you have your June reunion with your other brothers and cousins? Who else was there?

Take care,

F ~

Little could I know that things had indeed happened, and, after suffering the trauma of seeing her son accused of narco-trafficking, illegal gun possession, et cetera, young Gamaliel had apparently beaten the rap ~ not a small matter in provincial Mexico where public enemy number one is narco-trafficking. Thus, she responded as though nothing remarkable had happened:

~ Dearest Primo, we observed the Summer festival with a bit of nostalgia gnawing at our innards. At last they let my baby out, and we had, at last, occasion to celebrate something besides Campanita's birthday. We went to the movies in the afternoon. Campanita and Gamaliel are very close (I think I told you this before). Gamaliel had some money saved and decided to take her to the movies because she wanted to watch the new Disney feature, so we did that and came back home around 9pm. Dinner was ready before we left, so we just came back and ate. Enrique actually deigned to come, so it was only the five of us. We waited until midnight watching TV, exchanged hugs, Enrique returned to his own home, and the rest of us went to bed. The next day we exchanged gifts, which was a total failure because Campanita's MP3 player did not work, Enrique's television broke down so she couldn't play the video game that she received from Emanuel. Overall, to me it was the best reunion having my son with me. He came out so clean, thin, handsome and good looking. He has a very different mentality and I pray he continues that way, positive and eager to succeed in life!

Tu Becky ~

For my friend, I was genuinely happy, but the prison release came as a total surprise. It must have happened suddenly, and it just hadn't occurred to her to run and write to me. I did reproach her a bit for the oversight in the following reply:

~ Becky, Well, that is fantastic about the reunion and about Gamaliel. But Becky, you crazy woman you, how could you forget to inform me when he came out! I am over here thinking that maybe he was still in because you didn't actually confirm it. Well, now that is all over, I am so happy for you. You must have been overcome with emotion at having this early Summer reunion. Your wish did come true, so you must be so hopeful and optimistic about the future. Looks like better days are ahead, and all possibilities are laid before you.

My very best regards to you, Gamaliel, Emanuel, and the rest for all that the future holds. It's a new beginning for us all.

Freddy ~

I suppose I did catch her off guard, and she was quick to reply and offer her apologies:

~ My dear Primo, I am so sorry! I thought I did tell you. I am truly sorry, I was really excited. It happened like this: they called me from the court house around 2 pm on the 23rd to tell me that he was being released, cleared of ALL charges; I had to drive all the way to Puerto Veracruz, whereto they had transferred him, to pick him up, and the traffic and hassle with the paperwork were demoralizing. We came home late because of all the return traffic (due to one of the festival parades, which congested the streets). The next day we went to see his Parole officer, then got dressed, then I treated him to the movies, since he loves the cinema above all else, and then dinner. I guess it all happened so fast, and I've been so overwhelmed with all the stuff that I totally thought I had told you. I am so sorry.

I wish you had been here to share the reunion with us.

take good care of yourself,

R ~

The news of his release truly heartened me. So much has been at stake, and so much has been in the news about drug traffickers. The violence, police actions, government intervention, et cetera, and then to have this nice boy accused of being in the thick of it, the stress of the situation was great even for a detached party like myself, let alone my pitiable friend. All I could offer was my felicitations and hopes that things truly improve with her family, which I fear I may not see for a very long, long time:

~ Dear Prima, That's alright, babe, I am truly happy for you guys. How wonderful for you that this nightmare is over. May this never, ever happen again, even if you are chastened to the realities the experience thrust before you. I know it must be of no comfort to consider that you are a better, stronger person for having come through it all, and Gamaliel as well, but you are, and things can only get better from now on.

Take good care of yourselves, may you all rest and sleep truly happy now. I hope and pray that we have a big family reunion (assuming that would please you) very soon.

Take care, and may blessings rain on you all,

Freddy ~

That was sweet enough, but somehow I sensed there would be no grandiose family reunion considering the recent altercations regarding Don Pedro's legacy. It was in the offing, so to speak, and company would part ways, and another chapter in the annals of a family's history would come to a close. For the moment she betrayed no doubts or resentments, and was gracious with her reply as always:

~ Dear F, I also wish for that family reunion to come soon! And I also wish that, as for the feeling I have, all things will be getting better for me, although it's just a feeling. I know good things will happen to you too, and very soon. They just have to.

R ~

At this point it was obvious she had a lot on her mind, and proceeded to send me another email without my having a chance to reply:

~ Freddy, What joy it has given me to be able to correspond like this with you for certain. And, I am truly sorry that, without intending it, you should have been involved in this thread of emails. They were indeed disagreeable for all concerned, but it feels like it was all part of some awful reckoning. My boys are grown up, the rest of the family is disintegrating, and now we face the reality that we are no longer idealistic youths, but mature, weighed down with responsibilities and the cares of domestic life.

But look, in the last analysis there is something extraordinarily good and truly positive about all of this, all that has transpired. We learned to stand for ourselves, and to defend our convictions and opinions by the force and presence of our own minds. If this means that the price I have to pay is to stand aside and no longer participate or contribute anything more to these frictions and commentaries, polemics, whatever---it's all so destructive---well then, I believe that it was all worth it.

I mean, even though it is sad that we have to go our own way, live our own lives apart, at least we know that each is following his or her own happiness, and each one has a right to their own thoughts, their own soul, and above all to protect and defend them as they see fit. I will stop being a coward and live now for my children.

The only thing I objected to all the time was that I was never in accord with this relationship my brothers and sisters maintained, of losing respect for each other, just as it was.

Nonetheless, from then on I had no problem. The poison of their suspicions and resentments is out of my system. My brothers and sisters, and all of my cousins are truly lovely and good-hearted persons, but, perhaps, some are accustomed to treat others, especially the helpless, the defenseless, in a disrespectful manner. Being as simple as I am, I cannot abide such behavior. I insist on being treated with the utmost respect, including by my own mother.

It was better for me to treat them from a distance, to be detached from these familial concerns because I accept that I too can be difficult at times. In such a case it is precisely, with respect to everyone else, that I believe we should all continue dealing with each other as Destiny has decreed ~ from a healthy distance.

You cannot imagine how I have come to admire and respect your tranquility and presence of mind, though, in the final analysis, you had such an awful time with your own family. It has given me such satisfaction, notwithstanding, to see how your soul has also escaped the torments of their humiliations, has protected itself and has survived so much filth, so much dolor.

I wish I knew you better now as a mature adult, but I admire you all the more, and feel genuine affection for you because between sympathetic souls there is no distance great enough to separate us. It is enough to have found each other, understand each other after all of these years since we attended school, and empathize in the truest and purest sense.

You are my cousin like all the others, precious to my soul. I offer, in the same way I have done with all people who have crossed the path of my life on this road we call Destiny, an open heart, a sincere heart; a heart that knows dolor, but is, for the same reasons, always struggling and persisting before all challenges.

Always with love, always with hope and faith, I will survive.

Love you always, my primo,

Becky ~

It felt odd, but upon reading her closing thoughts I felt a chill run up my spine. Somehow I knew that this would be the last correspondence I would receive from her, at least for the length of my stay in Mexico. I worried at first that, if I should have a run-in with the authorities, she would not be able to vouch for or against my Wetback status. Eventually I got used to the idea, and later inquired from Santiago of her whereabouts; apparently, with her son back in her arms, the legal headaches associated with the battle for the legacy, and the problems associated with the maintenance of the Finca, she had decided to abandon it all and moved, but she failed to inform anyone of her decision. She had formerly promised to take her family to Mexico City, to partake of hospitality from other relatives, and opportunities that would help her to get back on her feet, figuratively speaking. I honestly felt bad for her, and prayed for her well-being. But, like she often said, life goes on, and she went on, defying disaster, the unexpected in all of its forms, and hardship. She lived only for her children, and would sacrifice everything to ensure their future well-being. She was just that kind of person and offered no apologies, and I honestly admired her for it.

So, Becky, until we meet again. Too bad there was no reunion to be had. Too bad there was no one around that I could talk to, like a Fulgencio San Roman, about this email experience with my old friend. It had been eerie, sometimes disturbing, but it all had to have some meaning, even the fact that so much drama and feeling had been revealed by way of emails.

Now, time enough for introspection.

HUMOR TO BE FOUND IN THE PORCINE FLU

The hour had come to board the ADO-line bus, and this time around I was headed for Mexico City, at last. Oaxaca had been a great adventure, though her people certainly did not charm me. Oaxaca City is a lovely, old colonial town with civic pride and cultural sophistication ~ as much as could be had from a population of not so hygienically-minded Cro-magnons. The architecture was lovely, the overall touristic atmosphere was lively, but the food was mostly disappointing; I can't honestly explain how these people survive on culinary crap. It is true, though, that I did not really get to meet anyone of note since my concerns were occupied with Becky's saga. Yet, the hours flew by, and I occupied them fully.

I did have some fun during those final days, and while the most memorable night forays of this trip included a full-moon *pinta parranda* (fun-filled party) beside the sea in Oaxaca, that wanderlust of mine was biting at my guts, and felt I had to move on. One thing about entrusting your life to the people of another country is that you are practically obligated to place your safety and well-being into their hands. Forging and renewing a new social circle of friends is essential to your overall experience of travel and exploration, wherever you may go. One must always keep in mind that the intended destination might fail to live up to your imagination, so you must be flexible and adjust to circumstances as they are served to you. Yet, I leave the state with some sense of satisfaction ~ I had entered a region that reflected my romantic image of the "real" Mexico. Mexico City beckoned, however, and I just had to get out lest I allow sloth and the warm sands of Puerto Angel, a truly magical spot on the coast of Tehuantepec, to entice me to wallow away the Summer in lecherous self-indulgence.

The bus-fare wasn't costly, but the company on board was typical of what you could expect on one of these interstate vehicles; one fellow, typically, had a flatulence problem, and no one thought of offering him Rolaids, or some other anti-gas tablets.

The bus-ride took over 12 hours, but we rumbled into the great metropolis on a chilly, drizzling night. The Summer rains were just arriving, and it would be a humid time in the old town.

Mexico City beckoned, and guess what? The alert was raised, again, to watch out for the Porcine Flu. This time, however, changes were to be noted that Mexicans, at last, had remembered their sense of humor. Specifically, instead of panicking and wondering what new horror the virus would bring, there was a lot of talk about how humdrum the experience of enduring the scare was becoming.

To begin with, popular TV soap operas were taking out all "nonessential" kissing and fondling, leaving the actors to fake it somehow. Secondly, and quite laughably, a song called the "Influenza Cumbia" was climbing the ratings charts, and the damned tune was heard everywhere. It was fast becoming annoying. Vulgar, yet hilarious, swine flu jokes were spreading faster than the illness ever could ~ a sheer sign that Mexicans had found their stride and were making the best of the danger.

As Mexicans incarcerated themselves within their own abodes for fear of catching the virus, they couldn't help but have a little fun with it as well. Times were bad, so why not poke fun at misfortune.

It was becoming quite evident that the surgical masks that Mexicans had reluctantly put up with by the millions had become canvases for creativity, as some news-paper pundit put it, while others took to embellishing their masks with painted-on gorilla lips, enormous "Zapata" or *Walrus* mustaches, or even cute animal faces, and certain taxi-drivers had fashioned protective "bras" for their vehicles. It made for a silly spectacle, but at least the fear factor had abated. Dog owners walked Mexico City's streets with matching masks for their none-too compliant pets, though veterinarians had yet to confirm that chihuahua-to-chihuahua infections is a threat to the public safety. I wasn't planning any sallies with a chihuahua, anyway.

Mexico's ebullient society and colorful culture were still trying to make sense out of the poorly executed anti-flu campaign after months of scratching their heads. Hugging, handshakes, kissing, public fondling, standing in crowded places, or eating crap from street-food stalls are all a part of a routine life that no one in this city of 20 million would prohibit just because of a little flu anxiety. The signs of discouragement abounded, and the authorities were making the most of it. For my part, I did not plan to get intimate with anyone, just yet. I wanted to see some of the sights, contact some old friends, perhaps inquire into Becky's whereabouts, and most certainly begin the search for my family's origins, which, everyone I spoke to assured me, had to begin in Mexico City. I wanted to find out why I was named for the name I was given. Perhaps then, I could make sense of my life.

There might not be much to the daily round of getting up, going through morning rituals, dodging traffic in the busy streets, and interacting with the ruder locals, yet it was pleasing to see that the same people were laughing, and acting as though nothing was unusual. Most people I'd run into delighted in gallows humor, and made frequent mention of what some wags referred to as "*The Aporkalypse*." This new reference to an "imminent doom" had been going about the metropolis, and everyone was having fun with it.

"Did you hear that Mexico has become a world power?" goes one joke. "When it sneezes, the whole world gets the flu."

The laughs did not reveal the practical mess that the people are dealing with on a routine basis. The government of Mexico had decreed a country-wide shutdown that lasted for five days, causing a paralyzing problem for parents. Because schools had been closed, the hapless mothers and fathers had to bar their brats from going insane, while ensuring the government's directives were met, or else.

As any parent might confess, there was always a way out of a mess.

Two days into my visit, I tracked down an old acquaintance (by way of my cousin Alfredo) named Renato Gomez-Mateos. I'd known him since the early 1990s, but hadn't spoken to him in nearly 10 years. He *seemed* as jovial as I remembered him to be when we met up at the historic Sanborn's restaurant down-town. Regrettably, he occupied our reunion mostly with complaints about his young daughter, Yvonne. It seems the little brat refused to wear one of those surgical masks, and she was particularly sensitive to air-borne viruses that attack the pulmonary tract. Her mother, Micaela, managed by decorating the mask with embroidered butterflies, and making a fairy-tale game out of wearing the thing as they walked to and from her pre-school. Renato proceeded to bore me with fulsome adulations for his clever wife (I never did get to meet her, though).

"She made it for her because little Yvonne didn't want to wear it, so she made her a special one," Renato went on. "And I'm the good fairy Flora," Yvonne supposedly said in response, as she shyly peered through the mask for the first time. This revelation clearly demonstrated that Renato was no longer the foul-mouthed rake-hell I remembered, but a doting father sickening me with quaint tales of domestic cuteness. I tried to meet my old drinking buddy again some time before I'd left Mexico City, but for the moment the reunion was more reality than I could handle. We bade our adieus, finished our coffee (quite good as I recall), and parted ways, and none the sooner.

Speaking of fairies, once I had parted Renato's company, I found myself wandering about the streets, from the Sanborn's near the cathedral and zocalo, to the Zona Rosa and Garibaldi Street ~ the epicenter of Gay culture in Mexico City. There was nothing in evidence to suggest that Mexican Gays were worried about a minuscule annoyance like porcine flu. On the contrary, they proved delightfully risque' when considering the measures their community took to spread awareness and encourage responsible behavior. Not only were the local residents induced into taking preventive medicines, but the latter were placed, free of charge, in contrived dispensers shaped like gaping mouths, elongated penises, or a muscular buttocks. The squirting penile projectors were especially popular, and many who hadn't thought of seeking protection were suddenly very enthusiastic about indulging themselves in "preventive care." The term *vaccination* soon became an epithet for an esoteric form of sodomy, and "getting vaccinated" became the hip thing to do for awhile, figuratively speaking.

I asked around what the response had been to such wily measures, and, much to my innocent surprise, it had been "extraordinary" (according to a very flamboyant narcissist who had crept up behind me, and solicited a "vaccination").

Just wandering around allowed me to take in some of the more remarkable landmarks like the Bellas Artes palace, La Catedral, the Palacio de Gobierno, the post office, the ruins of the Great Aztec temple, and elsewhere. There was not much to do all alone in the big city in any case, and tracking down any relatives or old acquaintances proved to be a minor nightmare. With no place to go except to the hotel, located a couple of blocks behind the Torre Latina, watching television had become the only available distraction during most of my evenings. Even on the boob-tube, the wicked little malady had imprinted itself on that typically Mexican past-time: the *telenovela* (akin to the American Soap Opera).

Nothing typifies the formulaic telenovelas more than melodrama and risque- tongue-kissing. But Televisa, Latin-America's most prolific producer of the soap-operas, had decided smooching would be reduced to a minimum in accordance with government guidelines to avoid close contact. So, here I was expecting to be aroused by adult themed entertainment, only to get sanitized foreplay that simply made no sense without the perversity!

"When the script of a telenovela requires a kiss," reported a Televisa spokesman for the Press, "the kiss will be given in accordance with the guidelines so as not to expose the actors to any risk."

Strangely though, this fellow leaked these details on condition of anonymity because he hadn't been authorized to speak to the Press.

He played dumb, and wouldn't divulge exactly how the "safe kisses" would be feigned. Perhaps they'd be air kisses? Or, perhaps cheek kisses? In any case, it was left to the viewing public to grin, bear it, and to speculate.

My guess was that until the whole shebang was resolved, we all would have to get by on telepathic kisses. I am sure others were of the same opinion. In any case, for the sort of horizontal affection I was looking forward to in the streets of Mexico City, kissing and other forms of facial contact weren't to be issues of contention.

The local music culture had also embraced an irreverent view of the epidemic. One notable band, the "Agrupacion Carino," whose songs were polluting the radio waves wherever I'd go, came out with the song "Influenza Cumbia" shortly after the disease alert was given. The lyrics smacked of a persiflage worthy of the common folk, with references to Superman and Indiana Jones.

"It's better to commit suicide with tacos," the lead-singer croaks to a resounding synthesizer. "They say it's the perfect flu. They don't know Mexico City folks live in the smog."

The previous lyrics should be a good indication of just how well Mexicans were taking the epidemic. Just like the pig flu, dark humor had infected all sectors of society, and even beyond Mexico's borders. Actually, I saw in a TV commercial that an American company was promoting T-shirts featuring a pig-shaped Mexican flag: "I went to Mexico and all I got was swine flu," it reads.

And, of course, the Internet was bustling with dark, pig-flu fun. In a game called "Swine-Fighter," players fire at viral-looking porkers with hypodermic needles. I heard the silly game was becoming quite popular at the kiddie arcades, or at Internet cafe' where net-surfers could download the game for free. And, what global catastrophe would be complete without its own Facebook page? Yes, I discovered the ridiculous thing as I was preparing to write to one of my correspondents.

After doing a bit of sleuthing myself, I learned that the page's creator boasts on the page: "There's more people infected on Facebook than in real life."

Oh, hah, hah! It was so funny I forgot what it was all about.

Though it is so that Mexico City is one of Latin America's largest cities, it still has the mentality of a small town, and rumors will abound of the most personal and puerile sort, while truly important issues are brushed aside because the common folk don't like to be troubled with issues that are beyond them. Nevertheless, something truly extraordinary occurred on the Monday after I had arrived, which shall rank as outstanding in the annals of Roman Catholic Mexico: same-sex marriage and adoption by same-sex couples had been legalized in a tumult of legislative fervor and festering Catholic reaction. Having grown up in an atmosphere of homo-phobia and religious intolerance, not to mention aggressive Mexican machismo, I have to say that I was aghast, shocked, delighted ... I really did not know how to feel or react. I have to hand it to this society, however, because not even America has accomplished such a socially progressive feat on a national scale, in spite of all the talk about freedom and pursuit of happiness.

Specifically, by a vote of two to one, the legislative assembly approved revisions to the civil code to permit same-sex marriages.

In a separate motion, the assembly voted in favor of legalizing adoption by same-sex couples, with nine abstentions. One could not avoid or ignore the news since it was blasted all over the place.

In any case, all this led to impromptu parades in the streets and other celebrations, which I too participated in just for the sheer fun of it. I wasn't going to pass up a chance to get drunk with the rest of the city, for sure! Although, I did have to watch out for unwarranted "vaccinations."

According to the specifics of this history-making legislation, the revision will effectively redefine marriage to a union between two people instead of the current explanation, which specifies a union between a man and a woman. No one knows if Civil groups in favor and opposed to the vote will fight it out, and I certainly won't be around to see any heads roll. They had gathered, nevertheless, since early Monday morning outside the congressional halls. As I understood it, the debate had been raging for some time now, and the legislators had already approved same-sex civil unions back in 2007. Politics is politics, and there were bound to be delays, filibusters, appeals, legal suits and counter-suits, but with a uniquely Mexican flavor to them ... Spicy!

This polarizing controversy wasn't new to Mexicans because Mexico City was the second major Latin American city to legitimize Gay marriage; months before, a court in Buenos Aires, Argentina had ruled that two articles in the metropolitan civic code, which stipulate only heterosexual matrimonies are permissible, are in fact illegal, hence breaking down the last barrier to gay matrimonies. The mayor of Mexico City cited Argentina's example, and declared that he would not appeal the ruling in spite of the brewing back-lash from conservative groups and the Church. I could see protesters gathering, notwithstanding, in the streets to oppose the intrusive Church whose clergy should not have been meddling in secular affairs anyway, according to the Mexican Constitution.

... What could old Fulgencio San Roman have said about all this talk of same-sex marriage? I wonder ... beats the Hell out of me!

STOCKING UP ON HOPE

It was a dark and stormy night in Mexico City near the ancient and still impoverished sector of Atzcapotzalco, the so-called "place of the ant-hills"; the acidic rain fell by the bucketful on unprotected heads ~ except at infrequent intervals when it was tempered by a violent gale which swept up the muddy streets, pelting the poorly constructed rooftops of wretched working class hovels. Power outages were provoked, which intensified the nearly freezing darkness and inflamed the exasperation of the residents. A gale of laughter ensued, and the strange weather departed almost as quickly as it had arrived, leaving the soaking poverty-borne populace to bemoan the irrepressible. In spite of flash flood warnings, no one stocked up on provisions, let alone hope, which wouldn't have comforted them in any case.

In an old cemetery near the park of the ancient *Ahuehuete* trees, the few remaining landmarks planted by the Aztecs in the heart of Atzcapotzalco, a couple of wet and exhausted sculptor-carpenters had just put the finishing touches on a poem carved upon a hastily erected marble memorial before the stroke of midnight on the 19th of June, that was titled, THE FEAR OF TIME:

>I knew fear and I knew dread,
>It is a different world, a different time,
>Didn't let them trouble me in bed,
>To lust, to covet no longer is a crime,
>
>No longer am I a baby,
>The family boom is sadly over,
>Fear in life ~ inescapable it may be,
>Under the ideals of youth I take cover,
>
>The fear is always there to scare you,
>I may be timid, but ain't no coward,

A Wetback in Reverse

The pathetic masses depend on the chosen few,
Return to happy thoughts or play it forward,

Childhood, what became of my dreams?
The sorrows of yesteryears plague me like flies!
The dreamer from false hopes forever gleams,
The fool for delusions always cries,

There was a time when I tasted of passion,
There was a moment when I knew happiness,
Escape into unreality was once the fashion,
Into oblivion I jumped and met craziness,

I hoped and hoped against inevitability,
Voices echoed in the darkness of despair,
Only for dread was there probability,
Hence, to the void I offered my prayer:

"May your troubles be less,
May your blessings be more,
And may nothing but happiness
Come through your door!"

... Come through your door,
and nothing more?

And now my young ones for wishes pray,
The fear then goes after their hopes,
The generation of ideals is now old and gray,
Our dreams of peace were narrow in scope,

So, I knew fear and I knew dread,
It is a different world, a different time,
May our children by our ideals be led,
Towards inspiration may they always climb!
the end

This poem was probably written by, and dedicated to the memory of the recently departed uncle of Cecilia, a distant cousin of mine, who was actually the oldest brother of the former husband of her aunt, who is the twin sister of her mother ... I think.

His name was Rafael Ramirez Rojas, and I never knew the man, but he had supposedly worked with Fulgencio San Roman as a co-writer, actor, and editor, thus his cinematic input had been significant. Much to my chagrin though, he had passed away just as I was delving more into the historical background of the subject of my fascination. He could have revealed many a nifty secret and nugatory rumor with respect to his long relationship with Fulgencio, and the fact that I came so close to meeting him without realizing his importance just made me want to call it quits and head for home. Fortunately, there were the living, and perhaps they could divulge a thing a two about their beloved relative before I hopped on the bus for another town.

The strange thing that arose from Rafael's death was controversy, for no sooner had his memorial been erected when his body was burned to a crisp, against the wishes of surviving loved ones. But, he wished it, and thus was he honored. The latter brought to mind my own controversy regarding cremation. It had involved my late brother, for whom I suffered no love loss. I only repented of not having been present to light the match that ignited the bonfire of my brother's mortal remains. Ashes to ashes, dust to dust, but all the euphemistic reflections aside, I was most pleased to learn that even his bones were no more.

If I had known about all the hassles involved with burying one's loved ones, I would have repented of my repentance with respect to cremating my *dearly departed* long before they had repented for not repenting for their sins. But, since they did pass away before repenting, then it was apropos that we, the *dearly beloved*, bury them in a way that really would have made them repent for how they demeaned and denigrated our lives as a matter of fact, as well as a lack of repentance!

Now, the thing I mostly repent of is my ignorance about how the cremation process works: indeed, it is a question most people would prefer to avoid, especially here in Mexico. But, death is a fact of life, especially for Mexicans, many of whom still hunt and trap their daily meals, and the survivors have to grin and bear with the nitty-gritty of burying their dearly departed. I had occasion to face the decision twice, and on both occasions cremation seemed to be the best, most viable option to the traditional, and hyper-expensive burial. First, there was my father who had once fancied a burial at sea, or perhaps a cremation, even though his most Catholic conscience prohibited him from countenancing such an option for fear of losing his soul. My mother decided to exercise an option presented by her church group, and had the old fart buried at the bargain-basement price of $5,000 USD, complete with professional "mourners" to wail at his funeral ~ it was a nice way of showing repentance by proxy, even though there was no real repenting to be had on your part.

Next on my agenda of repentance was my brother who had finally drunk one too many bottles of cheap whiskey, thus his heart gave out, and leaving us to fuss over his festering cadaver. I was the first one to be told of his decease by the officiating police, so it was incumbent upon me to prepare my mother for the sad tidings, and gather my siblings for a decision about what to do with his remains. In the end, no one did squat about it, and we left him to the tender mercies of the police, who had actually discovered his corpse dumped in some West Los Angeles alley. Afterwards, they informed our mother that they would keep him stored in some communal drawer, nicely tucked in between the other cold meat, until all the paper-work attesting to his demise was completed. Then, they would exercise the civic policy of disposal of the refuse by setting it ablaze ~ that is, the cremation option.

Now then, the process worked thusly; first they, the authorities, had the responsible parties affirm his identification (in this case, it was his only daughter Dorothea, who was inconsolably disappointed in her grandmother because she refused to handle the matter herself, and was forced to confront the issue alone, obliging her to travel several hundred miles to the morgue and identify the body, sign papers of release, and accede to the cremation option); then they performed the autopsy ~ six months after he'd kicked the bucket, literally. The taxidermists, or embalmers, or whatever those people are who prepare the body for disposal, were called, and they took their sweet time to make him look pretty enough for the roasting. The court order arrived with the permission for the procedure granted. Then, the transportation of the corpse to the designated crematorium, where the only ones who gave a crap were waiting, namely Dorothea, her husband, and her three children, followed en suite. Finally, the fuse was lit, and the human barbecue was on, full blast. Within an hour, the creature who never should have been was reduced to ashes. Dorothea was asked to sign a few more papers attesting to the fact that she had witnessed the ghastly sight of her father being cooked, that she still agreed with the procedure with or without condiments, especially since there was no going back, and that the responsible experts had done their job diligently and competently. The rest was then up to God whether to send his soul to cool off in Limbo, or send him down to get another roasting, courtesy of Lucifer, because the cremation had left him only medium-well-done, which is what everybody who knew my brother wanted for him! Hence, to all who are wary of repentance for having repented, one should countenance a cremation as a viable option to the traditional burial. One would say that it is, in this environmentally conscious world we now live in, a sound and ecologically friendly way of disposing so much trash, which could then be mixed with the mounting tide of human and animal feces, which could provide a great fertilizer, and then sent to developing countries facing desertification. We can all sleep soundly in the knowledge that we are no longer contributing to the awful pollution problem that faces 21st Century societies, Mexico in particular, right? In that way one's conscience can rest easy, and one need not repent, or face repentance, from anybody ever again. Mexico is no place in which to have latent pangs of remorse. One need better do something before we all end up repenting for our lack of brains, or end up with a troubled brow heavy with repentance!

I know I've done my part for saving the earth, how about the rest of this over-populated country? Not bloody likely!

Henceforth, what could have impelled Cecilia's uncle to desire cremation instead of a traditional Mexican burial? Well, more and more people want to exercise their freedom of choice without suffocating from the Church's moral constraints, so Uncle Rafael's decision was no big thing. On the other hand, his choice had something to do with the cinematic, and romantic, notions he'd inherited from his old boss. In fact (and according to Cecilia, who'd proved difficult to track down in a city of Mexico City's size), Uncle Rafael's favorite collaboration with

Fulgencio had also been his very first in the movie they'd made as young college-age bachelors back in 1938 titled *Cuauhtemoc* ~ a free adaptation of Lew Wallace's *The Fair God*, which attempted to retell the story of Cortes' conquest of the Aztec nation from the Aztec perspective. It was, reputedly, Fulgencio's reply to Cecil B. De Mille's 1917 film, *The Woman God Forgot*, which also dealt with the Conquest of Mexico, and heavily influenced him to make movie-making his career choice. I have as yet been unable to track-down a presentation of the film in any of the important cinema art-houses so I can't say much about it, but this film, according to existing reviews written at the time of its premiere, and originally running at nearly four hours, was also Fulgencio's first major film, and the generally positive notices it received set the stage for his subsequent works.

My cousin subsequently informed me that Rafael had willed his letters, which could prove to be very valuable to film buffs and movie historians, to her supposedly because she worked for the big television broadcasting network TELEMUNDO and would thus appreciate such a bequest. He had also willed them to her aunt, for whom he nurtured the warmest feelings even after she'd divorced his younger brother. Biting my nails with anticipation, I begged her to send me copies of them, and she did, eventually and unperturbedly, after much needling and pestering on my part. Thanks to modern conveniences, I received some remarkable epistles by way of faxes, and they were truly loaded with cinematic history. One of the first things I discovered in letters dated in 1939, when he was barely 19 years old, was that he nurtured pangs of repentance for his family's part in the *Cristiada*, complaining of his father's support of the rebels, and of his having killed at least two federal officers "just for the sheer hatred of their uniforms."

At this point, with my illegal status compromising my very being in this besieged country, I can assuredly comprehend his attitude.

He also admits that the scenes he'd filmed for his boss, of Aztec human sacrifices and ritual immolations, influenced his incidental desire to be cremated, and to have his ashes scattered atop Mount Popocatepetl, the *thinking warrior*, or on Mount Ixtaccihuatl, the *sleeping maiden* ~ the two sacred volcanoes of the Toltecs and Aztecs in the Valley of Mexico. Though his first wish was carried out, I very much doubt the second would be executed. Too bad.

Apparently, there was a great deal of controversy surrounding the production and release of the movie, which caused its young makers more than their fair share of anxiety. In a letter dated January 7, 1939, Uncle Rafael agrees that the first viewing of *Cuauhtemoc* in Mexico city was well received despite its atypical running-time (not including intermissions). One legend that seemed to make him chuckle every time it was recounted stated that, fearful of the audience departing, Fulgencio stopped the clock in the auditorium. In his later memoirs, which Rafael was privy to, Fulgencio recalled:

"No subsequent experience has given me sensations remotely similar to those I had on the night of the premiere of *Cuauhtemoc*. The well-founded distress as to their exeunt satisfaction has so adumbrated my feelings at all subsequent movie premieres that I could no longer enjoy them or take much notice of the way the audience was reacting. The initial popularity of *Cuauhtemoc* was to be expected beforehand. But the uproarious way in which the Chilangos declared their partiality for me was truly unexpected.

The movie-going crowds had been predisposed to accept it out of ignorance because everyone connected with the cinema had been forwarding favorable notices, and the entire population was looking forward to what was touted as a masterpiece. Little could they know otherwise what would come. In trying to recall my overall mood during those early days, I can remember it only as possessing all the features of a dumb-founding nightmare."

Subsequently, Rafael found his own stride by sticking to his mentor. They experimented both with giving the movie a showing over two evenings (at the suggestion of their financier), and making minor cuts while re-filming desultory segments leading up to the conclusion, to enable a less down-beat, more acceptable showing in a single evening. According to Rafael, his boss was not happy.

In the original reels, Cuauhtemoc's final words are bitter and angry:

"May Tenochtitlan and her weakling dwellers be accursed and destroyed! Disintegrate and wither, Mexica! Your degenerate ways have willed it so."

For the 1947 re-release, which coincided with the Ariel Film Festival in Acapulco, however, Fulgencio substituted rhetoric that was more upbeat: "Ever while the Eagle and Jaguar Knights stand sentinel against our enemies, ever while Huitzilopochtli commands us to shed blood that our sons may inherit the light of tomorrow, you will see Cuauhtemoc's return!"

Fulgencio later perceived *Cuauhtemoc* as an embarrassment. In his 1977 autobiographical essay, "A Communique to My Com-padres," which Rafael claims he dedicated to him, he wrote:

"I saw it only in the shape of 'six reels', with six brilliant 'anti-climaxes', with hymns, parades and the musical clash of arms." In another fascinating epistle, Rafael recorded Fulgencio's comment dated June 20 1971:

'*Cuauhtemoc* is very repugnant to me, but the damned critics should at least recognize the fire my audience has taken from it; I was a movie director and I filmed a historical epic that eventually pleased my inspiration, De Mille. The fact that it was this same movie director who gave them some hard nuts to crack - that's what should astonish them. As far as I am concerned, these critics should be buried in a dung-heap of their own words and jealous criticisms."

Thus the movie has remained outside of today's San Roman canon, and has never been performed at film festivals outside of Mexico. Although the movie-maker disclaimed it, it can be noted that *Cuauhtemoc* prefigures themes (romantic relationships, social order or break-down, foreign intervention and revolution) to which Fulgencio San Roman was often to return in his later movies.

The success of *Cuauhtemoc*---his first real success of any kind---was crucial in both Fulgencio's and Rafael's careers, launching the former as a film-maker to be reckoned with, and the latter as his trusted collaborator. It was followed, within months, by a contract with Azteca Film Studios of Mexico City (February 1940), which also gave him considerable prestige. It also received critical acclaim elsewhere in Europe, in the Soviet Union, whereto Fulgencio and company were invited, and regaled in by the eminent Russian film-makers of the time (such as Eisenstein), and in Hollywood.

The story that President Lazaro Cardenas was so influenced by seeing *Cuauhtemoc* after he'd left office that it changed his political outlook (and that he later told party loyalists "in that hour it all began") has been exposed as 'apocryphal'. What is more probable, according to another anecdote, is that he requested viewings of both the original cut and the later, edited version, and that he had studied the film on several occasions before his death in 1970. Regarding the stories of Cardenas' interest in *Cuauhtemoc*, Rafael commented in a letter dated October. 31, 1968, following the Tlatelolco massacres committed by federal soldiers earlier that month against marching students:

In every step of Cuauhtemoc's career - from his acclamation as successor to Moctezuma and Cuitlahuac, and leader of his people against the Spaniards, through military struggle, violent suppression of mutinous factions, betrayal and final immolation - all Mexican leaders have doubtless found sustenance for their fantasies.

All the political references aside, several mentions of Fulgencio's relationship with certain Jalisco mentors left me somewhat puzzled. In certain letters dated as far back as 1940, Rafael complains that his boss was often ill-disposed to continue work on their present project because of his contentious dealings with certain financial backers who'd happened also to be distant relatives on his mother's side. The latter, according to Rafael, was named Carmela Martin de Najar and, "a mean old she-wolf that eats the balls of her latest amorous interest before HE has a chance to 'cry wolf' or cross his legs."

Her other male relations weren't safe from her oppressive grasp either. Fulgencio was obliged to defer to her on all issues for the family's sake, and his own artistic ambitions. This left me with a big "why." What did this reference to a mysterious source have to do with Rafael's association with Fulgencio? According to the former in letters written to his cousin Rigoberto between 1944 and 1948, Fulgencio was obliged to travel to Tepatitlan, Jalisco quite often because of "business interests and family problems." Later I read that not only was Tepatitlan the place of his birth and the home of his mother's family, but also where most of my father's ancestors had resided. Could this be just fortuity? Or, had I tapped into a well-spring of epiphany? How was it that I encountered Fulgencio for the first and only time in Reynosa, of all places? Why did Fulgencio end up in Tamaulipas, anyway? And, what about this coincidence with Rafael Rojas's decease coming at such a crucial juncture in my travels? Cecilia proved unable to answer any of my questions; she knew him well, but never thought to ask him anything about his fascinating association with the old master ...

Wait a minute ... "San Roman"? What about "Martin"? My ancestors from Tepatitlan were surnamed "Martin." Could there be some incredible link here?

THE VAGARIES
OF WAYWARD VAGABONDS

Ah, Mexico City with all of its foibles will be the death of me yet! Nothing that I could do wasn't in some way hampered and harassed by this pig cooties outbreak, and it was likely to stick around so long as the locals clung to their less than sanitary ways. The big-wigs kept trying to convince the people that the epidemic was in its "declining phase," and that it was being effectively checked in other countries. No one believed the officials by now, however, and it really proved to be a ruse, a way of placating the people should they start complaining again about real issues like joblessness, exorbitant food prices, horrific utilities costs, and the damned IVA, or Federal taxes. And, people were really upset that the cost of riding the metro-subway had jumped 50% over-night, in Mexico City specifically. Surely, they would start a new revolution!

Memorable in a funny way during my second week in Mexico City was all this news going around that the Chinese had quarantined four-score Mexican tourists, citing charges that they were "importing the Bird Flu back within their frontiers." This was almost too risible to ignore. Then, many more Mexicans, along with other travelers, had been isolated in a Hong Kong hotel, supposedly as a precaution against the spread of cooties. All of these developments gave the Mexican government a head-ache as they enraged a disquieted Mexican public with respect to their compatriots. Therewithal, the two countries were trying to pass off credit for the epidemic to each other, the one insisting that it came from Mexican pigs, and the other that it was all due to eating so much Pork Chow Mein.

Provincial authorities, especially in Mexico State, Morelos, Colima Hidalgo, weren't going to have any of the debate, and simply rounded up and killed all the suspicious pigs as a way of shutting up the screaming-meemies railing about the undesirability of having pigs around in the first place. Expectedly, pig ranchers clashed with the agents sent to dispose of the offending porkers, and nothing salutary came out these regrettable confrontations.

This fight for the honor of pigs had degenerated into an insensible contest between the "civvies and the cops," each one vying for the favor of public opinion. Upon examination, it became evident that each side was more afraid of backing down, lest they lose all support from divergent sectors of their society, than interested in prevailing. The contending parties were nonetheless animated by a common spirit. They agreed on the necessity of some rapprochement; but the time, the place, and the manner could never be ascertained by mutual consent, except that it would take place somewhere in Mexico City. The fracas distracted the people from all the Flu anxiety, at least, and was regarded by the authorities as a welcome relief. Nevertheless, If the one advanced, so said a spokesman for the mayor Mexico City on the TV news, the other retreated; the one appeared like a beast fearful of the land, the other a creature phobic of the water. And thus, for a short remnant of a pig's life and procreative instincts, did these contrarians endanger the peace with their contretemps. There was still the Flu to contend with, after all.

During this time I tried to locate Becky, but I was Hell out of luck. No one I asked could answer the simplest of questions, and her relatives, most of them residing in the respectable Claveria district, were dumbfounded as to her whereabouts. It was really upsetting me by now, and not finding Becky was the biggest disappointment of them all. Meanwhile, people kept dying, one at time, and the cowardly authorities played to the muck-raking journalists who made it seem like nineteen deaths added up to a terrible holocaust. Never mind that twenty times as many were dying from all causes, but the figure of 506 of both infected and dead was just too much to support, and those responsible for containing the epidemic seemed like they were about to "throw in the towel," figuratively speaking. Even so, one could not avoid overhearing by whatever means that the officials kept harping on the line that "evolution of the epidemic is now in its declining phase."

Give me a freaking break!

Regardless of so-called drastic measures taken to protect the people, like the shuttering of business, closing the schools, prohibiting public gatherings and the such, which they insisted have curbed the virus's spread, everyone in the street believed that the epidemic had peaked a couple of months before, so why all the willy-nilly hypochondria?

Elsewhere in the country, especially in the northern states, the number of confirmed cases just kept rising, so that fact at least gave me an idea about where to go for my next stop. The swine flu was killing mostly the poor and disgusting Mexicans, so I had little to worry about, nor most Mexicans who really didn't give a pig's ass anymore about the whole thing. Still, the authorities weren't convinced, so everybody's actions, including most damnably mine, were once again restricted until the alert was revoked. The national caseload since the beginning of the outbreak was topping 800 and growing the vast majority in central and northern Mexico. In the Deep South, which I would not be visiting unless the hot weather had abated somewhat, reported their first confirmed cases a day after I had arrived in the Distrito Federal, and that was enough to send them all screaming to the nearest pharmacy.

The following day I thought to go to the Health Ministry to pick up some brochures and to find out where I could get a free vaccination, and it all went well until they started asking around for my "official" identification; I felt like I was going to defecate in my panties before being forced onto the first airplane headed for California, but the simple lie that I did not have it was enough to placate the disinterested clerks, thank goodness. They were mostly worried about an influx of local Indians, which could have led to a riot as far as they were concerned. Most victims who had somehow escaped death were mostly Criollos, which pleased the discriminating bureaucrats. They had all mostly recovered by now, and all but two were known to be residents of Mexico City.

The surrounding states of Zacatecas, Hidalgo, Morelos and Colima again reported new cases, but no one paid any attention. Whatever direction the virus took, it remained an unpredictable fuddle that managed to piss off a lot of people, yours truly included.

All that was left to do was wait ~ wait till more cases or deaths would be announced, and at least a dozen more people had contracted the virus in the previous 24 hours. The alarm proved to be much ado about nothing, but alarmists will be alarmists, and the warning came after the outbreak's toll in Mexico seemed to be tapering off.

At the international airport in Toluca just outside the main city, where a lot of Volkswagen Beetle-taxi-drivers where yelling for attention in between coughing and sneezing, and probably spreading more of the virus, everybody around was being asked to identify themselves on descending flights and were then isolated from every other traveler after landing, so advised the anchor-man in the national news broadcast. Expectedly, no one had presented symptoms, everyone had been isolated needlessly, many among them insisted they were hearing about the pandemic for the first time and had no idea Influenza could have so many strains!

In Guadalajara, Mexico's second biggest city and one of my next stops, the civic authorities were being harassed for having delayed quarantine measures. They were worried about other illnesses, but they eventually sealed down their hotels where a few sickened tourists had been lingering about and causing much grief. No less than a dozen police officers wearing masks showed up at my hotel, and had guarded it since the Sunday before, despite the fact that everyone within ear-shot was obviously healthy. Other guests just turned up their noses to the inexpressive officers, and casually sauntered on passed them to go about their social pursuits, or to alleviate the noxious boredom affecting everybody around. I'd asked another guest, a mature man who was on a business trip and had just arrived from the Orient, what he thought: "It's highly inconvenient ... Highly inconvenient." He said. "That's what's driving people crazy, because it knocked us over with the shock of it all. And now a frustration is setting in that's driving me crazy!"

After following this situation for months, I still could not make heads or tails of it, and the scientists in charge of informing the public were none the more clear on the matter. All that they kept pounding our ears with was that the virus had the potential to mutate into something really deadly. *Whoop Dee FREAKING Dee!* "Influenza is unpredictable," they kept telling the interviewers who looked them over like they were telling fibs, or perpetuating the government's "red herring" since more bad economic news was in the offing. "There are so many questions to be asked, but few answers to look forward to.

This is a virus we'd never examined before. There's a great deal we cannot understand about the human factor in relation to the virus."

For the present, the greatest obstacle proved to be a breakdown of information within Mexico, and people would rather trust the garbage removal workers than the expert doctors. Health sleuths tried to piece together the epidemiological puzzle which explained where the transmission began, and what sort of people were dying the fastest. Sadly, as long as they were aboriginal folk the White and Mestizo majority did not really care. It was soon revealed that indeed three of the dead were Amerindian children: a 9-year-old boy, a 12-year-old boy and a 14-year-old girl. Five of the dead were older than 60. The other ten were between 21 and 39, in spite of their stronger immune symptoms, but it was more of the same. Details were emerging slowly, but they also attempted to uncover *the way* it was attacking its victims with the severe sickness. In any case, it was still too much ado about nothing.

It was obvious to me, as to any rational person, that this was a still newer strain of the flu, and because we humans haven't developed an immunity to it, the virus has more potential to wreak havoc with our health. Unlike the other towns I had passed though, this thing was coming from different suburbs in a metropolis of 20 million, and there were no similarities linking the medical backgrounds of the infected. If it did spread further, there would truly be an infection of epic proportions. Frankly, in my mind the realization of this possibility just made me laugh like the proverbial fool who doesn't know just how close he stands to the edge of his own damnation. One of the explanations for the deaths was that perhaps the destitute Indians had sought treatment too late ~ falling ill about seven days before seeking medical help. Another reason being passed around was that the authorities were playing around with the imminent pandemic alert, but then would withdraw the alert at the last moment, giving the poorest citizens a false sense of comfort, and causing them to delay action before it was too late.

From the state of Durango came news that agriculture big-wigs had decreed that more than two hundred porkers should be quarantined after being infected by a field laborer who had recently returned from Mexico. Freaking fantastic! That is all I needed to make my laughter fatal to my own sense of balance ~ a human was responsible for having infected the pigs!

They would go on assuring the natives that porcine viruses were common among swine, and no one should give up their barbecues, ham tortas or taco-fests as long as people maintained sanitary conditions (fat chance), and so long as the situation was handled with care by them. The pigs were all recuperating nicely. Still, people will be people, and out of sheer anxiety some farmers and townsfolk formed posses, along with some anarchists in disguise, to help the police. They proceeded then to fire shots in the air and tear gas at pig owners who stoned them in an attempt to prevent government workers from slaughtering their animals as a way of containing the potential spread thereof once the first documented case of the H1N1 human flu was passed to another species. A Durango security official, who spoke on condition of anonymity because he was not authorized to talk to the news-hounds and their television jackals, said twenty bystanders, mostly Tarahumara Indians, had been injured outside of the Pancho Villa slum. In Durango, the capital of the state of Durango, officials killed wild boars at their zoo because of swine flu fears, even though the veterinarians argued that the virus could not be transmitted by pigs. So, what the Hell is one to do?

All of this was just so distracting that I nearly forgot about my present purpose: finding out what Fulgencio San Roman, or Uncle Rafael for that matter, had to do with my quest to find the origin of my existence. Nevertheless, I was determined, and I would not end the quest come Hell or more pig flu outbreaks.

WAITING AROUND FOR SOMETHING NICE TO HAPPEN

As long as I was in the old capital, and Mexican officials had lowered their flu alert level, I thought to go about exploring like I had intended in the first place. On the Monday following the big alert, I lived it up at the cafes', museums and libraries which had reopened, but which now offered disinfecting gel and facial masks gratis to their patrons. Elsewhere in Mexico it wasn't so simple, and some towns actually raised their epidemic alert to the highest level. As I sipped my delicious Chinese style coffee in one of the more pleasant cafes' on the Alameda, all that I could think was, "*Tsk, tsk*, those poor unfortunate fools ... and, I wonder, what the Hell is Fulgencio doing right now? Does he even know that his old behind-the-cameras comrade had passed away? *Tsk* and more *tsk*!

It wasn't all together so pleasant since the Mexican officials had declared the epidemic to be waning because the five-day long closure of non-essential businesses, that was decreed to halt the spread of the virus, was called off. Hereon, a lot more noise and traffic was in evidence. Students were kept off the streets until Government officials finished inspecting schools before decreeing that it was safe enough for them to return to class. It was no skin off of my back since the youngsters of the flirting age in Mexico City left me cold. It is a fact that the pandemic did not necessarily mean the illness was deadly. The past two pandemics in 1957 and 1968 had been relatively mild. A pandemic may refer to a disease's geographic extent rather than its severity, but that couldn't concern Mexico all that much. Other countries weren't exactly chivalrous about the whole thing, and were all too happy to blame Mexicans for the disease's spread. And, with the un-measured scope of the pandemic, several nations, namely China, had taken urgent measures against incoming Mexicans or those who had traveled to Mexico as of late.

President Calderon' went on the news to complain: "I think it's unfair that because we have been honest and transparent with the world, some countries and places are taking repressive and discriminatory measures because of ignorance and disinformation." ... which goes to show how ticked off he was over the whole thing, and went on to say: "There are always people who are seizing on this pretext to assault Mexicans, even if just verbally."

He didn't mention any countries or name any names, but everyone of us knew to what country and persons he was referring!

The Health Ministry also decried Argentina, Peru and Cuba for discouraging flights to Mexico, and said Argentina, of all the audacity, was sending a plane to Mexico on Monday just to pick up any of their lingering citizens who wanted to leave Mexico.

Well, if that ain't a kick in the proverbial balls!

One of the worst slights to be felt was the revelation that most of the victims had been females: 2 to 1 male. Malcontents were already complaining that women get poorer medical assistance throughout Mexico because of the macho manipulated culture ~ all of which is bullshit. It so happened most of the gynecological victims had jobs or were house-fraus who may have picked up the cooties from their own children, who themselves contracted the illness from each other. Most were ignorant, and with no means to fight the illness in their own homes, never mind seek care in a hospital. Curiously though, it was noted that there were no deaths among health care workers treating pig flu patients ~ a clue that the virus was not as *virulent* as the fraidy-cats had feared.

All this brings me to discharge all of the simmering emotions I had been repressing since I got trapped within the borders of this glorious prison called *Mexico*.

I've traveled through many places around this country, and have stopped at a number of them. ~ East, West, North, and heading South. Almost every stop, and many along the grand highway of disillusion, have their *Points of View*.

Hitherto embarking on this journey, I had always carried my own, but it would serve me well to handle the stress from now on. Starting with this Federal District sojourn, whenever a few things make sense and trigger my mind, from time to time, I'm going to sort out the events of each day and make sure I understand what is going on before I go insane. Whether anyone agrees with me, it is of no consequence. Absorbing the local color is not enough to inspire me.

Accordingly, in the mess that Mexicans have made of this epidemic, with the help of most willing countries, other Mexicans and well-wishers had sent fully staffed, fully operational medical units, and were up and operating on infected people within hours of setting up. Other countries from the other side of the world got here first and were very forth-coming, but America was short and slow in coming to her neighbor's aid.

America is just a few hundred miles away, and they couldn't get things straightened out if their own health depended on it, and it did. There is no one in charge, so supplies and vaccinations or other medical equipment remained sitting in warehouses everywhere. It wasn't Mexico's fault for sure. It was just *Reality*, that's all. The pandemic was transformed by responsible politicians into a comedy of errors at which everybody forgot to laugh. The latter were too busy figuring out the cost of containing the illness, and cringed at the thought that it would take away money from their political sacred cows. Too many nitwits were calling the shots, and no one really took charge, not even such a lauded statesman like President Calderon', and too many of said nitwits refused to give up their rights, or vaccinations, for the public good. Had not the nastiness of nature shown us all that our illusions needed to be discarded, and we needed to take care of the more important matters in life rather than our illusion of power?

There were groups that seemed to know what they were doing all along. They had no problem controlling the unruly masses and taking charge. Too many others were there jockeying for the best news-bytes, going by some script, worrying about looking bad in front of their bosses while more cases were being reported. It did not bother them that the disease was escalating by the minutes, hunger for some drastic action escalated the potential for anarchy, and the potential for complete social disorder and violence was imminent. The entire country could have erupted into anarchy, and still no one cared. This very intransigence is what saved this society from turning on itself. So, much as I hate to admit it, maybe this national contempt I've been writing about turned out to be a blessing for Mexico after all.

A Wetback in Reverse

Nonetheless, pomposity and sloth ruled the day, and the rest of us were left to decide whether this day or the next would be a good one in which to die.

This is what's happening in Mexico.

And, that is also what was happening and will happen...

President Calderon' vowed to give his people all the necessary resources, which include money, with which to fight the disease. The first of what will certainly be many handouts to cronies and other business contacts will determine the failure of this containment campaign ~ it is like giving a dying drunkard a ton of money and gently informing him that it's for his rehabilitation, accompanied by a slight slap on the wrist that he'd better wise up, but, of course, he goes out to buy a warehouse full of Tequila.

What a waste! What a waste!

Oh, I'm not whining because I am cold and heartless. I gave my fair share to The American Red Cross disaster relief fund; they are the only organization I would trust with giving money to do the right thing for the sake of the public good. My core convictions have little to do with politics or social philosophies, or with cynicism or contempt. It is simply reality with which I am concerned.

But in all this chaos of grief and death, troublemakers have managed to make things worse by going about their business like they always have ~ stealing, rioting, and raking Hell for the benefit of journalistic hell-raisers. Even where the epidemic had touched most people, such troublemakers intended on selling stolen food on the black market to their own people, thus profiting from the death and pestilence.

As evidenced, if watching, reading, or even slightly aware of Mexico's inability to stem the tide of illegal emigration and curb the activities of narco-traffickers over the past decade or more, the millions of dollars in aid given to Mexico has accomplished little but to make a few unscrupulous Mexicans so much the wealthier.

I pray that a few people observe this illuminating example that is unfolding, and they begin to adjust their priorities. Most Mexicans will go on begging for money, though, and billions upon billions of pesos will go on being mis-spent, unaccounted for, or flat-out stolen. That's just how things are in Mexico.

All of that money has been wasted by the corruption, greed, and vileness within people, so people are to blame for the sort of leadership they trust to handle their affairs. Mexican government people are in a position to slice their "piece of the patrimonial pie" without, and sometimes by, ever getting caught in the massive confusion and disarray. And the miserable folks in desperate need? They will keep on shaking their heads, insisting they don't give a damn, going without, and electing the same old crooks because there are none better to take their place. For tens of millions, even in a land as rich as Mexico, there is no clean water, no respectable schools, no decent system to assist in their needs, no real government that gives a damn ~ but many will assuredly be better off before the last charitable donation is counted. And the hundreds of millions in aid will line the pockets of many ungrateful bureaucrats and cynical legislators. But, then again, what would the rhythm of life be here in Mexico without all of that corruption? It's like asking what would Mexican food be like without chilies?

It is a sorry truth that so many drug-traffickers, corrupt officials, and other crime-mongers have profited in Mexico without ever having helped the people, or provided basic services. Everyone was expected to ignore the reality and allow the massive corruption to continue unabated, and the few continue to profit exorbitantly from the grief, despair, loss and pain, and death of their fellow Mexicans.

The Red Cross and Health Ministry bureaucrats had medical assistants in various health-care centers, most with limited supplies, and some had the effrontery to charge the hapless and ignorant for essentially "free" services.. The Health Ministry brought a truck around in Mexico city and ordered all the medics and nurses to leave because of a rumor of a coming labor riot; there has been a lot of labor unrest since I got here, and coming mostly from grade-school teachers. Mexico, needless to say, is rife with rumors. On a Thursday night, a rumor began that an early hurricane season was coming and there was mass panic brewing within the quiet of Mexican homes. I tried to imagine myself in such a state at this time. But, to the point, a field care center for the Pig Flu, with over 25 critically infected street-bums, was abandoned by the Health Ministry workers.

A Wetback in Reverse

They just packed up, picked up, and pecked at most of the supplies before leaving. Why? Because the Ministry spokespeople said they were not secure there.

So what happened? Some dedicated altruists were single-handily taking care of these people with hardly any supplies. And, fortunately for all concerned, there had been no security threat. Some dedicated people, a few religious volunteers and students, have been on their own with few supplies to take care of these people while the government had just bailed out. I was frankly stunned upon learning of their cowardice and disaffection. You could see it on their bureaucratic faces. Upon reflection, I could believe what these people and their disinterested medics and nurses had done. No one was taking control, and not much was getting done, which is inexcusable. The Mexican Government, minus a few devoted and loyal patriots, is a blight upon the history of this nation. They fool everyone, and they seem proactive on the surface, but it is incontrovertibly, irrefutably, and it seems irrevocably riddled with waste and corruption. It is, in my objective estimation, a rotting boil on the back of the humiliated Mexicans. And who is to blame? It's a rhetorical question. Ever since I could remember, everyone I've spoken to regarding the future of Mexico complained that their own elected government was counterproductive to aid, progress, or peace. When things truly get rough, when they are truly required and should help, where are they? They cringe in sinful shame, and giggle away the troubles of the nation till someone discovers them, and then it's off to replacing them with other incompetents. And, the county not only gets worse and worse, but the corrupt officials, along with their mafioso supporters, go on increasing their power and wealth, more and more. And, Mexico goes on suffering, standing against the winds of change with resignation and disillusion.

From the look of things, inflation continues to be on the rise. I don't need to tell any Mexican that, but their government finally admitted it, and it has been growing quickly too. Although Mexicans go about their business attempting to put tortillas on the table, fill up their cars with gasoline, and pay their utility bills, they regularly fear that inflation will be on the rise. After months of negating inflationary growth, their government reacted by raising taxes once the diminishing returns from crude petroleum sales became apparent. The voters never put their faith, trust, or hope in anyone in their government, anyway ~ even Felipe Calderon', who is basically honest and proactive, is regarded as cynical and impotent. Their government reacts about as forthrightly as a sea turtle set down at the base of El Popocatepetl and then is forced to climb it. The inflationary rise destabilized a steadily collapsing NAFTA driven economy. Most people in this country were aware and smart enough to know the statements about *Recovery* from President Calderon' and his ponderous ministers (and I do mean ponderous considering just how metabolically challenged they all seem to be) were all words blowing with the dust of many a ruined public work or social project. Things are still in decline. Things are vexing the cynical populace. No recovery is in sight, the pig flu remains a convenient "wag of the dog," and the hours of indecision tick away as real cases of infection turn deadly with the exposure of negligence.

The jobless rate kept increasing, not decreasing as the same government charlatans had claimed. When confronted with reports to the contrary, they naturally reacted with surprise and decried the increase in joblessness, that it was America's fault for not guarding the integrity of the dollar against her own banks.

Really? Since they have single-handedly ruined the Mexican Economy, one was left to wonder how next they would voice their surprise at the mess they purposely created.

Foreclosures are in evidence all over the place; around the Atzcapotzalco barrios alone I counted 134 homes (hovels rather) in foreclosure, and many more were up for sale or rent. All the hundreds of billions of dollars (trillions of pesos) the Mexican Government has taken from her sub-soil riches, where is the accounting? The great social projects and works, what became of them? And the pledges to alleviate hunger by providing starvation stipends to the poorest of the poor? I still see too many beggars and bums roaming the streets of the capital to be convinced of any good intentions. All has been in vain ... all in vain. And so, public confidence continues to collapse. More people lose their homes, estate values continue to decrease, and official promises once again are quietly broken.

Meanwhile, as visual news outlets focused on the foiled efforts of the Calderon' Administration, the contending legislators with their confrontational party loyalists have been creating their own *red herrings* without anyone paying attention. They've been affecting, adversely in most cases, every Mexican living *and* dead. They have been busily about passing laws granting gay marriage, raising taxes to stem the recession, hampering flood disaster relief efforts, and voting contrary to the best interests of the majority of Mexicans. And why not? The silly masses believe in them still, so why shouldn't they get away with proverbial murder? Never do they ask themselves this - when was the last time anything came out of the Mexican Congress that was good for the majority of its people? No one can answer.

New Question: In the next Mexican disaster, will the exhausted people have to wait until some other country, namely America, can come to their rescue and save them from their socio-political atavism, which has left them incapable of doing so on their own at this point in Mexican history?

I wonder: if Mexico suffered another devastating earthquake, like she suffered in 1985 and the entire area was in total ruin (an all too real possibility), and all the people that survived were blindly wandering the streets scrambling for scraps of tortillas or handouts of beans, would it take their own government a week to get their act together (like it took them after the 1985 quake)? Well, I know America might be there, ready to help control the inevitable wave of illegal immigration or attending to those in real need, but would it also take whole a week for the *rest of the Mexican nation* to finally get their act together and save their country from themselves? Only questions and more, but few convincing answers.

Nevertheless, as long as they force their lies and excuses down their citizens' throats, the frustrated survivors have to ask why it is that whenever a catastrophe occurs, some event that devastates and captures the compassion of the entire world, America and many other nations always are on the scene, always offering help, always providing aid and millions worth in logistics ... yet, very wealthy Mexicans are nowhere to be seen? Can they not offer aid and help? I have been reading that oil prices are escalating a lot, and perhaps they must first skim the money off the top of their profits to finance native narco-traffickers intent on siphoning billions of pesos from the tax rolls as well as their pathetically addicted clientele to pay for their ridiculously opulent lifestyles. Their own drug-abusing victims would think they'd have a few pesos to spare for help in situations such as this, but they are rarely forthcoming, and when they make a big show that they are, it is usually with a paltry offering hardly worth accepting. Questions remain, notwithstanding, and few are brave enough to ask them, thus the masses feign belief in official propaganda, and their leaders are all too glad to continue feeding it to them.

... And so, my quest goes on. The riddle of Fulgencio's origins now confounds my search for fulfillment, and nobody knows like Mexicans know the troubles that Mexico knows!

BEATING A DEAD HORSE

As long as there was much to see and do in Mexico City, I did not mind much the prolonged and forcible stay. The remarkable variety of people assuredly piqued my interest and, sometimes, provoked my baser nature. The carnal pleasures were not forbidden to me so, as long as nobody was obviously sick, I made the most of the lascivious opportunities before me. As long as I was stuck in this town, I had few options before me.

I was well in to my second week in this grand old metropolis, and the shimmering lights of the down-town *Zona Rosa*, or Red-Light district, delighted my evenings, and provided many distractions for my fancy. I have to say though that Chapultepec and its historical and recreational attractions together with the famous national Anthropological Museum were the most satisfying local landmarks. Everything else was no more remarkable than anything I had experienced in other great cities. Much of what is typical of everyday life in Mexico City proceeded without incidence or hindrance, and some semblance of normalcy was to be had despite the recent social upsets. The bad economy in any case found the residents mulling around with drooping spirits, and the signs of hunger were everywhere ~ situation hopeless as it were, but never serious. There were signs as well that measures were being taken by the city meisters to jump-start the stagnating economy, so badly battered around by the confounded epidemic. Many locals, however, sarcastically observed that it was more beating of the dead horse, or *burro* in Mexico's case. June holidays, however, would not be the same this year, and the more well-to-do people I'd inter-acted with were as sullen as the poorest of the poor surviving in the grimy streets. Local events scheduled for the latter part of the month remained canceled even though no casualties had been tallied in the previous days, and most of the city was going about doing business. Nevertheless, the death count left many disturbed. Some tourists had succumbed to the virus, including a couple who had stayed in the same hotel in which I had taken refuge.

It soon became apparent that the big-wigs would try and stimulate important industries, resist prohibitions on Mexican pork products, and were going all out to convince tourists to return and enjoy the pleasures of their country. As one fellow said, to "rapidly rebuild confidence in our country." And, that said it all.

It also became apparent that pork products would have to learn to fly before some discontented tourists would ever return to this country.

Meanwhile, I battled traffic as it picked up in the Zocalo and Bellas Artes districts, but the lovely cafes' had been re-opened and serving some of that great coffee for which Chinese immigrants are famous. It was also nice to gaze on the lovely, swarthy faces of the locals again without the irritating surgical masks everyone was wearing as of late. The recovery seemed to be going ahead of time, and a palpable calm was descending on the harried citizens. The much decried nation-wide shut-down was meant to rein in on the spread of the virus, but it ended up causing much resentment. Some people believed the severe measures had helped, but others were worried the illness would rebound as the unwashed masses would gather again. Just in the Metro-subway alone people are in such close proximity that it is a wonder that things never got worse.

Some would argue, in between sipping that fresh-brewed Veracruz coffee, that their society really needed to weigh the pros and cons of keeping the country under high alert. On the one hand they were showing the world that Mexico was on top of things, impressing the richer countries in the process. On the other hand, tourists were being scared away left and right, and it is a fact that Mexico lives on tourism dollars. Hence, in terms of how the epidemic was handled, they would keep every option in mind, and the affrighted politicos refused to make any forecasts of what new disappointments the epidemic could bring.

It was all really a bad case of *Post hoc ergo propter hoc*, or Latin for "after this, therefore because (on account) of this." As the academics would say, a logical fallacy (of the "questionable cause" variety), in this case the repercussions of the epidemic, which states, "Since that event followed this one, that event must have been caused by this one." Well, not for the tourists or the tourism industry!

A Wetback in Reverse

But it is so typical of my fellow Mexicans ~ They cling to any fallacy that lies in coming to a conclusion based *solely* on the order of events as they perceive them, rather than taking into account other factors that might rule out the connection. Most typically, much of Mexico's magical thinking and many of her superstitious (religious) beliefs arise from this attachment to the very principle of fallacy.

To the contrary, Fulgencio, in the body of his work, would insist that Mexicans simply maintain their aloof attitude of "minding not the times but the eternities." If this be true, then they complain out of habit, but without malice in their hearts. They complain out of compassion for their fellow citizens, but with thoroughly egotistical intent at root. They prefer to leave each man and woman to workout their individual salvation, as it were. Considering all the steps backward their own leaders were taking, they felt all vindicated for their dissatisfaction. Fulgencio, according to Uncle Rafael, believed that a strong leader is what they should always aspire to, like a Porfirio Diaz or at least a Lazaro Cardenas, but they end up relenting to their obligation toward democracy. Fulgencio would often say that so long as their government was thus limited, they would, "prefer to be ruled by a lion (strong-man; dictator) than one of their fellow rats" (democrats). They do not take themselves too seriously in any case, but, in between sipping his Pedro Domecq, Fulgencio would reflect on the days' disruptions, and would lay the blame for the corruption and decadence in their country squarely on the shoulders of his people. He would remorselessly disparage his countrymen as being stupid and dim-witted, often saying that, "For a Mexican, it is even good to have somewhat lengthy words in his mouth for he thinks slowly, and they give him time to reflect."

Anyway, the events of the week that were canceled included re-enactments of some famous revolutionary battles and accompanying parades. This would surely be a downer since many had been looking forward to the festivities. Then the president himself appeared on television once more to compare the threats (the civil conflict vis-a-vis the epidemic) in a speech some of my fellow patrons believed was not quite apropos:

"Almost a century and a half later, Mexico is facing a new threat, this time of a very different kind; an unusual threat, specifically the appearance and spread of an epidemic that has put at risk the lives and health of Mexico's families."

Well, if the president of the country no less wants to compare revolutionary heroes and the battles they fought with diseases and germs, well then that puts the reason why Mexicans treat each-other so badly into proper perspective.

After 26 confirmed deaths, nobody had actually perished from the porcine flu in Mexico since late April, giving some the courage to re-open their restaurants and other local commerce before the curfew had been lifted. The five days of the shutdown had proven salubrious to no one and nothing except the virus itself. Despite the longer days, bright sunshine and Summer heat, the mood of the city remained somewhat lugubrious.

Hereinafter, the economy had lost, according to the local news-papers, billions of dollars, and the rumors of the government stimulus for small enterprises and tourism, which had been hit the hardest, would have little salutary effect. So, what do the big-wigs decide to do next? They just slash at health benefits and payments, but would reduce taxes for foreign airlines and cruise-ships making money in Mexico. Will Mexicans ever get their dignity back from the rapacious outsiders? Funny though, but hereabout I learned the true meaning of the racial slur *Gringo*: it basically translates into "outsider," or foreigner, someone from the outside wishing to despoil the beauty and riches of their national patrimony.

Universities and other academic institutions were being thoroughly sanitized to allow their student bodies to go back to their studies lest they get too comfortable with the idea of a life without purpose. Younger students would be looking forward to Summer recess in any case, thus avoiding certain pools of contagion that their mommies and daddies worried would make the virus return.

The schools would nonetheless reopen even as teachers and parents demanded more resources to deal with potential flare-ups, and begged local commerce to assist them in controlling their children, which most especially involved sports and other recreational facilities. The pathetic adolescents and pre-pubescent rascals were further upset to learn that sports events and weekend ball-games would not be allowed for awhile. That caused me much annoyance since I was planning to attend a few before taking off for Colima.

Despite what others had called it, a return to "normalcy" would have sufficed for most people, but it was not in the offing. Everyone had to remain on guard, and it was evident everyone was throughout the city. They were not by any means out of the woods, as they say, and severe cases could surface at any time, anywhere, and my quest for meaning would be plagued by all this. The search for the pieces to this unexpected puzzle of Fulgencio San Roman left me feeling sick in either case ~ just where did he fit in to my search?

I did try again to get a vaccine, but the local clinic had run out of them just as I got there, and the prices of anti-flu drugs were jacked up despite anti-profiteering laws. Not even because this country had been hardest hit by the outbreak, or was rather "most in need," as the Health Ministry spokespeople would say, did merchants stay their hand from feeding on the misery of their compatriots. Thereunto, they continued to stockpile the drugs while the poorest of the poorest resigned themselves to the worst.

As of the following Tuesday, Mexico had nearly 840 confirmed cases, and few details had been divulged about the most recent porcine flu death in and around the government center,. The same officials said the victim was a woman with chronic health deterioration who lived on the poorest part of Tepit, the filthiest, rottenest part of town. World health officials had said a pandemic could be declared in the days to come. Again, this could be terrible for me for once again I would be forced to stay put while the screaming bureaucratic pansies would go about scaring everybody about the relative severity of the spreading infections, even though nothing really exceptional had been going on, and no more deaths had been registered than in previous years.

For the time being I thought to tract down a contact of Renato's who, he'd said, might help me to make sense of Uncle Rafael's letters. It took me a couple of days to track him down in and about Tasquena, a rather unpleasant district on the other side of the city. This fellow, Jose' Pino, turned out to be (small, dark and humble fellow that he was) quite gracious and helpful. From what I gathered, he had known both Rafael and Fulgencio well, and shared some amusing anecdotes with me about their days at the Azteca and Churrubusco Movie Studios, and all the magic they produced for the Cinema Industry. This placated me for the moment, but I was anxious to learn about the possible connection Fulgencio had with my recent ancestors. Once the initial pleasantries had passed, Jose' did confide to me that Fulgencio's mother, Carmela Martin, had in fact originated from Tepatitlan. She had erstwhile been promised to, and had earlier birthed a bastard child by, her second cousin, Arturo Gutierrez Martin. Sadly, the bastard child did not survive infancy. All this had transpired before having to run away in shame and marry her secret lover of four years, Ramiro San Roman: Fulgencio's father, and a rather sodden union boss of some repute. The marriage lasted about 18 years until Ramiro had drunk himself to death. At that point Carmela, never one to mourn for her dead, found herself a wealthy liquor distributor, Ernesto Najar Pereira, and married him on the spot; the fact that he was 23 years older and suffered from heart disease left him quite impatient to exchange vows as well. But, what of Arturo? I asked impatiently. Where did he fit into this mystery?

It just so happened that Arturo, who I had never heard of before, was my grand-father's second younger brother. He was the chosen inheritor of the Martin estate, thus leaving my grand-father, who was a libertine and dissolute asshole, to fend for himself. He managed alright and piled up a fortune of his own in the process, so there are no unread missives or eulogies regarding him. Nevertheless, Fulgencio, by way of his mother who had re-established relations with the family clan following her marriage to Najar, ending up meeting and getting to know well some of my ancestors, including my grandfather and his children.

Well, if this didn't feel like a kick in the testes! I was just overwhelmed, beside myself, dogged by an immanent and imminent sense of elation ... I was just left speechless. How strange the ways of Fate, I thought to myself. What do the workings of Providence, I asked myself, add up to in the final analysis? Only silence sufficed for Mr. Pino. Only silence made sense of these outrageous revelations. Where to go next? What to do next? What to think now?

It would be quite a challenge and it stumped me before the riddle.

For the time being, it would be back to worries of community-level transmission; back to pig flu anxieties, and all the incompetence that exacerbated it to the umpteenth degree!

CRY DAMNATION FOR THE PATHETIC

After bidding my adieus to Jos thanking him profusely for the information he shared, I returned to the hotel to mull over what my next actions should be. Peripatetic as my musings may seem today, they reflect all that was going on in reality, all things subject to capricious chance, and I was no less vulnerable to this unseen danger than the next guy. I thought to go next to the colonia of Claveria, one of the more decent neighborhoods in the entire city and, to reiterate, where Becky's relatives were to be found.

It turned out many were out of town or occupied with affairs that prevented them from getting back to me, but I did run into Lazaro, Becky's eldest brother. It wasn't surprising, especially since he led such a quite domestic life raising fighting-cockerels and managing his taxi-service business from his own home. He explained that Becky had not in fact returned to Mexico City like she had promised, but instead took refuge with intimate friends in the state of Guanajuato, the actual home state of her father's family. Naturally, this came as a disappointment to me, but I swallowed it and inquired of Lazaro about Corazon Salvaje, a mutual college friend of Becky's and mine whom I'd promised to contact once I was able, and thank her for having set up the logistics and contacts I would need during this pompous and lately frustrating voyage of discovery. I had much difficulty getting used to calling her *Corazon'*, but she eschewed her real name, which was Gloria Trebiniani, for artistic reasons among others. She wanted a straightforward break with her past, and she never appreciated having inherited the name of an aunt she really despised. So, that's how *Corazon'* came to life. The reunion, though, would have to come later.

As I wandered about the streets looking like a homeless mendicant, I decided to partake of a free tour of UNAM, the national university of Mexico. It was fascinating to see the outsized murals of Jose Clemente Orozco, and the *Student Body* was seething with many beautiful student bodies of all varieties. I made no illusions about my intentions, however, and took advantage of their grand library to look over some ancient genealogical records stored in their official archives. I could then compare some of the information gained therein with some of the claims Uncle Rafael had made in his letters. This would not be an easy task since I was traipsing on Terra Incognita as it were, and incognizant as I was about towards what the new discoveries might lead me.

As I explored the grounds and whistled at some coquettish sophomores, news was circulated among them that dozens of quarantined Mexican nationals had been given their freedom by the Chinese government, even though they never had the damned virus in the first place. They were returned to their families all flustered and whining about "humiliation and discrimination," but at least they got a government-paid-for chartered jet of their own. We were all recovering from our own quarantine of sorts here in the big city. The number of casualties continued to mount, and I remained fearful of what the next few weeks might bring.

Mexico City displayed its typical ebullience during the obnoxious pre-noon rush hour. Thousands of newspaper hawkers, street vendors foisting trinkets, and vagrants all dropped their surgical masks and added to the irritating clamor of truck horns and musical cacophony. Cafes' encouraged haughty customers again, and many corporate offices went about business as usual. Lazaro, who offered me several rides around town in his taxi, would walk through the capital's Chapultepec subway station without a protective mask (He had accepted work as a construction worker in order to make ends meet in the rough and tumble economy), which just goes to show how little he, along with countless others, really cared about the whole epidemic and the constant news-flashes.

I asked him about his attitude towards the nerve-wracking circumstances, but he wouldn't say much, contenting himself by musing, "The news-people insist that all of this is over, so I trashed my mask, and a lot of other Chilangos are doing the same wherever you go. I told my own children they had nothing to worry about, so they too abandoned the annoying masks."

Many others fretted about this nonchalant attitude rapidly catching on, and would argue not to let their guards down so precipitously. Many of the biggest whiners were idealistic high-schoolers and university students, and those bearing the most nonchalant attitude were their fellow students. This could prove to be a problem with schools and colleges reopening by that very Thursday, followed by secondary and elementary schools the following week.

My wandering about the hallowed grounds of North America's most ancient functioning university forced my eyes to fixate on the beauty of so much youth and vitality about me in the fine forms, figures and physiognomies of the clueless students, enjoying each other's presence more than worrying about their studies ~ as indeed it should be. Once I was able to pry my wistful eyes from the luscious apparitions crossing my path in between the formless, box-like academic edifices, I focused on one of Fulgencio's letters regarding his aesthetics toward the tribulations of sex. This was revealing since he applied his philosophy to his art. Sex is generally represented forthrightly in most expressions of art, but he seemed to want to impart his reasonings about it through metaphors as well as his characters. He did not seem overtly impressed by the whole concept, but he addressed it in almost all of his work, and Rafael was always there helping him to make his point. In a letter dated June. 6, 1951 he wrote:

...one should be surprised that sex and all the silly games attached to its pursuit, which plays throughout a being's existence such a vital and vigorous role, has up to our present age practically been ignored or disdained by our intelligentsia, not to mention scoffed at and condemned by the ignorant, and lies before us as a raw and untreated *tabula rasa*.

He gave his own expression to an inherent power within all humans which he felt had incontrovertible precedence over the quiet of the mind: *Quiero-Meresco*, "I want, I deserve," or his version of the Will to Live (a thing he truly believed in like the good little Nietzschean that he was), and defined as an innate energy within all creatures, to stay alive and to reproduce. Fulgencio refused to conceive of love as either trifling or accidental, but rather comprehended it to be a tremendous, almost uncontainable power lying latently within an individual's psyche and dramatically shaping the world at once:

The ultimate objective of all love pursuits ... is more significant than all other pursuits in a human's life; and therefore it is quite dignified in the profound gravity with which all hapless, unwitting souls chase it.

What is decided by it is more than than the seeding of the future and the generations that will shape it ...

In his closing paragraphs he answers the question many had asked him about his attitude towards posterity and what the future will manifest:

"My art is for the ages. My art defies Time itself, and yields only to the ideals of youth, which redefine it for the generations to come. It has been the solace of my life; it will be the solace of my death!"

His words did not surprise me. His feelings transcend any commentary I could add upon the study of his philosophy. It makes sense of my own indecisive feelings towards sex and the siring of children. His attitude towards his own art puts this transitory epidemic panic into proper aesthetic perspective.

As I folded the letters and put them in my knapsack, and pondered the real meaning of what I'd just read, my thoughts then turned back to the mundane issue before all of Mexico. The preventive shutdown was meant to minimize the dispersion of the virus at its heart, and deaths were avoided as the nation got its act together, and aggressively responded to it.

But the virus kept spreading and setting patience aflame. Like any normal person, I was sick and tired of the reports of miserable wretches succumbing meekly to deadly symptoms. What could anybody do but wait, and wait, and wait some more for better news.

At the same time people all over the city had a good laugh upon reading of Mexico's chastisement of China's quarantine of its citizens as "discriminatory." The victims had complained that they were held without water, without food, and without the use of a lavatory. Others insisted that they'd been delighted by Chinese hospitality in spite of the shut-in. The Chinese, notwithstanding, had to let them go home someday, and they finally did. Crowds formed in the streets to welcome them home; none had suffered any of the flu symptoms, so it was all just a big misunderstanding. To me the whole controversy was more than a misunderstanding; it was a hilarious joke on the country itself.

The strident measures would be continued and enforced, and traveling outside of the country would be discouraged. This was no skin off of my back since I had only to worry about trains and buses.

Lazaro and I talked about these quarantines and restrictions while he drove me to and fro, and he was more phlegmatic about it all. He figured the big-wigs had their rationale and had seen many a health alert come and go throughout his 53 years. To him, the effectiveness of official interventions was and would always be minimal.

That's just the sort of person my friend was, he never worried about things over which he had no control or influence. Neither did he recommend anything or course of action I should take. He just wished me well, and smiled.

He was, nonetheless, adversely affected and saddened by the epidemic when he received word from Tijuana, Baja California, that an old girlfriend of his, for whom he still carried a slow-burning torch, had succumbed to the disease, complicated by her diabetes and other conditions. He had tried to find any excuse to go and see her while yet she lived, but the very measures taken to contain the flu prevented him from leaving the capital. Now that it was over, Lazaro was left with only his memories and sadness. He'd be the first to urge caution, and typically said that none could make predictions of what will happen. The passing of his old flame, however, may have allowed for the escape of the reckless spirit trapped inside him.

There was the future to contend with, and he would never be the same, though the same old troubles would afflict Mexico in times to come. In this metropolis of 20 million, there are 20 million stories to be heard, but the pig sickness forced many mouths shut. Many of the corrupt officials were glad to comply and kept their's shut.

Enough with the bullshit! The time had come to wipe their mouths of it and get busy cleaning up their act.

"I WANT, I DESERVE"

Looking forward to my third week in Mexico City, a sense of complacency infected my adventurous spirit, but I had good cause to keep my cool. Thanks to Lazaro I had established contact with Corazon Salvaje, a most lovely Morena whom Becky and I had known for many years now. She was sweet, effervescent and caring, and already I owed her a great deal for making my trip possible. Our reunion was reaffirmed by a warm embrace and boisterous welcome. She had lost none of her sensuous allure and luscious beauty, but was more adept at exploiting both when circumstances demanded them. She would offer me hospice in her ample and comfortable guest cabana adjoining her home near Chapultepec, in an even more posh neighborhood crossed by elegant boulevards and shaded by lush and fecund grandfatherly trees, and with a clear though distant view of the historic castle of Chapultepec. She was obviously doing quite well, and was in the midst of her third romance while collecting two generous alimony cheques from 2 former, yet quite wealthy, husbands who still loved her sincerely and remained her best friends; this domestic arrangement truly revealed something of the magnanimity and munificence of her character. I had no intention of taking advantage of course, but I would continue to depend on her so long as I did not try her patience.

Upon my arrival at her house, she regaled me with a great lunch she had prepared. We talked of old times, shared many wicked laughs, she introduced me to her two lovely, equally sparkling teen-aged children, guided me through her elegant villa decorated with Napoleonic and Art Nouveau-style furniture, and then invited me to stay for as I long as I wished. Accepting lodgings from her would be a welcome retreat from the stale hotel, so I gladly acquiesced. Upon reflection, I felt like her invitation was a just reprieve for all this trouble with the porcine flu; I had to decide, and then reasoned that I want, I deserve, so I should have!

Then, she got personal and started asking me about my love-life, but without self-interest of course. Since I had known Corazon for many years I did not mind confiding in her, and she was very sympathetic in any case. I told her how much her generosity overwhelmed me, that I did not know how to repay her. She would have none of it, however, and insisted that what was hers was mine. I honestly was not used to such open-hearted goodness, I could only think, "no wonder her ex-husbands still love her ... she is worthy of the name 'Corazon' (Soul)." When she got more personal and wanted to know what feelings drove me, and, specifically, why it was so important for me to discover my roots ~ why had it been so important to me to embark upon this extended roving, which on the surface seemed aimless, but was very purposeful and important to my future, I did not know how to respond at first.

As we sat down to sip some fine Spanish *Jerez* (sherry), and to delve into the inner recesses of our psyches to extract the constituent feelings that would accompany our responses, I timorously confessed that, "Some sensitive souls out there have told me that I cannot love, have never loved, because it is a defense mechanism of mine ~ a shield to avoid being hurt again.

But, then a real human being comes along, like you, and I just don't know how to behave, how to handle it, especially when my life is still being adversely affected by the same old Neanderthals who fight tooth and nail over the same old bone, so to speak.

I hope you can understand me ... Oh, of course you understand me! Who else but you could? You are our angel."

I admit, my response had been somewhat maudlin, but she saw right through the shyness (or false humility), and, typical of her affectionate nature, she said, "You are very special to me. I rarely get that involved with anyone as I had with Becky and you, but I felt a bond with you both from the beginning."

I was surprised at her admission, but she continued, "Freddy, I remember how long it took you to talk to me that one time to ask me if I could provide you information for your grand journey because you said you don't like to talk to people on the phone. You said you were 'nervous,' but you sounded so wonderful, and it was wonderful to hear from you after all these years. That day sealed our family bonds for me. You always had inspired me when I was down, encouraged me when I was running out of steam, and kept me laughing. I will never hurt, disparage, or ignore you ... ever. I value you as a person and a definite family member. I wish I could do more for you. *Yo te amo*! Don't let the assholes of the world kill your spirit! Nothing is forever!"

I didn't know what to say to her after that. I never imagined my friendship meant that much to her. I was embarrassed and delighted at the same time. Then our conversation went off on a tangent, and I related the details of my quest, but also the details of what I came to regard as the "Fulgencio Factor." She admitted that she knew all about him, had seen many of his movies and just loved them. Furthermore, she had no idea he was still alive, and she feigned great surprise when I whispered that my sleuthing had uncovered a probable family connection. After absorbing the compelling secret, she reflected on, and told me all about her own search for a long lost father, which absorbed my attention with all the intriguing secrets: "... I had previously sent Pablo (Pablito) Mitre de Lorca, my cousin on my father's side who lives in Oaxtepec, a note. Our papa, Mauricio Trebiani De La Fuerte, had one sister, Anita, who was a few years older. She was a lovely lady, always kind to me. She passed away about 8 years ago. She had two sons, Pablo and Carlos, together with four daughters. We were very close growing up until we were 14 ~ we were a year apart. They lived in Nuevo Leon'; we, in La Paz. I used to spend time in the Summer there. After they moved, my parents divorced so I lost track. We met up about 7 years ago after I'd tracked him down in Puerto Vallarta, and when I go there he tries to go so we could have another great holiday together. He is married to a Cuban woman, so his children (he has 3 of them) are Mulatto. He is in the clothing manufacturing business like his father was. He's a great father and husband. He taught me a great deal, including a love for the cinema."

Her last admission was revealing, but she had only begun to talk.

"My father's name was originally Joaquin Pablo Llaguno." She went on to explain. "He changed it to Mauricio Trebiani when he moved to Baja California in 1967 so no one would know him. That's just for your information! His father, Grandpa David, was one of 11 children who came from a very rich bakery family. He was the 'black sheep' of the family because of his notorious gambling and womanizing, and they paid him off to leave Nuevo Leon' and go south to Puerto Vallarta. They settled there in the mid-1950's and opened a bakery. The family moved here in Mexico City in 1962, six years before I was born, and started another bakery. At around this time Grandpa David got to meet, and interact with Fulgencio San Roman ~ something having to do with a bakery contract he won from Azteca Studios, and even maintained a friendly acquaintance with him for some time. Don't ask me how or why. Perhaps Fulgencio shared my Grandpa's weakness for card-games and gambling ~ I have no clue. Maybe cousin Pablito will know. Actually, I'll ask him how Anita, his mother and Papa Joaquin's sister, ended up back in Nuevo Leon'. I never thought about it until now. Incidentally, Pablito is an ally in the battle for Grandpa David's bequest against his own family. You are really helping me drudge up the family history!"

Corazon got me curious by now, but I was anxious to know what else she could tell me about Fulgencio. In any case, she would have to verify any details with Pablito, all else would be speculation on her part. Then she went on to say: "Anyway, I asked Pablito if he has any pictures of our grandfather David because you look very much like him. I have no pictures, but I'm sure he does. I'll keep you posted. You never know, Freddy! It's so funny, but I have felt like you were right here by my side like my special *hermano* all this time, and now here you are. By the way, how are things with your own family? Are you still thinking of staying put in Mexico?"

With respect to my family, I did not want to talk about it, so I tried to subvert the conversation. As for my waning enthusiasm for Mexico, I kind of figured that would happen, and Corazon well understood the reasons why. This country, I complained, is so "voluble" (unpredictable), and I did express my hope that as soon as I accomplish my purpose I would get out of this dump without the Federales ever getting wind of my *wetback* status. My friends Billy, Cecilia, and Becky and so forth over somewhere else were just pushing and pushing me to get out before anything worse than the flu epidemic happens. Corazon did reassure me that she could do so much for me if I needed her and could stay longer in Mexico City. I appreciated the offer, but the overall situation made me more desperate to get roving again. Yet, I knew to take everything with a grain of salt, so to speak. It would be a big ordeal to pack up and leave if I were to prolong my stay, but with the situation as it was with the *embargada* (or "embargo" on my passport), and the general state of health of the country, this was no "capricho" on my part.

Yes, it would be a pity to give up my dream and all that without trying harder to figure out the puzzle whilst I had the pieces in hand, but even Corazon admitted to how crushing it is to the individual to abandon hope as the realization of one's goals are within sight. As she wrote me in a previous email, referring to her first love Victor Inarittu who had passed away long ago, she'd lost heart to go on with her dream of becoming an explorer-archaeologist because it just would not be the same without Victor. And, worse still, she recently learned that her beloved elder brother Andres had come down with the porcine flu, and the prognosis was not promising. Naturally she feared for the worst, and she ruminated about how he had never realized his dream of founding a college for the study of eco-friendly technologies. For the present, she confided that she was in a bind and did not know how to proceed; regardless of her comfortable circumstances, she wanted to leave, start a new life in America, but worried for the welfare of her own children. They were old enough to look after themselves by now and even encouraged their mother to follow her dreams, just like I was doing in spite of myself (I was following something more in the nature of a nightmare).

Here I was just hoping to discover the origins of my name!

After we had supped together in a swanky Chapultepec restaurant, we had some brandy, and I then assured her, "Corazon, all I can do is give a bit of advice: as you know all kings and queens have a moment when they need to be relieved from their decision making power, and delegate to their offspring whether they like it or not. You, and I and every one else know and say out loud that you would be well off wherever you go if you stay together. I am sure you want better things for your children, so you have to have a serious talk with them. You have to be who you are. You need to make all the moves to make the move happen. I understand you must feel way too tired to start it all yourself again, even with the support of the men in your life, but it can be done. I had to face the same decisions, the same obstacles, and like I'd told you before when we first talked on the phone, I can only regret not doing more. Now I wish I had."

She nodded in agreement, we hugged, and then she explained that she wanted to analyze her circumstances more carefully, because there was a lot to ponder on her part, especially if she was to be suddenly thrust into a position of decision in view of her present state of utter dependency. One thing she disputed was the part about imposing her hardships on her children despite their support.

Up until the present moment she had viewed herself, and felt treated by life like a "prisoner," or the "slave of the palace." Why? I never could figure it out. Oddly though, for many months I had been crying to others of having the same feelings, of the fears I had about undertaking my quest. I felt like Life didn't respect me, doesn't listen to me, so, in spite of the same serious issues we faced, it was very doubtful that Corazon would suddenly change her attitude towards the future for the better. She did like the idea that I would start investigating moving options for her, but all she could tell me in response was that she would see how things would unfold.

In fact, she had tried to move to America beforehand, and I couldn't help noticing that she made resentful mention of her siblings with respect to the problem of helping her to move. A couple of them had made a nice life for themselves in Florida, but they did not offer to help with the move. They kept egging her on, and insisted they wanted her to move as well, telling her that they loved and needed their little sister, but it was always she who had to shoulder the burden alone, and put up with their *berrinches* and *muleria* (tantrums and grudges)!

Later I would learn that Corazon would make things somewhat difficult on them when they had stepped forward to help. At one point her sister Mariel had informed her that it would cost around $30,000 USD to contract a moving service to take all of her stuff to Florida, and Corazon (according to her sister) angrily responded, "What, are you crazy? Where the shit will I get so much money for a simple move? I should just pile everything on the roof of my SUV and do it myself! No, no, no! Forget about that. I am screwed and that is the end of it. What notions you have, stupid!"

If Corazon had actually said that, then no wonder her siblings were reluctant to go on assisting her.

Well, she was only at the beginning stages of her goal, and she would remain determined in spite of her darker nature.

As we talked about moving back, she mentioned something about not being worth it to bring anything with her, *Ni siquiera la ropa* (not even her clothes) because she wanted a complete break with the past. This got me to thinking of my own options, as well as the irony that I was actually in search of the past. I had thought to do the same, to sell and bargain away all the furniture of my California apartment. It would force me to take control of my life without strife and violence, and feel better about myself. I cannot control what others do or do not do (I kept telling myself), I can only control my life and what I want of it. Corazon, Becky and I were in the same boat, and now that our siblings were dealing with us in evil ways, now that we could not be there to stop them or confide in our parents, it made the outcome all the more certain if we were to forsake dependence on these old attachments. We understood how others felt and how difficult arriving at our decisions had been. But, we would do things for ourselves, not for them, and if we must lose all material concerns, so let it be! (I'd say). To save only what is worth saving ~ Ourselves!

Ah, of course the truth of our Fate stands between fear and illusion, and it grinds in the pit of my belly. All this time I have been doing everything for myself, my own well-being and survival since no one else gave a shit, and yet found time to look after my family; a fact which, surprisingly, they have acknowledged in a most hypocritical way. The same truth plagued my dear old college friends. We all have to vent, even though we conscientiously know exactly what we were going through. Yet, at our age, one finally gets sick and tired of having one's filial "enemies" screw with one's better nature. One has to scream out *FUCK*! Otherwise, if one doesn't at least scream to let off the steam, one will resort to violence, against oneself as well as others.

Upon hearing Corazon speak of her troubles, it fortified my resolve to pursue my ends. I would unravel the puzzle of Fulgencio San Roman, and come to the end of my quest with my identity in hand. Anyway, if Corazon was fine with losing everything, well that is great! I too could face a future with nothing left behind me. I mean, I just couldn't go home and start up where I'd left off. Nobody would help me, and it was a life I happily abandoned. I would still need some logistical help from them as well as access to my funds, which only my mother could withdraw. If I had anything to ship back, I could rely on a couple of old friends in Los Angeles to receive the packages. Other than that, I would really have nothing to look forward, or come back to, except for a few manuscripts and the files of my writings, recorded music, a few DVD's, legal documents, et cetera. If I were to lose even all of that, I would not panic.

Once we'd returned to her home, our conversation focused back on the objects of my quest. Corazon was genuinely intrigued with the work and convictions of Fulgencio San Roman, and her interest grew as I related the experience I'd had in Reynosa with him, and the trouble I was having in trying to establish any contact once I'd learned who he is, and what he really meant to the history of cinema art and to my own ancestry. She reiterated that she loved his movies and had studied his writings, a fact which piqued my interest since I had just gathered bits and pieces of them but could draw no conclusions about him. According to Corazon's notes (from a Cinema course she'd taken at USC when she'd studied there some twenty years before, and had saved), Fulgencio believed sincerely in the force of Will as being above the play of senses and mind. This belief drove him to uphold his art above any prosaic matters that occupied the rest of society. His personal analysis of Will drove him to the conviction that affectional, physical, and procreative lusts can never be sated. Consequently, he advocated a lifestyle of denying human lusts, similar to the wisdom of ancient Greek stoics.

For Fulgencio, human lusts, or "willing," and wanting cause agony or pain. A fleeting yet profound and moving way to escape this pain is through aesthetic contemplation (a method comparable to the theory of "sublimation"). This is the second best way, short of not willing at all, which is the best way. Total surrender to the world as manifestation restrains the individual from suffering the world as Will. Art diverts the observer's attention from the grievous everyday world and flies him or her to a plane of consciousness that consists of mere play of images and sounds. With music, the hearer becomes captive to an ethereal form of the Will, which is otherwise deadly serious. Music was also given a special place in Fulgencio's aesthetics as it did not rely upon the matter of phenomenal manifestation. Music manifests the will itself artistically, not the manner by which the Will appears to a participating beholder. According to an anonymous biographer of his,"Fulgencio believed that Music was the only art that did not merely replicate cognitive content, but actually was the avatar of the Will itself."

This might explain my own worship of Music as an invisible manifestation of a deity! These newest revelations uplifted my heart, and refreshed my resolve to find the meaning of his legacy in my life. They were certainly revealing of a greater truth that joined our souls to the metaphysical source.

Corazon, for her part, had more on her mind than trivia about Fulgencio San Roman. She changed the subject on me, and expressed a frustration that her cousin Carlos, Pablo's rakish and manipulative brother, who had also met and knew a lot about Fulgencio San Roman, had also caused her family a lot of trouble with regard to family holdings (Boy, did this anecdote rag on my nerves!), and she was reluctant to ask him for any favors. "WHAT is this you say about Carlos?" I asked her. "I thought he was a darling favorite of your family like Pablito against his own branch of the family? So, the shit has hit the fan with Carlos? You cannot keep this to yourself. You have to give me all the dirt on this situation. It sounds really explosive!"

To my surprise, she was quite forthcoming with the dirty details, and in any case wanted to vent with me. I assured her that she could vent all she wanted, and that her venting would be safe with me. With respect to my goal of gathering all the information about the objects of my fascination, and then some, she sympathized and assured me, "I know, Freddy, for me it may be simple because life is so different in the States. I understand your concern for what you search as this represents your whole life, and please let me apologize if I sound insensitive. Maybe I tell you this because I know that my worst defect is that I move around too much. People have told me many times in the past that I am 'unstable' because I do not stay in one place for a long time. I do not have any love for material goods. I do not care how many times I fall, because the falls allow me to see that I can get up again and again. I am well aware also that this is a double-edged sword for me as the same things that I pride myself for are the ones that do not let me sleep at night. They leave me thinking how much my moving around has affected my beautiful children's well being."

Corazon's admission made me think only of my own wanderlust, yet the big difference between us lay in the fact that I still maintained attachments to material things. Mine was, arguably, the greater burden. Now, about Carlos she went on to explain:

"You must remember when you previously visited us here in Mexico about 10 years ago how my brothers and, especially, my older sisters, Alicia and Monica, felt about him. Whether they liked him better than *Chivis* (sobriquet of Silvia, wife of Corazon's elder brother Andres and her favorite sister-in-law, and who once had a fling with Carlos), or not, I DO NOT HATE HIM like others have said. I have never been blind to his true evil intentions, however, with regard to manipulating people, especially my sisters. We were happy with him in the past, so I did not give a shit about that. Now, you must also remember or at least noticed that Monica peculiarly loved him. Well, when they visited Mexico in January this year, I told my sisters that I did not want Carlos alone in the house. Mariel, and my other brother, Mauricio Jr., were alright with that, and I knew (and every one else as well) that our mother Helena did not like him much, and did not trust Carlos.

When I saw my mother so deteriorated and helpless (from heart disease about 2 years ago) in that hospital bed, I knew that she would not have wanted Carlos there, and told my sisters so. Alicia, the oldest one and being the way she is, immediately went and told Carlos ... 'Oh, Corazon doesn't want you near our mother, so be very careful around her. You know what an imbecile she could be, and she might be rude and nasty if you happen to run in to her.'

Monica, being who she is and loving Carlos more than Alicia, once said to me.. 'If you don't want Carlos anywhere near our mother, I don't want Silvia to get anywhere near her!'

Then I responded, 'To what do we owe this god damned attitude? In any case, maybe you're right. Only we should be there with our mother, not the daughters-in-law or unappreciated cousins. Just the daughters and sons, Damn you all!'

I was bitter for a long time, especially after I broke my leg and could not be with my mother any more. It got worse when I learned that Carlos was the last person to see my mother alive!

WHY? He was also the first one to know that Andres had come down with the porcine flu. I tell you, that man is evil. I know him probably better than I know my brothers. I practically grew up with them both, Pablo and Carlos. Silvia's mother had lived next door to Anita, Pablo's mother, and across the street from our own. Ever since I can remember, my best childhood friends were Pablito and Carlos's little sisters, Chely and Jaqueline. Chely is Carlos's favorite sister, and, ironically, is still my best friend of all. Jaqueline, Pablo's favorite little sister, was also one of my best friends. So, Chely and Jaqueline shared in all of my happiest moments from Kindergarten through High School. Jaqueline, sadly, became too vain for her own good and a stupid whore; mind you, I have nothing against being a whore, but being a *stupid* whore is a *NO, NO* in my book of rules. Consequently, Chely and I stopped hanging out with her. I can tell you that living around the corner from them all my life had its advantages. I spent more time in their houses than in my own, so this is why I am telling you all of this. I know Pablo and Carlos are like day and night, and I know them better than I know my own sisters."

Now, I was getting a bit flustered with the family history and details of the genealogical tree. I wanted to know about the connection to Fulgencio. How did Carlos come about knowing him? Well, she went on with the background to her story, and it behooved me to listen. Thus, she assured me: " Fred, you also have to remember that I was married to Manuel Andrade (Corazon's first husband), who is Pablito's cousin on his father's side, and I lived with him for more than ten years, hanging out with their family all day, every day of the year for as long as I lived in the colonia of Gabino-Barrera. Manuel's mother always told me .. 'Don't confide in Carlos, nor in Chely who runs and tells Carlos everything. I tell you for your own good.'

Pablito's own aunt warned me about them as well.

I always complained to my sisters about these things, and to which they always replied 'Don't be a snake! they're good people, especially Carlos!'

Yes, he is good, very good ... GOOD FOR EVIL, If you let him! He will eat you if you trust him, but I know for a fact that he is also a coward. He is helpful and has good feelings, but he will take advantage of you when he can. I compare him to a 'hyena.' As long as he needs you, he will serve you and bend over backwards for you. At the same time he is rending service to you, in order to be close to you and learn of your weaknesses, he would soon bite you in the ass and turn against you as he gets the opportunity. All along, whether he serves you or bites you, he will be laughing!

Finally, Silvia got sick of dealing with the 'ingratitude' of Alicia and Monica so she told them about two months ago that she no longer could take care of our beloved grandmother Ramona. Alicia had no other choice but to ask and pay Monica for taking care of her. For the past two months or more, Monica has gone to Popotla to take care of our grandmother, every day. Now, she has close contact with Carlos and sees how he handles his life and those around him. As I once told you, Grandma Ramona lives next door to Carlos's family. It only took Monica a month to see from up close who Carlos really is, and now they do not even talk to each other and have declared war between them. Monica and Alicia have both called and asked me to step in, go to Popotla and put Carlos in his place because they feel that he is eating them alive.

Speaking of this ravenous predator, can you believe that Carlos had the balls to demand that Alicia give him the papers to my father's property? Supposedly it's because he feels that they really belong to his mother Anita. Then, he wants her to go and fix the bakery-inheritance that Grandpa David left. There's no turning back. Monica and Alicia are screwed."

Corazon almost choked with emotion as she recollected this story, and asked me to sit down to hear this one: "Carlos demands MONEY because he firmly believes that Alicia has to give him complete accounting of the rentals our father left behind for us. Furthermore, Alicia is obligated to give him a monthly allowance from our father's trust.

I, of course, enjoyed this moment. I warned my sisters of this, and they both turned against me, stabbing me in the back more than once to defend Carlos. Now, they cannot control him. Although the situation does not make me happy, I want them to learn their lesson."

At this point Corazon became reflective, wondering whether it was worth going through all of this psychological torment. I tried to be reassuring and she smiled, but her troubles weighed all too visibly on her brow. She then went on to say, "I will not stay in Mexico to rescue them from the monster they created. They got caught in their own web of lies and deceit. Now, let them twist and turn until he has sucked the stupidity and hubris right out of their conceited hearts! I'll stick around at least until I see them squirm. I hate to be so vengeful, but they put me through this special kind of nightmare!

So, there you have it my dear *hermano*. This is just one small part of the whole story."

... And quite a small part of the story it was. I listened to all that, and she still hadn't arrived at the point!

We hugged, encouraged each other, and went off to bed, and that was it.

As for the riddle of Fulgencio's family connection, I would just have to wait a bit longer for the next piece of the puzzle.

THE MUSIC OF 'GOOD-BYE'

A couple of days passed on by before we had a tete-a-tete again. Corazon had been busy attending to problems involving her children. I occupied my time checking with the Hall of Records and Civil Registry, and by arranging my next leg of this crazy journey. I knew she wanted to unload more repressed emotions on me, and I was just as anxious to listen, especially if she did in fact want to share something about Fulgencio.

The whole issue about inheritance nagged at Corazon. She protested that all this in-fighting between families over properties and legacies was getting to be the great unspoken problem in Mexico. According to her, many families were in a similar fix. Apparently there was a lot of wealth to spread around, and Modern Mexicans scrambled to get their share of it. Hence, Carlos was unapologetically doing what many others his age were doing.

Once we got settled down back at her house, enjoyed a great lasagna meal she'd made, and got tipsy on some very dry Chianti, she unburdened her soul once again: "Listen, Freddy, I appreciate your advice about moving. Now we shall see how my silly sisters respond once they get back. It must have been really hard for you to move around so much, but it was equally interesting to note that you have no material attachments. That is generally a good thing, and wish I was more like that."

I had to interrupt and confess that if I had been unstable about staying in one place, my problem was that I couldn't retain anyone's friendship for very long. It just happened that way ~ it is as though people got a close look at me eventually, and realized that I am not the affable, bumbling, funny ass that they thought I was. They find I am a very complex, dark-moody skeptic and deep-thinking cynic that doesn't let anything get past him. I could be flattering myself, of course, but others, including Becky and Corazon, have drawn that very conclusion and surmise that they just don't know what to do with my friendship. This is especially true after I demonstrate that I am perfectly content not to have to go through all the bullshit and lies attached to most friendships. But, when it comes to the intellectual pleasures, I just can't let go, while death permits, of books and music. Now, I have to worry about these archives on hard disk ~ given his philosophy, I think Fulgencio would approve of me.

Corazon, regardless of her fears on behalf of her children, felt that I was best suited to advise her on the pitfalls or advantages of moving to America. She just plainly admitted: "I think I will need your advice, and have you walk me through this, assuming I could store everything safely by some other medium, or have to give up entirely the idea of taking with me the remnants of my life. There is that consolation at least, and thank you for pointing it out for me."

Then, she started unloading about her sisters and Carlos again. It was all so remarkable I couldn't help but react with hyperbole, and unload all of my questions in one heap:

"Incredible! All I can say is *Incredible* to all of it! I can't believe it. The more you reveal to me, the more incredulous I remain. So, Monica was all chummy with Carlos? I thought it was Alicia with all the guile and bullshit? Now, after a couple of months, Carlos has stabbed both of them in the back? Honestly, what can, or do they expect from you? Why don't they fix this problem on their own, especially if they helped to create it by giving Carlos wings?

And where is everybody else on this issue, especially Andres? What about Mauricio Jr.? It is just so astounding, the unmitigated gall of this person. How dare He! And, he really expects payment ... for what? Why should he be entitled to anything? What an evil bastard.

But you, you were so close to his family once? And, Manuel is actually related to him? All this is just too close for comfort. I am going to spend all night digesting all that you've told me.

You can hang tough in any case, Corazon. Enjoy the irony for the meantime, and I must admit that I do feel a little pity for Monica and Alicia ~ that was rather stupid of them to trust him so much, and now they are in such danger of unseen plots that will leave them without anything to call their own.

Anyway, so what exactly did Carlos do to alienate Monica, especially if Monica once 'loved' him so much?

And why do Alicia and Monica need you so much now? Are you the actual 'inheritor' to Grandma Ramona's fortune? Is that why they need you to step in? What is it with these people? And what did Carlos or Pablito have to do with Fulgencio San Roman?

Sorry, I don't mean to be so nosy, but I can't help myself. The details are all so juicy!"

After such an avalanche of an interrogation, Corazon just sat back, finished her Chianti, and replied, "Look, my dear *hermano*, The only reason that they want me in Mexico is that they are afraid of him, really afraid of what he is capable of, and they want me to put a stop to him. To my eyes, he is not a threat but my sisters are very easily intimidated and disturbed by him. I have always told Carlos how I feel about him, that is why they told you that I hate him. They have it all wrong. I just do not need to fight or be a bitch to people to tell them how I feel about them, there is no need.

I think I am the only one crazy enough to kick his ass. I've done it before; I can do it again, easily. Carlos is from the barrio, and when he hates someone he uses *chingadazos* (physical violence). Monica and Alicia are always afraid of that, and although I am really calm, I am also a a girl of the barrio at heart and will gladly kick his ass.   There are things I negated to tell you. Carlos cruelly dumped his first wife Rosario to marry one of my mother's favorite nieces, Julia. He worshiped the ground she walked on. He committed all sorts of dastardly deeds to win her love. When she died, a very ugly side of Carlos emerged, and we would be on guard against him ever since. The fact that his children, Alejandra and Sergio, are directly related to our branch of the family makes him very aggressive about protecting their interests. He really has come to threaten us with violence, excusing himself that he is doing it all for the sake of his children. Naturally, I think that is bullshit and would extract eye for eye, tooth for tooth if it came to that. Now, that is not what I want, mind you. That sort of comportment is not my preference, but I am not afraid if there is a need. I will avoid physical fights, specially with family members at ALL costs but, like I said, if there is no other choice I will do it. I think that is what my sisters want of me.

Therefore, this is the principal reason why I will not go to America just yet. My sisters only want me when they need me, and I have always put up with it because I love them. I know they love me too, but there are so many things, Freddy, that it is like re-opening Pandora's Box: once you open it, a whole bunch of demons come out and you just don't know which one to catch first."

It was my turn now to sit back, shake my head, and gulp down the Chianti, and then I continued: "My sweet Corazon, you don't need to tell me about Pandora's box ~ we created it in our house. If you think it might take chingadazos, then, by all means, go for it!

In any case, this is surprising about Carlos. It just seems like such a shame considering how well, or fond you seem to be of his sisters and his own children. Well, at least when you guys visited last Spring, you seemed fond of them; boy, that visit seems like ages ago now. I never figured Monica and especially Alicia to be such idiots, especially in regards to someone of such little import like Carlos. It is a good thing they have you, but what can I say but support your stance to the hilt. It is bullshit that on the one hand they are conniving behind your back, and then when the demon had revealed his true colors, they ran like *mariquitas* (pansies), expecting you to 'put out the fire' they'd started, right?

On the other hand, Carlos cannot really do anything, am I correct? What freaking right does he have to anything of your parents'? The children maybe, but very little considering there are the rest of you, and all of you have equal rights above mere 'distant relatives.' It is just so fascinating, from the time Carlos and you guys were children and right up to the present moment, this could be a great project for Fulgencio San Roman. It would be a great family saga of trial and tribulation.

Alicia had once recounted some of the drama that went back decades, and it would make a great story; a kind of perverse and twisted *ROMEO AND JULIET* mixed with *OEDIPUS REX*, and the saga of *MEDEA*. Carlos certainly does seem like a male Medea incarnate; doing everything for the hero Jason (in this case, Julia) to divorce his old wife, then connives through witchcraft to gain power, commit murder, arson, blood-feuds, pestilence, evil spells which bring madness, diseases. Then, when his beloved Julia dies, our male Medea casts a spell to have your sisters do his bidding, and ruins everyone's life in the process. He then abuses and exploits his children by her to get what he wants from your family. It's everyone's hope that, like the

Medea of myth, he'll hop on a chariot drawn by dragons, and ride off in a dark storm cloud never to be seen again. The rest of you though will end up ruined and cursed. Your sisters will just sit under the bough of their own *Argo* (the famous ship of the Argonauts), and, ironically, it will fall on them, killing them softly with his song, so to speak. All that after they had courted his favor, and the same devices that he used to rescue our male Medea from his own worst impulses.

I tell you, Carlos, without all of the mythology, magic and mayhem, reminds me of this ancient Greek character of tragedy and horror.

As for the part you play in this grand drama, Corazon, you seem like Hera, the queen of the heavens, who always tried to help. When the others turned their backs on you to do the male Medea's bidding, your Hera would no longer intercede, basically telling them to their faces, 'Ya se chingaron, cabronas, por no escucharme!' ('You're screwed, bitches, for not listening to me!')

And, after the disaster, no matter how much your sisters pray to you, your Hera will not heed their begging. Later, after this controversy dies, you know as I do, you will get your men and others to go after the male Medea, and punish him for being such a cold-blooded, conspiring bastard, then stuff his eye-balls up his own ass that it might have a point of view as you're kicking the shit out of it.

It is nice to see and learn that throughout our lives we are tied to the ancients by the same mythological themes and moral issues!"

Corazon laughed her head off, enjoying the idea of physically attacking this nemesis they'd taken to their bosoms. We had some more Chianti, and she admitted: "I love the idea of recreating the Carlos and Julia saga, and perhaps twist it a little bit by making it into an Aztec fable. This would make a great project for Fulgencio San Roman. He is like a Mexican *David Lean* and would bring out the dramatic sweep and romance of the story.

About their kids, they really had nothing to do with what their father has done. I truly love all of them. I have always liked Alejandra a lot. She was for a long time my favorite because she was so cute, and I spent a lot of time with her when she was a baby. She was like my toy when she was a toddler, she would do everything I told her to do. She loved it because like all children, whatever you do bad and makes people laugh she would do. I used to take her out to the streets of

Gabino-Barrera with my street friends. I showed her how to fart while pointing her fore-finger like she was shooting someone.

Of course, she was not supposed to relay any of my street secrets to her parents or that would have put an end to our outings. These kinds of things made us 'accomplices.' I remember when she was in Junior High she gave me an essay that she had to write in one of her classes about someone who had been a role model for her. She wrote there that she admired me. That was so very sweet and I will always remember that. This happened more than ten years ago so, to tell you the truth, I do not know if she still feels the same way. She's always polite and loving to me, calls me and we chat online from time to time. She's admitted a couple of times that she wants to go to America, but she does not want to leave her father alone. He fears that she will like it so much, she will never go back to Mexico.

Carlos's older children by Rosario, Nancy and Nathan, are sweethearts to me. They have always been very respectful and even to this day they confide their frustrations to me about their father. Just this past January, when I broke my leg, Joaquin (Mauricio's son) and Nathan spent most of their days with me. Nathan spent most of the time telling me about his feuds with his father, why he left the house to go live with his mother's family, and how bad everybody's relationship with his father was. Carlos really treats them as if they were his worthless step-children instead of his real offspring. He always has since they were very little, that is why we all appreciate them at the house. They have suffered too much at the hands of their manipulative father. We all know that because they used to confide some of those frustrations to our Mother as well.

About Sergio, I really didn't spend much time with him. I think he is a lot like Carlos' family---the bad side---but I am not saying he is a bad boy. I just have nothing to say about him. I do love him like the nephew that he is, but he is certainly not part of my list of favorite nephews. He has never done anything bad to me, I just do not bear the same affection for him that I feel for Joaquin for example; now here is a nephew I truly love! He is an honest, kind and pure soul. A blithe and generous spirit worthy of our love.

Sergio was born during a transitional period, after Carlos had worked in Fulgencio San Roman's home office, over in Jalisco."

(At last, Corazon had finally let the cat out of the bag about Fulgencio!)

She then went on to explain, "I am sure Carlos met him several times. He introduced Pablito to him, as I remember, and then Pablito worked as an intern or something, helping the great director to organize his memoirs. San Roman had endured a bitter legal battle with the studio regarding the retention of rights to his own movies, while the studio argued otherwise. It was a contentious case, and though San Roman got most of what he wanted, the whole affair left him bitter and disgusted with the Mexican Movie Industry as it devolved, as he saw it, into a purveyor of pornography. Before that, the director had shared anecdotes and secrets with Pablito about the Mexican Cinema going back to the 1930's, including stories about going on drinking binges with (legendary singer) Pedro Infante, and he had been there to warn him (unsuccessfully) not to take the flight that led to his death, way back in 1957.

Ultimately, he shunned the Industry which had lent him so much prestige and glory, and retired to a ranch near Reynosa in Tamaulipas, a region he had grown to love. No goodbyes to anyone, no music to commemorate his life, career and marvelous art. The silence of an unspoken farewell was enough to sate his Will, so he packed up, hugged the few he still cared about, and left, and that's it. Pablito was fortunate enough to be there and helped him with the move. I think they corresponded for a time, but that was a long time ago when Pablito was barely 20 years old or so. He talks to me about all this from time to time; he gets pretty wistful about the subject. I envy him in a way, for having been in close contact with such a great genius of the cinema.

Well, that's it, Freddy. It's all about the final music, and saying your goodbye's before you begin to stink. That's the way it is in life. That's how things are going for me, and I'll be saying my goodbyes before the music is over!"

TOWARDS THE WESTERN HORIZON

I had spent four long weeks in Mexico City. What an experience it all had been! Once the moment had arrived to depart, Corazon and I would tearfully exchange our farewells, a couple of gifts, hugs, fraternal kisses, and part ways ... but not quite yet. There were still a few more things to hammer out between us, and, naturally, I'd impose on her a bit more regarding the next leg of my journey. The danger of getting trapped by my own devices hung over me like the Sword of Damocles. There have been days since I'd arrived in this shadowy country when I felt like I would never get my identity back.

I had been fighting now for a year to get a new birth certificate apostillated after the damned Mexican consulate had taken mine to give me the worthless "matricula consular," which is supposed to be the official Mexican national identification card, instead of an extended traveler's Visa, which was what I wanted to get in the first place. No one, after all this time, NO ONE in this wretched country has recognized it as legitimate. Therefore, because of them I am regarded as no better than an illegal "wetback," and have been treated as such by all government agencies and most commercial enterprises; this might be great stuff for my new journal, but for a real life adventure I was left desolate and lost amid the hostile environs of a people that have forsaken my destiny as I have repudiated my heritage of it.

Like I explained to Corazon, the damned responses I'd get from the Consulate, after all these months, were entirely negative. To re-establish my legal status, I would again have to present proof of my identity, namely an apostillated birth certificate, which they had taken from me and for which they never compensated me. The cherry on the cake of audacity was that they insisted I pay them what amounted to a bribe, but they are not to blame; one cannot blame a rat for being a rat. This is all my stupid brother's fault; for his negligence, stupidity, and willful sabotage I cannot re-establish my identity until I cough up more money. This may just be a detail, but it's details like this that grind into one's conscience as well as cause one unending frustration with the Federales. They have torn away at the fabric of my existence, leaving me to face legal and political oblivion until I get back, and that will prove more difficult than I'd supposed. I cannot do it quietly. I will have to pay the bribe!

In the meantime, the July elections had come and gone. The ruling conservative PAN party had lost seats in state houses and the national legislature. The losses of the socialist PRD left them irrelevant, but the lately disgraced PRI party, which had wielded dictatorial rule over the country for seventy years before being toppled by the PAN, made impressive gains by winning control of the Chamber of Deputies and Senate, and numerous governorships. They wouldn't take office for a few months, but already I could feel that the shift in power would adversely affect me because in past decades the PRI governments were notorious for their unwieldy and stifling bureaucracies. Many disaffected voters feared aloud that official functions would grind to a halt, that the government would atavistically revert to its former ponderous inefficiency, making it very miserable for fools like me to get any justice or consular services from them. This PRI victory truly spelled DOOM for my quest. I had to move fast!

Stepping in like the angel that she is, Corazon had called some acquaintances working in the Secretariat de Gobernacion' who owed her a few favors, and told them about my sorry case. What would have taken months if I had proceeded on my own, my friend was able to do in a couple of days and procured domestic transit passes for me. This tremendous favor she had done eliminated the hassle of presenting an identification to the inter-state inspectors that periodically boarded commercial long-distance buses. What a load off of my mind! I was squirming and sweating till the last moment when my sweet friend presented me with the truly delightful surprise. Yet, all I could do for her in response was to thank her sincerely and give her an extra special hug, "Thanks for letting your friends in Gobernacion' know about my case. Without the transit passes you got for me I would be stuck here without an umbrella, as it were. Too bad I couldn't be convinced to stay longer, but I have a purpose to fulfill and couldn't wait around till things are happier. Oh well, I didn't expect otherwise."

I was truly curious to see how her demeanor would change now that she'd resolved to go to America. I was curious to see how Mexico was outside of the capital since the last flu alert. Even if it took a year to get back to California, it would be a very short time in view of the bullshit I'd endured thus far to accomplish my purpose. It makes it so ironic that if and when I do leave, it will be due in no small part to the dirty double dealings with corrupt officials I'd been reduced to, as well as the incompetence of the *Jurado* that put the damn embargada on me in the first place. I would nonetheless think of Corazon a great many times once I'd departed for Colima. I couldn't have done anything without her. She was the first to send advance warning about taking care to cover my face from people. This influenza epidemic had become more than a national emergency. It seemed to have stunted the growth of the whole country!

Another thing before leaving, Corazon confided that she'd finally contacted Becky. That was great! Old bonds were re-affirmed, and each exchanged sound advice regarding their mutual desires; Becky to start a new life for her family, and Corazon to move with hers to America. Strange, I thought, how life had brought us together during a time of indecision, and a time when we'd resolved to redefine ourselves for an uncertain future.

In fact, after we'd graduated from college and parted ways, I had returned to America while they maintained contact and helped each other to settle down. Corazon and I conversed about this just before leaving. I kind of suspected that Becky was still special to her, but didn't know that she had maintained such a great influence on her.

Since both were now mothers with children, naturally they would feel human nature more keenly than most of us do. I could say with out worry of contradiction that people generally recall with the sincerest and tenderest fondness those people that delighted and made them feel special as youngsters, just as it had been between Corazon and the children of Pablo and Carlos. She confessed that the hardest part about the feud with Carlos and her decision to leave Mexico City was becoming alienated from her nieces and nephews. I tried to re-assure her that if indeed she had shown them off to her friends and made them feel like part of the gang, I was so positive that they would always harbor the most affectionate feelings for her that probably superseded their love for their acquisitive father. The fact that Alejandra wrote that essay listing her as a role model said it all. People just don't forget about those things, unless something really terrible happens between them. Most likely she still felt that way about her.

As for her wanting to go to the USA, I did say to her that no one and nothing should limit her ambitions or actions. "Who cares if you like it too much and want to stay!" I assured her. "You'll never abandon your feelings for Mexico anymore than you would your own children, so I think your worry is spurious, and with your pretty looks and personality, you could easily take care of yourself. Even if you have to dance on tables at some tittie-bar, you'll make a lot of money, right?"

Corazon laughed, and socked me in the arm.

I had occasion to meet some of these characters before heading for the bus station, if only in passing. They all bore the trademark prettiness of the Trebiani family, which made the reality of the family feud all the more lamentable. It was interesting to note that she once had such close ties to her sisters as well, and, I must say, after I'd met them I thought they were quite lovely; it is also funny that Carlos boorishly marginalized them, despite their worship of him. Little could I guess what she told me about Carlos's relationship with his progeny by Rosario, that he indeed treats Nancy and Nathan like step-children! That Carlos has survived all these years doing what he wants is a genuine *rompe-cabezas* (puzzle), yet he has all the markings and attributes of a real psychopath. Her sisters should consider denouncing him to the medical authorities, and have him interred in an asylum.

About Sergio? I did find him to be a curious character. He was nice and all that, but mysterious, too quiet even. My own opinion of him had been prejudiced by her brother Andres', of all people, who'd related some disgusting rumors about him long before I made his acquaintance, so I couldn't vouch for their accuracy. One rumor about Sergio had something to do with his alleged attempt to stick his erect penis into a cousin of his, the son of Corazon's brother Andres'. I heard other versions, that it was the other way around. I doubt the whole thing, and yet I don't. If it so happened in either case, it was because he was trying to imitate something he'd seen in his father's bedroom, according to Corazon. He was only nine at the time, but she doesn't know the related circumstances for certain.

"I sometimes do not pay attention to *chismes* (rumors) that I feel are exaggerations." she told me. "If it was true, I don't know what anybody could have done to prevent it."

In any case, the silly rumor has dogged him and marred his relationship with his father to the present day. Indeed, I hope all the allegations are false, otherwise I am surprised that more hasn't been said or done about his unique case. When I finally got to know him, I thought he was a decent, friendly fellow who obviously feels lonely and misses his mother a lot ~ assuming, of course, that he loved her.

As for Corazon, I cannot see how she could keep so much love for so many people. I have enough trouble just loving one person, and right now I don't know that I feel love for anybody. Oh sure, I do feel affection, fondness, great or small respect, and even admiration for certain people, but I can't say that it translates into "love." Take this for example, love is supposed to bear all things, gives you the courage to lay your life down for the person(s) you love. I don't think I could do that for anyone, not even, or especially, my family.

I am not doubting, of course, my friend's capacity for love by writing all this. It is just that I find it hard to believe that anyone can love so many people. But, I shouldn't talk; after all, since I have been deprived of love, it is understandable for me to feel like this.

I did tell her brother about my emergency. I had spoken to him on the phone the other day, and we would meet the next day for lunch to say goodbye. Yes, I did try to bribe Corazon one more time into coming with us, but she said she honestly needed to start pulling down her house, as she put it. I did understand that.

The accusal that Corazon has too much love is insensible. I think her filial passion is normal. I think the tender influence of Grandma Ramona and of her mother was an inestimable blessing. Regardless of what everyone said about him, her father was a great and loving father to her. Her Grandma Ramona was always nice and attentive to a fault. Corazon's brothers and sisters took sound and sincere care of her, and although they are not perfect and she complains about shit they do now that she is not willing to put up with any more, she had a very good upbringing. As for my not being able to love someone, could that be a defense mechanism? The example of many taught me to be afraid. In view of Corazon's explanation, maybe I am just trying to shield myself from getting hurt.

A Wetback in Reverse

She makes a good point.
And now I was off for Colima!

UNDER THE VOLCANO OF FIRE

Dawn broke with a piecing vengeance. I was off to Colima for no good purpose that I could readily explain. Suffice it to say, going there just formed part of my desire to see and experience the most I could of Mexico. It would be a side-trip before entering Jalisco, and heading straight for Tepatitlan. In this city, I could find out more about Fulgencio and the roles his mother's family background and personal past could play in realizing my genealogical quest.

The bus ride was a bit uncomfortable, and the other passengers were disaffected towards one another and indifferent to the local surroundings. I disembarked already feeling wistful and introspective about Mexico City, not to mention Corazon and all of her troubles.

For such a small state Colima surely had many municipalities, which proved to be a bother because the bus-operator was stopped at the border of each one, and the vehicle inspected for possible narco-trafficking, and, of course, for possible carriers of the damned pig flu. These municipalities could be best compared to Counties in the United States, in that they have their own government, police, and civil services. We'd soon find out they also hold their own cultural traditions which culminate in creating the state's unique culture. Each has its own songs, dances, clothes and traditional foods. While exploring the local landmarks we partook of the *Jamaica*, or Summer Festival, which takes place in the towns of Colima, Manzanillo and Cuyutlan. The only thing I'll remember of the latter, which is a gray and sandy beach-town found in the municipality of Armeria, was that I was attacked by small, roving crabs (not of the genital type).

The area wreaks of Tarascan Indian customs, but their living purveyors charged tourists at tourists prices for their artifacts and other native wares like any self-respecting money-grubbing vendor.

I took a tour of a famous volcano in the area called the Volcan' de Colima, also known as the Volcano de Fuego (of Fire). In fact, half of the time I didn't know if I was in Colima or in neighboring Jalisco because half of the volcano is in Jalisco which, the resentful Tarascans asseverated, has been taking over more and more Colimense territory since the states were divided. This was one argument I did not want to touch with a ten-foot tamale!

I hadn't been touring around more than two days trying to absorb as much of the local atmosphere as I could when the porcine flu issue cropped up again. Once again Mexico's high schools and universities opened for the first time in several weeks. The big-wigs ascertained that the porcine flu break-out was again on the decline, but I gauged the Colimense attitude, and they were as worried about it as ever. Just in Manzanillo alone, a most congenial spot that reminded me of Zihuatanejo and Puerto Vallarta, I could see that that students were being checked as they entered the grounds of their local schools for the flu symptoms, and some were obviously hostile about being sent home.

In other places, like dance halls, movie theaters and bars, it was clear that they had no trouble operating and attracting customers so I had little to fear, and that's the only thing that mattered. I could attend pro-soccer matches with other fans the following weekend once the officially mandated curfews, which did not curb in the least the spread of the virus, had been lifted. I did find it somewhat irksome that businesses were still required to screen for any suspicious characters along with their own workers for any signs of sickness, and practically rammed those inconvenient surgical masks down our mouths!

It was only more of the same old crap that nobody noticed anymore than I cared to worry about coming down with symptoms.

I did find it curious that that the Secretariat of Public Education displayed signs all over the town calling on local citizens to show "strength of spirit," whilst encouraging people to emerge from their holes and allow their children to go back to school. I think television and radio broadcasts would have done a better job since most people seemed to ignore the silly, bright yellow signs; an unfortunate choice of color since passersby noticed it before troubling themselves to read the warning. Thus, despite efforts, no one was really assuaged of their worries, only disgusted with the whole thing a little bit more than they had been.

Laughing and joking, high school students gathered at the entrance of the local clinic, and had waited there for about twenty minutes only to have several of their peers display symptoms of the flu, including nasal congestion and coughing. Naturally, the authorities there made a big stink about it, and scared the Manzanillo populace all over again. Parents were notified, ambulances showed up, the police harangued the bystanders, and it made for a pretty deplorable spectacle. I tried to enjoy myself despite the circumstances. I was also waiting for word from Corazon, to whom I had forwarded my contact information and cell-phone number. Meanwhile, everyone was being observed by the police and other uniformed civil workers, making many of us rather uncomfortable with all of their staring. The officials, afraid of popular backlashes, just couldn't accept that the sickness was still around, despite their unceasing exhortations that the people be careful with their contacts.

After a few hours of checking out the local Manzanillo sights, I received a text message from Corazon: apparently the virus had picked up steam in Mexico City and more deaths from it had been confirmed. Worse yet, she informed me that brother Andres's condition had taken a turn for the worse. He seemed so healthy that afternoon of farewell. What could he have neglected to do that worsened his illness? She also informed me that one of Andres's co-workers had perished from the conflux of symptoms, which confirmed Corazon's suspicion that her brother had picked up the virus at his place of work.

All states had mobilized to disinfect their schools before re-opening, and Colima was no different. Most importantly, the students did not seem to care, or were unconcerned. The last thing that Mexico needed at the time was a bunch of panicky teenagers on their hands. "I'm not scared. They say it's getting normal again," said a 17-year-old boy I'd asked while in transit to his school. "I'm just pleased to be back. I was bored witless all these days, far from my *carnales* and *chavalas* (schoolmates and girlfriends)."

Others did seem under the weather to me, and would have exhorted them to return home, at least so that I wouldn't catch their cooties. The notice about Andres had me really worried, and I'd be wearing the facial mask again.

It was evident that youths at Colima vocational high schools were allowed back with a dollop of liquid sanitizer and the said mask.

Anxious to embrace each other again, the lascivious adolescents slobbered over one another, some through the masks.

I still think the danger of the epidemic had been blown out of proportion. The confounded media had exploited the issue so much that now they were seen as the purveyors of the sickness, for sheer exasperating mention of it. Another fellow I'd spoken to said he was all gung ho for getting his mates to take precautions.

"I know it's not the best 'look' for you, but it's important," he said he told them, about half of whom had clearly taken off their masks, and paid no mind to the warnings.

I also saw that the little brats were being commuted by their parents as primary schools reopened the following day. Parents expressed alleviation that their brats, cloistered for so long in their homes, could be corralled back into their classrooms. But they also fretted that the illness could strike back once all the less than hygienically minded youngsters gathered in one place again. So, yes, they were afraid again. They all knew they'd have to go back and did not want to, but even in such a charming town like Manzanillo things had to get back to normal. Parents with their progeny were all about town with their masks on. In a tiny roasted-chicken restaurant I patronized, the owners were obviously having a good time with the epidemic as they displayed their raw chickens or dolls of them wearing surgical masks. Frankly, I thought they took the appropriate attitude; so what if a few people die of the flu, more people die from hunger or exposure to the elements in and around those parts anyway!

According to the newspapers and blogs, working parents have fought constantly to provide child care during the curfew. The struggle forced many to avoid work while they sought solutions, or they took their offspring to their jobs, or sent them to the movies or to go bother their grand-parents ~ Anything to alleviate the tension.

Corazon confessed that she had to leave her children behind unsupervised while she took care of Andres, which was no hardship on them. Teenagers will find things to do in the absence of supervision!

"I'm nervous about them going back to school on Monday." She complained. "But they will wear a mask, and I have instructed them to stay away from their common, dirtier class-mates who appear sick."

Beyond that, they would be on their own. Lord have mercy!

Outside of their high school in Chapultepec, she went on to explain, nurses stood ready to hand out surgical masks, antiseptic gel, sheets of paper with sanitary recommendations and a health questionnaire. Most students just marched right on past her, Corazon complained, including her children. And, she went on to say, many teachers draped their masks around their necks with an air of sans souci. This really irked Corazon as she cleaned up after Andres.

"If they come to ask for information," I answered her, "I'd ask them some serious questions." (she agreed).

Meanwhile, most commercial establishments in Colima had installed antiseptic gel dispensers, and increased shifts for cleaning crews. The local officials had also created an online manual, "What to do to restart classes without risk?" The silly thing called for parents and scholastic workers to wash down classrooms, cafeterias and other areas with water, soap and chlorine, and to provide running water for hand-washing. Of course, nobody read it.

Each business or office building, the bigwigs cried, had to be thoroughly scrubbed and inspected that very week. This porcine flu supposedly has a long incubation period of five to seven days before people begin to feel the symptoms. Basically this meant the virus could be spread around by unsanitary persons who just wouldn't stay at home if their lives depended on it, so it was urgent that they get busy with the washing. Complicating the task, however, was the fact that many schools are primitive buildings with dirt floors and lack proper bathrooms. It was reprehensible how students attending those schools could stick to their government's strictures.

In order to gain posture with the voters, so said the pundits, political hacks promised detergent, chlorine, trash bags, anti-bacterial soap or antiseptic gel and face masks to the locals for delivery to commercial and public places. Some local districts, even in a state covered with municipalities, apparently didn't get the word.

Mexico's public education department stipulates that students must accomplish the annual requirement of 800 hours in class, but did not say if the term would be extended because of the shutdown. This last bit of news fell on Corazon's children like a ton of bricks.

Officials in other states were no longer recommending that schools shut down because of suspected pig flu cases since the latest virus scare had turned out to be milder than initially reported. But, many Mexican schools had done so out of fear of the unexpected.

Things around the borders of each state had gotten so bad in fact that just trying to transport a refrigerator, for example, into Colima from Jalisco in the back of a pickup truck became near impossible, and would be seized by state officials. On the other hand, stick a couple of AK-47 rifles in your trunk, as Andres joked before I left the capital, and chances are you'll fly through every border crossing. Whether or not Mexico was owning up to its porous border as it commenced a new plan to watch for suspicious vehicles entering the country, the aim thereof was to measure and interdict cars and trucks bound for known illegal drug-distribution centers in hopes of snaring the surreptitious and slippery smugglers.

More inconveniences, more side-tracking, more frustrations. What could I do but bear it all. On the beaches of lovely Manzanillo I almost did *bare* it all if only to defy the stupid flu. Other tourists seemed to have the same thing in mind, and many lovely bare figures sauntered and sashayed on passed me. It was quite obvious that they worried not for the silly old cooties!

And yet, I was melancholy over this thing with Andres. He is a thoroughly good fellow, and if he does not recover, I too would be devastated.

DOMESTIC TROUBLES

July was giving out, the summer rains were descending across the heartland, stifling heat made it nearly impossible to get a decent night's sleep, other Summer Festivals only intensified the pervasive sense of frustration with the state of society as it was, and August heralded very few surprises or prospects for a return to an already defunct state of normalcy. A few days of exploring Colima had come and gone, and I began to prepare for the next leg of the journey before sauntering on over to the nearest station and hopping on the first bus bound for Jalisco. I had been referred to a contact named Felipe Ramayo Arias by the friend of a distant cousin, who not only hailed from Tepatitlan, but knew some relatives of mine I had never met. If I could succeed in introducing myself to them, perhaps they could lead me closer to my goal.

In the meantime, I had received some harried calls and text messages from Corazon. She reported that Andres's condition was not improving but had been stabilized. She had also forwarded messages she exchanged with, of all people, Becky. Somehow Corazon had managed it, but the correspondence also reflected Becky's need to have her situation known to sympathetic supporters. It concerned her deteriorating relationship with her ex-husband, Enrique Alvarez. It turned out the ol' boy had unleashed his spurious resentments on her, and by doing so suffocated the righteousness right out of his moral contention. In a written letter dated one month before, he rebuked:

~ I know that Campanita is very unhappy to see me. Every time she comes from spending time with you, she is alway very upset and unhappy, *malnutrida, mugrosa, piojosa y está bien pendeja en la escuela* (malnourished, dirty, flea-bitten, and is very stupid in school), or so you say. I think it's better if she has the good influence that her mother can provide by not having her around fricking *C*holo (Chicano gangsters) losers, while watching Cholo movies. I'm a loser dad, I admit it, since I failed with your *chiquillos* (little ones), oh, and you are such an example to all mothers by raising fricking loser Cholos. You are sure to be commended for that.

You and I have different perspectives, priorities, beliefs and views on or about life, especially when it comes to raising children.

Please stop attacking and insulting me every time you can, especially in front of Campanita, and do not preach to me how I should raise my daughter! Also, you cannot set the rules of the custody/visitation of my own daughter. If you have her one week, I should have her one week. When you have her, you can take her to school, pick her up and interact all you want with her. I'll do the same when she is with me. You can always go to her karate class when she is with me, and vice-versa.

I'm sick and tired of fighting with a bitch, that's why I'd rather avoid you. You don't have to be nice to me, just don't talk to me. You know exactly how I feel about you!

I regret *haberte recogido* (having picked you up e.g. from the gutter)

Enrique ~

"What do you think of this?" Corazon then asked me.

"Unbelievable," I thought, and yet it was so very believable. This is just the kind of bullshit Becky, Corazon and I would hear from time to time from psycho-emotional drug abusers. Some people, in this case men, really give the rest of us a bad name.

"So, he thinks he has rights?" Corazon asked of her. "He needs to be reminded that he does not live in the Mexico of his grand-father when men had dominion over their families. This is a new Mexico, sister! He needs to be reminded that as soon as it involves litigation he will see just how many rights he has."

I wanted to know who these "loser cholos" were he was talking about? Becky's own sons? And then the big phony doesn't want Becky to attack, or to insult him in front of Campanita?

As far as I would evaluate his motives and considerations, this boy is a pathetic, lugubrious, rancorous flea of a frustrated Chilango! He cannot win, I replied to Corazon. He is quite obviously boiling in his own juices. For that, Becky should cry victory! Now he is suffering from the same medicine he served her for so many years. Now he is burning with regret, anger and a sense of betrayal and helplessness. He must really be consuming himself in his own bile to have worked up enough gumption to write her that pathetic email. And just what the Hell did he mean by: *she is alway very upset and unhappy, malnutrida, mugrosa, piojosa y está bien pendeja ... ?*

Is this the line he will use to accuse Becky before his lawyer?

*Be care*fu*l!* I'd tell Becky. This is exactly what a LOSER ex-husband and abuser will say to try and take the child from her arms. And, then to accuse her of bringing up "loser" cholos as sons is just another ploy for his court case. No, she must have her own children testify against him, it's the only way. I think even his own mother and brother will turn against him.

Corazon whimsically texted her: ~ Hijo le, pero que pendejo Enrique is! Becky, you have both my sympathy for going through this stressful bullshit, and my congratulations for having struck a blow for freedom against despots and imbecilic morons! And this is the most galling point of all: *I regret haberte recogido ...*

What a bastard! ~

Becky's reply was concise:

~ I was going to respond, but I decided not to at the last moment. I am sure he wants a reaction out of me, and not getting any is going to make him wonder what I am feeling. ¿Como ves?

Becky ~

Corazon then brought up the subject of how they'd met and got together in the first place. Becky, pensive as always, replied:

~ I know, considering that he just moved in with me, without asking me, makes one wonder what was going on in my mind when I permitted this. He just landed and started spending nights in my home. I wrote him a letter telling how I liked him, but didn't like the situation; he got offended but never left. I felt sorry for his ass because he had just lost his job. Asi que el mendigo recogido es el (so the mendicant who was plucked from the gutter was him).

After I'd received that bitter letter from him, I answered him right back: "Enrique, You know it is not my habit to offend you or call you names. DO know that I have begun the process of freeing myself of your vengeful influence. I have also stopped fearing you like I did. For ten years you were the one who controlled, screamed, belittled, abused me, emotionally and physically, and my children; who by the way were only five and three years old when I met you. Know that if you scream at my daughter or me again, I will always ask you to speak to us with respect. That was all said to you last night, and I repeat: next time you demand something from me screaming and disrespectfully, I WILL ignore you.

1. I am sorry if asking you to consider our daughter's needs sounds to you like preaching. I do not mean to disrespect you. My requests are simple and are as follows:
2. I ask that you bring Campanita back from Karate classes no later than 9:30 pm. every Tuesday and Wednesday. Her classes end at 9 pm. and we live only five minutes away from the YMCA. It is not healthy for her to come home at close to 10 pm. She has to eat supper and do homework.
3. My only request to you is that you be considerate and pay attention to these things that hinder our daughters health; it is not good that she ends up going to bed at 11 pm.
4. I believe that six karate classes a week for a seven year old girl is too much, but I have said nothing to you in this regard because I know how much you enjoy these activities with her.
5. I know she likes it too, but I also want her to do well in school. She has fallen behind in her reading, math and has no time to play with her friends from Monday to Thursday when she is very busy doing and practicing karate with you.
6. I set up play-dates and fun days for her because playing with girls her age and doing creative activities are good for her emotional, social and intellectual development; it is not to sabotage your time with her like you accused me of the other day. I always offer the option that if she has an activity like this you are more than welcome to take her, which you have always refused like the field trip to the museum last Monday and the play date last week.
7. I am sure the activities I'd set up for her are a lot healthier than being locked up in your apartment, in your bedroom with easily accessible pornographic material and DVD's that you have under the TV, where she spends most of her time, watching TV most of the day when she is with you.

8. I don't think it's good for her either that she goes to your neighbor's apartment where there are two grungy male adults that smoke marijuana and a thirteen year old boy who has nothing in common with our seven year old daughter. Up until now, this issue has bothered me a lot, but I have said nothing because I know how defensive and verbally abusive you get, and most importantly I want to trust your good fatherly judgment and intuition that you will be alert to any perverse situation that may arise.
9. When we first separated, we vowed that we were going to do everything in our power to make Campanita's life a happy one. We had agreed that on school days she would sleep with me so that it will be easier for her. You recognized the fact that I am more patient and can understand her needs when it comes to dressing appropriately for school, and the fact that I have a bedroom perfectly set up for a little girl.
10. We agreed that the ideal schedule for keeping her best interest in mind would be as follows:
11. On school days - Monday through Friday she sleeps with me, either I take her to school or you do. (Based on your recent request, I can take her to school and you can pick her up.)
12. Every other weekend starting Friday after school we each keep her until Sunday morning, let's say at noon or so.
13. At vacation time we each keep her half of the time.
14. On holidays we alternate - one holiday with me, and one holiday with you, each.
15. I beg of you not to forget that we are both very important to her, and also beg of you to think about her well being. We have gotten into 'fights' or disagreements over who keeps the tennis shoes or the uniform for the week. Please! This is ridiculous. Let's keep the agreement we had, for our daughter's sake; not yours, not mine, only hers.
16. Here in my house she has a suitable bedroom with play-space and toys, appropriate
17. colors for her age and gender, friends and neighbors her own age with whom she loves spending time. She has two brothers, especially one that she loves with all her heart and has been

(ever since she can pronounce the words) what she always call…'her bestest friend'
18. Please put your bitterness aside and think about your daughter's well-being and happiness. You know perfectly well she does not like sleeping with you because she has no friends. You don't understand her dressing needs, you can't do her hair, you snore and she can't sleep, you scream for no good reason, you smoke at least a pack of cigarettes per day or marijuana, you have pornography all over your place, and that makes her very uncomfortable.
19. I am very sorry I have left nothing but resentment in your heart; I hope one day all these resentments and rebukes will pass and you find it in your heart to forgive me. I have forgiven you and want nothing but good vibes amongst us."

… And all this during one day in the life of a solitary Mexican household! I honestly could not see how either Becky or Corazon could endure so many inconveniences. I tried to reply to Becky, but for some damned reason Corazon was unable to transmit the message. Damn! In it I took exception, and offered my own thoughts regarding her state of affairs with Enrique:

~ Becky, to begin with, while reading your reply to Enrique I was reminded of what historian Edward Gibbons wrote about the Romans and Barbarians (and by extension The astonished Aztecs against the fanatical Spanish Conquistadors, or you and Enrique): between equally civilized enemies, the sacrifice and courage of one will bring out the admiration and respect of the other.

But, if one enemy is civilized and the other is savage, then any show of honor, nobility and chivalry by the civilized one will only provoke greater fury, hatred and blood-lust in the savage.

Well, Becky, your reply to Enrique was very well redacted, respectful, reflective, reasonable and more than rewarding. However, Enrique, I am sorry to judge him thus, is NOT a civilized enemy. He really is the savage who will fume, fuss, fulminate and become furious with your show of nobility. If this is what you want out of him, alright then, screw him! But, if you are really extending the olive branch of peace to him, I, for one, very much doubt he will correspond by releasing the dove of concord.

I would recommend you send it to him NOT for any real desire on your part to make him happy, BUT as a ploy to show the LAW that you tried your best till the last moment, but he was just a beast and could not be reasoned with. This reply should be for your lawyer's benefit more than anything.

If, as you observe in the note, that you guys had a prior agreement and he is obviously violating it, then it is also quite obvious that he will NOT respect your offer of detente. He will go on violating it, and traumatizing your daughter in the process. Even something like the karate class is turning out to be deleterious to her upbringing and psychological health since it is adversely affecting her studies.

I loved the way you harped on his terrible habits, like leaving pornographic material around and the malignant influence of his pot-smoking friends. This is a slam-dunk for you with regard to parental rights and custody.

Thus, dear Becky, I pray you get a worthy response out of him, but don't keep your hopes up. You, more than anybody, know that it borders on the hopeless. He has a savage side to him and your reply will provoke his ire and thirst for revenge. Be sure and keep it as evidence. Remember: whatever doesn't kill you makes you stronger.

Right now you are on the cusp of showing him just how indestructible you are.

Good luck, and let me know asap how he reacts to this. ~

After some time, however, I did get a reply from her, and once again through Corazon. I was naturally glad to hear from her, but that reunion we were supposed to have was more elusive than ever. In her reply she said: ~ Thank you *F*, that is precisely my intention, to keep my correspondence as evidence for the Law. I don't give a fuck anymore, and will no longer try to keep him content. The more angry and vengeful he turns towards me, the faster he tumbles in his own weeds, don't you think? ~

Being worried now about my old school chum, I asked Corazon to forward my latest reply as soon as she could: ~ Becky, one other point about all this with Enrique: since this a domestic-family case and if witnesses should be called for, there would be none except family members to lend testimony. Therefore, I would be most willing to testify on your behalf to the fact that his allegations amount to little more than libel, or at least to defamation of the character of the mother of his child.

To boot, when the subject had come up in the past with your friends and my family back in California, they had all unambiguously said that they would be most glad to lend you all of their support, even if it means having to go to court in Mexico as witnesses.

We all admit that it would be tough, but we would be most objective as witnesses because: a. we do not know you as well as your mother did and are not tied to you by any pre-existing arrangement or agreement, yet can provide factual answers should we be called upon to give them; b. we have nothing against Enrique, and in fact some have said that they like him, which more than demonstrates their legal neutrality; c. we have all seen you many, many times interact with your children, and know too well how good you've been, and how you are with them on a daily basis, especially la "malnutrida"; and, d. we firmly believe that Enrique is a slanderer for accusing you of all this, and so would defend you like your own mother would, should we be called to the witness stand. And, if I should still be in Mexico when the case arrives before a judge, I would be willing to go to Veracruz, or wherever the case would be tried for that express purpose. Incredible? Take care, my friend ~

A couple of days later, I received her reply: ~ It is incredible what you tell me of all this. But from inside something bad, emerges something good.

Amor y besos, Becky ~

And so, that was the end of my correspondence with Becky again, and the close of this peculiarly pathetic chapter in her life.

FAMILY FEUDS

August had just turned, and no sooner had I concluded this dialogue with my dear friends when I would find myself in the middle of a contentious situation involving Felipe Ramayo, who was just supposed to serve as intermediary between myself and my as yet unfamiliar or estranged relatives. I had said my farewells to Colima, and boarded the Express bus for Jalisco. I was bound for Tepatitlan de Morelos; a city and municipality in the central part of the state. Getting there proved to be a bit rough on the buttocks, and it did not help that the vehicle's cooling system was malfunctioning. The city itself is located in an area known as Los Altos de Jalisco. I remember my father would speak with a love/hate wistfulness about the region, the fact being that he had spent his adolescence amid its dry and cold environs. Another seventy kilometers or so to the east is Guadalajara, and I'd end up there eventually. Tepatitlan meanwhile would be my place of residence for the next week. I found it amusing that the name means "Hard Stone Place" in the Nahuatl language, because almost everything about the damned place, including the beds, were quite hard on the body. No wonder other Mexicans complain that *Tapatios*, or natives of Jalisco, possess hard souls and a heads full of stones.

I enjoyed visiting its most distinctive landmarks like the Fine Baroque Cathedral and wasted sometime watching the lovely young forms at the State Agricultural University campus located nearby there. Tepatitlan, or "Tepa" for short, lived up to its reputation of being the largest producer of eggs in all Mexico; eggs, eggs, and more eggs everywhere, but no less expensive than anywhere else. Fortunately for my frustrated temper, it is also one of the biggest producers of Tequila. Many people here, mostly Criollos, practically deny that they are Mexican, insisting rather that they are French. Interestingly, the classic Fleur-de-Lys symbol is to be seen in many public areas and edifices, including on the Santuario de Guadalupe, another notable landmark.

I finally caught up with Felipe, who turned out to be a decent

Mestizo of decent parentage, gray-haired and mustachioed, soft-spoken, shy and awkward. He was courteous to me throughout our interaction, but when we spoke of my relatives, mentioned Carmela Najar or Fulgencio San Roman, he'd grow tense, nervous, almost irritated. I couldn't draw enough information out of the stoical native at first to understand exactly why he felt the way he did, but I could surmise that the rancor went back many years. I also learned that his family had worked for my ancestors across many decades, perhaps centuries. I could therefore understand his natural aversion to social rank, or perhaps it was a repressed inferiority complex that was threatening to creep out of his system.

One of the first things we discussed involved Carmela Najar's long fight with her relatives to keep the rights to her son's films and other works, which my immediate ancestors had contested. It was a fight which ended in a draw with her death because Fulgencio would have none of it. The fight was being renewed, however, by some cousins who felt that as long as the studios had deprived Fulgencio of "intellectual hegemony over studio properties" they were in their rights to renew the contention, and get the studios to own up.

There was something to be said about the intense days they'd all been having. Cousins on both sides of the tribe had met, and it was clear to everyone that everyone hated each other ~ now I know why my siblings had turned out the way they did! The oldest members were exhausted from dealing with all the litigation. They'd fought, they'd cried, but ultimately they agreed to stand firm together against the rapacious studios. The next day, Felipe and I met with Abigail, a second cousin and a most pleasant woman with pronounced Spanish features, and her lawyer. After receiving me with courtesy and affection, she confided that respective branches of the clan were behaving like the Medicis and Pazzis in Renaissance Florence ~ engaged in an internecine family feud. Both sides are directly related through Grand-uncle Arturo, and they were now fighting over much more mundane matters. We went to visit her sister Consuelo's tenant-manager who oversees her apartment complex, but had been paying rent to someone from the Gutierrez side of the family. He had recently been notified that the real owner was Consuelo Martin and not the Gutierrez family. This was significant because the Martins were facing a renter's revolt while the Gutierrez's were illegally collecting all of the rents. I had stumbled upon a family feud I knew nothing about, and it was about to get worse.

The tenant tracked Consuelo down for us, and the introductions went smoothly. She turned out to be the sweetest and most warm-hearted relative I could ever hope for, and I instantly grew fond of her. Unfortunately, she had been engaged in a long struggle with Sandro Gutierrez, also a second cousin and who over-saw legal and financial matters for his branch of the tribe. No sooner had Consuelo served us coffee and *empanadas* (pies) when Sandro, who couldn't be bothered with introductions, came storming in and screamed that Consuelo and her siblings had taken advantage of his situation because he is alone with the responsibility. In the heated exchange he went so far as to accuse them of robbing the Gutierrez portion of Arturo's legacy. After growling like a rabid wolf, he broke down and cried, squealing like a pig in front of other inquilinos (tenants) in attendance and passers-by. We were all embarrassed for him. Also, his behavior assuredly confirmed my kinship with him since my own immediate family members howl like hogs when they are overwrought and emotional. Samuel, his teen-aged son, showed up to investigate the fracas but ended up calling everyone, including me, a venomous snake, and provoking Consuelo's teen-aged son Juanito to fisticuffs. After separating them and introducing myself, which made no impression on either of them, I tried to reason first with Samuel, and asked that he not call us snakes. I tried to assuage his hysterical breast, but he wouldn't listen, just like my own family members! Juanito was more amenable to reason, and quickly simmered down.

It was truly amazing to see this spectacle unfold before my innocent eyes. Despite how awful this was, it was also comforting to perceive that justice was being served to the Martins since I had heard rumors going back a few years that the Gutierrez folks were not to be trusted.

I felt really bad afterwards for the respective teen-agers. They would inherit the feud for no purpose. For the present, they were left crying alongside their parents. Each side continued hurling invectives at one-another, accusing each-other of being harpies, and that each one had been the victim of the other. It was also obvious that the younger generation had been brain-washed by their parents, and refused to listen

A Wetback in Reverse

to reason.

After the smoke of the invectives and denunciations had cleared away, explanations emerged that shed a clear light on the matter. Allegedly, it had all started about eight years ago. Abigail had taken their mother, Dona Marta, who had been the chief arbiter of all matters related to inheritance, to America when Consuelo was pregnant with her youngest daughter, Evita. Consuelo was the only one who did not exercise physical possession of her own property, and I learned they all had inherited a good piece of real-estate. They each derived a hefty income from rentals, and weren't about to surrender their rights to the Gutierrez usurpers. Javier, their younger and now deceased brother (may he rest in peace) and who had been married to a Gutierrez cousin, Silvana (these sorts of in-bred arranged marriages still exist in parts of Mexico), offered to help Consuelo take possession, and provided her a small loan to cover the transfer of possession, legal fees, maintenance, et cetera. When some old tenants had passed away, Javier immediately took possession of, and rented two vacated apartments without their mother's approval, ostensibly to ensure that Consuelo would pay him back before she was again solvent.

Rumors then ran about that Consuelo had sold the apartments to Javier, which is something they could not legally do since they were as yet not legally hers. The arrangement between Consuelo and Javier was that he would eventually buy the whole property. Everyone understood, however, that Consuelo did need to take possession of her property and present the owner's documents to the notary. Others had intervened by trying to convince their mother, but their well-intentioned involution regrettably provoked many fights between them. Because they had defended Consuelo's cause against Dona Marta's stubborn contrariness, most of the siblings were not on speaking terms for months. Dona Marta had always been angry about this move, and in reality she never got over it.

At this point, the long simmering feud between the Gutierrez clan and the Martins erupted. Felipe had inveighed against the Martins and lent his support to the untrustworthy Gutierrez's even after Sandro had exploited him, and suffered him to spy on Dona Marta. Accusations and calumnies had flown back and forth for years, and the strangest was that Sandro had maintained a gay-incestuous infatuation with his cousin Javier, but despised Consuelo because she threatened to expose them. As a consequence, their respective wives, Silvana and Leandra, mutually despised each-other, and actively inveigled their husbands to participate in their duple-faced treacheries and domestic trouble-making.

Javier finally proposed that he and Consuelo should exchange properties. He had already taken possession of a valuable commercial property next to Consuelo's apartment complex. He now wanted to exchange the property in question for a property that, much to my astonishment, my own father had sold to Dona Marta decades before, and Mario, the eldest brother, was poised to inherit. Not long before Dona Marta had decided to bestow her consent, it was discovered that Javier had promised to share the revenues of, and eventually turn over the whole complex to Sandro if he would keep their sexual affair a secret, and deny all accusations should Consuelo or anyone else unmask them. Felipe Ramayo had acted as their go-between, and stood to benefit from the exchange. Mario abruptly intervened, and forced Consuelo to refuse the offer since he had always known about Sandro's evil intentions. Felipe would lose his pay-off, and thus nurtured a scalding hatred for Mario.

Some very tense days were ahead of them, but eventually Javier informed Consuelo that he did not want to go through with the property purchase because the deal he wanted to strike with Mario fell through. They agreed thereon that Javier was going to rent the rooms until he'd recovered the amount of the loan.

Well, it has been eight years since that tumultuous period. Felipe had not recovered from the loss and harbored acrimony for all the Martins. When Javier died, Consuelo felt *sooo* guilty about *pooor* Sandro (and Leandra) that she promised she would hesitate a bit longer before moving to regain possession of the rents; by this time Javier had already collected four times the money he had originally loaned to Consuelo. Furthermore, Consuelo gave Samuel, who'd adored his uncle Javier, her promise that she would turn the collected rents over to him until he graduated from the University.

Two months before my unexpected arrival, Samuel had graduated from UNAM with a Bachelors degree in Business Administration.

Consuelo then talked to Sandro and said, "four years have passed,

Samuel graduated, so I will now take possession of my rentals." Sandro flew into a rage busting up furniture, and Leandra went about screaming that the deal with Javier had been a sale and not a repayment, and she was truly a venomous "Medusa."

Sandro, who had reconciled with Consuelo after Javier's death, and after a hypocritical profession and show of unconditional love and loyalty for her, had now declared *war*, refused to allow his children to inter-act with their Martin cousins, slandered and insulted her every time he could get away with it. Hence, that is why they had to bring in lawyers, so Consuelo informed me, and notify the tenants that she was and is the real, legal owner of those confounded apartments.

It was very sad; it was also obvious that they mutually loved their respective nieces and nephews. Regrettably, the Gutierrez children were led to believe that the Martins are assholes and bitches, that they had taken advantage of their poor witless parents, and left them hanging until they'd made vengeance their own.

God! What a welcome this family feud had proved! All that I had come to do was beg for some family records. With this war I had stumbled upon, I was left doubtful of ever realizing my goal.

My distant cousins, however, especially the Martins, were very hospitable and solicitous, and I was most pleased to have met them.

They insisted I stay longer than I had planned, and this allowed me the opportunity to get them to share relevant family anecdotes with me. I was, however, most distressed with Felipe Ramayo and the part he played in this conflict.

After things had simmered down I inquired about the property my father had supposedly sold to Dona Marta. All innuendos of cheating and double-dealing aside, I learned that the property in question, with a fine Italian style villa built behind some majestic almond trees shading the enclosed entrance, had in fact once belonged to Carmela Martin ~ it was the home in which she had given birth to her son, Fulgencio San Roman.

I begged Abigail and Consuelo to show me around the premises, and they cheerfully agreed. It was truly a stately home, but was now devoid of personal items. As we inspected the premises, my cousins confessed that the arguments with the Gutierrez relatives had drained the fight out of them, and weren't certain if they would proceed with their lawsuit against the movie studios. They further admitted that no one had contacted Fulgencio about their intentions, and had not convinced themselves that they had a legal right to the intellectual-artistic properties in question. Much to their consternation, they'd recently learned that the survivors of Rafael Ramirez Rojas were also contesting the film rights, and were putting up quite a fight against both the studios and my relatives. The Gutierrez cousins were just as interested in getting their hands on them, but had no intention of sharing the spoils should they win. The emerging facts together formed one ugly, amorphous, and despicable truth of which I wanted no part.

DRUG PUSHERS AND DOPERS

Terrible news was had out of Reynosa: Fulgencio San Roman, accomplished film-maker and writer, was stricken with the porcine flu. The fact that he was over 90 years old cast a dark shadow over his prognosis; the sad revelation just made me wonder how Andres was doing. Would Fulgencio perish before I had a chance to meet him again, but this time knowing full who he was and his importance to the culture of Mexico and World Cinema? Would either of them die before I had accomplished my mission? There was still no word to confirm or deny his knowing of the scathing feud being fought over his movies. He'd probably and typically reply that he once thought that old-age had made him more patient, but the truth was that he just didn't give a shit anymore!

Furthermore, he had long since disavowed possession of his natal home, and refused to arbitrate ~ an action which would have resolved the feud between all sides, including the Rojas relatives. Thus I would leave, eventually, my newly acquainted cousins just like I'd found them ~ feuding. Meanwhile, problems were blurting forth all around cousin Mario over his small operation merchandise distribution business; it turned out that his employees, a couple of them nephews of Felipe Ramayo, had been using his transport vehicles to run contraband goods, and perhaps even illicit drugs, between state lines and occasionally the Mexico-U.S.A border. Mexico checks only 10 percent of the quarter-of-a-million vehicles that cross the border each day, according to statistics the police, who had arrived to harass Mario, shared with us. By measuring the volume and carriage of cars to detect if they are unusually ponderous, and running out-of-state license plate numbers through a database of registered vehicles operating in questionable locales, the local drug-control enforcement agency hoped to trap more hidden contraband. Regrettably, Mario's employees, for whom he was directly responsible, had gotten away with some pretty heavy stuff. If I recall properly, the American enforcers had long weighed and reviewed the license plates of incoming vehicles, but this measuring technology is relatively new to the Mexican officials who are now installing it at all border and interstate customs inspection-points.

Since finding out about the dirty little habits of his workers, Mario had great cause for concern. One of them would admit, eventually, that they had been smuggling electronics, drugs (mostly marijuana) and even people for a few years now. Mario was aghast and on the brink of panic. What could I do but feel terrible about the whole thing; Mario was a genuinely sweet and trusting guy, and I'd hate to see any thing bad happen to him. An outstanding shipment, incidentally, was in transit from Matamoros, across the Rio Grande from Texas, and the new technology, the police also informed us, had recently been installed at check-points thereabout. The three workers in question, one of their peers asserted, had gone intending to transport undocumented workers to the fields of Western Texas, but knew nothing about all this. To me, this was an irony par-excellence.

Gathering details of this concerted effort to stem the tide of contraband goods and illegal drugs proved easier than I'd supposed. This systematized endeavor would be a troubling change: Inspections would now be mostly enforced by lights that alternately flash green or red. Regular border-crossers agree that they rarely see red, no pun intended. Inside the country, strict gun control regulations proscribe weapons sales with calibers above a .38 pistol. To purchase one, like Mario himself wanted to, all citizens must get a license from the Defense Ministry. North of the Texas border, notwithstanding, the narco cartels cheerfully pay *straw buyers* to receive pre-paid arms at gun shops, gun shows or flea markets, then resell the guns to dim-witted smugglers like Mario's workers.

It is said that officials have traced almost all of the arms procured at places of drug-related violence all over the country to American distribution networks. The said arms are usually .50 caliber or higher powered rifles and ammunition that can pierce the armor of Mexican police and soldiers ~ this fact really scared them.

Prior to my undertaking this journey, guns like these were hardly seen in, let alone transported to, Mexico. Mario said he had known about the increasing troubles Mexico was grappling with, having previously dealt with the local bureau charged with controlling the flow of alcohol, fire-arms, tobacco and explosives. Yet, these dangerous and easily concealable guns had become the weapons of choice for these modern desperadoes.

The modernization trials coincided with the Mexican government's campaign to recruit hundreds more special agents to root out the narco thugs using drug-rooting dogs and sophisticated X-ray screening detectors to halt the illegal traffic and the spreading narco-related violence as well as contain the gun trading. The federal security agency and the law-enforcers were trying to step up their commitment to this containment and to reinforce the borders against out-bound as well as inbound delinquency. None of this, naturally, was comforting to a disappointed and brooding Mario.

The Martin siblings worried that Sandro and Leandra would conspire with the snooping agents, much to the Martins' humiliation. Moreover, Felipe Ramayo was rumored to be carrying out his long-desired coup against his nemesis by informing the Federales that Mario was guilty of what his nephews had done. This slander would rank highly in the annals of treachery! If he'd known I fully sympathized with the Martins, he would have ratted me out as well. Their presence was too close for comfort, and I squirmed every moment they were there investigating every detail, right down to Mario and Silvana's underwear drawers.

The stumbling police were skeptical about their prospects of retarding the illegal weapons traffic. Dedicated gun-runners easily transport thousands of arms in small quantities each time, breaking them apart and tucking them in valises or even inside household appliances, and no one would get hurt ... so they say.

One of the officers warned Mario that, "If the vehicle has no criminal past, and is verifiably legal, it shouldn't be stopped or inspected. Questions will be asked, though, so be ready to answer." Contrabandists can also outflank inspection-points all the time, running weapons in other directions along the same desolate corridors that bring undocumented workers and narcotics north.

While the crafty cartels get most of their high-caliber weapons from America, they turn to Central America for additional military-grade ordnance like bazookas and hand-tossed bombs.

"You're seeing truly military-worthy weaponry, like grenade launchers," the officer said. "They're not arriving from *Gringolandia* (America). The grenades they use, you're looking at items smuggled in from Central America."

I had previously heard that the Mexican military, which is often outmatched and outwitted by the narco-traffickers, has not been an important source of weapons despite all of the corrupt soldiers known to have sold out to the cartels.

Many of the cartels' weapons could be spare-parts from Central America's civil wars. Raymundo Francisco-Capote, an heir to the Juarez cartel, one of Mexico's most despicable narco-trafficking empires, was snatched by the Federales as he jogged through a city park before I arrived in Jalisco. This came just a couple of days before Mexican and American ministers rendezvoused to coordinate interdiction of escalating narco-trafficking related murders and destruction.

To my dismay, I later learned that one of Felipe's nephews, Jose Arias, would inherit a top position in the Juarez cartel from the father of his recently killed comrade, Amado "El Lagarto" (the alligator) Francisco-Capote, brother of Raymundo. He bore the additional pseudonym "Pharmacist of the Friendly Skies" for sending jet-planes crammed with marijuana and crack-cocaine to American states. The father was considered one of Mexico's top narco-traffickers when he died in 2000 during gastric-bypass surgery ~ he weighed over 350 pounds, but was only five-feet tall. Mario explained that the besieged remnant of his organization was still "one of Mexico's most ruthless organized criminal gangs, which once controlled the primary transportation routes for illegal drug shipments into the United States."

Mario also informed me that this Francisco-Capote was second only to his uncle Venustiano Feliponcio Francisco-Capote in the gang, whose vicious fights with upstart cartels have spilled the blood of nearly 2,000 persons, innocent as well as guilty, in Juarez alone.

During the week I was in Colima, Mexico's government posted a 30 million Pesos reward for Venustiano Francisco-Capote and 34 other top gang-lord suspects. Another suspect on the list already had been taken captive, as had two alleged cartel runners facing less tempting bounties. Neither of them was a nephew of Felipe.

A Wetback in Reverse

During my third day in Tepatitlan I witnessed masked police officers wearing helmets and bulletproof vests haul off a number of suspects operating just a few hundred yards from Mario's and Consuelo's homes. The young men, looking a little like average college students (and probably were) wearing square-framed glasses and a track suit emblazoned with "Abercrombie & Fitch," showed little fear before the automatic weapons pointed at their faces.

We'd all heard that something like this would happen, but were nonetheless surprised when we actually witnessed the proceedings. The whole shebang had been the local *Chota's* ("cops") way of aiming at ways to halt the smuggling across the border as well as original tactics for combating the cartels, which have promoted violence in both countries.

Before we had a chance to finish our thick, Veracruzano coffee and *Campechana* cakes, we learned from a radio-broadcast that the "Tepa" police had apprehended Raymundo Francisco-Capote as he was trying to escape custody, and was shot through the chest. He was expected to recover, nevertheless. Apparently, he was heading for the mansion-lined neighborhood of Las Lomas, a very swanky area north of the city. No one could say what he was attempting, but most were relieved to learn of his bloody capture.

Two weeks prior to the shoot-out with Capote, police had arrested Jacobo *El Gavilan* (the Hawk) Tamargo, a putative top- figure in Mexico's Michoacan drug cartel. The government described Tamargo's father, Ismael *El Negro* Tamargo as "perhaps the most crafty leader of cartels in Mexico." Among his cronies at the scene was Arnoldo Ramayo, another of Felipe's rascally nephews. Furthermore, he had been using an alias, Romulo Peralta Menendez, supposedly the name of his now deceased mentor in the contraband business. He was trying to pass himself off as a businessman, but his common, almost sleazy features raised many an suspicious eyebrow. A chota friend of Mario's later confided to us that the local posse comitatus tracked down the rotten bums through their jilted girlfriends, who'd complained that their beaus owed them money for services rendered. The Tepatitlan rubes possessed records showing that the sister of Arnoldo had been married to Rodolfo Durazo Tamargo, a brother of the cartel leader. Interestingly, I'd also learned that Rodolfo was a convert to Judaism, and allegedly had paid to train with the Mossad, the national intelligence agency of Israel.

Boy! What these desperadoes will do to secure and perpetuate their felonious organization, eh?

How terrible ... How senseless! Before I ever set foot in Mexico I'd learned that over 9,000 people had been slaughtered in narco-related violence in Mexico since Presidente Felipe Calderon took office in 2006. What could come after he departs? Alas, better let the foxes take over the hen-house, Mario complained, "they're already in there doing what they want, and all the stink about interdiction is just a front to keep the common herd complacent."

And, I would agree!

JEWS IN MEXICO

Jews have survived and thrived in Mexico since the dark days of the Inquisition. Today the community numbers over 50,000, concentrated mostly in Mexico City. Additional communities exist in the states of Jalisco, mostly in big cities like Guadalajara, and in prosperous sections of Culiacan, Monterrey, Veracruz, and the border town of Tijuana.

There weren't too many Jews in Tepatitlan, but the number of Jewish people in Guadalajara has been contracting for a long time. There are only about 250 families left. The remnants are made up of an equal number of Sephardic and Ashkenazy Jews. Beforehand, the two groups had their own synagogues and did not intentionally mix; in time the separate groups got together with the result that practically all of the younger families are presently composed of Sephardic-Ashkenazy unions. There is a community center similar to that of a Jewish Community Center in the United States, which is the center of Jewish activities in the greater metropolitan area. The center serves as a gathering place for family support in the midst of a sea of Roman Catholics, and also houses the synagogue. Because the Jews of Guadalajara rarely fool around with the non- Jewish community, most of the younger rakes and rapscallions who are only interested in sowing their wild Semitic oats are inclined to move to Mexico City, which has a larger Jewish community. This is the main reason for the lack of Jewish pornography in Guadalajara.

In the last few decades the community became Modern Orthodox, which caused a sizable part of the community to separate and form a new Conservative temple and community center. This move to Modern Orthodox cemented deep divisions within the community, tearing families apart, and having them choose between the two temples, intermarriage and conversions are the principal problems irritating the divide. Among well known Jews from Guadalajara are actors, comics, producers, promoters, agents, singers and other entertainers who have enjoyed as much fame and respect in the Spanish-speaking world as they do in Hollywood.

There are also some Mexicans who consider themselves descendants of so-called Conversos, or Jews who converted to Roman Catholicism to escape the Inquisition, but retained some Jewish heritage ~ such as burning candles on Friday nights. For example, the famous painter Diego Rivera was a Converso descendant. Another one who I never expected to be a Converso on his father's side was Fulgencio San Roman. In a recent article I'd researched about him, he purportedly said back in 1945 after learning about the Holocaust: "The Jewish factor in my ancestry is the motivating element in my life. From this has flowered a compassionate understanding for the downtrodden masses which illuminates my imagination and all my art."

All of which brings up an interesting point about my object of fascination: Fulgencio had actually translated an edition of the MIDRASH in to Spanish during his college days, and the version is putatively still used in some campuses around Jalisco, and Estado de Mexico. This discovery just left me dumbfounded, and as I dusted off old archives in Jalisco I couldn't help but wonder what he was doing in Tamaulipas!

In the edition he translated he included a short list of questions he'd asked himself, using it as an introduction of sorts to the book:

1. Were you brought up on the MIDRASH?
2. What exactly is it? Is it worth getting into?
3. What about Rabbi Hillel? Did his writings influence your way of thinking?

Strangely enough, he didn't answer his own questions. He simply included a personal definition in the prologue to the translation:

~ *Definition of Midrash* (according to Fulgencio): While the Talmud deals primarily with questions of Jewish law as deduced from the Torah, a parallel body of work developed at the same time, using the Torah as a source for homiletic discussions. The different works of the Midrash are generally (but not always) linked to specific books of the Bible. Thus, for example, the most important work in the field, the Midrash Rabbah (the "Great Midrash"), is a commentary, as it were, on the Five Books of Moses. While the Midrash does on occasion contain items dealing with Jewish law, its major purpose is homiletic, offering insights into both the Torah and human nature and giving guidance as to how a person should live and behave. ~

That was concise enough, but as the curator of the film-art library remarked, "Jews learn some of this growing up in Sunday school. It's been over 40 years since we've had actual Jews come in to borrow or study this book. I once read it, but it was so boring I don't really remember it. I wouldn't spend too much time on it.

However, if you become wealthy or realize a dream of yours once after reading the Midrash, I think you should consider becoming Jewish because it will mean that Jewish prayers work!"

Fascinating! Now I was thinking that I could make a good Scholar of Jewish Studies. If I were to convert, it would be to gain access to a considerable store of philosophy and knowledge ~ it wouldn't be to get my own dreidel or a free circumcision. As I considered the issue more, I did want to study more. There is that rich tradition, from Philo, Josephus and Eusebius, right down to Hillel, Maimonides and Benedictus de Spinoza, that is inspiring. Thence-forward I would be hungrily taking in this fabulous, older documentary I'd found in the film archives that is presented and narrated by Fulgencio San Roman called CIVILIZATIONS OF THE AMERICAS AND THE JEWS. It was the most fascinating documentary work about the origins of civilizations I had seen since LEGACY-*The Origins of Civilization* by Michael Wood. After all, it can and should be said that both Christianity and Islam are the wayward children of Judaism, right? Mexican Catholics are taught and are all too aware that Jews have made great contributions to Mexico's society as well as to Christianity by its very meaning, existence and teachings.

For me, therefore, it wasn't a stretch of the imagination in the least. I just might feel very much at home in such an environment. After all, the Jewish ritual seems so much more akin to the Roman Catholic or Greek Orthodox ceremonies that I've witnessed here in Mexico than that which passes for church-services amongst Pentecostal and Baptist Christians; weird gatherings that look nothing like something I would ever want to get involved with, and are filled with singing and screaming about casting out sin, ...just ridiculous. I know all this for a

fact, having traveled with missionaries way back in the early 1990s!
Once I get through my present challenge without the Federales ever finding out about my illegality, maybe I'll check out what I can about furthering my Jewish Studies.

And, if and when I return to California before getting caught, not only will it lend gravity to the power of Jewish prayer, but it will be the fulfillment of a great omen that my finding out about Fulgencio would lead to a meeting of, and with Destiny!

Before leaving to attend a dinner hosted by cousin Consuelo, I pondered over the additional fact that Fulgencio's distant Jewish relatives actually pretended not to be Jewish, but rather agnostic Catholics, if there is such a thing. A half-sister of his who had vociferously denied her Jewish ancestry, Celestina, sent the film-library an old letter with his deranged writing (or so she described it in an accompanying addendum) she'd found about a year before I undertook this journey, with the proviso that the curators never inform Fulgencio of its procurement. In the letter he talked about Mexican orphans in the Pacific Coast states of Baja California, Sonora, Sinaloa and Nayarit, which he loved to visit because of the fantastic fishing to be had, and the serene beauty of the topography.

More importantly, he remarks about how proud he was of his movies because in them was shed a critical light on the corruption and inefficiency of local and state agencies and the federal government with respect to the care and treatment of innumerable, anonymous orphans ~ that the secular governments never ceased to attack and divest the Church of its traditional roles as educators and care-takers of the downtrodden and helpless, but when it came to the issue of orphans the respective governments both turned a blind eye. Celestina had sent it to them in order to silence many speculating critics who'd perpetuated the rumor that Fulgencio had disavowed his own films. Worse yet, he complains in the same letter that some anonymous vagrants knocked on his door a couple of times insisting they were long lost children of his and had decided to search for him, showing up at his home 25 years later. His detractors were all too willing to believe the worst about him since he had been complaining about the Mexican Orphans problem for more than 30 years. The impostors probably believed their own lies and thought they truly had a chance to become his adopted sons!

The hours passed, and I attended Consuelo's dinner party in a state of mental turpitude. She served a delectable roast turkey stuffed with peppers and sweetened ground-beef meat-balls. The atmosphere was as tense as it had been when I first visited their home. She was sweet and solicitous as before, but caveated against my staying long in *Tepa*. Yet, she hoped that I could somehow help by procuring documents that attested to the legitimacy of the Martin claims to the San Roman movies, since my family blood-ties to his mother were stronger than theirs. Otherwise, they'd all be moving in to the depths of the hell they all helped to create. "Please tell our relatives in California that we'd adopt them into our immediate family," said Consuelo, "if they help you to pull this off. We would dedicate the recovered films to you as thanks!"

Well! That last offer certainly tickled my fancy. How could I refuse?

The following day I went to dinner with young Samuel and his friend, Vicente; he had lost his brother Ricardo 3 months before to heroin at the age of 20, a victim of an addiction foisted on him by Felipe's nephews. Vicente complained that he'd been a true mental wreck, and found comfort in being with Samuel. As for the latter, he apologized for his prior comportment, and wanted to get to know me better because I had been around and had published a couple of books, a fact which intrigued him. Pride he took in our relationship, albeit distant, but Vicente's problems took up most of our conversation. Our hearts ached for him, but there was nothing I could say to console his grief. Worse yet, he felt he couldn't return because it was too painful for him to come home every evening and sleep in the same room where his beloved Ricardo had died. So, he was staying with Samuel and his family during this time, and would stay until he could decide what to do next.

After wasting two hours in a cantina, we dined in a restaurant called *Benito El Holgazan'* (Benny The Bum). I had a savory shrimp and oyster cocktail followed by barely palatable broiled scallops.

The next day would make 10 since I'd arrived in Jalisco, and was getting restless to visit other states on my agenda. For the time being, both Samuel and me agreed to Vicente's request to put out a prayer chain dedicated to his brother's celestial care.

THE TREATY OF HIDALGO AND THE TROUBLE WITH WETBACKS

Article VIII of the Treaty of Hidalgo (which ended the Mexican - American War back in 1848) guaranteed that Mexicans who remained more than one year in the ceded lands would automatically become full-fledged American citizens (or they could declare their intention of remaining Mexican citizens); however, the American Senate modified Article IX, changing the first paragraph and excluding the last two. Among the changes was that Mexican nationals would "be admitted at the proper time (to be judged by the Congress of the United States)" instead of "admitted as soon as possible."

Apparently, some people never got the notice, and Mexicans have been battling for their rights to American residency ever since. Every time a Mexican crosses the border in to America, documented or not, he/she enters a territory that belonged to Mexico but was torn away from the motherland by fraud and illegal conquest, or so he/she had been taught in primary school. Many historians would agree. Americans do not! So, the sad spectacle of ignorant, illiterate, utterly destitute peasants entering illegally to grab at any opportunity for work has perpetuated the human tragedy till the present day.

Whilst I prepared to tour greater Guadalajara, news was had that no less than 70 hopeful migrants had suffocated to death in the trailer of a transport truck coming out of Saltillo, Coahuila that was headed for the border with Texas. Dozens more had been rescued, though were unconscious at the time, after Saltillo police acting on suspicion forced open the carrier on a foggy Sunday morning.

Raul Benavidez, a senior police official in the city of Saltillo, said the bulk-load container the truck was transporting was attempting to enter Texas and was purposely headed for Chicago, Illinois. He remarked that most of the victims were Lipan Apache peasants who had been desperate to escape their drought ravaged lands, and feared that their own government would expropriate them for their failure to pay taxes. More than 100 people had been forced into the 50-foot-long (15-meter-long) metal container, Benavidez reported. Furthermore, survivors were rushed to the Red Cross Clinic, many of them unconscious. Worse still, the corrupt clinic workers, employees of a gratis charitable organization, had the audacity to present the patients with a bill for medical services!

How pathetic, I thought. Here I was afraid I'd be caught for enjoying myself in their country without papers, and there they were losing their lives for a chance to make a buck in America and save their traditional lands! All that the senior Saltillo official could report was that 70 had been pronounced dead without ever having set foot in America. Once the trailer had been forced open, television footage ensued which showed more than three-score dehydrated corpses. Most were stripped to the waist while others were fully naked. Then, to add insult to tragedy, volunteers where shown brutishly tossing the corpses out to be lined up eventually on the gravelly road next to the vehicle. The stink from the container led to suspicions that some might have perished days before, but not even the survivors were willing to talk about their horrid experience. All that the local officials could say was that they'd be "detaining" the *coyote* (the smuggler/driver) while they prepared for their investigation.

It is no mystery that South-Western Mexico lies on a well-trodden path for smugglers whom export hapless desperadoes from destitute countries like Guatemala and Mexico praying to find work and liberty in America, Europe and elsewhere.

Elsewhere during that sodden week, Michoacano police captured Antonio David *El Caca* (the "turd") Garcia, notorious as one of a dozen Zacatecas-based narco-traffickers mixed up in the bloody killings of a dozen Salvadorans aboard a bus some months before. Stumbling sleuths reported that Garcia's smuggler-gang was allegedly searching for a rival trafficker's cargo when they forced the bus to stop in eastern Michoacan. They didn't find any pot or cocaine, but killed and flayed the bodies of the passengers, some of whom they were convinced were members of the rival gang. Garcia, I was to learn, was the second suspect arrested in the case.

I must apologize for overly-concerning myself with all this drama. The issue of drug-trafficking and the explosion of the number of related crimes being committed throughout the country give a poor impression of just how perilous lies the state of civil matters in Mexico. The thing is that I was so excited that I had the chance to view the documentaries and obtained other information about my ancestors, that I blocked out most news until the shock of them awakened me to the impending reality. Since I was constantly on the move and depending on public transports, I had to be mindful of the possibility of a kid-napping or hijacking by local narco-traffickers.

Speaking of kid-napping, while in Guadalajara I'd learned that another crime I had to worry about was taking place: Enrique had tried to kid-nap Campanita, and intended to smuggle her into the United States. To him it was a question of migration and getting back "his property," according to his macho-chauvinistic Mexican perspective. Thanks to trusty Corazon, I was able to communicate via web-cam and Internet with Becky. I just had to make it to the nearest Internet Cafe' near the grandiose Gothic-Baroque cathedral.

When we were finally connected, it took a while before I could get the video camera to work, and Corazon suddenly appeared in a window-video screen and said aloud, "Freddy has connected to us, and we can see him live. I think he is available to chat with others."

I sat behind a desk with malodorous busy-bodies behind me peaking in. My friend and me then exchanged pleasantries, a few reproaches about not maintaining contact, and then laughed about the wayward, feckless fate that brought us together, then tore us apart and hurled us in opposite directions. At that point Becky appeared on another video window, and we started to chat. It was nerve-wracking because they referred to Enrique right away. I wasn't sure of the topic so asked, "Who are you two plotting against?" and they confided that they'd been arguing about the threatened kid-napping. Afterwards they skirted the subject as much as they could especially since it was so painful to Becky, and Corazon promised she wouldn't say more about Enrique, but my curiosity had been whetted. Overcome with sudden emotion, Becky broke her composure and blurted out, "Hey, it is time to feed my daughter. It is very late, so this will have to wait for another day."

That's what happened, so Corazon and I were left to squirm.

While she and I chatted about recent events, Becky suddenly reappeared and begged, "Please forgive me, both of you, that I had to make you wait, but we had already spoken about my not feeling comfortable with this subject."

Corazon and I pardoned her, and assured her of our indulgence.

She went on, "You guys know that I am sick to death of putting up with Enrique's character and comportment. How he treats my sons and me is beyond contempt. I have been really depressed because of what he yelled at me. With the threat of kidnapping, which he is capable of attempting, I just felt like dying, like wishing I had never been born. I also wished I had never had kids."

Corazon tried to assure her that we understood her feelings, and I expressed my sympathy considering the violence I'd put up with in my own family. Becky went on, "I felt like a cockroach because Enrique feels he is so good, and he had the audacity to say that I'd abused him. He told me that he is going to take our child no matter what happens. I'm really afraid of what he might do ... I'm a weak hen. Forgive me, but I don't want to speak of this right now."

She tuned out, and once again Corazon and I were left to squirm.

Perhaps her rantings revealed a part of her personality that no one knew about, and it was obvious that she desperately needed help. She wanted the world to know how she felt but couldn't bring herself to admit to her failings. She reappeared after a few minutes and tearfully uttered, "My bones hurt ... I feel trapped, and don't know what to do. At times I feel like a big turd because I see that Enrique succeeds at troubling me at times. He tried to be nice when we'd meet at some restaurant to talk about the welfare of our daughter, and at the close of our conversations he hugs me, and tells me that we have to try harder to overcome our problems. If I relent to his supplications, my children will get the worst of it. If I defy him outright, my children will get the worst of it."

At this point Corazon interrupted and asked what she meant to do, to which Becky replied, "I want to give him another chance because I still love him, and I have to be honest and admit that he is not totally bad. But, I despise it when he yells at me. If I go back to him, I feel like I am betraying my sons. If I sue him for divorce and spousal support, I feel like I will put them through a special kind of Hell. They don't deserve this life. They deserve a peaceful life, so what can I do?"

I then intervened and assured Becky, "First of all, please, never apologize for something like this. Your drama is our drama, and we certainly have burdened you with our selfish bullshit."

Then Corazon interrupted and said, "Truly, Beccita (her pet-name for her) you are facing a great burden. You know, since my mother knows all about your drama, she's always asking if anything new has happened with you. I have shared a very few tidbits about your wanting to divorce him and move your family to America and such, not much else. But, our mothers, having merciless opinions as you can imagine, said, 'Enrique will not change, he will go on with his malevolent ways, and Becky will go on regretting her decision; regretting not having left him the sooner.' And yet, Freddy and me understand them, that you don't want to do it for fear of what might happen to your children, even though they suffer more than anybody else in any case."

Wishing to express my sympathy, I interjected my own thoughts, "Look Becky, from this point of view, and speaking as one who went through the same shit with my parents, you are caught in the middle of a terrible dilemma: you are damned if you do, and damned if don't! How can you justify one decision or the other when, clearly, you still love the man though you can't stand to be with him anymore!"

Corazon quickly picked up on the point and remarked, "From my point of view, if you don't mind my imposing my thoughts on you my girlfriend, to live with fear is to invite death to the dinner table, metaphorically speaking. Nothing, absolutely nothing is more horrible than to accommodate your life to make room for fear. This is when you most need your courage, and you must do the right thing for your kids. If they, specifically Campanita, really don't need him, and you pay all the bills anyway, this is the time to serve Enrique the lesson that, despite the love you share, in the end he does not matter. He is *Nothing*!"

My lovely friend made an important point ~ he really did not matter in their lives, any more. Her cause was righteous, and if he could learn this once the divorce papers are finalized, she could look forward to closure. Regrettably for her own conscience, she felt her relationship might still have a chance, and that Enrique might truly change. Becky deluded herself that he would do anything to get her back after seeing how determined she was.

I warned her, "If you give in to his entreaties, together with the veiled threat that he will keep Campanita, he will never respect you. That is human nature, and it WILL happen that way."

As Becky squirmed with doubtful resignation, Corazon pressed her, "Your fears are justifiable, yet, Becky, you are in the Right. Don't make the mistake that my mother did with my father. She never made the effort to educate herself about the rights you and your children have against an often abusive, often cruel, sometimes violent person, just like my father was. Enrique is all these things, and you can't afford to vacillate when the lives of your children are at stake!"

The last statement almost shocked Becky into speechlessness, and I tried to remind her, "The Law is entirely on your side, and will force Enrique to support you and Campanita, like it or not. Even if you are just bluffing, you might consider telling him that you spoke to the police and to a lawyer, and they both told you that the Law is on your side. He does not stand a chance of legally taking Campanita from you. If he tries to run away with her, the authorities already know about your case and will be watching him, and that kid-napping he'd threatened will get him 20 years in prison, even if Campanita is his daughter. We are not living in The Middle-Ages. It is good that this is the Age of Respect for Human Rights. You are in the drivers seat!"

"Even if you end up staying in Mexico, Becky," Corazon averred to our trembling friend, "he has to learn once and for all that you have him by the balls, *ACCORDING TO THE LAW!*

If fear and love for him are what have you indecisive right now, this is all that anyone can tell you, that this cannot be about sentimentality and worries of family ties. These worries only led you to feel like you would rather be dead. It has to be about what is right, and what your legal status is under the laws of this land."

As she was making her point and Becky was sobbing, I followed up, "No tears, no more begging, it has to be about the Law, especially if he is threatening to kidnap Campanita and steel her away illegally to America. That is another lesson we learned with my family after my brother Alberto had committed so much shit against the rest of us. Our mother begged and cried, and gave him chance after chance, until, finally, she called in the Law. He surely suffered and had to go rehabilitation, but finally he was broken of his arrogance, his violence and dependence on drugs. He begged my mother to forgive him, and pleaded with her to intercede on his behalf. It took a long while, but it happened, and we have been safe and secure from Alberto ever since."

To which Becky abruptly responded, "If only the stupid old hag of Enrique's mother had done the same with him, god damn it!"

Corazon continued, "Needless to remind you, but you have your whole life ahead. You may end up having to call the Law, once you have surmounted your fears of Enrique. Again, you just cannot live your life in fear. It is a living death sentence ... A sentence that you are still living through."

... And with that, our somber and tearful web-cam conversation came to an end.

DRUG ADDICTION IN THE FAMILY

I was left doleful because our long vaunted web-cam reunion had ended with sorrow and lachrymose au-revoirs. Previously, I thought I'd never get another chance to talk to Becky again, so I put all of my hopes in this video-conferencing. Now I was more confused and perturbed about her case than ever. Would there be another chance to hook up again by way of resourceful Corazon? I think we both were anxious to be kept abreast of new episodes in the heated drama. For my part, I just had to wait, pray, and continue with my investigation of genealogical references, and looking up literature about Fulgencio; the latest news out of Reynosa was that his condition had been stabilized, but he was far from recovering his health.

After another day of brooding and gloominess in Guadalajara, I took advantage of a special "pilgrims" tour of San Juan de Los Lagos; a gorgeous Churrigueresque colonial gem in the highlands of northeastern Jalisco. Other pilgrims arrived in a series of pedestrian, cyclist or horseback processions, which took days, weeks or months. The basilica is very beautiful with its looming twin towers, and is the second most visited shrine in Mexico. Upon arriving, I gasped at the sight of innumerable pilgrims lining the city streets. They had covered a great distance on their knees with the help of relatives who extended *petates* (mats made of dried palm-leaves) in their path right up to the altar of the basilica. It was an inspiring ... sickening sight!

San Juan (I could see for myself) was hurting from a rising level of violence. While there was no regular newspaper or other sources of information I could rely upon, some residents I spoke to admitted to having witnessed (or participated in) a number of violent affrays between the police and ne'er-do-wells. My God! This place is so quaint, elegant, historic and touristic that I would not have been more surprised than if it was Disneyland we'd been referring to; in this "sacred" town, violence of that sort was heretofore not known in their daily routine. The war declared by their president against narco-traffickers changed everything. Some of the destructive reactions have been attributed to the growing salience of drug abuse amongst Jalisco youngsters. While narco-trafficking from this state to America was a rumored concern amongst some enterprising San Juan families, addiction to these drugs was surfacing as a deadly anxiety for the community. San Juan is no longer a point of access and transit but sadly an end destination for these illegal substances.

As I got acquainted with the sights and reveled in the stupefying clang of tolling bells from the great towers of the basilica resounding boomingly in our ears, I over-heard heated discussions between locals. Gulping their flagons of beer in the open cafe' and gesturing wildly and angrily, they had a row about a recently appointed tribunal in Guadalajara that was on the verge of sentencing the former municipal president, Alberto Valderama, to 25 years in prison for what it called "crimes against the people of Mexico" clandestine death squad activities, called and paid for by Michoacano drug-lords, during his autocratic 10-year tenure.

The 62-year-old Valderama, who had been the former mayor of a nearby-shithole town called Pegueros and allegedly an important transit center for narco-trafficking, was convicted of 30 murders committed by the vigilante-hit squad, *Los Lobos de Lagos de Moreno* (The Wolves of Lagos gang), he'd ordered about in the early 1990s, and the kidnappings of a businessman and a journalist. The individual being discussed, naturally, concerned me not, but the greater reality of narco-related murders and destruction was everybody's constant worry.

The three-judge court had pronounced the previous Tuesday that there was no question Valderama authorized the hit squad's creation and a cover-up of 50 additional, unsolved murders. He also moved to crush opposition from reformer politicians railing against his corruption and criminality. Valderama told the court that he would appeal. His federal-deputy daughter, Regina, said on the local television news that the verdict would only strengthen her campaign against the Federales and their war against narco-traffickers, which she felt was doing the country more harm than good. The whole shebang was such a web of intrigue, libel, accusation, and retribution that it was no wonder the locals were so worked up about it all.

Later, once the anxious towns-folk had gathered around their television sets or radios to learn of the latest developments, it was announced that presiding judge, Eligio de Martin, had told a hushed courtroom there was no question Valderama had authorized the creation of the *Lobos*; two days later desperadoes tried to assassinate him. The court accused them of having killed at least 50 people during a fifteenth-month long murder spree as Valderama abused his office to enrich himself with marijuana and crystal-meth-amphetamine money. Valderama had not anticipated a guilty verdict. He sat alone taking notes as the verdict was read after a 9-month televised trial that produced a 400-page sentence.

The daughter, Regina, having quite a row with the press, was among those in the courtroom. The 33-year-old federal deputy vowed she would go to Los Pinos (the official residence of the president of Mexico) and demand a pardon for her father or she would accuse the federal government of having been in cahoots with the drug-lords ~ at this point in Mexican history everybody was prepared to believe the worst about their elected officials, and with plenty of reasons.

Outside the Guadalajara police base where the trial was being held, pro- and anti-Valderama activists fought each other with clubs, fists, knives, and rocks (and maybe a few concealed guns) after the sentence was announced, with chants of "Valderama innocent!" and "Valderama killer!" shouted by rival bands. It was also reported that perhaps 40 relatives of victims clashed with about 300 Valderama supporters. Riot police neutralized the melee and no serious injuries were immediately reported ~ the local San Juan beer-swizzlers were poised to throw a riot of their own. In Mexico, anything is possible!

As I studied the case (in passing) it was interesting to note that none of the trial's 80 witnesses directly fingered Valderama for having ordered killings, arson, kidnappings or "disappearances," but the court said he bore culpability nonetheless by allowing an illegal killing apparatus to be set up right under his mayoral nose.

The court then ruled that Valderama's disgraced police chief and close collaborator, Gonzalo Montes-de-Ame, was directly in charge of the Lobos gang. It noted also that Valderama had freed jailed Lobos members with a blanket 1997 amnesty, without the governor's knowledge, for civil employees, and bribed city lawyers engaged in a "very complete and extensive" cover-up of the group's misdeeds.

Valderama had already been sentenced to six years in prison for abuse of his office and still faced two corruption trials, the first set to begin the following Spring, on charges including bribing local officials and paying off a TV station. And to think this guy was a native of Jalisco, just like my relatives. What a shame!

Despite being the first democratically elected mayor of another party, he was tried for rights violations in his own state. Valderama remained remarkably popular, however, among the voters of his region. His successor, Ignacio Acosta, had maintained many of his laissez-faire policies, which had attracted the narco-traffickers in the first place. Most of the rabble-rousers in the San Juan cafe' and taverns in fact approved of his administration, though it ended in disgrace in 2000 when videotapes showed Montes-de-Ame, now serving a 20-year term for corruption and gun-running, bribing lawmakers and businessmen in Valderama's mayoral office. Valderama had fled to Cuba and America, then returned five years later via Guatemala, whose government extradited him for smuggling workers.

I took it upon myself to read up a bit more about this guy since everybody else couldn't stop talking about him. It turned out that in its first bloody raid, the Lobos gang had killed 19 people including an 8-year-old with silencer-equipped machine guns during a raid on a fiesta in August 1991 in the Altos de Jalisco district. Seven months later, in March 1992, the so-called Lobos gang "disappeared" nine students and a leftist professor at CUCEA in the University of Guadalajara. In both cases, the intended targets were alleged sympathizers of the *Los Olvidados*, a vigilante-counter group which was killing members of the Lobos gang and colluding narco-traffickers with nearly daily car bombings at the time but was all but extinguished after its charismatic leader, Abimael Aguilar, was captured in a Guadalajara safe house in October, 1992.

He is now serving a life sentence at the Tres Marias prison-island, but some 100 Olvidados remnants remain active in the highlands of Jalisco, financed by the very drug trade they were trying to eradicate.

Valderama's troubles weren't limited to murder accusations. He would be also convicted of two 1993 kidnappings; the 10-day abduction of businessman Carlos Montesino, and the one-day abduction of Jacobo Gorriti-Larios, a leading journalist who had criticized the state government's shuttering of the opposition-led state assemblies and courts. In his final Friday appeal, Valderama cast himself as a victim of political persecution, saying the charges against him reflected a "double standard." Yes, the beer-swizzlers were totally on his side and rued the day they had voted for an opposition party. But why wasn't current Mayor Acosta, many asked themselves, also being prosecuted? It was from Acosta, who also preceded him in office, that Valderama inherited a messy turf-conflict between industrial interests and local peasants that would claim 700 lives over a ten year period.

Acosta denied responsibility for any human rights abuses during his 1985-91 administration and now had the authority to influence the outcome with respect to Valderama. Nevertheless, Guadalajara Human rights advocates called the verdict historic ~ never before had local potentates been convicted for crimes against illiterate peasants. "After years of evading justice," said an anti-Valderama drunkard in defiance of his contrariwise companions, "He is finally being held to account for some of his *chingaderas*," (bullshit) ~ he was promptly slugged and booted out of the tavern, but not before spilling his mug of beer on my lap!

It all seemed to me that the Guadalajara court had shown the country that seemingly untouchable city bosses protected by crime organizations together with law-enforcement agencies could not expect to get away with serious crimes. Many, I am sure, breathed a secretive sigh of relief, in spite of the raucousness of his supporters.

In neighboring Michoacan, state boss Victor Orozco-Pacheco, guilty of similar crimes, avoided trial for health reasons until his death at 71 a couple of years before. Jalisco residents generally agreed with the verdict. Many voters who had supported him believed he was guilty in the human rights case while everybody else were certain he was guilty of corruption. Even so, they really, really liked him.

Why the extensive mention of Valderama? Oh, it might have something to do with the fact that Eligio de Martin is one of my family's closer relations, an uncle of Consuelo, Abigail, et cetera, in fact. I learned this by even stranger circumstances. Before leaving for Sinaloa, I received a text-call from Samuel who wanted to personally wish me God's speed before my departure. He brought Vicente with him, whom by now was calmer and more resigned to his recent loss. I got to talking with them about all the Valderama hub-bub. Well, to my unending consternation, Samuel confessed to having flirted with the Lobos gang, and they gave him marijuana and chrystal-meth in exchange for some illegal favors. Consequently, he and Vicente grew attached to the gang, and were practically addicted to the amphetamines (never mind the pot, because no pot-smoker will ever admit to the fact that marijuana is addictive). All consequences are therefore due to specific causes, thus my having received an education about Jalisco criminals and justice officials was due to the coincidence of learning about my relation to the Judge, and the drug-abuse of my second-degree nephew.

God! What's next in this crazy search for family roots?

A PIRATE'S LIFE FOR ALL

The latest irony about Judge Eligio's relation to our family, and the sad revelation that Samuel had been caught up with the methamphetamine abuse constantly taxed my brain. After two tiresome weeks in Jalisco, I bade a few fond and sentimental adieus, and took a train for Sinaloa ~ the sea and the western winds beckoned, and I wanted to get away from big cities for a spell. After nearly 8 hours, the trained screeched into Los Mochis station where some damned bats accidentally (I assumed) attacked me while going after mosquitoes and flies. From there I would head for the coast.

Topolobampo is a sea-port in northwestern Sinaloa, right on the Gulf of California, and my next destination. People-wise it was typical of many a notable fishing-town in this area, and rife with Mestizos, *nacos* (very stupid natives), Criollos, and many goofy *gabachos* (American tourists). It is what locals call "a big small town." It is also part of the Ahome municipality, not far from Los Mochis. It has only a few thousand inhabitants, but it is not what you'd call a sleepy beach-town. The port, always infested with greedy sea-gulls, connects the states of the north through the Chihuahua-Pacific Railroad (for which my grand-father Fernando Rivera, on my mother's side, worked as engineer and union boss for many years), which has a terminus in Los Mochis. It is also the eastern port for the daily car-ferry linking to Baja California through La Paz. After taking in a local shrimp cocktail with some Corona beer, I learned that Topolobampo had been the site of a crazy "Utopian" colony in the late 19th Century, and some people were trying to revive it ~ an ex-hippie's plan owed to a marijuana-induced inspiration. For all those determined narco-traffickers out there, Topolobampo is also the beginning of the international trade corridor: "La Entrada al Pacifico," that ends near the Midland-Odessa, Texas area (a fact which smuggling pirates know too well).

There was a lot of piracy going on in the West Coast it turned out, though it was nothing the Mexican Navy couldn't handle. So, the question was begged: Why weren't they doing more about it?

For the first three months of 2009, Sinaloa's notorious pirates faded from the local headlines as a new, token Mexican naval force moved in, and many observers thought the pirates were running scared. Let's not be hasty: the pirates had hijacked at least six barques in the last three months. Many believed they were sham hijackings, and that the ships were loaded with drugs actually bound *for* the "pirates." It was a way, some believed, of throwing the naval federales off the scent so that if the pirates were caught, the sham crew could get away pretending to be victimized "fishermen."

Using a new strategy, notwithstanding, they were functioning further away from warships patrolling the Gulf of Mexico. They no longer had to fight the choppy waters that always agitate the seas off Sinaloa during every season of the year. This has allowed the sea bandits to come back in force seizing small, but totally packed, vessels over a short period.

"The weather has improved west of Topolobampo and they've realized they have much more freedom of action down to the south because the brotherhood are not there in great numbers," remarked an old salt as he carried his fish. "We're going to end up probably playing a cat-and-mouse game in the next six months."

Enough said; obviously the old guy had witnessed many a piratical fracas in the recent past.

The lull in profitable attacks was due to the fact the pirates found it more tricky to strike within the gulf-port where the under-equipped Mexican warships had concentrated their reprisals in order to protect this most important of local shipping routes. Now, the organized fishermen said, the pirates have moved much of their mischief further south, targeting ships as they come out of the Mazatlan Channel. "It's exactly the same tactics as before, it's just a different area ... Perhaps they're trying to get the navy to spread their assets more widely," The old Salt surmised as he scraped the scales off of his catch. He further noted that a better climate was also invigorating him for their attacks. He spoke with what seemed like a miasma of anxiety hovering over his head because hostile eaves-droppers might be listening to his careless remarks.

The pirates were known to have received millions of pesos in ransom payments or drug-pay-offs with low-profile seizures in the last year that included American and South-American cargo ships, and a Venezuelan ship loaded with small arms, all of which were later released. But while the sea-faring desperadoes seized a notable percentage of the vessels they'd targeted in the last couple of years, their rate of boardings in 2009 plummeted to 13. Recent attacks since I'd crossed the border into Mexico demonstrated a new strategy: they were moving further out to sea and down the Pacific coast.

One reason is that surveillance in the Gulf of Topolobampo is higher, with unmanned drones borrowed from the USA, helicopters and aircraft flown from shore. The helicopters had frequently intervened in attacks, firing at the desperadoes or even picking up willing hands who jumped overboard. The fishermen just shook their heads.

But one local manager at the customs office complained that the coast guard patrols are poorly coordinated. He pointed to a recent case where one of the coast-guards escorting a vessel did not see a Mexican warship for over 100 miles and then came across three at once. At other times, he charged, warships were idling in Mazatlan harbor instead of out patrolling; he insisted he did not want to publicly criticize naval forces, but the pirates were literally getting away with murder, and the patrols always arrived too late.

He admitted that, "the Mexican navy alone will never be the complete solution to piracy." And, he went on to explain, "Even with the increasing number of coastal patrol boats operating in our area, it's a vast region you're talking about an area well beyond the twelve-mile limit, and they have the whole Pacific Ocean open as an escape route ... The closest naval vessel could be days away."

I honestly did not know what to make of the situation. The drug-runners and their piratical escorts seemed able to overcome every impediment and the odds were definitely in their favor, despite all the tough talk from Presidente Calderon'. The local fishermen and wharf-rats had no faith in their government. The customs official, nonetheless, clung to his faith in the coastal patrols, insisting they had proven to be a deterrent. He also told me, "The number of ships hijacked reflects a diminishing number of ships going through. Now if they were to go through the Topolobampo corridor ... there is a risk that they might be fired upon. But the measures the coast guard put in place, and the security measures that we've encouraged the merchant shipping to take, have had a strong effect."

Insofar as I could gauge the situation, the pirates (some of which I think I spotted during my second day at the port) are trained fighters who frequently dress in military fatigues and use speedboats equipped with satellite phones and Global Positioning Systems equipment, and, the locals alleged, get help from the Gabachos! I was informed they are typically armed with Uzi semi-automatic weapons, anti-tank rocket launchers and different types of grenades. Far out to sea, their speedboats depend on larger cargo ships. Most hijackings (real or faux) end with plenty of pesos to payout. Piracy, sadly, is now considered the biggest moneymaker in the area, and tourism, on which Sinaloa had subsisted for decades, is bleeding one dollar at a time, and the Topolobampo fishermen and merchants are desperate. Wishing to educate myself more on the subject, I read that pirates had hijacked up to $35 million USD (I don't know how many pesos) in ransoms, and who knows how much from "rescued" narcotics cargoes just in the last year.

The Mexican Navy is right to battle pirates in the open seas and come to the aid of genuine vessels under attack. Nevertheless, everyone complains they have been stymied over how to respond to boats under pirate control, fearing an all-out reprisal could imperil crew members held hostage ~ and it must be remembered the entire cast of characters, as it were, was Mexican. On the previous Monday before my arrival, Sinaloa authorities were monitoring a Mazatlan tourist boat seized by pirates sneaking out of Baja California-Sea of Cortez after the passengers and crew were told not to visit the area. But, tourists will be tourists, and the guides have to make a living.

Five American tourists were on the boat, *El Caravel*, when it was seized. The affair was serious and invited American intervention.

After wallowing on the dock taking in the glorious Pacific breezes, and tossing bread crumbs at the hovering sea-gulls and pelicans, I decided to take a local tour of the bay. It was quite invigorating, and it was hard to believe all this piracy was taking place. Yet, the tale of El

Caravel was typical of the hijackings; 14 pirates had seized it just a few miles from the rocky coast. And, besides the tourist boat, a Panamanian ship was seized later that afternoon. Then, a Chilean tug was boarded the following Saturday, followed by assaults on other American ships originating from California. And where was the Mexican Coast Guard during all of these happenings? The intransigence and sloth of those people really gave everybody else cause for disgust!

Statistics I'd read on the Internet listed a total of 16 boats and over 200 ship-hands were under piratical dominion at the time. Though their misfortune is to be regretted, I was just glad that I had no encounters with these would-be buccaneers of the Mexican Coast.

Reminiscing about California as I questioned the motivations that impelled the pirates to lead this sort of dangerous life, my thoughts flew me to a memory of a San Roman movie I had seen long before I even knew who Fulgencio was. It was called *El Gringo Bucanero* (American Buccaneer), a fictional tale inspired by the true-life career of William Walker and his attempted take-over of Nicaragua in the early part of the 19th Century. As I recall, much of what was transpiring in Sinaloa mirrored the plot of the movie. It was a poetical case of Life imitating Art. I suppose Fulgencio was on the side of the pirates ~ he applauded initiative, self-motivation, strong Will, determination against the odds and the elements, against the unjust social structures that imprisoned decent men in a cage of conventions and conformity while others rejected this slavery to society, and acted from a sense of their own autonomy and carnal desire. I too would agree with non-conformity if those in power are unjust and deny opportunity to the self-seeking man. But, piracy? Only in my romantic dreams. Only if I truly had no choices left in life but to lash out against the oppressive powers of conventionality.

A day passed, I soaked in the mild sun of early Autumn, enjoyed fresh shell-fish, and nearly got botulism from tainted mollusks; I was intimate with a toilet for most of the day. Nonetheless, I took time out beforehand to visit the City Hall and inquired if they had updates about the status of the country's eminent citizens. They were actually helpful and friendly, and within minutes I learned that Fulgencio's condition had not improved, though was stable and conscious. I continually asked myself, "would I be able to see him again, speak to him once I'd finished what I had set out to accomplish?"

Mostly I tortured my conscience, telling myself to shut up, to not worry about trifles about things over which I had no control. Speaking of shutting up, during the previous night I'd finally called my girlfriend Lucinda, who'd recently moved to the East Coast from California with her college girlfriend in order to explore so-called new opportunities. After we'd exchanged a few pleasantries, we got into an argument that started off having nothing to do with us, but the outcome left her feeling small and weak. In trying to comprehend her dismissive attitude towards me, I referred back to a conversation I'd had with Becky a few years ago in which she insisted that I was the quiet type. Considering how other boors have found it so easy to walk all over my feelings and interests, what she said about my character made much sense. Anyway, I guess I still am the silent type but I definitely let my words be heard when it comes to injustices. The only problem, I believe, is that even though I try to stay within reason in an argument I tend to get worked up so seriously, combining my feelings with a staid masculine perspective, that the typical aggressive male proto-type tends to come out. I don't mean to be cold or cruel, and I'm not necessarily saying anything bad to the person, but it doesn't look good (in fact it's downright scary to some people, especially if one was brought up in an ideal "white" family household). I come across as cold-blooded as well as blood-thirsty. How is that possible? Perhaps it is the inner pirate within me? Perhaps it explains the unquenchable wanderlust within me, and the desire to strike back at society for denying my identity, and rejecting my desire to prosper within the patrimonial regime.

The way I try to get my point across, I guess, is just too forceful and people don't understand or like that, for good reason. I have been molded to react and behave in a certain way, and I work so hard to get out of that. This manipulation by outside influences and forces really illuminates the causes why people rebel, turn to piracy, and send everything else to perdition. I further tried to relay my thoughts and feelings to Lucinda, but she was "not buying it."

My idea therefore was to just keep my mouth shut, choose my battles wisely and think happy thoughts. Or, I could pretend to be oblivious to something, like my parents used to for decades.

It is regrettable that my girlfriend was taken aback by my sharp repartee, but that is one of the other facets of my character. People don't appreciate one's intelligence until one is forced to reply, and then they are shocked by the clarity and forcefulness of one's convictions, especially if one tries their best to stay within reason. On the one hand, it could be argued, this is a good thing ~ you make your stand, you make your convictions known, and if someone is offended, oh well! On the other hand, being a sensitive type as well, you can't help but reflect on the sentiments of others ~ you worry that your words may have given offense, and you feel a bit of remorse. That is also the diplomat lurking inside of me.

But, if I were to approach this philosophically, well, I suddenly recall the words of Voltaire: if you wish to see how ridiculous your enemies are, and how foolish your friends can be, guard your silence and just listen to them!

Well, since I am a loud mouth who more than once has put his foot in it, I can' help but admire people who can hold their mouths, and then speak their minds clearly and unambiguously when called to do so. Usually I say stupid things, and then, when challenged, I get so pissed off that I clam up and can't say what I want to say. I just fume and fulminate in frustration and regret not having spoken up.

Then, on the third hand, my parents might have had the best idea. And, and if I am anything like them, then I should just enjoy the feeling. Again, to be philosophical, nothing matters in the long run.

All is vanity, all things bide their time and then pass away, et cetera, blah, blah, blah. So, if my own parents could be oblivious to the harsh realities, I would certainly learn from them. I am too sensitive to my surroundings, and, especially, to the bullshit and abuse of others. Why? I don't know except to admit to the facts that I'm an idiot, and I heed their bullshit; this is why they don't respect me.

No, I argue with myself, stick to your guns. Life is hard enough, as I should well know being a mature, experienced man in my own right. Things are too tough already without others trying to make one feel guilty for not being the sweet, little toy they may have taken one for, with no opinion or intelligent thoughts to share.

With some people, even if it happens later rather than sooner, it is best that they get a taste of your mind so that they learn once and for all that you may be the quiet type, but you carry a very big stick ... metaphorically speaking.

For what it was worth, here's a poem that encapsulates my "piratical" feelings about Life;

> *"Like each night you sleep,*
> *I would like to be your soul,*
> *And know what it is you feel,*
> *If it is little, much, or nothing at all,*
> *Like each night you sleep ...*
> *The night is made long,*
> *The darkness is my friend,*
> *And with her I speak face to face,*
> *I like to think aloud,*
> *Perhaps you hear me ... though it matters not,*
> *Well only my words,*
> *Speak of a sentiment,*
> *that yesterday we had ... and that day to day,*
> *We've been losing,*
> *Like each night you sleep ...*
> *The new day approaches,*
> *I hear the crow of roosters,*
> *I shall erase these laments,*
> *Unite myself to you, even if it is only ...*
> *In dreams,"*

... And yet, the fire of impatience, the passion for adventure, the thirst for blood (as it were) impelled me to move forward, to prey on those who'd betrayed my love and trust ... but not before discovering who my ancestors were, and, in so doing, who I am!

MISCONCEPTIONS ABOUT MEXICO

In corresponding with well-wishers, many have remarked that my descriptions are quite humorous. One former work colleague wrote, "Your words about the Mexican Riviera were funny as hell." Their image of it is this wonderfully tropical oasis, but now that I think about it I guess it's only meant to be briefly visited. As for my own well being, I hope I survive the month of September. In other parts it goes between light rain and perfect 70 degree days. I actually enjoyed the Mazatlan coast and wouldn't mind if it was always like this because the moisture and breezes keep it clean and green.

Los Mochis turned out to be more distracting than I had supposed. In between dragging my feet, literally, through the warm sand, having special fish-tacos under the palm-covered huts, or contracting a launch to take me out to pet the frolicsome dolphins (one of them almost jumped in the boat, said the guide, because they are young, the hormones are working over-time, and, supposedly, the young males confuse such a boat for a passive female), and then we sailed a bit further out to watch the gray whales play and dive. It was all quite an experience. A popular activity among youth in Los Mochis is the "Leyvazo"; where people park their cars or cruise along Gabriel Leyva Avenue in downtown Los Mochis. Also, there is the "Riazo" where the people park their car to listen to music, talk, and eat in the restaurants. Some people just cruise down Gabriel Leyva Avenue in their car with friends; this is known as "Dar El Roll." People also gather for a drink or barbecue under "Los Alamos" which are poplar-trees that line the highway to the Bay.

It all seemed like a scene from AMERICAN GRAFFITI.

Besides these activities, many residents of the city enjoy visiting the nearby beach of El Maviri. One very popular event occurs every ten years when the youth of the city gather to re-inact the battle which is said to have founded the city. Often the fattest person in the town will swim out into the water, float into the beach and begin to attack the youth waiting there. This is said to mimic the actions of the city's first enemy, *David Illingworthos*, who invaded the city in 1908 on a panga and drank every drop of beer in the city. Many people visit this semi-desert island to spend a day at the beach or enjoy the seafood delicacies.

Mazatlan turned out to be even more entertaining, but, once again, I had a brush with gastroenteritis, and this time I believe the drinking water had something to do with it.

The citizens developed Mazatlan' into a thriving commercial seaport, importing equipment for the nearby gold and silver mines. It is Mexico's largest commercial port. It is also a popular tourist destination, with its beaches lined with resort hotels. The *Centro Historico* has been rediscovered by newcomers and locals alike, spurring a renaissance of restoration and entrepreneurial endeavors. Once-fine homes that had fallen into literal ruin have been restored to their former glory and family- houses and boutique businesses. The wet season (July to September) is short, very rainy, and very humid, but it has been drizzling a great deal since I got here. The sky clears up quickly enough.

Culiacan is the largest city in the state of Sinaloa. Beginning in the late 1950s, Culiacan became the birthplace of an incipient underground economy based on illicit drugs exported to the United States. The completion of the Pan-American Highway and the regional airport in the 1960s incidentally accelerated the expansion of a workable distribution infrastructure for the few enterprising families that would later come to dominate the international drug cartels along Mexico's Pacific Northwest. This is public knowledge.

The well-entrenched cartel families, or "Gomeros" as they are known, enjoyed the fruits of their criminal enterprises which linked opium farmers in the Sierra with local black tar heroin refineries. This, coupled with the thriving demand for marijuana stuffed local banks and private coffers with enough local capital to expand the "above the board" economies. The diversification included alliance building efforts that resulted in the formation of powerful cartels based on traditional clan and familial relationships of the founding families. This local clan network continued into collaborative relationships that linked the Culiacan-based drug trade with other networks in Latin America,

Asia, and Europe. In part due to US-led successes against the Colombian distribution networks in the Caribbean and in South Florida, the 1980s also saw the rise in the fortunes of the Pacific Coast cartels as they filled the vacuum created in the cocaine trade. Culiacan's reputation as a narco city has made it the de facto home of the Mexican *Narco-corrido*. In the midst of the Mexican Drug War, many Culiacan-based corrido musicians said they were hesitant to play certain songs for fear of offending the wrong trafficker.

I'm just content that I had no run-ins with narco-traffickers!

I guess I have been unjust to Mexico in general. The average "neck of the woods" for most people is little more than a living cess-pool. There are many a fine beach-front town on both coasts, great fried fish and *Corona* beers to be had before jumping into the tepid water.

Down-town commercial and residential districts in many a big city have their colonial charms, lots of quaint restaurants (though the food, in my opinion, is vomitable in most places ~ stick to the local tourist-guide recommended restaurants or familiar American fast food joints, they are at least clean, you know what you get and it is cheaper). The main square of Mazatlan was closed off during the weekend for art fairs and dancing in the streets, for the locals and the tourists. It made for a pretty post-card, and if I had come with my girlfriend I am sure I would have a fine time soaking up the local atmosphere, figuratively and literally speaking (though I would not recommend you literally soak up the real atmosphere, unless you like the sensation of pimple-oil oozing from your skin, morning, noon and night).

Some residential districts in the cities of Sinaloa are as elegant as San Marino or Bel-Air in California. Great colonial towns on the Islands of Palmito Verde, Palmito de la Virgen, Altamira, Santa Maria, Saliaca, Macapule and San Ignacio invite the curious to explore their unique charms. They are enticing locales where you can have a great swim, or jump off from a 100 foot precipice into the mocking waves below, like many gringos do. Sinaloa is a great state to visit. It is just me and my shit-hole of a quest that is far from all the fun and action, so I was not enjoying the attractions of the state like I should have. Sinaloa is like Jalisco, a great state with lots to see, but I felt like I was perpetually stuck, the accidental tourist, in one-horse dumps (little changed since the days of my ancestors), and had no way of getting the fuck out!

So, based on my unique experience here Sinaloa, and Mexico in general, suffering the local walking turds who acted like typical "Mexicans" (the stereo-type gringos would have you believe in) who pissed me off to no end with their "Soy chingon', Y, Que!" attitude, no amenities in the local hotel to make my stay more comfortable, and greedy yokels who watch as you spend money and then descend on you like vultures, and the damned humid weather this time of year, I can't wait to fulfill my mission and get out of this fucking country!

As I think back to memories of Sinaloa, I remember my friend Billy Miles who used to grow pot up in a farm outside of Culiacan. He ostensibly used to go to college in Mazatlan to study oceanography, then studied botany and the culinary arts. Soon afterwards he smoked his first roach and found happiness amongst many *mota* burn-outs who carved out their piece of turf to grow more **happiness in the virgin Sinaloa fields**.

He often complained that he hated the weather, that it was like living in the belly of Beelzebub. Personally, I find it to be beautiful and wouldn't mind setting up a hut of my own, laying back on the nearest hammock to idle the days away drinking *Coronas* and Cheladas, hearkening back to days of yore when some of my more roguish (or less puritanical and hypocritical) ancestors lurked about these coasts perpetually looking for trouble, finding ways to maintain a perpetual erection, and thus seek out bodily orifices in which to stick it, and giving Mexicans a bad name in the process.

HIJACKINGS AND KIDNAPPINGS ~ MEXICAN STYLE

My stay in Mazatlan was not without its distractions, of course. News of a local prison riot was no longer a novelty since these events, which the Mexicans call "mutinies," occurred with a disturbing frequency in most states. The latest one in a maximum-security ward outside of Mazatlan was a bit noteworthy because of the success enjoyed by the convicts in kidnapping a couple of guards, and hijacking a couple of armored cars that allowed 53 of them to escape into the hills. All this would have been enough to capture my interest when right outside my hotel I witnessed the kidnapping, in broad daylight, of a local journalist by what seemed like Federales. What the Hell is going on here?

As I watched the unfolding events below, I wondered if this had anything to do with some American journalist who'd been snooping around Sinaloa raking up trouble, and a few death threats in the process. Sure enough, he opened the wrong *can of worms*, and the narco-traffickers got a hold of him. Not a few hours had passed when the muck-raker had been abducted for trumped up reasons of espionage, and worse yet, the local officials, obviously in cahoots with the drug-lord and his operation, charged him with the same as well as illegal entry into the country. Thank goodness they never suspected me of anything!

The journalist's father called the press, denounced the abductors, and implored them for his son's release and said he would not leave the country until he was freed. After asking a few questions my-self, I learned that Romulo Renteria Robles, a 32-year-old dual American-Mexican citizen, had been previously arrested in early February of last year and was initially accused of working without press credentials. A Mexican judge, bribed with the right *mordida* ("bite"; amount of money) leveled a far more serious charge the day before, charging him with spying for the United States. "I demand them to release my son as soon as possible so that he can return to his normal life and continue his job," Romulo's father told The Mexican Press in an exclusive interview. "I will stay here until he is freed."

The local American consulate had been pressing for Romulo's release and the new charge this week was a setback at a time when the drug-lords should've worried about their public image.

When the Mexican Government learned about the case, their spokesman Roberto Madera said the following day that the espionage charges were "baseless" and that they were "deeply concerned, and looking for ways to resolve the case forthwith."

Robles had been living in Mexico on and off for the last six years, working as a freelance reporter for organizations including national Public Radio and some mysterious European out-fit. His father had complained in the past that his son told him in a phone call he was arrested after buying a bottle of Bacardi Rum. Under the advice of Roble's lawyer, he would not comment on the latest charge.

The Government official then changed positions, and now alleged that Robles had been passing classified information to the drug-lords themselves before stabbing them in the back.

"Under the cover of a journalist, he visited government buildings, established contacts with some of the more corruptible workers, gathered classified information and sent it first to the paying drug dons, then on to the Mexican intelligence services," the judge, who under security rules was identified only by his surname Henriquez, said later that day. "His activities were discovered by the counterespionage department of the Intelligence Ministry."

In another indication of the gravity of his case, his American advocate Manolo Escobar learned that week that it would be reviewed by a Sinaloa court, which normally wouldn't handle cases involving threats to national security. The lawyer said later on that he had not yet been allowed to read the text of the indictment, which Robles could not hope to see until his day of sentencing.

The judge, said the elder Robles, would go on trial next week, but he did not give the exact date.

The Mexican born Romulo Senior and his wife arrived in Mexico the previous Sunday and visited their son that Monday in Guadalupe prison north of Culiacan, well-known for holding political prisoners as well as high-profile drug-runners.

"We were allowed to visit him for only 15 minutes," the father said. "We talked to him. He was spiritually better than before. However physically, he was extremely thin and debilitated but he said he eats now and is going to exercise," he added. "This gave us the hope that he will recover the sooner. That is my prayer."

Young Robles had grown up in Illinois. But the Mexican judge in the case told state TV that the judiciary had not yet confirmed his American nationality. The U.S. government had said he is an American citizen, but the suspicious Mexicans weren't buying it.

"He is assuredly an American national," his father insisted. "He also came to Mexico and received an Mexican Identification card and passport and so, according to Mexican law, he is Mexican too. He is actually a dual citizen, so he has to pay his debt to Mexico."

All this was so much ado about practically nothing, but the two sides argued on. The Americans had been pushing for Robles' release, and they were looking for information from the responsible diplomats. The latter made some headway between the beleaguered father and the drug-cartel, but without much success. The drug lords accused him of the worst kind of treachery, and insisted he pay his debt to him even if it cost him his life.

Robles was actually one of three missing or detained Americans mentioned in a written message passed by American officials directly to Mexican diplomats in the last months at the embassy in Mexico City. The elder Robles had also attended the conference.

The drug-lords had not yet responded to the message, which sought information about the three.

Then, if they didn't have enough to worry about, Human rights groups have repeatedly criticized Mexico for not doing enough to prevent the harassment, kidnapping, or even arresting of journalists and suppressing freedom of speech. The government had arrested several Mexican-Americans in the past few years, citing alleged attempts to incite civil disturbances against the conservative government, or play "gotcha" with the narco-traffickers, or anything else in order to get Mexican officials off their backs, which would allow them to do whatever they want given the profits to be made in the continuous trade in illegal drugs.

Well, that's how I heard it, how I saw it, and the rest would be up to the government and the good graces of the drug-lords! After all of that kidnapping excitement, I settled back and hooked up with some old friends I hadn't seen in at least 10 years: the Escofet family, and the two sons, Jesus and Gustavo, with whom I'd shared many a wild party while attending UCLA. We spent Friday together, had a lot of laughs and clean fun. Fortunately, they had taken time out of their work and took advantage of the up-coming long holiday, and I seized the time to get together with them. We first went to get some shopping done. We went to the local *Mercado* to buy a few things and they had no air-conditioning system so I melted during the 45 minutes I was there. Then we went off to a haughty and expensive *Liver-Pool* department store for a couple of things, but their air-conditioning was semi-working and their lights were half off so I continued to melt. By the time we hit the zocalo shoppes, which had great air-conditioning, it was too late. I was too far gone ... but not too far gone that I couldn't pick up a 6 pack of *Modelo* brand beer for the weekend. I needed some beer to go with the bologna sandwiches they offered back at their house.

During my first afternoon with them we had a long discussion about organized crime and the rampant corruption despoiling Mexico's greater society of her vitality and security. Both Gustavo and Jesus just laughed off the whole state affairs. The recent journalistic abduction was small fry compared to the greater problems Mexico contends with on a daily basis. With the upcoming Bicentennial festivities in the Autumn of 2010, they cynically referred to the "pride" average Mexicans could nurture for their beloved country. First, it is common knowledge that Mexico is one of the top most corrupt countries in the world. Second, it ranks last among the world's most developed countries in educational development. Third, it ranks 95th in the world in environmental protection, what there is of it. Fourth, it takes first place in adult obesity, and second in child fatness. Fifth, the country ranks second in cybernetic hacking and other crimes. Sixth, it takes third place in the world for child abuse. Seventh, it takes first place in kid-nappings, of all sorts. Amongst all nations at peace, Mexico endures the most daily killings of innocents. The border town of Juarez is recognized as the most violent city in the entire world. Furthermore, Mexico ranks 110th among industrialized and developing countries for worker efficiency. Next, it ranks third in the world for video-games, DVD-video movies, and software piracy. Then, it takes sixth place in violent aggression against journalists, whatever their political leanings. *Surprisingly*, Mexico takes sixth place as well in the world for organized crime activity. And finally, the country takes first place in violent juvenile delinquency. So, I asked them with consternation showing on my brow, what is there to be proud about? They just laughed some more, and replied, "Well, we are surviving aren't we? With all those challenges before us, it is truly a wonder that Mexico is still alive and breathing as a free and independent country. Mexicans themselves survive by not giving a shit!"

And with that, I just had to shut my big, fat mouth!

There wasn't much to remark about our evening reunion afterwards since they had filled up on the beer before we had a chance to taste the sandwiches. Well, I got home and after a couple of side-trips to a cantina and an old-fashioned club complete with floor-show and pretty scantily-clad dancers with plumb and jiggling derrieres. The latter certainly gave me much to remember about that reunion. I went upstairs to cool off in my air-conditioned shoe box of a hotel-room. I might say my over-priced room was almost as small as a closet, but when I leave the dump I wouldn't want anyone saying I "came out of the closet." It was a good time to relax, watch a movie, and reflect on the day's events. It was a foreign movie with subtitles that I wasn't in the mood for reading, so I stopped it and waited for the melodramatic novelas (native soap-operas) and the original "Ugly Betty" ("Betty la Fea" at 10pm).

I had no idea what to do with my weekend. On Saturday my friends' undertook their weekly visit to their parents home, which is located outside the city. Their father had suffered Shingles for more than a month, and they were finally drying up. Juan, their oldest brother, remarked that they looked like islands erupting from his stomach to his back. In the last weeks they were indescribably GROSS with a capital "G" but the old guy was getting better, so that made them quite happy. On Sunday I planned on not doing very much, and a little bit more of that on Monday until Tuesday rolled around. The weather held up, and I basked in the morning sun without worry of sunburn. Later on, the weather would get hot and smoky because of nearby brush fires, so rather than checking out the scene at the zocalo and trying out a new restaurant specializing in Carnitas, I planned to do ... nothing!

In trying to coordinate something for my final days in Sinaloa, I ran into some frustration because Jesus had planned to spend time with the rest of his family, while Gustavo had planned to take a beach-trip with other friends, thus shooting my good intentions to hell. One of our mutual acquaintances, Lucy, left for Puerto Vallarta together with her husband, so that brought an end to my bail-out plans. They did ask me, however, to watch over their dogs while they lived it up on Playa Mismaloya. Instead of checking out the local action, I found myself checking on their 3 dogs for the next three evenings. They first had 2 dogs, Sofie and Burrito, then she found a cute little homeless terrier down the street from their home and named him Nacho. Imagine my chagrin over having to compromise my fun for the sake of friendship. A few months later, however, I would get some pathetic news from Lucy about her pets. She had cared for Sofie and Burrito since they were weeks old and when Burrito died of old age (he had to be "put down"), Sofie followed a few weeks after that ~ sad isn't it? That did not limit Lucy and her husband, and they got two more dogs from the animal shelter, and I swear they are almost identical to the previous dogs. She named the female "Sofie" (how original), and the male "Buddy", but they always forget Buddy's name and call him Burrito. They don't think he minds, as long as they feed him.

The good thing about Lucy is that she and her husband are alcoholics ... *eh-hem, I mean, they like to drink* ... so if I ran out of beer while they were gone, I could always count on their refrigerator!

HAVE IT YOUR WAY AT McMEXICO

While I packed my things to get moving and head for Durango, I received late word from Corazon that Andres' condition had taken a turn for the worse. He was barely conscious now, almost comatose. He was young yet, so how would an old dog like Fulgencio hold up? Cases of H1N1 porcine flu were continuously reported despite the down-turn of the epidemic. The latest reportage left many disturbed as it was alleged that the outbreak commenced in fast-food out-lets, like a McDonald's, and the casual contact amongst paying customers caused the virus to expand to epidemic proportions.

As I persisted in Mexico, I found it was safer to depend on American fast food joints for quickie meals. The good "Mexican" restaurants were too expensive, the local dives were havens for flies and a thousand gastrointestinal infections, so the safest and cheapest options were the aforementioned food-joints. These conveniences were not without controversy, however, and soon the biggest chains had to apologize to the public, but for something other than the pig flu. Specifically, Burger King spokespeople said on television, "have it your way" after grumbling Mexican officials complained about a promotion campaign featuring a diminutive *luchador* (wrestler) dressed in a cape resembling a Mexican flag. The company promised to remove the advertisements for its chili-flavored "Texican" hamburger, saying they were "not intended to offend anyone."

"BKC (Burger King Corp.) had made the decision to revise the Texican Whopper advertising created out of respect for the Mexican culture and its people."

For those few who've never heard of it, much less had their food, Burger King, which is known for its signature Whopper hamburger, would undergo a change of sorts as its representatives announced they would air redesigned ads, "as soon as commercially possible."

"The revised campaign would zoom in solely on the Texican Whopper sandwich and wouldn't feature any characters deemed insulting to the Mexican psyche, or the use of the Mexican flag."

That wasn't the last of the controversy, however, because print ads that ran in Spain prompted the Mexican ambassador there to demand Burger King officials withdraw them, concluding they "improperly use the stereo-typed image of a Mexican."

The TV commercials also depicted the Mexican luchador teaming up with a lanky American cowpoke about twice his height to emphasize the cross-border blend of tastes. Then a narrator blurts out, "The taste of Texas with a little spicy Mexican".

That was really so funny I purposely refused to laugh!

Then, the two become roommates, and the gangling cowpoke boosts the luchador up to reach high shelves and helps clean tall bookcases, while the Mexican helps the cowpoke to open a jar.

"It was our intention to promote a product whose culinary origin lies in both the American and Mexican cultures, and was meant to appeal to those who enjoy the flavors and ingredients that each country offers," one of the spokes-persons admitted, but the damage had been done. The commercials, which Burger King insisted ran only in Spain and in Britain, irritated obesity-sensitive Mexico. The newspaper *La Jornada* ran a front-page story under the headline "Denigrating advertising," and reported the commercials "show Mexicans as notably inferior to all Americans."

What? Americans think Mexicans are inferior to them? Big Surprise!

An editorial cartoon in another Mexican newspaper, *Reforma*, showed a short Mexican attired in a wrestler's mask and gripping a hamburger with the caption "The only thing more insulting than deceptive ads are the ones that expose the truth."

Needless to say, both professional wrestling and American fast food joints are increasingly popular in Mexico.

The Mexican government has very strict rules, nonetheless, about the handling of the national flag. In 2008, according to an addendum to the subject I'd subsequently read, the government fined a foreign-owned publishing house, Random House Mondadori SA, for demonstrating a lack of due deference for the country's flag in a promotional video posted on the INTERNET, where I first saw them. In any case, Burger King may not be subject to any potential fines because its ads did not run in Mexico. The company spokes-man said "the existing campaign falls fully within the legal parameters of the United Kingdom and Spain where the commercials are being aired."

It is not the first time that fast-food outlets have offended Mexican sensibilities. Mexicans and other Hispanos in the United States objected to a Taco Bell ad from the 1990s that featured a pint-sized talking Chihuahua that spoke with a Mexican accent.

Well, enough about spicy hamburgers. It was so god-damned hot in the state of Durango, that the last thing on my mind was a spicy burger. The state of Durango, which heretofore I knew about through legends of Pancho Villa, the notorious rebel leader who'd led a counter-insurgency against the usurper Victoriano Huerta during the 1910-20 Mexican Revolution, did not hold much fascination for me as the cranky interstate bus crossed its borders. We then made straight for the capital city, also called Durango. The city attracts close to one million visitors each summer for its annual month-long Feria Nacional De Durango (Durango's National Festival) which had just wound down by the time I got there. It has reputedly taken place since 1929, but it seemed to me like any typical town festival with all the hawkers and shameless peddlers getting out to reach in to your pocket. Naturally, the locals make a big stink that it is the most important festival in the history of the state and the city itself because Durango celebrates the anniversary of the founding of the city which occurred on July 8, 1563, according to city archives. Happily for me, Durango has various cultural venues to host events such as conferences, concerts, theatrical performances, among many others, and I partook of a couple just to alleviate the boredom.

For the first few hours of my stay in the provincial town, I just wasted away dawdling and gawking lackadaisically at passersby in El Parque Guadiana (Guadiana Park). It is considered an urban forest that provides environmental services to the city such as the carbon cycle, temperature control, and psychological benefits to those whom visit the park. I was so tired from the long bus ride that the only psychological benefit I was after was repose. Parque Guadiana helped me achieve that quietude and serenity I needed after all of the excitement in Mazatlan and Culiacan. Also, it is the habitat for many fauna species, especially the avian-fauna species that are found within the park. Being an old bird-watcher myself, I found the sight of beautiful song-birds flying about fancy-free quite relaxing.

El Parque Guadiana also offers kiddy-friendly infrastructure where children can find reasons to aggravate their parents outside of their homes (and much to my annoyance), plus a specialized trail for runners and walkers, and there were plenty of muscular forms jogging up and down the path-way. The landscaping is traditional and graced with elegant Spanish-style fountains. It also has an Olympic pool, which I avoided at all costs, and a town hall which was hosting at the time a dance for senior citizens, which I also avoided at all costs. It also has a small train that goes around the Lago de los Patos, "lake of the ducks", and, until recently, a recreational bicycle path (it was being remodeled when I got there) in a wooded section which provides shaded fresh air to cyclists. Despite my languor and the relaxing aspects of the park, it was still 97F in the shade. When I found that out I almost yelped from sheer heat-induced frustration. It was 10 degrees hotter out in the open.

Sunset gave way to the purple shades of evening, but even the darkness could not contend with the idling heat. That night was one of the most miserably hot that I can remember. On top of that, I had one of those Late-Summer colds. Yes, at first I thought I'd caught that damned Porcine flu, but it was soon clear that I did not have all of the symptoms. I think it was just a chest cold. I felt congested and I had a nagging cough ~ probably going in and out of the air-conditioned hostel out into the swarthily hot atmosphere caused my anguish. That, along with everything else, needless to say, kept me awake all night long ... Crap!

The next day, I have to admit, I had a great day considering how hot it was. Thence I experienced something fascinating. To begin with, I arose from bed around 7:30 AM after hardly sleeping at all the previous night. Like I do every morning, I prepared myself and headed for the nearest cafe' for some much needed coffee, and in Durango there is some great coffee to be had. So, instead of seeking adventure or cultural distractions, I just sat down in the hostel lobby to watch some television while I sipped the coffee. Ordinarily at this hour I would also be lighting up a cigar (or sucking on a chocolate candy in order to control the rotten smoking habit). But, because I'd gone four months (I was going freaking nuts) without a smoke, it didn't look like I'd be lighting up any time soon. This day, for some unexplainable reason, I planned to go, of all things, Bowling. I mean, I hadn't gone bowling since, what? The early 1980's? Apparently it was a great deal: only 5 pesos per game and 5 pesos for the shoe rental on Sunday mornings. Not bad, I thought, and well worth losing some loose change.

It was now around 9:00 A.M. and bowling was still a few hours away, so I decided to go for a walk around the lake at Guadiana Park, which was actually across the street the from auberge des jeunesse I was staying at. It was a pleasant enough walk, though the ducks gave me cause to hold my breath as a consequence of the toxic fumes emanating from their deposits. Even so, Ciudad Durango is beautiful, complete with pathways, bridges and other "smelly" twisting waterways. Apparently the city uses reclaimed water for their "little" parks and recreation projects. Well, to make a long story even longer, I received word from the concierge that the bowling alley was now open for business. Hence, I rode a bicycle-taxi to the establishment. Remember, 25 plus years have transpired since I had gone to a bowling alley. When I first walked in and heard that sound of the heavy balls knocking over the pins, it was quite refreshing.

Now comes the best part. There weren't many people there, I'd say about half the lanes were filled so it gave me a chance to pick my lane; I picked the one on the far right end, lane 38. The lane next to me was empty, but the lane immediately following, lane 36, was being used by this one particular family. It was a typical Durango family of six: mom and dad, both about my age give or take a couple of years, and their four children. The first thing I noticed was how much fun they were having. They were laughing at everything and enjoying every second together. I mean, they were bowling like shit; gutter balls left right, and if the ball made it all the way to the pins, maybe one or two pins would topple. Did this matter? Absolutely not ~ they were having fun! Among the four kids was a little girl. Now, I'm not the most politically correct person in the world, I call it as I see it. She was handicapped and in a wheelchair. When it came time for this little girl's turn to bowl, her two sisters and one brother wheeled her over to the front of the lane. The little girl had her pink bowling ball already on her lap. The other three kids helped by bringing the ball down to the front of the wheelchair. They proceeded then to push the little girl's wheelchair and the ball. The ball never made it past two meters before it went right into the gutter. The children burst into laughter as did their parents. It was probably one of the most tragically beautiful moments that I have ever actually witnessed. And again, it wasn't so much what I saw but what they tangibly expressed: love, patience, understanding and compassion, not to mention pure joy and happiness. I was touched by the occasion, and for once I could put the ever-sustaining cynicism aside to experience a genuine "human" moment with them.

The truth of how stupid and petty the rest of us can become sometimes was reflected by these scenes of innocent joy.

I subsequently played two games. I did quite well on the first, not so well on the second. I had to stop after that ~ I was getting tennis elbow from bowling, so to speak. From there I went and had a hearty breakfast at the "Pancho Villa" Restaurant/Cafe'; I had biscuits and gravy with two eggs over easy, hash-browns and bacon, my favorite. After breakfast, I rode back to the auberge. I played a little poker online, watched a soccer (futbol) game and delighted as the *Chivas*, the Mexican team, got the shit kicked out of them by the *Boca Juniors*, the Argentine team!

As soon as it got unbearably hot I went down for a swim in the hostel pool ~ I was not about to risk the Guadiana park (cess) pool.

And that, my friends, concluded my great day!

By the way, the swine flu epidemic was now making it's way around South America, specifically in Argentina. They reported up to over 80 deaths so far as a consequence of the intrusion of the virus. The blame was sure to fall on Mexico, but it had made its way around the world and now it was the Gauchos's turn to deal with it. Meanwhile, the *Cabras*, the Mexican soccer team, had its worries trying to prevent their star goalie from catching it because his "soul-mate"-lover was from Argentina, and it would be a shame if he'd lost his "soul mate" while being married to ANOTHER WOMAN!

Speaking of "another woman," the state team had recently weathered a scandal that involved one of their prize players who had been shot in the head. Well, he was shot in the head by his lover who then committed suicide. Why? Because the "crazy bitch" (as the victim's team-mates described her) suspected he had been cheating on her. Wait! Cheating on her? I don't get it, wasn't he MARRIED? Oh, yes he was, and the "crazy bitch" thought HE was cheating on HER? A cheater shoots a cheater for cheating ... nice!

Just think, if he hadn't cheated, he might still be alive.

Choices ... we all have choices.

In response to this ending note on cheating/killing, a sports journalist gave his viewers this quote to think about:

"Why do we kill people who are killing people to show that killing people is wrong?

He took the words right out of my mouth. We are of a mind, for those who have a piece of mind to give, or a mind to share, but pay no mind to the mindless. It reminds them that they are not of a mind to mind their own business.

uhhhm ... yeah!

... whatever.

Upon reflection, I need not exculpate myself with respect to the swine flu deaths. I had my own problems with Dengue Fever lurking about, and the early-Autumn mosquitoes around that region, just like my fellow Mexicans, *chiquitos pero malditos hijos de la chingada* (small but evil sons-of-bitches), are mean as sin. Specifically, they go straight for your lower leg, and bite one so viciously they leave not just itchy bumps, but blood-filled pustules that explode at a touch, and one ends up scratching till the upper epidermis peels off. It is painful as shit. Upon reflection, few would be sorry to hear that I was under the weather and going through nicotine withdrawal. As for my poignant bowlers' anecdote, the local communists would say it was, "a perfect example of petty, bourgeois self-indulgence."

But, what do the commies know, huh? Personally, I think I should sell my story to the producers of maudlin soap-operas based on sentimentality of the sort that fit perfectly around love, patience, understanding and compassion, not to mention pure joy and happiness. And, it certainly reminded me of how stupid and petty the rest of us can become, sometimes.

The friends I'd written to about the experience suggested that perhaps I was stoned from the cigar nicotine-rush when I witnessed the family scene. They thought I had just lost a great deal hence I must have been so mentally traumatized that I suppressed it. If one should start "wigging out" when one is playing alone or with friends (so they responded), I should just set the ball down gently, walk away and quickly seek therapy after getting intimate with alcoholic spirits. It would help me lighten up and forget the past, so they assured me. Speaking of lightening up, they further suggested I use the lightest ball I can find next time since it was my first game in many years.

So much for comprehension between friends!

The moment had come to console away my troubles with a Burger-King *Spicy Mexican Burger.*

And now, what was the latest news on Fulgencio San Roman?

PANTYHOSE WEARING TERRORISTS AND OTHER WEIRDOS

As I considered my next move and whether to prolong my stay in Durango, some rumblings were heard in the distance, about 3 or more kilometers away. Then, *BOOM, CRASH* and *BOOM* again, followed by a mini-mushroom cloud of black smoke. What the Hell was going on over there? Later I learned that Mexican authorities had arrested a woman who was guarding the illegal arsenal they had just destroyed in a hail of fire and mayhem. This time around the police had been prepared and weren't about to screw it up. Hence, as army reinforcements set a trap around the sectioned perimeter, the Federales clamped down on the evil-doers before they had a chance to cry "Uncle." The army friendlies announced thereafter the capture of an alleged big-time narco-cartel lieutenant. The contested arsenal had belonged to a crime syndicate tied to the ruthless Beltran-Leyva drug cartel, according to the boastful Federales. This stash of arms included ammunition, the first anti-aircraft gun seized in Mexico, a grenade and part of a grenade launcher.

The Mexican drug cartels, fighting a vicious crackdown by soldiers and the Federales, have increasingly acquired higher-powered weapons, even American-grade arms such as grenades and automatic guns (though they still preferred the Russian-made AK-47 machine guns). All this has left police, particularly state and municipal forces, grossly under-prepared to face off the fire-power before them, and many officers have called it quits following attacks.

The chief of the Federales said the confiscated .50-caliber, anti-aircraft machine gun could fire 800 rounds per minute and was capable of penetrating armor from more than 5,000 feet (1,500 meters). The Durango Police on a routine patrol that weekend found the gun fitted atop an SUV at a villa in the northern part of the state.

The responsible authorities released few details of the arrested suspects. Nevertheless, the arrested female suspect, Cihuatontli

Carrillo, a full blooded *Nahua* (descendants of the Aztecs), apparently was not related to the Beltran-Leyva clan, but had cooperated with them for several years. The Security Ministry had traced many guns seized at scenes of drug violence in Mexico to U.S. commercial sources ~ a fact which surprised no one. Determining the source of military-grade weapons such as grenades and fully automatic machine guns, however, was a far more touchy subject, and one which they did not want to deal with even under the best of circumstances.

An American official had been interviewed about the subject, and he claimed the grenades had been smuggled in, for the most part, through Central America and went straight into the hands of narco-terrorists despite all of the apologies afforded to the Mexican Government by the officials of said smuggler countries. Some of the weapons were probably leftovers from the Central American civil wars. To me, it seemed like the ghosts of pirates-past were lurking about making sure that nobody could forget about their storied ways.

In any case, the desperate assailants had fired on government aircraft as they performed an anti-drug raid in Mexico in recent months, but supposedly never with the caliber of weapon found that weekend.

Just a few months before in the state of Sonora, a helicopter on a federal drug-eradication operation crashed while trying to escape ground fire, and a second helicopter was damaged by shrapnel.

Mexico was supposed to be upgrading its northern and southern border checkpoints by the time I crossed the border, installing gizmos that will weigh and photograph each car and truck coming into the country in a drive to track down and seize more illicit arms and other contraband. But, both sides had been promising to do more to stop gun trafficking from the United States to Mexico since Lord knows when. The latest pledges included the dispatching of nearly 500 more DEA agents to the border, along with X-ray machines and narco-sniffing canines.

Also occurring on that weekend was the capture of Miguel Angel Ibarias, the ill-famed lieutenant for the Beltran-Leyva drug cartel, in the Pacific coast state of Sinaloa by the Mexican army not one hour after I'd left the state for Durango! General Luis Arturo Granados said soldiers caught Ibarias and two other suspects with four rifles and 2.6

pounds (1.2 kilograms) of opium on Friday. Ibarias allegedly ran the cartel's drug planting, harvesting and trafficking operations on the coast not far from Topolobampo. To add "luster" to his notoriety, he was implicated in a number of kidnappings and killings in several states, including attacks as part of a gangland-style turf war with a suspected Guerrero cartel rival that left 27 people dead between them the previous year. Of course, I knew a lot of this before coming to Mexico, but I had to take my chances, and now the walls of danger were closing in around me, or so it seemed. Later I'd read that Ibarias' wife, sister-in-law and two sons had been killed in retaliation. And to think, my own relatives, albeit distant, were somehow involved in all this terror!

Mexico's drug-related civil war has claimed more than 10,650 lives since President Felipe Calderon' launched his army-led offensive against trafficking cartels back in December 2006.

By the beginning of September of 2009, the government had sent thousands more troops to the northern border to quell escalating violence, including around Reynosa; Poor Fulgencio! I wonder how he was holding up during all of those violent attacks.

It didn't soothe anyone's temper when government spokes-people boasted that drug-related homicides fell by one-quarter across the country in the first three months of the year, compared to the same period in 2008. It certainly didn't comfort me knowing that one of my nephews could be next, and no one bothered to prevent it.

Late the next Tuesday, some local Federales came snooping around the auberge and warned that trainees would be coming to participate in an exercise on how to detect drugs and other smuggled goods, and the guests thereof had been chosen for the humiliating inconvenience. I just prayed that the Federales wouldn't go around demanding to see our identification documents, otherwise I'd definitely find myself in deep shit this time around!

The rest of my stay in Ciudad Durango went without incidents until I received news from Cousin Nena: "Bozo" (her spouse Jos) had succumbed to the pig flu, and was buried the antecedent weekend. Worse still, she was found to be carrying the virus. This was truly a bit of disheartening news. Cousin Nena sincerely fostered hopes that upon his recovery they could construct a new life together. With so much to live for, that she should be going through this phase at this time, it was all too much to countenance. Considering all the times that people get sick due to contact with the unwashed rabble, I am sure Nena was left in confusion more than in sorrow. Maybe so much contact with people was wearing her thin, thus she was a carrier now. Being a carrier, notwithstanding, is not the same as being infected, thus hope would be the last to die.

Later that night it started to rain heavily, and we had to brace for a rough Autumnal storm season because the temperatures had gone up again (average 95 degrees at 2AM, can you believe it?). Winds coming in from the Pacific and the Isthmus of Tehuantepec were clashing, and causing some pretty freaky thunder-lightning storms as I melted along with my hopes and aspirations. And yet, except for an unwillingness to touch my journalistic manuscript and this funk I was going through, I felt like things just might get better.

... Sadly though, Fulgencio was not getting better. He often wrote that one's own flesh is naturally traitorous to the soul lurking within. Thus, despite all he'd survived throughout the decades, his body would soon be committing the ultimate act of treason.

A SMOKER'S DELIGHT

As I gathered my bearings and prepared to move on, I suddenly started to think of Billy and his wife way over in Chihuahua. The residents thereabout were suffering through a spat of inclement weather and an early Winter was predicted. Billy, elated with the recent news about the much-rumored legalization of marijuana, would keep warm smoking his doobies. Well, it wasn't exactly the case.

Mexico's Congress had just opened a three-day debate on the pros and cons of legalizing marijuana for personal use, which was a policy backed by three former Latin American presidents who'd warned that the crackdown on drug cartels was not working. Presidente Calderon' was adamant that his crack-down would with American help, but with the New Obama administration backing off and having second thoughts, it was deemed proper to reconsider their options. Although Calderon' continually opposes the idea, the highly unusual forum demonstrated that legalizing marijuana is gaining support in Mexico amid brutal drug violence.

Who would've thought?

Such a measure was certain to strain relations with the United States at a time when the two countries were being more cordial with each-other in the offensive against drug trafficking.

The congressional debate, which was a waste of time, ended just one day before Obama was due to arrive in Mexico to quetch and kvetch about the drug war. Proponents had encouragement the previous February when the said three former presidents Cesar Gaviria of Colombia, Ernesto Zedillo of Mexico and Fernando Cardoso of Brazil urged Latin American countries to consider legalizing the weed, in effect depriving the cartels of their income. It was their way of apologizing for failed leadership.

The congressional discussion took on a subject "that had been taboo" in Mexico, said a local pot-smoker I'd run into in Durango, adding that his Democratic Revolution Party supported its legalization for personal "medicinal" consumption. *BULLSHIT!*

But, that is what all dopers hope for, and he further insisted, "What we don't want is to criminalize youths for consuming or possessing marijuana."

At least now he made some sense.

Calderon', whose six-year terms ends in 2012, had proposed changing the law and to make it easier for users to get treatment instead of jail time but stop short of decriminalizing its sale and use.

Before I arrived, Mexico had considered acting on legislation that would have abolished prison sentences for drug possession in small amounts, but America squawked and that was the end of that.

"It's clear that a totally prohibitive policy has not been a solution for all ills," said a local police big-wig. "At the same time, it's illusory to imagine that complete legalization of marijuana would be a panacea."

Though not according to the smokers!

On the streets everywhere one could see activists urging voters to pressure lawmakers to keep in mind that drug use and abuse were still rising in Mexico. The number of people who have tried drugs rose by a million in 2008, while the number of addicts rose from 307,000 to an estimated 465,000 ~ according to newspapers' statistics. Frankly, I was surprised the numbers were so low, unless the officials weren't releasing the actual figures.

Drug-abuse related violence has surged to unprecedented levels since Calderon' launched his offensive against the powerful trafficking cartels in 2006. Most, however, ask themselves how Calderon' has managed to escape assassination. Lawmakers refused to deal with specific proposals in either case, and the fight was not expected to result in concerted action. Lawmakers have said they want to continue the study before they even begin to consider proposed bills for legitimizing Pot, and thus make Billy Miles happy.

The time had come, inevitably, to depart Durango and head on somewhere else. I had thought to make for Coahuila, but the weather was not permitting, so I changed course and ended up in *Aguascalientes* (literally "Hot Water"): Although this state is not often billed as a tourist center, international busy-bodies, as well as yokels from all over Mexico, are attracted to the San Marcos Fair, which is considered the national fair of the whole country and contributes much to Mexico's economy. Recently, Aguascalientes, also the name of the capital city, has gained some notoriety as a "hot" destination for its superb colonial architecture visible in the colonial centre, as well as the modernity and dynamism in the outskirts.

The city is also popular for its ambiance of relaxation and for its security and cleanliness, as it is often lauded by people when traveling to this part of the country. The place is indeed known for "Hot Water," and the haciendas, hot springs and baths scattered around the state are also of recreational relevance besides the historical landmarks. In the city of Aguascalientes one of the most enchanting sunsets in the world can be seen in the Cerro del Muerto (Hill of the Dead); the hill resembles the shape of a man lying down. The city of Aguascalientes is called "el corazon'" which means "the heart" of Mexico because it lies in the middle of the country.

Coming here was significant to me because I would meet a couple of distant relatives on my mother's side who are, or had been Roman Catholic priests; a fact which was unusual only because most of my mother's relatives are, or had been clergy-bashing Freemasons. Bernardo Lugo Rivera, related to my mother once removed, was the first one of my local contacts to receive my introduction query, and warmly welcomed me to his home. Oddly enough, I arrived to discover he was in the middle of quite a controversy of his own. If the inheritance squabbles between the Martins back in Jalisco weren't enough, now I would be a reluctant observer of a sex scandal. Ostensibly he had admitted the previous month that he is the father of a child conceived while he was still a Roman Catholic priest. Bernardo, a middle-height and lanky figure, quiet and shy though somewhat cave-mannish in appearance, surprised his parish by acknowledging he had suffered an intimate relationship not only with some local church-mouse named Victoria Vargas, the child's mother, just five days after lawyers for Vargas announced they were filing a paternity suit against him but also with a fellow named Nicolas Mejia, an effeminate though handsome, faux-blonde and pot-smoking gay man who claimed to be Bernardo's partner. For a minute there I thought I was in the middle of a scene in some updated version of Tennessee Williams' *Night of the Iguana*!

Before I had a chance to ask questions, he was harangued by the local press and a parish lynch-mob, forcing him to respond, "Here and now, before my people and my conscience, I declare with absolute honesty and a sense of duty and transparency in relation to the controversy provoked by the paternity suit, that there was a relationship with Victoria Vargas." Then he went on after swallowing his pride along with some emotions, "I assume all responsibilities ... and recognize the paternity of the child, and promise to protect the boy's privacy. He will lack for nothing as long as I can help it."

I was aghast at the personal drama I had stumbled upon. I had really to think hard whether to stay and take in all the emotions, or flee for quieter prospects. After all, I didn't know this guy, he was just a distant relative I'd heard about in passing years before. Hence, would it behoove me to experience a real live sex scandal? I caved in to my baser instincts, and resolved to take in all of the juicy details.

After the commotion had died down (somewhat), I approached him with my own questions, but he said he would not comment further on the matter for the rest of the day, and would instead focus on his responsibility. It was not known if Vargas had immediately responded to Bernardo's surprise announcement, but her lawyer, like a true blue vulturine opportunist, said he was pleased. All that I could express was my dismay and sympathy for this fellow who, like my Jalisco relatives, I had never met before but now found myself in the middle of his worst tribulations. He did later complain to me that, "By recognizing I am the father of the child, I proved my persecutors right. But I had no intention of inventing anything."

He also confided that he did not know immediately what would happen with the lawsuit. A couple of weeks before, he'd said he would withdraw it after Vargas denied approving it.

But, the Judge said the law required the case to continue, even if Vargas's lawyers withdraw it. Bernardo would be notified in three days of the content of the lawsuit in any case.

Frankly, had I known about this scandal beforehand I think I would have braved the cold winds of Coahuila. While Bernardo would remain silent about the allegations until the forthcoming Wednesday, he did plan to say that the paternity claim "must be false." His legal adviser called it a smear campaign by Vargas's lawyers, so what advice could I give him? He was very humble with me and very generous, but so preoccupied nonetheless that at times I felt like he was unaware of my presence.

Nicolas came in soon-after, and we all had a long conversation about it. "Generally speaking," said Nicolas, "people get more in trouble for lying about what they've done than for what they've actually done," which was some advice he admitted he should have used after he had initially denied his relationship with uncle Bernardo. Then, to my consternation, Nicolas pulled out a *roach* and starting smoking away, and suffused the atmosphere with the noxious fumes. I almost gagged. But, his face lit up and he exclaimed, "Ah, such a smoker's delight!"

With Bernardo joining him, I had little choice but to shut up!

As I saw this affair (which really concerned me not), by acknowledging his son Bernardo could steal thunder from the opposition and would be able to move forward and focus on his more compelling problems--namely his active support for the legalization of marijuana, and more importantly, his position on gay matrimony in view of the fact that he was currently involved with another man, and his Roman Catholic convictions prevented him from accepting such unions. Bernardo, 48, had resigned in 2004 as pastor of San Pedro, latterly his Aguascalientes parish and the poorest in the region. I also learned that in December 2006 he announced that he was renouncing the priesthood itself to run for local office and fight for legalized marijuana and Gay rights. But it was not until July 31 of last year that he was given "consecrated" permission to resign by his archbishop, thus relieving him of his chastity vows, and freeing him to pursue the kind of love that dare not speak its name in provincial Mexico.

With all the details of a troubled vocation flying back and forth, I learned that his boy was born on May 4, 2007, and that the child is named Armindo Primo de Rivera in honor of Bernardo's grandfather.

The mother is now 26, but her relationship with the priest-turned-political hack began when she was 16, according to Bernardo's own admission. His opponents in the state legislature called on the Church to excommunicate him for allegedly having a relationship with an adolescent while he was a priest, but nothing came of that.

Monsignor. Mario Medina Villalobos, who had been present at the gathering in Bernardo's home and had initially supported his onetime pupil, was the first member of the local clergy to react.

"Bernardo lied to the church, but better late than never, as the saying goes," Medina said to the group. "He won't be the only one who lies to the church, but he recognized his mistake and that is a courageous act. Truth be told, courage is a trait rarely to be seen in the Church."

I personally think that Bernardo's acknowledgment of his paternity effectively stopped the growing scandal dead in its tracks. The monsignor further remarked, "He is not the first priest with a child."

Unfortunately, many of his parishioners considered the scandal a black eye for the Catholic Church, which 90 percent of Mexicans identify as their faith, and residents of Aguascalientes are particularly touchy about the subject. Others believe the church should examine its celibacy (rule for clergy), because it's an embarrassment that more and more priests have had sex with parishioners, and a boy was born out of Bernardo's relationship. Fortunately, he was accepting his responsibility as father, that's all I could say. The episode was like another "telenovela" (soap opera), but fewer and fewer people were tuning in to watch the almost formulaic melodrama.

When we finally had a few moments alone together, I explained the reasons for my adventure, he explained the finer points of smoking marijuana with Nicolas (among other things), and the revelation he'd had which led him to emerge from the closet of sexual shame. We further exchanged laughs, anecdotes, and a few hopes for the future.

GETTING MY MOXY BACK

At this point in my journey I felt like I was losing my drive, my motivation ... my "moxy." Everything seemed to be falling apart on me, and at each point of arrival I was being met with more and more controversy rather than enthusiastic assistance, which, to reiterate, was all I wanted. The anxiety surrounding, and conflicts within the family relations were putting a damper on everything, and the more I crossed state borders, the more I antagonized the federales, thus laying myself bare to dishonorable deportation.

After talking and dealing with Bernardo for a couple of days, I started to feel a turn-around in my mood. Nicolas would poke fun at me (and that's all he poked) that it was the pot fumes that were working their "magic" on me. My "humors" were in tact, none-theless, and my reason unclouded, despite Nicolas's arguments to the contrary. After much reflection and introspection, the light of inspiration slowly flickered again, and I could focus on my purpose once more in spite of the pot and silly insinuations.

The next morning I exclaimed with glee, *Praise Heaven!* I found the will, if not the energy, to work on my journal again after a 5-day lapse ~ the very days since the arsenal explosions in Durango.

I was getting my moxy back! But, there surely had been a lot of distraction. Hopefully, from now on I could return to my goals without confrontational interruptions from nagging parishioners or loitering lovers with a penchant for ganja worship.

Bernardo and I talked calmly about the scandal. He meekly apologized for allowing the affair to become so damn *caliente* (hot). But, in a few more weeks it would all be OVER, or so he wanted to believe. I shared with him a letter of introduction written by Consuelo, whom he knew very well. He then showed me pictures of his grandfather Armindo, and offered to scan them so I could have a copy of each before I left. From them I could see my family resemblance and get a feel for our family heritage. I thought it all too curious considering how Corazon had compared me to her Grandpa David. Did I possess such a common face that I could be confused for anyone, albeit old grandfatherly types?

Bernardo insisted the pictures would show me how well I fit in to the overall scheme. Moreover, without pressing him, he shared stories Grandpa Armindo had told him about his run-in, and experiences with Fulgencio San Roman ~ stories about politics and their mutual association with an underground writers' group that opposed the increasingly patronizing hold the PRI Party was tightening around Mexico's democratic institutions back in the 1950s. For the present I needed only to hang on a bit longer.

I was quite curious and anxious to learn more about my family heritage, albeit loosely connected with respect to Bernardo.

I think it was finally settling in that it was not just a symbolical adoption, but the return of a long lost half brother of mine! At this point I felt like I had three grand-fathers; I wasn't just a Martin, but the grandson of Armindo and Fulgencio. Yet, what of Fulgencio? His life was hanging by a thread, to coin a phrase, and a death watch had commenced. All that I could think about was whether I could make it back in time to Reynosa and pay my respects before this great and mysterious institution of cinema-art had passed away.

Even though it was more of a coincidence than anything else, it was so ironic that my own great-grandfather Alberto Aldama, father of my father's mother, was of fine Sephardic stock (speaking of the latter, I swear to you, my grandmother Justina looks just like Menachem Begin if he were a drag queen), and, like Armindo, had made good money in the meat-packing business. He put my own father to work, and he did so until he was 21 ~ yes, my "old man" could have inherited the whole enterprise and could have died a millionaire, but, way back then, he decided he'd had enough of the stench of dead carcasses stuck up his nose, and waved off Great-Grandpa Alberto. He'd decided on the life of a male whore until he met my mother about 8 years later, and the rest, as they say, is tragedy.

Furthermore, it seemed like the family meat-packing vocation asserted itself now that I had discovered I was related to Bernardo.

I found it also quite funny that Grandpa Armindo, just like Corazon's grandfather, had moved to California so that no one would know him. Why? Who was he running away from?

Neither Bernardo nor anyone could tell me, but it happened way back in 1952, the very year my parents were married.

Drudging up the family history was turning out be a lot more interesting than I'd supposed.

Bernardo wasn't sure when those pictures he showed me were taken, probably in the 1940's. Grandpa Armindo died in the 1970's from cancer. He was a tough bird, hated by most ~ but he was always nice to those who knew him best. He was just a typical Mexican Macho-Gentleman who wouldn't tolerate crap from anybody!

The hours came and went, and I bucked up and decided to get moving again. No sooner had I resolved to take a side-trip to one of the natural hot-springs of Aguascalientes and thereafter soaked my travel-weary carcass in a boiling bath, when another scandal exploded over Bernardo's head, and this time involved many priests and their parishes. Thus my new found relative, who was long gone from his sacerdotal duties, was attacked again, and this time it really involved Nicolas; for years he had served as Bernardo's private secretary and personal manager, hence much of what they were being accused of fell on his head. The press had a field day interrogating poor saps like them and other priests and bishops they had exposed. Bills for porn movies, horse manure, a chocolate Santa Claus, all listed as expense claims by the respective bishops and priests to pay for an array of items. They were initially exposed by a disgruntled former priest who had heretofore fled to Spain. Then the regional newspapers ran away with the juicy rumors the following Friday, stoking public anger over congregational excesses amid the protracted recession. The Aguascalientes Daily published details of claims related to 13 priests and offered examples of hundreds of other bills submitted by them to their respective dioceses, and their bishops seemed to have participated in the graft. The documents revealed how some diocesans used lax regulations to accumulate hefty bills to pay for their relatives' housing taxes and costs of furnishing homes, while others claimed for trivial amounts including a packet of pork rinds worth about $1, two cans of cat food and an ice cube tray (these belonged to Nicolas).

One shameless small-town pastor claimed the cost of servicing the swimming pool of the country home his parishioners had bought for his relatives, without their knowledge, while another paid for a hunter to catch coyotes who'd invaded his garden, according to the newspapers. A minor monsignor in the municipality of Calvillo, then the diocese treasurer, paid his brother 65,000 pesos ($5,000USD as of 2009) for cleaning services between 2003 and 2006. A spokesman said the cleric's brother had handled payments for a cleaner the two men shared. The figures released to the state government (which was in no position to cast aspersions of their own) showed that the priests and their assistants claimed 93 million pesos ($7.2 million USD) in allowances and expenses over the said period. Under the Mexican Church's own rules, parishes could claim expenses for a second home, rent and furnishings, and expenses incurred when staying away overnight from their parish.

The price for such furnishings was colloquially known as the "Liverpool list," named after an upscale Mexican department store chain. The list was being axed under reforms of the system currently under scrutiny by the laity and the grueling Press.

The crooked secular government officials had long refused to offer receipt by receipt breakdowns of their claims for public money, until a ruling under Instituto Federal de Eleccion' (IFE) ordered them to make the details known. Hence, it behooved them to keep their mouths shut about the Church finances. Thousands of receipts for claims by both secular and clerical big-wigs would be published in July after the congressional elections, but the newspapers railed they had obtained the material ahead of its planned release.

Members of that part of Mexico's public that still cared for what happens with their leaders complained the expenses system is too generous, isn't independently audited, and follows rules drafted by the lawmakers themselves. The first to benefit were the clergy who were really outside of government jurisdiction yet subject to income laws. Then, after much haranguing, some rogue journalist got the offending monsignor to make a statement: "There can be no greater proof of the need for urgent and wholesale reform of the expenses of these priests than the fact that so many people at the top of government have been making such dubious claims."

A Wetback in Reverse

In other words, he was passing the buck!

A spokesman for the bishop of said diocese claimed the cost of housing taxes he'd never actually paid though later reimbursed authorities. In a handwritten note explaining his mistake, he wrote that "accountancy does not appear to be my strongest suit."

Then the bishop urged congregations under his watch to speed up an expenses payment. His secretary confided to a conniving reporter "he might be in line for a papal suspension" if he didn't receive the money quickly. To me it was just a lot of hub-bub. As I told Bernardo and Nicolas after we'd discussed the issue, the system doesn't seem to work. I knew it doesn't work, and it had to be changed. For their part, they half-heartedly agreed.

I was rather disgusted to learn that Bernardo had been receiving about 18,900 pesos per month for his priestly work ~ that is, doing mostly nothing. By comparison, many grade-school teachers, police and fire-men earn a base salary of about 4,500 pesos per month working their arses off!

I just had to shake my head in disgust in front of Bernardo who was forced to concede the injustice of it all.

A key concern for critics of the system is how Mexican lawmakers routinely switched the house they called their "personal" residence. Those changes meant they could claim second home allowances like the costs of furniture, decorating and repairs on several different properties. Other bills show how priests, invoking the necessities of their respective parish, were prepared to claim even small amounts, including designer hand-bags, imported chocolate Santa Claus-shaped snacks, and very expensive silver-service sets. One particularly wealthy parish curate charged the parish for a bag of manure for his country retreat. Previously, the curate's secretary (and probable live-in lover) acknowledged she'd claimed the costs of two pay-per-view porn movies watched by her "man-of-the-cloth."

For shame ... for shame ...

Thence, with so many vicious little scandals emerging from the very bowels of the Mexican Church, how could I not get my writer's moxy back? It was all just so titillating that I forgot about my woes and my purpose in Mexico for a spell!

A MULTITUDE OF SINS

The whole shebang with the Roman Catholic priesthood was, in the opinion of many Mexicans, long over-due. The awful pederasty scandals in America were just the tip of the iceberg as it were, and Mexicans, long under the oppressive shadow of the Church, were now emerging in force, with courage and rage bursting in their breasts, to accuse their spiritual leaders of the rottenest of interpersonal crimes for which there'd be no remuneration of any kind. Poor Bernardo, I just knew that the erupting scandals were hurting him as much as the next guy. Though he had gladly given up his vocation, he was still faithful to the Church that had educated him and fostered his spiritual yearnings.

Guadalajara, long the seat of the Catholic hierarchy, was now the epicenter of the condemnation. Aguascalientes, being so close culturally and geographically, was sure to suffer from the backlash. The fiercely debated, long-delayed investigation into Mexico's Catholic-run institutions said that priests and nuns terrorized thousands of boys and girls in workhouse-style schools for decades and government inspectors, who'd always carried a contempt for the Church going back to the days of *La Revolucion'*, failed to stop the chronic beatings, rapes and humiliation.

Surprise, surprise!

Decades in the making, a recently released official report sided entirely with the horrific reports of abuse from former students sent to more than 300 church-run, mostly residential institutions. Victims' advocates said it didn't accomplish squat, peculiarly because none of the abusers had been fingered (no pun intended).

The report surmised that church officials always shielded the worst of pedophiles from arrest to protect their own reputations if nothing else and, according to documents uncovered in the Vatican, knew that many of the priestly pedophiles were serial attackers.

The investigators said irresistible, irrefutable testimony from still-traumatized individuals, now in old age, had demonstrated beyond a doubt that the entire church apparatus treated children more like prison inmates and slaves than people with legal rights and human potential. Bernardo reluctantly concurred.

"A climate of fear, created by pervasive, excessive and arbitrary punishment, permeated most of the institutions and all those run for the benefit of boys. Children lived with the daily terror of not knowing where the next beating was coming from," so concluded this pervasive study of Mexico's Commission to Inquire Into Child Abuse.

The cardinal-archbishop of Mexico City, leader of Mexico's 100 million Catholics and religious orders at the center of the scandal, offered immediate apologies, though not without some typical self-righteous justification ~ that maybe the brutalized children brought it upon themselves, thus *requiring* the abusers to beat them good.

Nonetheless, the cardinal went on to say, "I am profoundly sorry and deeply ashamed that children suffered in such awful ways in these institutions. This is not worthy of a Christian nation. This is not worthy of our Lady of Guadalupe, who is the mother of all. Children deserved better and especially from those caring for them in the name of Jesus Christ."

Whether anybody believed him, no one would say. I surely did not!

The Sisters of Mercy, which ran several refuges for girls and so-called fallen women where the report documented degenerative brutality, side-tracked the issue in a statement that said its nuns "accept that many who spent their childhoods in our orphanages or industrial schools were hurt and damaged while in our care" (no wonder nuns are so universally despised). One of the head mothers went on, "There is a great sadness in our hearts at this time and our deepest desire is to continue the healing process for all involved."

And, a priestly spokesman for the Christian Brothers order that hitherto ran dozens of boys' schools, said that reading the report's "presentation of the history of our institutions, it is hard to avoid feeling shame." (oh, so NOW they feel shame!)

At least 50,000 children deemed to be petty thieves, truants or from (stereo-typically Mexican) dysfunctional families, a category that often included unmarried mothers, were sent to Mexico's austere network of industrial schools, reformatories, orphanages and hostels from the 1910s until the last church-run facilities shut-down decades later. The scandals, unveiled by the Jalisco Supreme Court, found that molestation and rape were "endemic" in boys' facilities, chiefly run by the Christian Brothers, and their clerical over-seers pursued policies that increased the danger. Girls supervised by orders of nuns, chiefly the Sisters of Mercy, suffered much less sexual molestation but frequent beatings and humiliation designed to make them feel worthless. But, then again, that is how Mexicans typically treat each-other with or without participation from the Church.

"In some schools a high level of ritualized beating was routine ... Girls were struck with implements designed to maximize pain and were struck on all parts of the body. Personal and family denigration was widespread."

Victims of this medieval system have long decried the truth that has kept them in religious shackles, thus they demanded reportage of their experiences be documented and made public.

But several victims, who were prevented from attending that month's debate and scuffled with police outside a central Guadalajara hotel, complained the promised measures didn't go far enough and rejected the church leaders' apologies as insincere. Even the church leaders themselves didn't believe their own excuses.

Bernardo, trying to view the whole thing with an detached observer's eye, commented, "Victims will feel a small degree of comfort that they've been vindicated. But the findings do not go far enough."

Well, obviously ~ that's all I could add to his prosaic comment.

But my relative went on to say the report should have scrutinized how children like himself were taken away from parents without just cause, and demanded more answers from Mexican administrations after World War II that ceded control over their lives to the Church.

There was no argument on my part, but, as if trying to atone for the sins of his former bosses, he insisted that any apologies offered now were "hollow, shallow and have no substance or merit at all. We feel betrayed and cheated today."

And this is from a former priest who may have molested Nicolas before he decided on a life of gay activism!

In any case, the activists fighting against the Church proposed 21 ways the government could recognize past crimes, including building a permanent monument to the victims, providing counseling and education to victims and improving Mexico's current child protection services. But their findings would not be used for criminal prosecutions, regrettably, in part because the Christian Brothers successfully sued the commission to keep the identities of all of its suspected pedophiles, dead or alive, unnamed in the official public findings. No real names, whether of victims or perpetrators, appear in the final document.

Mexican bishops and religious orders all declined to comment on the scandals, citing the need to read the massive document first. The Mexican government already had funded a parallel compensation system that has paid abuse victims for stress and suffering. Thousands of claims remained outstanding, and would probably never be compensated. Victims received the payouts only if they waived their rights to sue the State and the Church. Hundreds have rejected that condition and had taken their abusers and those church employers to court. Fortunately for Bernardo, no one was around to point the finger at him. Furthermore, the anti-clerical activists said children had no safe and easy way to tell responsible authorities about the brutality and sexual degradation they were suffering, particularly the sexual aggression from church officials and older inmates in boys' institutions. Nicolas interrupted, much to Bernardo's embarrassment, "The management did not listen to or believe children when they complained of the activities of some of the men who had responsibility for their care ... At best, the abusers were moved, but nothing was done about the harm done to the children. At worst, the children were blamed, as though they were unruly miniature adults who knew what was going on, seen as having been corrupted by the sexual activity, and were punished severely."

Then he looked over at Bernardo and added, "Disgraceful. Just, disgraceful. How could they do such things?" Bernardo just nodded.

The laity bigwigs, much to their credit, dismissed as implausible a central defense of the religious orders that, in bygone days, people did not recognize the sexual abuse of a child as a criminal offense, but rather as a sin that required repentance. *BULLSHIT!*

In their testimony, religious orders conveniently cited this as the most compelling reason why sex-predator-pervert priests and man-hungry monks were sheltered within their organization and moved to new posts where they could go on perverting and fondling children to their hearts' content. Once again Nicolas just shook his head in disgust.

But the big-wigs said their fact-finding, which included unearthing decades-old church archives, principally stored in the Vatican, on scores of unreported abuse cases from Mexico's industrial schools, demonstrated that officials understood exactly what was at stake: their own reputations, and personal secrets they dared not expose.

They cited numerous examples where school managers hypocritically told police about child abusers who were not church officials, but never did when one of their own had committed the diddling and piddling.

Bernardo, of course, had to have the final word on this controversy: "Contrary to the Church apologists' claims that the recidivist nature of sexual transgressors was not understood, it is clear from these tragic cases that they were aware of the propensity for these perverts to re-abuse!"

And Nicolas just shook his head, "Disgraceful ... just disgraceful!"

Later, I was to learn that Fulgencio, himself a victim of monkish abuse, made a movie about the subject back in the 1940s:

Memories Of Ghosts To Come.

PLAYING CAT AND MOUSE IN THE STREETS

After overcoming a "smoking" farewell party given to me by my hosts, my flight out of Aguascalientes couldn't have been more precipitous. The bus-ride to my next destination, San Luis Potosi was quiet enough, and the arrival in San Luis Potosi City was pleasant. The city is beautiful, full of colonial charms, not to mention charming Criollo-type people. Today, the downtown is one of plazas and colonial architecture. The "Plaza de Armas" is home to a cathedral and an 18th Century governor's palace, and chatting couples and families enjoying popsicles can be seen around the city at times. The nearby "Templo de Nuestra Senora del Carmen," with its colorful tiled domes and famous altars, is considered among Mexico's finest churches. In addition, San Luis is home to the building Plaza de Toros Fermin Rivera. Potosinos (as residents of the city are referred to) are proud of their bright orange *enchiladas potosinas*, often served fried with refried beans and guacamole. I suppose they were right to feel proud because the examples I choked down were quite tasty, in spite of the gastritis they later gave me.

The nearby town of Santa Maria del Rio provides the state with its sparkling mineral water, *Agua de Lourdes*. The water fills both store shelves and the cocktails of Potosinos, who claim the water can cure a hangover, and I needed some in a hurry. I learned about the latter through their newspapers, and they are known for their objectivity. I've depended on them while in Mexico to keep me abreast of current events: El Sol de San Luis, Pulso, El Heraldo de San Luis, La Prensa, San Luis Hoy, La Jornada San Luis y Tribuna. On-line journalism is pretty good, and their "Noticiero Cuarto Enfoque" has been a reliable source of developments through the Web. The Laberinto Museum of Science and Arts, quite an impressive modern structure, allows visitors to make an interactive tour that will switch themes of the art museum with samples of science and technology, and considering the restlessness that was presently overtaking me, I found it to be a relaxing distraction.

Here in San Luis they were preparing for the Grito de la Independencia (Independence Cry), always held at mid-night September 16th. Well, that date was a few days off, and I had hoped to make it to Dolores- Hidalgo in the state of Guanajuato where the historic event actually took place in 1810, to witness the proceedings.

There was, however, no rejoicing to be had for the time being (what a surprise!). And, I did not make the best of my time hereabout. Actually, things were as bad as they could ever be. I was just feeling so run down, and the latest spat of the *Aztec Two-Step* really drained me, literally. Then, to top things off, as I was rummaging through some merchandise at a side-town *Fayuqueros* (unlicensed swap-meet) the silly hag who had just taken my money for the web-cam and related attachments I wanted, went ahead and dropped a bombshell on me after I'd just wished her a happy day: considering she'd brought me the equipment, which I did not expect, and talked to me about the uses of the mobile web-cam and the communication programs, and even proposed, out of her own volition, she would eliminate the middle-man mark-up of these toys from the base price if I would refer my friends and family to her, just up and accused me of thieving from her the second she saw some police-men approaching her stall!

Well, when the two officers arrived to investigate her show of paranoia, I showed them the receipt I'd just been handed as well as the equipment, which was already placed in the bag she gave me. So, how could I know that she was selling me stolen goods? They examined her hand-written receipt carefully and saw with their own, crusty brown eyes that everything was accounted for and that **no** extraneous materials were included in the bag. That insane, demented old bitch was clearly feeling guilty about her illegal activities and was deflecting the crime upon me with all of her yammering, but her actions had just put the last straw on me with respect to my tolerance for the imbecilic yokels. We had a terrible argument match right in front of the bemused police, who ended up doing nothing, and it degenerated into a screaming match with all the Mexican expletives one could think of at the moment. This, by far, was the closest I got to being discovered for an illegal alien.

I was so overwrought with anger and sadness afterwards that nothing could calm me down. I had taken aspirin already, several Tylenol, and this blue pill that was supposed to knock me out, but my tachycardia was getting worse. I could feel the bile seeping into my blood, I just couldn't calm down. This undue experience brought my late-great Aunt Carmela (Fulgencio's mother) to mind. She had reputedly been attacked by her drunken brother, Damiano, and died just from such a condition; her blood sugar shot up and no amount of medication could calm her down, and her heart just pumped away madly until she passed away a month later.

I thought I stood on the precipice of a similar disaster. I kept thinking, how dare that old hag accuse me, after all I had suffered in this country? I could have been exposed to the Federales right then and there!

Damn! All she had yelled at me just left me sleepless that evening. She made me feel like a fucking leech, and put the fear of deportation right back into my gut. I mean, it was an ugly exchange, and, of course, I didn't miss a chance to scream at her, that she was a "miserable spicko who will wallow in your own filth for the rest of your years!"

I may have left her sleepless as well.

Nevertheless, the wretched exchange inspired me too. I would trudge on despite my doubts. I would realize my goal despite the threats to my safety. Yes, it is finished, practically, between me and Mexico. I want to get out of this country, and the sooner the better. I thought to stay till Christmas, but I felt really fed up by now. I would go on just long enough till things got better for me. I needed to divorce myself from this creeping dementia. It was not a case of my health withering away. I still had enough of my resolve to trudge on and had always to remain on guard against atom-brained street crooks, con-artists, shysters and swindlers, always craftily concocting ways of getting at one's honestly earned dinero. *Damn!* was all I could scream regarding these evil demons I felt were lurking about and making it their business to screw with my rotten life, using native simpletons as their agents of damnation. I was in serious shit here, and didn't know to whom to turn this time around. I could not get over it.

Not 8 days had past since I'd left Durango and traveled through Aguascalientes, and already the people and local environment had sent my soul plunging into the depths of Hell! And, with the heat, 102 degrees and rising, again I was wondering what I could do to forget the pitfalls of this quest of mine that now seemed like a waste of time. These Potosinos finished me off emotionally (or so I thought at the moment), rendering my purpose vile and untouchable. I was so sick to my stomach, always figuratively and now literally, and thought I would vomit on the police.

The next day, Mexican Independence Day preparations were evident throughout the city. I called some local acquaintances, the Aguilars, who I did not know very well, and they couldn't answer any of my family questions nor even knew who Fulgencio San Roman was, but they invited me to a pleasant luncheon. They were very nice to me, but their conversation left me a bit tearful. They'd recently lost their mother, so they were seeking solace from whomever would give it. I supposed, at the time, that I didn't mind, but the sight of me offering condolences was pretty mawkish in retrospect. Yes, it was very pleasant but sad as well. Moreover, The pre-celebration activities left me wistful for Old Glory. I missed my country and all of its distractions, most of all on this day of remembrance for patriotic values. My friends were sorry that I was going through such hell with the Federales, and there did not seem to be a way out before I'd accomplished my goal.

Would I survive for a couple more months down here until I'd reached my goal? If they did catch me before doing so, I could ask my cousins back home to help in bringing me back. Even if I were to suffer more confrontations with native officials of any type until this business had been settled, it would have to be better than living in the Hell of failure and self-defeat for the rest of my life. I reflected upon those fears of leaving before I had finished, and they just didn't make sense anymore. All I wanted was some affirmation. All I wanted was some human vindication. Nothing mattered anymore. Nothing ever really mattered.

On a few occasions, I briefly thought to take a bus or train back. Others encouraged me to do so before the Federales caught up with me. If I got back to California, I could re-apply for an extended visa until things got more settled. Hell, I could go on just as I was, get drunk and forget my woes for a spell, cry to the American embassy... anything, so long as I could find closure to this journey and return with vindication

A Wetback in Reverse

in hand. This cat and mouse game I was playing with the Federales and the uncooperative natives, in the streets or on the road, was wearing me thin. I had had enough of the contemptuous attitude and mortal threats that greeted me in almost every city. And yet, I couldn't be worse off than I was.

I wouldn't give up till the puzzle had been solved.

INDEFENSIBLE ... IRRESISTIBLE

My stay in San Luis Potosi ended up quiet and without glad recollections. I prepared myself for the journey to Guanajuato, the cradle of my mother's ancestors. It is also one of the finest colonial architectural treasures in the whole Western Hemisphere. It is also a bastion of Roman Catholicism, even though most of its residents are secretly anti-clerical; this was especially true of my maternal relatives. The bad news for the Church didn't end with the cases of abuse, and Bernardo was good enough to inform me of the newest developments. Thus, in Guanajuato and elsewhere, the Catholic orders responsible for abusing Mexico's poorest children whined that they were struggling to come up with funds to help their pathetic dupes. Yet some vituperative sleuthing on the part of anti-clerical groups into their net worth painted a very different picture ~ that of nuns and monks with billions' worth of carefully sheltered assets worldwide. *Jesus!* And here I was giving alms to help them!

Mexican government leaders said that week they'd expected the 18 religious orders involved in mistreating children in workhouse-style schools to pay a much greater portion of recompense to 34,000 state-recognized victims. They also exacted from the secretive orders the truth be revealed about their wealth for the first time in face-to-face deliberations with the government, which seemed shocking because of so many anti-church laws on the books. The average folk didn't like what they were hearing, so they had to ascertain how rich they really are. The government was adamant and determined that they would make an appropriate contribution, but to many it seemed like one crook was demanding an accounting from another.

The pressure followed the previous week's publication of a ten-year investigation into the widespread sexual, physical and psychological humiliation of children in Church care from the 1920s to the 1990s, when the last of the special schools, reformatories and orphanages had been scrutinized.

Some days before, about half of the 18 orders agreed they would meet with the federal officials. All reiterated excuses along with half-hearted apologies for their part in harming children, but none said they would "donate" more than promised in a 2002 deal with the government that left Mexicans paying practically all of the settlement to conciliate the abuse claims. Under their proviso, the orders received a state indemnity from civil lawsuits by the victims in exchange for a preposterous contribution. Church leaders reluctantly admitted, though not before protesting, they hadn't given the Mexican government all that money yet, because their earmarked donations were largely in properties they were not supposed to accept, some of which still remained in church hands, and most suffering heavy falls in valuation amid Mexico's recession.

The orders had ruled out paying more compensation that week, even though the impeachment found them principally to blame and guilty of far greater abuses than they admitted to in past years. Instead, the orders have offered unspecified contributions to a new victims' compensation fund.

The Conference of Religious Orders in Mexico, an umbrella body, reported the 18 orders were planning a private strategy session in Guanajuato to decide on a common approach to the outstanding claims. Insiders in the global resistance against abuse claims said the orders won't shed light on their finances voluntarily.

First off, no one could trust anything they said. The claimants needed a champion of abuse victims' rights. And they had to be prepared to follow up the urging for voluntary donation or contribution with some form of force, which really got the priests and nuns shaking under their cassocks and habits. The Mexican orders had to be forced by a power greater than themselves, and that was the courts and the Mexican government, to make sure the payments for damages come, even to the point of forcibly divesting them of their goods.

The order most deeply implicated in the unfolding scandals, the Christian Brothers, was founded two centuries ago but has spread across the globe. It has the biggest property empire and is vulnerable to exposure to abuse claims ranging from the United States to Canada, Australia and other countries.

The order still owns hundreds of boys' schools in 20 countries worldwide. But, the Mexican lawyers who expected to win multi-million-dollar sex-abuse cases against the Christian Brothers accuse the brotherhood of making itself appear as destitute as possible by transferring school ownership to individual members, trusts, corporations or offshore bodies ~ just like the rottenest of crooks.

Bernardo commented, "Their assets and how they hold assets is of Byzantine complexity. They have unlimited financial resources to mount litigation, and they have absolutely no shame in doing so."

I couldn't agree more. Previously, A bust by Mexican broadcasters (circa 2000) into Christian Brothers' mounting legal fights world-wide estimated the order's global property assets, including its Rome headquarters, in excess of billions of dollars.

A spokesman for the Christian Brothers in Mexico estimated the previous month that its approximately 100 schools in Mexico alone are worth billions of pesos.

Last year the order allegedly transferred control of its Mexican school network to a Guadalajara-based trust. The same priests insisted the trust was designed to defend the long-term credibility of the order's schools, not protect the order from lawsuits. They further insisted the order was ready to relinquish Mexican assets but was struggling financially to care for its 300 mostly elderly brothers in Mexico. Other apologists came forth to say the order would try to beg more money to placate the victims, but weren't sure that was feasible. At this point in time, I didn't believe they could either.

Still others commented that the Christian Brothers often sought to negate their hold over particularly fat assets that could be handed over to, or awarded, in any judgment in favor of the aggrieved.

Nothing of this surprised me, it's what corporations do when they feel like they're in deep shit. The question was whether it was lawful.

I spoke later on with a local journalist who really hated the Church and had exposed church abuse cover-ups in Mexico, and he said Christian Brothers' leaders in Australia and Canada behaved the same way during 1990s abuse scandals in those countries as they were doing now in Mexico.

None of this made much sense to me. They denied the abuse, accused the victims of lying, and set about ensuring that their assets were protected from survivors and lawsuits by either creating trusts or splitting various schools and assets away from central control, and still acted as though they were innocent and beyond judgment.

Disgraceful, like Nicolas would say, just disgraceful!

Other Church orders, like the Legion of Christ founded by the pederastic priest Marcial Maciel, exposed as serial abusers have big footprints overseas. Others, like the Sisters of Mercy who run scores of girls' schools in Britain, Australia, Canada, New Zealand and the United States, have ruined a few lives in Mexico as well. The Sisters of Mercy also own key hospitals in Mexico.

Their nuns were identified as serial abusers of girls, chiefly in the form of beatings and humiliation rather than molestation. Like the Christian Brothers, they have vowed to cooperate with the Mexican government, but made no promises to give more money for victims.

The Mexican Press urged the government to go harder after the orders, which was not surprising considering their liberal leanings.

Many journalists agreed with me that their foolish and self-serving efforts to guard their greedy interests were rapidly aggravating whatever little support they had. This is how institutions perish. The gross imbalance which left the hapless people paying 90 percent is indefensible ... yet following the scandals was so irresistible.

Some victims want the government to hold a national referendum to amend Mexico's constitution, which is already very hostile to the Church, so it would permit seizures of church money and property.

Some people couldn't wait to divulge their own experiences with brutal monks and cruel nuns. A certain Gabriel Cisneros, 72, I'd spoken to confided that he'd been separated from his seven brothers, sisters and cousins when they were placed in separate church-run residences in the 1940s. He suffered repeated rapes and beatings from age 8 onward in an industrial school run by the Oblates of Mary Immaculate order in a town of Oaxaca.

Cisneros electrified many viewers that week by denouncing a government minister on live television, detailing the degradations and terror he endured as a boy and demanding a constitutional crackdown on church rapacity. He exclaimed, "Don't say you can't change it! You are the government of this state. You run this state. So, for God's sake, stop *cagando el palo* (shitting the stick) because I am sick of it! All of Mexico is sick of it!"

Well, the week ended on a sizzling note, and I would have plenty to fret over while I made for Guanajuato. Poor Mexico, I thought. If this sad country didn't have enough to worry about, now the Church, their only spiritual solace, was eroding about their knees as the faithful genuflected to receive communion or a blessing from the very men who'd soiled their hands with the blood or sexual excretions of their victims!

... Disgraceful! Just, disgraceful!

A SEASON OF EVIL AND HATE

After inquiring of the local cinema museum about the works of Fulgencio San Roman, I was privileged to attend a late night viewing of *Memories of Ghosts to Come*, which proved quite prescient considering the unfolding church scandals.

Once going about the town and exploring the mystical charms of Guanajuato, which seemed more like some Renaissance town in Italy or Spain, the glaring paradox of the place standing as a metonym for the whole country somehow made sense for the first time since my arrival several moons before. I then hunkered down to catch up on my journal and iron out the riddles that withheld my comprehension from the resolution I sought. I don't know, but with everything that was going on, the infinite distractions served the very essence of abstraction. I had to trudge on in a season of doubt and anxiety. I would conclude this during a season of evil and hate.

First, all that I was going through, *Jesus Christ!*

And now, what? Malcontents decide they want to set the house ablaze, figuratively speaking? Mexico was the edifice that would be consumed in the inferno. Specifically, today, this morning, the 13th of September, I woke up and felt like it was going to be a fabulous day, but I noticed that others were looking at me suspiciously (actually for a couple of days now, especially after I'd interact with the natives, express my conclusions about what was going on, and related my needs to them). I couldn't pay much mind to them. Nevertheless, these ignorant wretches have been harboring suspicions about all strangers, and they probably thought I was a drug smuggler or something like that. I couldn't let these yokels impede my way, so I went straight for the ancestral home of the Riveras on Pocitos Street. It was quite a homecoming, and an eerie one at that. Things would never be the same afterwards.

I knocked on the rustic door, and a maid with Indian hair-locks opened and meekly presented me to Micaela Rivera, a great aunt of my mother. She was very gracious and curious about my particular branch of the family. She hardly remembered my mother, but knew very well how I fit into the family tree. She invited me to an old fashioned Spanish breakfast, and after we'd sat down to eat, her son and daughter entered. After we'd exchanged pleasantries, they excused themselves and went ahead, almost in cold blood and right before my eyes, and accused their mother of stealing. Yes! of charging many of their property's expenses to the family account. Aunt Micaela cried, and complained that after scrupulously managing the tenuous account all this time without touching it, they should come forth with such a spurious accusation. The fact that the others were always complaining and crying about how their mother withheld money from even herself should have been proof enough that she was not guilty of malfeasance, let alone stealing by charging expensive stuff to the damned account. Only a prisoner who has no freedom or can't do anything to help him/herself, as I saw it, is always complaining and crying. My distant cousins regarded themselves as prisoners. Furthermore, I was later to find out that she still had over $4 Million Pesos in her private account, acquired from the dowry she kept after her husband Rodrigo had died. She had every right therefore to buy anything she wanted, with or without the approval of her ungrateful children.

But, no! They insisted she had charged half a million Pesos to the family account and then, out of sheer paranoia, suggested that I, a mysterious presence who'd just shown up out of nowhere, might be her accomplice! Could a sane and rational observer objectively believe this? Of course I had no idea this was going to happen, but it was obvious that their personal hostilities had been simmering for a long time. I think I did receive an email from one of them a couple of months ago, and I asked him/her if I could bring anything to ingratiate myself with their mother. The response was positive and gracious. All I did bring in tribute was a bottle of *Sangre de Cristo* (Blood of Christ) Sherry, a favorite wine of Micaela's. Thus, I asked myself, why were they squawking about poor little old me?

"One man's family," I tells ya'!

But no, I do this out of the goodness of my heart, and I think they even said that they had been informed that I was coming to inquire about "certain information." Unfortunately, because they over-looked any specifications they automatically assumed that it had something to do with their inheritance. Damn! First the Martins, and now the Riveras. Was it that *family* only meant inheritance to them? Then the boy, Rodrigo Jr., suggested we might do business by charging his expenses to the account over which he assumed I had control. He promised to pay me, that we'd be partners in lucrative deals, et cetera and what have you. It was just so outrageous I wanted to laugh in his face. The evil and hate were indeed written all over his face. The daughter, Celsa, was even more hostile and avoided me altogether. Poor Micaela, I thought. What a bunch a vipers she had to live with. She later wept on my shoulders, bereaving the fact her children took her for a swindler of sorts. Well, I had arrived here in peace and with the best intentions (I said to myself) *Pero no, ahora me traen como ladron'* (but no, now they took me for a thief). They also threatened to call the police on me!

Hence, her children insisted on examining the account online. I accommodated them by offering the use of my lap-top. They saw for themselves that it was all on the up and up, but their family relationship had just deteriorated before my eyes. They screamed at their mother, she screamed at them, called them *pinches mantenidos* (leeching bums), and all of them oblivious to my presence.

Between all that was happening with the Martins and the Gutierrez, and this latest altercation amongst the Riveras, this was a season of hate and evil, and I was squat in the middle. And now, after all the bullshit I had endured with these people, now I was regarded as a thief? This was fucking unbelievable! I was left so, so angry, distraught, I didn't know what I would do. It wasn't enough they were helping a great deal to ruin my life. Out of patience and a sense of benevolence, I had allowed them to ruin it. Still I had no options, except to get the hell out or die starving in the streets, or allow the Federales to take me. These petty squabbles were draining me like the bites of a thousand mosquitoes, and I had no way of controlling the anguish. In retrospect, I could have gone on pretending nothing had happened. As I reflected on the events, I was boiling over with an undue anger, and was suffering another case of tachycardia. Nothing calmed me down, and I was really getting sick over this.

Frederick Martin-Del-Campo

The meeting ended in a draw, so to speak. I bade my aunt to take good care of herself, she wished me the same and expressed her dismay over the demeaning display and accusations of her offspring. She was clearly very hurt and sorry about the whole matter and invited me to return under happier circumstances. I prayed things did calm down eventually with her and the family.

Yes, things were very bad within the respective families. They were, for the most part, not speaking to each-other (I certainly wouldn't be after all the things I had witnessed; if I did get involved it might lead to something terrible for me, so it was better that I kept my big mouth shut). I had thought to call Consuelo or Abigail and inquire about how things were going with them, but this last experience only left me with the desire to crawl under some rock for a spell. Actually, I had really nothing to worry about, I was not directly involved in any of their bellicosity, and they were more disposed to deal with me than with each-other, on both sides of the family coin.

All this was a god-damned dementia that was growing in most of them, a consequence of in-breeding I thought. I was now, with this accusation between the Riveras, bereft of family ties. The rancor endured left the situation just hopeless between them. There could not be a real reconciliation. Either they could live in a truce, or things would undoubtedly get worse, and I would be hopping on a plane or bus or whatever to get the fuck out regardless of what happened to them. But, since I was wallowing in self-pity, my only concern was what could happen to me after all I had sacrificed, all I had endured, all I did to realize my fondest hope of discovering my roots. I had nothing to fall back on. Sticking around for another round would spell disaster for me. All that they could think of was their supercilious accusations, unrequited bitterness, living through the worst periods of their life, and family genealogy just did not matter a rat's ass to them. I really made terrible mistakes in allowing them to affect me in such a way, and especially in depending on them for family trivia.

All I got from all this journey was a nascent hatred for the country of my ancestors, and they were opening wider this gate of hatred with their petty calumnies and viciousness. I had better stop this fulsome ruminating. I was just writing out of vituperative anger, but I feared the anger would never subside. It had been growing and festering for many years now between members of my immediate family, and the last 2 had been the most intense ~ Now that I had met many of the members of the extended clan, it was obvious that these conflicts were endemic to the family nature. In time I would respond with a powerful indictment of my own, but for the meantime I had to endure and make the best of things. As for my cousins, it was a lost cause. I couldn't know what would come of all this, and I certainly did not want to participate in some fight in which I was at a disadvantage. The accusation by Rodrigo and Celsa was the last straw. They were helping, or conspiring, to ruin my life without my suspecting it till it was too late.

When I had a clear opportunity, I would call and try to put them in their rightful place, make them see all this objectively, and make them realize how wrong they'd been. I was sorry about what the hate was doing to gentle souls like Aunt Micaela and cousins Consuelo and Abigail. I prayed that the calm of their individual circumstances would eventually be restored. I would never know, however, if their disagreements and grudges were reconciled.

I would simply participate in the rites of state for the rest of my journey, seek to enjoy myself, and fit the last pieces of the puzzle together before I went completely insane!

RED-LIGHT LIVELIHOODS

September 16th celebrations were inspiring and elegant in Dolores-Hidalgo. I had a great supper of Pozole soup and Sopes in a restaurant across the park from the cathedral. After fireworks celebrations, I determined to head for Leon' City and take in some of the nightlife. I mixed in with a few rake-hells from the large Argentinian immigrant community in the city because the local Mexicans weren't all that friendly. The city's *Optibus* bus rapid transit colloquially known as "La Oruga" (The Caterpillar) took me all over the place so I saved a lot of money on taxis. I ended up wasting a lot of time at the La Plaza Mayor, one of the largest malls in Leon' and the sixth in all Mexico. I have to say that in spite of the commercial districts, which were ugly in my opinion, the heart of the old city is beautiful with its own colonial Churrigueresque charms such as the cathedral, the Expiatorio, the historic Teatro Doblado, the Casa Municipal, Portal of the Millennium, Arch of the Heroes' Pathway, and old Madero Street and its particular attractions. At the Teatro Doblado I did get to see ex-president Vicente Fox in person; he was there to give a talk about corruption in Mexico. *Big surprise!*

On Calandria Street, not far from the "Lechugueros" basketball stadium, I had quite an experience, or should I say dalliance, with the local solicitors. Calandria, one of Leon's most notorious red-light districts, go-go girls, or "ficheras" (literally "ticket-girls"), count their livelihood by the number of sex tourists they entertain. "Three inches, three minutes, 3,000 Pesos ($230USD)," laughed Griselda, a 25-year-old bar-girl who insinuated herself to me not five minutes after I'd entered the crummy night-club. She was pushy and gregarious, telling me that last summer she and her fellow pole dancers at the *Castillo de Leones* bar-club entertained scores of men every night ~ first in the bar, where they scrounge for a monthly salary, then at the "patron's" hotel, where they wrangle over their own rates or base prices.

But as cash-strapped patrons have lost interest in Mexico - tourism officials say "night-life" revenues would plunge 35% this year due to the epidemic, bad weather and narco-terrorism - the ranks of horn-doggers cruising Calandria have fallen off considerably. On a recent Saturday night foray, just three horn-doggers watched a visibly disgruntled Griselda wiggle her lovely fundament around her pole. Getting to her wasn't so easy, nonetheless, but I managed to get around to asking her a few questions about the state of the economy. She whined that, "My base salary was 8,000 Pesos ($615) a month, but now they are giving me 6,000 Pesos ($462)."

Yes, things were pretty bad for the sex industry as well, and if sex falls off in Mexico, that could prove to be a truly horrendous calamity! "I haven't had a customer in five nights," Griselda cried, "and I'm to consider myself fortunate if someone buys me a drink."

Then, I watched her warily as she slithered back to her pole, sliding down and, having kicked the clothes off her coppery form and laying prone, her nates were silvered by the Mexican moonlight to the likeness of a meringue or a caramel-frosted cake.

As the recession continued to bite, sex workers from Leon' to Tijuana to Cancun' shared Griselda's frustration. One of the drunken horn-doggers sitting there, privileged to get a front seat to Griselda's esoteric gyrating, managed to murmur, "People just don't spend that freely anymore. I heard visitor numbers have dropped up to 20% since the crisis began. Customers who used to come two or three times a week now limit themselves to once a week, including me."

Obviously, the fellow was well-versed with the statistics!

In any case, that newfound restraint had already forced some brothels to shut their doors. In the more sedate states, where many men admit to having slept with a prostitute, up to half of all sex establishments outside of the big cities have closed in the past year.

This situation has actually caused more problems for prostitution-outreach groups than helped to solve them. Others had forcibly reduced their labor pool, so to speak. Based on other information I gathered, one was led to conclude that in villages where there used to be 10 girls, there were now two working to fulfill copulatory needs. In Mexico City, the biggest market for such things, working girls have suffered too. The *Rancho de Rameras,* one of the biggest of the slut corrals, recently laid off one in three of its staff after its highest-spending clients started staying away, and the pig flu had a lot to do with frosting their weenies as well.

The world's oldest profession wasn't about to take the recession lying down (no pun intended). Brothels and bathhouses had recently launched promotions (don't ask me how I know) - including free shuttle transports, old-folks discounts and matinee passes - in a bid to excite interest among wary satyrs. Annabel, one of Griselda's co-workers, told me, "Now we have to offer better incentives these days and individually suited packages. Our revenues have fallen 30% since the recession hit Mexico, *Chinga la madre!*"

Therefore, as part of a new deal she described to me, customers there would pay $150 to dance as much horizontal mambo as they want (or can) for one hour. At *Castillo de Leones*, recent loss-leader sales, so to speak, permitted horn-doggers to have jiggery-pokery for free on the Day of the Dead (November 1-2) and on Carnaval (mid-February) if they brought consumable goodies for their working pussy-kats or wore a costume on either occasion. And, Acapulco's Pussy Club charged guests a $100 flat rate for six hours to *make the beast with two backs*, access to a sauna and solarium and an all-you-can-eat buffet (the last incentive really fired the temptation in me).

Not everyone needed a tactical maneuver to arouse what needed arousing. In Jalisco, locals have remarked the recession hadn't affected brothels because the locals target the "common man"; horn-doggers pay as little as $40 for an hour with a hooker. And, while many former customers have left, individuals who would customarily go to the expensive clubs were looking to save some money, so it all evened out. Elsewhere, the weakening Peso had actually created opportunities for the sex trade. Mexico's currency lost 24% of its value against the Dollar and Euro since the onset of the crisis, a change that would further enhance the country's teetering tourism sector and thereby the number of satyrs willing to open their wallets for a thrill. A disapproving matron waiting at the same bus stop complained to me, "The country is becoming a paradise for sexual pervertourism before our eyes."

Upon returning to my hotel room, I read that police experts forecasted that the industry would more than double its income this year, generating $1.5 billion. Deepening joblessness would assuredly increase the exploitation of desperate women. Indeed, there were plenty of maidens without employment, and foreigners with cash who wanted companions who were fast and loose with their panties.

Back in Leon, the relative dependability of foreign currencies wasn't helping local trade. The cost of traveling to Mexico from far-flung places like Europe or even New York offsets any gains from the exchange rate. Paulina, a lovely mestizo who happened to be the supervisor of Calandria's *Malinche* Sauna, Bed and Breakfast, knew that all too well as her business relied on dollars to stay afloat. Described as "the most opulent and relaxing sauna ever seen in Mexico" by online gay guide Pink Banana World, Malinche attended an average of 800 visitors per day before the financial crisis struck. That number now hovered around 500. She confided to me that, "The entrance charge is already low, so cutting it further wouldn't make a difference."

So, what's a sauna supervisor to do?

"Pray for us," is all she could say.

As I weighed the pros and cons of getting involved with a *ramera* (whore) I noticed many of them offered "family rates." Naturally, this situation made many observers laugh. The rameras were actually popular with so-called family get-togethers, like Christmas and birthdays. For such a gathering I honestly hoped to be invited. With respect to Mexico's attitude towards members of the oldest profession, it is all due to our upbringing. We are made to accept misery in all of its forms. Many Mexicans would admit that we are a bunch of barbarians. They see someone in the streets starving or begging for help, and they'll just step on him, figuratively speaking. WE, as Mexicans of all types and backgrounds, are boorish, insensitive, uncaring, extremely selfish, self-indulgent, self-righteous, obscurantist, narrow-minded ... and these are our good points! They would be the first ones to argue, however, that their despair of and for life has imposed this sense of futility on their collective conscience, thus they step over people reminding themselves that we are creatures of causes we or our ancestors have made. There is nothing to be done, nothing to be ameliorated, and the wretched are left to their individual misery, "stepped upon" if you will, ignored.

The attitude that has most consistently greeted me in this country is, "oh too bad ... well good luck." ~ and that is it. I asked a clerk at the Ayuntamiento (city hall) of Guadalajara a couple of months back if she could help me, and this lovely maiden was supposed to be, according to the locals, representative of all that is fine in Mexico, but all that she replied to me was, "well, if you are in such need, why don't you get a job?"

Well, well, now why didn't I think of that? Why didn't I act on the suggestion, especially since I am an illegal in Mexico, and I even explained to her that I wasn't a citizen! She may as well have said, "Let them eat cake!"

I tell you, I was so pissed off, I should have spat in her face.

No, I have to say that we, my fellow Mexicans and I, are a tribe of gorillas delighting in throwing feces at each-other. It has nothing at all to do with hunger or despair. We all inherited this damned attitude from our parents, and they from their parents and so forth down the line. Provincials, not surprisingly, are the champion Christian-hypocrites who give lots of lip service to charity and piety, but delight in hearing of the misfortune of others. Our Mexican mothers, actually, are not so uncouth, but they have their cruel and merciless side. In fact, many local mothers think they are living representatives of the Virgin Mary for having given us birth in this hell-hole, so how does one argue with that attitude?

Despite my complaints about Mexico, there are other causes for cynicism. Politicians are really the most universally despised figures in all of Mexican society ~ their rapacity, their cynical opportunism, their hypocrisy, conceit. The threats of violence from their supporters do not make for a happy democracy. Before arriving in Guanajuato, I came really close to a bunch of malcontents who were splashing the headquarters and trucks of some political rival who'd won the latest election with gasoline and proceeded to light them afire, and damned be the consequences. With things as they are, there are no places of refuge for the average commoner except the dulling confines of intransigence ~ a particularly restful sanctuary for the ever-wretched Mexicans. The minute the natives lose that most peculiar sense of futility, the death knell for peace will sound throughout the land, and they could lose their independence of action as well as nationality. The wolves among them will find the audacity to boss the common herd around, or would have, if they get a chance, a reason to suspend all liberties and proclaim imminent domain on the whole country. It is so close to happening already that I could taste it in the air.

Henceforth, the hope for prosperity for all is dead, foreign investment pirates are here, and the masses are preparing to play victims of their vindictive, threatening ways. While they worry and beg their demons not to resort to vengeance, the average voter feels helpless before the opportunists. They are unable to help themselves. As for hating each-other, it is the same old relationship between Mexicans of divergent groupings and demographics. They finagle anything they can get out of a situation: a house, money, services, anything. The natives, despite themselves, carry a grudge against their own nation for trusting in national unity at the expense of tribal identity, culture and customs. Now it is going to be a bitch getting them to instill patriotic values in their children for the sake of promised stability and prosperity. Sometimes I get the feeling that they are all too willing to sell out to the Gringoes because they harbor naught but contempt for their leaders.

As a matter of fact, some of my reliable contacts, including Corazon, have spoken of promises betrayed. They fear that they themselves, the people, are their own nemeses. They fear they will leave the country to the reviled, yet idolized, Anglo-Americans. I felt this fear even amongst my own relatives. They really believe Mexico now belongs to America. But, the reality of the situation is that Americans are always up, the advantage is in their hands. Mexico seems always to be down, unable to care for itself. The index of stupidity amongst the average folk is the only thing that seems to be up, and their manipulation of self-pity and resentment for the crooks they had chosen and elected is entirely to blame.

That damned provincial contempt of theirs not only morphs into a kind of intra-national hate, but has brought out fear in the people too. Falsehood is taken for truth, and the lies they imbibe from unscrupulous politicians are like drugs that lead them to a self-deceiving complacency. Hence, the uncounted, silent masses are too afraid to act in their own interest. They are afraid to provoke the ghosts of revolution.

It all reminds me of something the scholar Eusebius wrote many centuries ago: "How it may be lawful and fitting to use falsehood as a medicine, and for the benefit of those who want to be deceived."

GUNS AND GANGSTERS ON THE RUN

Before leaving for Tamaulipas again to hunt down Fulgencio San Roman before he departed this world, I just had to swallow my worries, and take on the risk of visiting Michoacan ~ the cradle of Mexico's narco-terrorism. It is one of the most beautiful and enchanting provinces in all of North America, not just Mexico. Nowadays there are many cultural activities in Michoacan, especially in the major cities like Morelia, Patzcuaro, and Uruapan. Morelia, as the capital, has the highest number of museums, art galleries, film theaters and restaurants. Again, I had been ignoring my journal but this region, I'd hoped, would give me plenty to muse about. Every year in the month of October, Morelia hosts an international film festival, which is rapidly growing to become one of the top festivals in the whole country. It features international film stars such as Gael Garcia Bernal, Salma Hayek, and Martha Higareda. I would be arriving just in time to participate in the proceedings. Fortunately for me, this year around they were holding a tribute and film retrospective for Fulgencio San Roman!

Yearly, between October and April, tourism increases as more than a hundred million monarch butterflies migrate from Canada and the United States to the mountains in Michoacan to spend the winter in Oyamel Forests. It may be good commerce for the locals, but I had a rotten time finding a decent hostel for an indeterminate period. There are also several archaeological sites where tourists get to see ancient petro-glyphs of varied indigenous cultures, some of them still present in towns throughout Michoacan. Personally, I was getting sick of archaeological sites, but I sonambulated through the experience if only to boast that I'd been there. One of the most enchanting of these ancient sites, which was eventually turned into a colonial treasure and bordering Lake Patzcuaro, is Tzintzuntzan, or "Place of the Hummingbirds." I had to admit, it carried a special charm for some of us who cling to a romantic, if false, notion of a mystical, magical Mexico that never actually existed.

Morelia is often cited as the most beautiful city in Mexico, with its fabulous colonial architecture, the stunning 400-year old cathedral and its museums. I was truly caught up by the power and glory of the baroque-rococo structures if not the devious and sly cunning of the most mistrustful natives. The Museum of Masks, the Museum of Geology and Mineralogy, the Museum of Contemporary Art Alfredo Zalce and The Museum of Colonial Art are the most visited by tourists. Since I had nothing else to do to curb the boredom, I made the most of these cultural distractions.

A couple of days had passed, and just as I had decided that not much would come of this particular trip since the old friends I had hoped to visit, Israel Juarabe and his brothers, Tomas and Alvaro, no longer lived in this state, my hotel was suddenly surrounded by helicopters and armored vehicles. Mexican soldiers proceeded to fight a frightening two-hour battle with heavily armed thugs holed up in an old restaurant next to the hotel in the Morelia commercial zone, killing 12 of the vicious bums as I, along with the locals, cowered in our rooms or otherwise. One hapless soldier was cut-down in a hail of bullets and the wounded included three soldiers and five bystanders. If I had decided to descend to the bar I could have ended up in the hospital with the others. Several Gabacho tourists were evacuated from other hotels near the Alameda separated by the city park. When the soldiers arrived at the hotel on a tip, the vicious desperadoes opened fire and hurled some 50 grenades, according to an Army colonel who wore a ski mask to protect his identity as he led the stumbling reporters on a tour of the scene. He spoke on condition of anonymity for security reasons. I certainly had nothing on the man. Most luckily for me, not once during all the tense proceedings did any of the authorities ask me to present my identification or journalistic credentials!

Several of the desperadoes tried to flee, but crashed their cars into military APVs that were blocking the alley. At one point, more armed men with grenades arrived by SUV to reinforce their comrades in the restaurant, but they were cut to pieces in the shooting. Soldiers found four Michoacano state police officers handcuffed inside the kitchen of the restaurant, and one of them accidentally spilled blood on me as they were being led out ~ my fault of course since I just had to join the other vultures in glaring at the crime scene out of shear excitement. The officers, who were still bound and sitting on the floor when their rescuers arrived, said they'd been held captive by the desperadoes, and were too glad to answer reporters' questions the second they'd been liberated. Soldiers did not know the police were inside when the fiery exchange began late Saturday night, and the colonel said their claims would be considered. "We found them like this, handcuffed, and they say they were kidnapped. So if they were kidnapped, as they insist, then we saved them from a most violent murder," he boasted.

Residents and tourists cowered like feeble little mice inside their homes and hospices and at several low-cost hotels during the battle. I too got a bit scared with all the rapid-machine-gun fire. I tasted sulfur in my mouth, and felt at that instant that one of those bullets had my name on it. When the shooting suddenly stopped, many frightened bystanders, some of them having soiled themselves from the fear, were evacuated by ambulance, including 15 French tourists from a small hotel, a family of four from another hotel, a pregnant woman with her mother from their home, an elderly man with pronounced varicose veins, and me with my soiled shorts. Two men and a woman were caught in the gunfire and were killed. The gun-fight raged just blocks from classical old residences that once belonged to the cream of Mexico's aristocrats and nouveau-riche, which included many film celebrities like Fulgencio San Roman. He loved to fish in Lake Patzcuaro and wrote fondly of the stunning vistas of this particularly striking region.

It remained unclear whether the desperadoes belonged to one of the drug cartels that for decades have been fighting for turf in Michoacan, home to the monarch butterflies and birthplace of Jose' Maria Morelos y Pavon', one of the fathers of Mexican Independence. The Beltran Leyva cartel, in particular, has maintained a strong presence in Michoacan. In antecedent months, soldiers had arrested suspected cartel operatives as they stepped off private planes or limousines in between the towns of San Juan Parangaricutiro and Angahuan near the volcano Paricutin' on their way back from Acapulco. They said they'd met with the head-honcho himself, Arturo Beltran Leyva, at a christening fiesta hosted by this most-wanted cartel leader.

Soldiers confiscated 60 guns, grenades and ammunition at the impressive, gated house, which really stood out amongst more modest dwellings. Several armed hummers were also seized from the property, including a platinum-covered customized Mercedes Benz. President Felipe Calderon' had deployed more than 45,000 soldiers across Mexico to battle drug violence but they were making little difference in Michoacan. To reiterate, more than 10,800 people have died since the offensive began in December 2006.

Elsewhere near the crime scene, grieving parents buried their children Sunday after a devastating daycare fire killed 40 infants and toddlers as a consequence of the gun-fire, stunning Mexico and prompting the government to promise a thorough investigation. It would all be empty talk, however, everybody knew who and what was involved, and nobody was regarded as the "good-guy."

Funeral processions drove slowly to churches and cemeteries on the outskirts of Morelia, decorated with balloons and flowers.

The family of a 3-year-old girl dropped white roses on her casket and attached a *Dora the Explorer* balloon to the cross marking her grave at one of the first funerals held a couple of days later.

"I love you and I don't want to leave you here!" her mother screamed. Upon witnessing these proceedings first hand I almost lost my composure. It was truly pathetic and heart-rending.

I had the chance to see President Felipe Calderon' first hand as he arrived in Morelia late that day to console the victims and give a show of proactive presidential diligence. He wished surviving children a speedy recovery and promised families full government assistance and a thorough investigation into the actions of either the soldiers or the desperadoes which led to the accidental fire. In a speech near the town zocalo he declared, "I want to say to the mothers and fathers of the little ones who died that we share their profound sadness."

And with that, many a tear was shed.

The death toll had risen to 42 on Sunday after two of the children were found to have died from bullet-wounds, according to the attending doctor who had his hands full fending off rapacious reporters. Most of the victims had died of organ collapse caused by smoke inhalation, he said. Worse still, it was admitted that the soldiers had been so busy playing cops'n'robbers that they did nothing to put out the fire they'd helped to start.

The conflagration initially consumed an adjacent automotive warehouse after feral bullets struck highly combustible electrical machinery, which then led to the explosion that caused the fire. It then spread to the roof of the "Pepito" day care and sent flames raining down. All that officials would say was that once those bullets had struck the electrical mechanisms, it would be a foregone conclusion that an uncontrollable fire would result. I came across the grandmother of one of the victims who'd died of burns just three days after his fourth birthday. Did she care where the fire came from? All she could think of was the horror of seeing the roasted torso of her grandson. Everybody by then had watched televised reports about the fire Saturday, and many busy-bodies rushed over to make matters worse.

The old grandmother cried on my shoulders, dissolving into tears outside the morgue where she waited with 30 other victims' relatives. I commiserated with her and she said, "I thought he wasn't that burned and that we would find him safe and sound, but he was very burned. They operated on him yesterday, and he held on, but today he couldn't."

Firefighters carried injured children out of the day-care's front door, its only working exit, and through large holes that a civilian knocked into the walls before rescue crews arrived, according to a couple of soldiers who also spoke on condition of anonymity because they were not authorized to speak publicly about the fire, especially since they helped to cause it.

After the initial gun-fire exchange, a reckless would-be hero with a child in the danger-zone, who worked at a nearby auto parts store, had rammed his pickup truck through a wall and helped rescue five toddlers. What was not certain was if the man's child survived.

The deaths in Morelia again raised questions about building-safety in Mexico as well as the campaign against the narco-terrorists. Officials apologized on television that they would crack down on code violations after a deadly stampede at a Mexico City nightclub last year killed 12 teenagers, and a disco fire killed 21.

After the smoked had cleared up, figuratively as well as literally, it was estimated 142 children, ranging from 6 months to 5 years in age, were in the day care at the time of the gun-fight and subsequent fire, along with six staffers who looked after them. But, there would be no compensation for them, only for the hotel and restaurant owners whose establishments were losing money due to the scuffle.

After I'd asked around with the talking-heads about the significance of the fire that followed the fracas, I discovered that a May 26 inspection the previous year found that the day-care building, a converted warehouse with a few windows high up, had not complied with safety standards and was deemed a fire hazard. It was further conceded that security requirements needed reevaluation before the calamity struck. This is so typical of circumstances in Mexico: nobody does nothing till there's no turning back, and then nobody is responsible for none of the chaos that they insist never occurred! When I found a free moment to snoop around the smoking ruins, I found that the building's emergency exit could not be opened even after the disaster, and nobody could answer why. The place was in bad condition, it's a warehouse, there were no windows in the classrooms, and, suspiciously, the caretaker at the center was the only person not injured in the blaze.

Some of the children had third-degree burns, according to the Morelia fire department official. Thirty-three remained hospitalized, 23 of them in Morelia including 13 who remained in critical condition after I'd left town. Sadly, one of the "survivors" was brain dead. In a short time nine were transferred to Mexican hospitals in Ciudad Obregon in Sonora and to Guadalajara, which has a special burn unit. The official word after a couple of days was that four children were released, along with two of six adults who had been admitted. The adults included five women who had supervised the children at the center and the security guard who had been caught typically sleeping while on duty. Two 3-year-olds were being treated at a pediatric burn center in northern California. One of them, a boy, was flown there with his mother by a Mexican police escort, so said the reporters. He had burns over 70 percent of his tender little body and was expected to require many months of treatment. I later learned that the survival rate in such cases is about 50 percent, and that boy displayed no positive outlook on his tormented expression.

"A lot of it is how deep the burn is and where it's located and how bad was the smoke inhalation," a therapist also told me. In fact, the medicos were expecting more victims might be headed to California for treatment.

The arch-bishop of Mexico sent a telegram of sympathy for those killed or injured. The archbishop, always around to bask in the limelight of another's misery, was "deeply pained" by the fire and offered his prayers for its victims as well as "heartfelt condolences" to their loved ones. How typical, I thought, for one such as he to take advantage of the free press to make himself look good.

But, that's Mexico! What are you going to do?

The stay in Morelia turned out to be a big waste. I accomplished nothing but to watch as Mexico tore itself apart just a little bit more, and died just a little bit more.

THE PITY PROBLEM
WITH PROSTITUTES

Before deciding to head for Tamaulipas through Mexico State, I stopped in the lovely town of Ziticuaro, a stop en-route to see the arrival of the monarch butterflies on their return flight from Canada to spend the Winter in the forests of Oyamel. The surrounding terrain is mostly the pine-covered mountain-range of the Sierra Madre Occidental. Many of the locals spoke an indigenous language, probably Tarascan. Ziticuaro is an important intermediate point only because it runs from Mexico City to Morelia (following the route of the colonial royal road). It is a tourist destination, and fishing, camping and other activities are permitted. The area is especially popular during Holy Week when the municipal authorities organize various activities. It is also a popular area for football, volleyball, riding and other recreational pursuits. I thought to swim along with other people in the dam water because of its mythical curing powers.

It was past midnight in downtown Ziticuaro, and I had it in mind to get out and get a taste of local nocturnal recreations. Prostitutes paced in front of the "Presa del Bosque" Mercado stores. Evidently, nocturnal commerce was being hit really bad by economic realities even in semi-rural areas. Signs of a slow economy were everywhere ~ a sportswear store offered 40 percent markdowns, and bars advertised discounted drinks. Like so many other businesses, Mexico's semi-legalized prostitution industry was having to adapt to the economic downturn. Customers were fewer or more frugal, competition had doubled, and more clubs and brothels were offering discounts to drum up business. Even though brothels are technically illegal, street solicitation is legal so long as no pimp is involved. Well, that sure shot my Mexican career prospects to Hell!

Since late 2008, the number of English and American tourists had fallen off and the street dynamic had transformed for the worse, according to one prostitute in her mid-20s I'd flirted with named

Aracely, and who requested anonymity because she did not want her family to know where the tacos and beans were coming from. She still had enough customers, she admitted, but they now wanted extras *gratis*. "We have to be a lot more pushy now," said the pretty, happy hooker, wearing black jeans and a pink corset, who had worked the area for three years. "The *johns* used to come straight to you. Now they wait till you come to them."

Nevertheless, she admitted, the hookers in the area had been sticking to a standard price of about 650 Pesos ($50) for sex.

She then explained, putting her hands on her hips, "If the horndogger doesn't pay our prices then he can't go home with me!"

As for the tourist market to reiterate, Mexico is one of the favored destinations of pedophile sex tourists from Europe and the United States. Mexico City was one of the leading producers of child pornography videos. An estimated 5,000 children are currently involved in prostitution, pornography and sex-tourism in Mexico. Nearly 100 children and teenagers a month fall into the hands of the child prostitution networks, which are mafias or organized crime syndicates. Mexican authorities discovered a house in Acapulco where pornographic videos were filmed using children ranging in age from newborns to 18 year olds. Furthermore, Mexican police broke up an international child pornography ring based in Acapulco, which had at least 4,000 American clients and as many Europeans.

Mexicans and Americans together had set up the rotten operation.

A large proportion of the minors used in the sex industry catch sexually transmitted diseases, which leave them infertile, while others contract AIDS. Some 25 homeless children contracted AIDS in the past two years after being forced to engage in sodomitic acts. Many girls get pregnant, and are forced to have abortions. All suffered serious psychological problems. Children in Mexico City and cities along the U.S. border are at highest risk of sexual exploitation. Aracely then cried on my shoulders and told me about a sweet little girl she'd known named Rosenda who ended up sterile at age 12, and of a happy go-lucky boy named Tito, who'd always be there to help her with her grocery shopping, and ended up catching AIDS at age 14. Sadly, there were many more like them out there.

Mexico has no laws defining or sanctioning child prostitution and pornography as criminal activity. It wasn't enough that In mid-1997 the Mexican Supreme Court ruled that forcing a spouse violently to engage in sexual relations was not rape but the "undue exercise of a right." It wasn't enough that on July 1991, Mexico revised its rape law, eliminating a provision that allowed a man who rapes a minor to avoid prosecution if he agrees to marry her. The terrible yet remaining fact was that the Mexican justice system is inadequate to protect children from abuse such as child pornography.

Disgraceful ... just disgraceful!

Though the demand for the goods and services of hookers remains strong, the supply has increased manifold as young hopefuls lost their jobs and turned to the time-honored profession. The consequence was increased competition. In contrast, clubs and brothels were increasingly marketing themselves either as high-class and exclusive spas, or as bargain basements of delight; to reiterate, they were barred by Law from advertising sex, so they had to skirt the issue with euphemisms and the sort. Ziticuaro's biggest bordello, *La Diana*, is one of the former with a wide variety of enticements. For an entry fee of 80 Pesos, guests gain access, just like the naughty places of Morelia, to a gym, free buffet, a pool and two erotic cinemas ~ it was certain that I wouldn't find any San Roman movies playing therein.

The sex costs extra, of course. For thirty minutes, I ... uh, I meant other prospective clients had to pay 600 Pesos, with set rates for a variety of other copulatory attentions. On any given day, the bordello had about 70 diligent women, or so a regular customer confided to me as he gorged himself on free taquitos.

Juana, 28, a soft-spoken bottle blonde who worked at the same street corner where Aracely was stationed, had left a job in hotel hospitality two years before to become a prostitute. "It wasn't a stimulating job, and I wanted to try something more fun and *rewarding*," she said, pleading that her name not be mentioned to the local police.

Aracely, once calming down and having a couple of smokes, said she hadn't seen a decrease in the number of her daily patrons usually about 10 men but they had grown increasingly tight-fisted, except, of course, in the act of playing with her goods. She also bemoaned a drop in professional customers as fewer attended conventions or retreats at a nearby conference center ~ going to "check out the returning butterflies," they'd tell their families, "just wasn't worth the price and the hassle, anymore."

Aracely just mused wistfully as she shook her pretty, swarthy head suffused with dark make-up and bright lip-rouge, "This is what the girls and I have been complaining about. The number of dicks is pretty much the same, but they only find their way to us once or twice, not three or four times like before."

Notwithstanding, *La Diana* owners were working over-time at bringing in discerning patrons through other or additional incentives such as discount cards and lowered prices for taxi-drivers and older horny-boys. The incentives had translated into an increase in the number of regular patrons, and Aracely benefited from the "run-off" of excess trade. At the other end of the spectrum there was *Las Ficheras* club-bordello, which had branches in Mexico City and Monterrey. It opened in mid-2007 with a focus on the discount-minded "slam-bam-thank-you-m'am" shopper, and offered an "all you can sex" flat-rate. Thus I discovered, for my own curiosity, that for 400 to 500 Pesos, depending upon the time of day, patrons could enjoy any sexual services with an unlimited number of girls. For their work, the girls were also remunerated with a flat-rate wage.

I asked Juana about this, and she thought it grand: "All the girls get a daily wage of 650 Pesos, so they don't have to fret over money, which is good in this working environment."

She also noted a steady increase in "aspirants" ever since the *Ficheras* Club had opened, attributing this in part to the bordello's flat-rate salary. "Many girls in other dumps aren't earning a living wage anymore, and we offer steady, secure money."

Yes, there is nothing like job security!

Juana further explained that the pricing structure had helped the bordello avoid any money anxieties, despite the global market downturn, and that the number of horn-doggers had not diminished.

Back at the "Presa del Bosque" Mercado, Aracely, as she paced nervously with cigarette in hand, said she was thinking of a change in location. She then bent down to retie the laces on knee-high black patent leather boots with five-inch platform heels only to reveal remarkably ample glutes worthy of handling with care. She was planning to head soon to Las Vegas, to work in strip clubs that still catered to horny truckers, saying there was still ample work there as well. She confided, "I make more in one night just dancing than on the streets here."

Juana, meanwhile, said she would eventually return to the quieter life working for hotels, but that she was in no rush to leave the high pay and dependability of prostitution. "This type of job will always be in existence," she shrugged. "People will always have money for a little bit of *culiando* ("ass-play" = sex)."

WHEN THE LIGHT WENT OUT AT THE MOVIES

At last I made it back to Mexico City. Suddenly, I felt a presentiment of death. Suddenly, I felt I would not arrive in time to look up this strange figure that had been my object of fascination since learning of his existence. He dominated my meditations, thus totally redirecting the true purpose of my journey to this country. Fulgencio San Roman had completely occupied my spare thoughts and quiet moments since crossing the borders of Tamaulipas. Announcements of his worsening condition had made it to the international news broadcasts and were more frequent. Concurrently, I received word from Corazon that her brother Andres was getting worse and now they feared he would not recover.

Meanwhile, the attractions and distractions of the big metropolis remained the same. I would be attending a major Cinema Festival which, to my surprise, would be themed around the Gay genre, even while holding tribute retrospectives for revered antecedents such as Emilio Fernandez, Gabriel Figueroa, Luis Bunuel, Ismael Rodriguez, and, of course, Fulgencio San Roman. The first time director and movie buff Hugo de Mirlos Branco was appointed the chairman of the festival. He spoke of his inspiration, and mentioned Fulgencio in a number of (very boring) speeches. I was surprised to learn he had tried to hold a gay and lesbian film festival in the 1990s, but it was shut down by the Federales before it even opened. When he tried to organize a gay cultural festival a couple of years later, five dozen Federales swarmed the venue, closing it.

The forthcoming Wednesday before *DIA DE LOS MUERTOS*, however, Branco and other organizers managed to pull off the opening to the five-day Mexico Queer Film Festival with no police and no disruptions, but drawing only a low-key but an appreciative crowd to the Garibaldi Art District in the city's heart.

For Mexico's gay community, that week's film festival and an art exhibition on sexual diversity in Distrito Federal, along with the previous season's growing gay pride festival in most of the major cities, are quiet steps forward after years of slow but unmistakable progress. Branco, a professor at the Azteca Film Academy, said the events marked a significant moment for Mexico's fledgling gay movement. It has gone farther and faster than anything in America.

He was quoted as saying,"The biggest change is that I'm not the only one doing this. There's more support from the gay community. Society has become more relaxed and open-minded in its thinking."

And, based on what I saw first hand, I would say he was most certainly *NOT* exaggerating. But he sounded a note of caution that progress is often accompanied by disappointments, saying promoters would not consider the events a triumph until they make it to their closing ceremony the following Sunday unspoiled by protests.

"In Mexico, we were the first to put on queer events. In those events, we've had harassment and that had lasting influences," Branco went on to say. "(Now) we've enjoyed a successful premier and if we can also assure a successful closing to the event, it will have another kind of impact."

Mexico has indeed eased its control over some aspects of gay life, and made strident forward moves in others. Years before, sodomy was removed from the country's list of crimes, although homosexuality was still considered a mental disorder in some bigoted circles even though it is widespread throughout Latin-America; Latins themselves prefer to keep it a huh-hush affair for the sake of modesty if nothing else. In recent years, the gay community in Mexico has gone from being practically invisible to establishing a secure foothold in society. In large cities, gay bars are more popular than straight bars, and gay and lesbian activist and support groups have achieved a respectability in the Media. Internet access to gay groups online has helped ease the isolation for those who live in rural areas. At last the country boys could look forward to other, *human* partners besides chickens *and* goats!

Even so, many in the country's gay and lesbian population complain of discrimination and continue to face stigmatization. Many remain deeply closeted in a still highly backward society where illiteracy and hunger are still major issues. Gay Web sites are often blocked by the competing media's Internet firewalls.

Still, community activists see progress in the fact that gay-themed events that would have been banned outright when their parents were growing up are now being permitted.

I asked one of the curators, Salvador Mungia, who helped put together the Guadalajara art show a few years before, the first in the country to explore sexual diversity and gender issues, about the significance of the festival, and he explained, "years ago, this would have been completely impossible, it was that simple."

Now he was putting together exhibits for the works of 16 artists, which included explicit explorations of gay and other gender issues.

The auditorium for the film festival's opening movie, a story of a mulatto Mexican man from Veracruz who searches for the soul of his dead Gringo lover, was packed with a lively crowd of about 240 people, mostly young and proudly gay. Others who'd attended were simply curious to know more about gay issues, a segment lusted for by sponsors who sought to encourage dialogue between the gay community and the wider public.

One of Mungia's artists, a 29-year old artist named Dora Jimenez who lived in the area, told me, "I don't know that much about the lifestyle so I was curious. I really liked the movie. You see on-screen the raw emotions in the relationship between them. It's a very good opportunity for the public to better understand the gay community."

That's not to say that everything has gone smoothly with gay Mexicans. The art show curators ran into problems with local Church opposition just before opening day.

"I used to think Mexico's Catholic Church was becoming more and more open. On TV, movies and magazines, you hear more and more about these issues," said Gerardo Mariscal, a second curator who prefers to be called "Gargajo." He went on to reflect, "But before the exhibit started, they came and told us 'You can't do this. The Church won't like it.' That changed my mind a little about how ready Mexico's traditional Catholics really were. After all, most of their priests are gay or pederasts. What's the god-damned big deal?"

Good question. What was the god-damned big deal with them?

Accordingly, furious fulminations over the festival followed, and in the end only four works were removed including one photo showing a man holding a crucifix in one hand, a fish over his crotch in the other, and a crown of thorns on his head, as well as a painting depicting two naked men in a sexual act. Sponsors decided to leave the empty white frames hanging on the wall as a statement on censorship, and solidarity with the artist. In spite of the initial hostility, and the incumbent problems of putting it all together, the exhibit's opening drew an estimated 3,000 people--an enthusiastic public response that left its sponsors delightfully shocked.

The sponsors remarked they'd made a concentrated effort to keep the events low profile to ward off unwanted attention from lurking narco-traffickers because they too like to hang about the Garibaldi district. There were no fliers or public advertisements for the events only announcements circulated on Web sites. And they chose to hold it during business hours when they knew suspicious figures weren't normally around haunting the adjacent restaurants.

The same low-key approach was taken by sponsors of the country's gay pride festival, though the turn-out was overwhelming, something that nobody could ignore. They carefully planned a week's worth of movie screenings, art shows and sports events all held in Garibaldi's private venues instead of public spaces, which was just as well since I didn't want to be recognized either.

Despite the attempt to circumvent obvious obstacles, several events still ended up getting postponed or canceled by local officials who'd claimed organizers didn't have the correct permits, but they were just out to give the gay community a hard time (no pun intended).

The festival, nevertheless, got high praise from *El Alarma*, a newspaper with an internationalist perspective, and which ran a front-page article lauding organizers for sending a strong message about "greater acceptance and tolerance."

Overall, Mexico has been gradually, surprisingly moving in a direction of more openness toward the gay community.

"I think the changing governments, the fall of the PRI party from grace in the year 2000 gave us a lot of space for the local gay community to grow and flourish," Gargajo went to explain. "I've been in Mexico City for seven years and the changes in the gay scene I've seen in other cities around the country are tremendous. It's a metamorphosis."

On the other hand, the Church had to back off after a scandal erupted over the alleged abuse suffered by the secret son of one of their own: Jose' Ramon Gonzalez Lara, the presumed son of Marcial Maciel, the founder of the religious and highly intolerant order *Legionnaires of Christ*. He told reporters that he had asked the Legionnaires for 26 million dollars in exchange for his silence, but he demanded they not parade about like victims because he and his brother were ruined by sexual abuses committed by Maciel himself. So, that ended the Church's supercilious interference.

The festival went as well as anyone could have hoped, and the retrospective on Fulgencio was appropriately sentimental. They focused on *Memories of Ghosts to Come*, followed by *The Eagle and the Serpent*, then by *The Wind that Swept Mexico*, then *Tonantzin- Our Lady Of The Roses*, next by *Once Upon A Time In Old Mexico*. The sponsors, oddly enough, tried to pass them off as pre-liberation Gay oriented movies. Personally, I thought the claim rather ridiculous, and if Fulgencio had been present he too would have laughed them off the stage.

Then, THUNDER stuck! A page suddenly came running in with a news-flash alert. The host interrupted, read it, and quietly began to weep.

What the Hell happened? everyone asked themselves.

He asked them for silence, for everybody to bow their heads in memoriam and announced:

"Fulgencio San Roman has just died ..."

AFTERSHOCK

Although his impending death was a forgone conclusion, the announcement of the fact still hit me like a bolt of lightning. So, I was beaten by the clock. Damn! Would I make it in time for the funeral? Now that he was gone I felt a tremendous, indescribable void. All the horrors I'd experienced he had once addressed in so poetic a way through his movies. I didn't know who he was until coming to Mexico, and now he meant more to me than my own parents. What could this mean?

So, Fulgencio, my friend, mentor, idol, care-taker of my dreams, was now gone forever.

What would become of me?

I dizzily went about packing my bags to take the next train to Reynosa, and totally blocked out the rest of the world from my mind. As I boarded a taxi, I received a call ~ It was from Corazon. I answered, exchanged pleasantries, expressed my delight at hearing her voice again, and then she dropped her own bombshell on me: her brother, Andres, had just succumbed to the protracted after-effects of the pig flu. JESUS CHRIST! What the Hell? The season of death had arrived and nobody told me about it? I felt ridiculous more than sad for Andres. That poor, simple soul who radiated only positivity and wanted nothing more than to do good had fallen victim to some disgusting animal virus, what the fuck? And, true to my selfish form, I couldn't decide whether to console Corazon, or head for Reynosa to indulge in a caprice. Well, I took two extra hours to visit Corazon, and promised I would be back in time to attend the funeral ~ I never did. Then, I headed straight for the train station.

Upon arriving, I made straight for the civil registry. The clerk there shared the necessary details with me, but very reluctantly ~ 500 Pesos assuaged his misgivings, and he even gave me the exact hour of the memorial ceremony. I hadn't been in the town more than an hour when I learned that the mayor, Majencio Villaboas Moreno, was a nephew of

Fulgencio's on his father's side, and had actually facilitated his move to this state with promises of a land grant and a great new house built just for him. When he successfully ran for mayor of an adjoining town, *Tapetes*, three years prior, no one much cared that his brother and cousin were in prison on drug charges. Poor Fulgencio, I thought. I had come this far in search of my identity only to discover that he had been living in a house paid for with drug money, and his legend would be tainted by the naughty deeds of his younger relatives?

Deplorable!

I arrived at the ranch where well-wishers were permitted to view the body. I approached and shook with fore-boding. This man was so alive at the *Aguila Desnuda* bar, and now was just a carcass. I couldn't stand it. It was all a big let-down, and I practically ran back to the hotel. My illusions had been shattered once and for all.

Now, I'd just learned, Villaboas was running for governor of Tamaulipas state, and a banner appeared in the capital city mocking Villaboas's family ties by linking him to the Zetas, a gang of drug hit men: "Welcome to Tamaulipas! Soon to be territory of our boss of bosses, Majencio Villaboas Moreno. The Zetas support you, and we are with you until death!"

So, what's the poor guy to think?

The drug war was playing in Mexico's newest elections like never before. Usually a taboo topic hiding in plain sight, narco-terrorism had not figured prominently in electoral campaigns even in regions like the Pacific coast, or in the Gulf states where Reynosa's border-town status is a major transshipment point for America-bound cocaine. Villaboas's Institutional Revolutionary Party (PRI) denied any collusion with drug traffickers and accused the ruling National Action Party (PAN) of hanging the banner - which it flatly negated.

Ah, the free and open expressions of democracy!

In the previous July 5 midterm elections for 500 congressional seats, notwithstanding, six governors and 565 mayors, President Felipe Calderon's PAN party was ruthlessly painting opponents as weak on drugs and itself as the only party ballsy enough to defy the cartels.

To me it was obvious that these were the first elections where a party was directly linking itself to the drug-trafficking issue. In the past, it was mentioned in a pusillanimous manner, like an insinuation.

The PAN was banking on an *mean-asshole* image to keep its grip on power against Villaboas's PRI party, and which had continued to rule in Tamaulipas after it had lost presidential power in 2000. The PRI was indeed regaining support among Mexicans fed up with this economic slump and drug violence that has killed so many of their ready and willing fellow citizens. At the same time, a growing victim's group, disgusted with what it perceived as corrupt politics as usual, implored voters to erase all candidates in protest.

Now that was an idea I could support!

Anyway, if the PAN lost to the PRI, it would mean popular support had slipped for Calderon' and his bloody, American-backed internecine war on the drug cartels. It would also embolden his opponents to block his more polemical measures, including passing laws that would give more police powers to 45,000 troops deployed across the country to counter corrupt law enforcement in the drug war.

You have a corrupt law enforcement structure and their solution was to give the police more power?

The PAN had initiated a campaign featuring some of Mexico's most popular celebrities warning that a vote against the ruling party would signify a return to times when Mexico's leaders, namely the PRI leaders, let the cartels flourish and profited by them.

In one campaign commercial, popular masked *Lucha Libre* wrestler "Mistico" flexes his muscles, bounces around the ring and says: "A lot of people say the fight against drug trafficking has never been as complicated. The truth is, that for many years, nobody had fought against them. Now, the president and the PAN are giving it their all, and we have to support them."

That would never be enough, of course. Villaboas's detractors denounced him for manipulating the drug war for political gain. They insisted it was no accident that federal agents arrested 10 mayors after he'd just recruited them to campaign on his behalf for allegedly protecting drug traffickers just a month before the elections. But state officials assured they were merely going after the trashiest areas for drug violence and that PAN members were among those arrested, including the mayor of Ulipanes, where Fulgencio's ranch is located, and where gunmen on the Monday before I'd left Mexico City attacked an ambulance with a grenade and AK-47s just to kill a wounded rival.

Prosecutors then had levied organized crime and drug charges against seven of Villaboas's mayoral supporters, plus the former state attorney general. The other three mayors detained had not been charged upon learning of Fulgencio's death, but would continue to be held pending some detective work.

Federal Attorney General Eduardo Medina-Mora alleged the charged officials helped the *La Familia* drug cartel. He did not provide specifics about the charges, but whistle-blowers have said the suspects allegedly leaked sensitive "dope" (allegations) to the drug gang. The saddest part of all this is that Villaboas tried to use his great-uncle's revered name to advance his dirty ambitions, and even tried to get him to act as spokesman for his gubernatorial race.

Federal election over-seers remarked they were watching campaigns like never before to detect any illegal influence doing random checks, forcing political parties to report irregularities, and ordering investigations into anything suspicious such as more wasteful spending by a contender than reported by his campaign. Sadly, they even came to harass Fulgencio for his part in endorsing his relative.

So far, they couldn't find any evidence of narco-traffickers handing over money to their political puppets. The Federales were limited in their policing, as drug traffickers could offer bribes under the table or use threats to cut deals with ever-corruptible candidates.

The issue was dominating political discussions from sleepy beach towns to elegant suburbs. Candidates who used to focus on joblessness and pot-holes, even as drug violence plagued their states, were pretending to meet it head on while they, including Villaboas himself, quietly accepted the bribes.

After he had won the nomination in Tamaulipas, PRI leader Beatriz Paredes coolly remarked that the Federales assured the party he was not under criminal indictment. The candidate's brother, Humberto Villaboas, however was in prison for drug dealing, while his cousin, Rafael Moreno, was arrested in Los Angeles in a 1997 sweep that dismantled meth-amphetamine and cocaine trafficking rings across the U.S. South-West.

There is no evidence that Fulgencio was tied to drug trafficking, even if Villaboas was. Nevertheless, the PAN national leader German Martinez wondered aloud whether Villaboas would pugnaciously fight drug gangs, while consoling Tamaulipas voters that there are no such doubts about their own PAN gubernatorial candidate. But the drug-war strategy would backfire for the PAN when a plain-speaking PAN mayoral candidate was recorded telling supporters that drug traffickers had contacted all leading political contenders in the country seeking their loyalty, which admission took the heat off of Villaboas. The would-be mayoral blabber-mouth also suggested in the recording that he would avoid standing up to the Beltran Leyva cartel, which controlled his representative suburb, to maintain the peace. The recording was leaked to Mexican media, which broadcasted it nationwide last week (giving poor Fulgencio some negative publicity), prompting calls by political enemies for his withdrawal from the race. This suited Villaboas just fine.

The poor sap acknowledged making the remarks, but he said they were taken out context. For many Mexicans, the scandalous recording pointed out a weak spot for all the parties: Some voters preferred peace to the mayhem that comes with confronting drug lords. And, many Mexicans firmly believe that the recording revealed a truth long since taken for granted. The sacrifice of having a completely clean city would be too terrible in human terms, and I believe it is naive to think they could do away with drug-trafficking entirely. More violence would come without changing anything, and few people seemed really to care.

If I could vote, I too would mark "X" through my ballot and join the protest vote. All Mexican politicians, I have come to believe, belong to a criminal class uniquely their own, or at least have to work with organized crime to get anything done!

Therewithal, just as they were burying Fulgencio, tainted by the drug war with the final eulogies, narco-related recriminations were being carried out. In revenge for the assassination of Drug-lord Arturo Beltran Leyva, drug gang hit-men shot dead the grieving mother, brother, sister, and aunt of an elite Mexican marine who'd perished after taking part in a raid that killed the notorious drug lord.

Gunmen burst into the family's home in Matamoros in the northeast of the state just before midnight on Monday, firing assault rifles. They had ruthlessly broken the door down with a sledgehammer and sprayed them with bullets in the living room and bedrooms, or so alleged the local deputy police commander. A neighbor who'd witnessed it all reported, "It all happened in less than a minute."

It was clear that any legal reprisals could spur revenge attacks and fan fresh violence despite the simple victories of the flagging drug war, and as rival cartels seek to take over territory from the drug lord's weakened cartel. In separate assaults, *sicarios* (delinquents) shot to pieces the tourism secretary in narco-terrorist-plagued Sinaloa, and another gang fired on a restaurant in the northern border city of Piedras Negras where the state prosecutor was snarfing down some tacos with other government officials. It was just one story like this after another filtering through the official news agencies. Just Disgraceful!

Broad daylight shootings are typical of Mexican street justice. Torture, decapitations, and other atrocities are all too common.

The rising bloodshed had again alarmed tourists, which further damaged Mexico's image as a relatively secure destination for foreign investors. The attack on the family home in Matamoros came hours after Fulgencio's funeral, thus upstaging a ceremony which should have been a national observance. President Calderon' condemned the attack even while eulogizing Fulgencio, saying: "We must not be frightened by the unscrupulous criminals who commit barbarities like this, even while mourning the passing of one of our greatest artists."

Hence, Fulgencio had been lauded as a hero by respectful countrymen while his grand-nephew was indicted for associating with drug-traffickers. This was a tragic post-script to the life of a great man. Sadness now would accompany me back to America.

Goodbye, old Soul. I guess I will have to wait to see you!

THE STORMS THAT BRING OUT THE STRESS

November passed away, and all preparations were underway for the grandest Christmas celebrations of them all. Now with Fulgencio buried, and nothing left to propel my mission, I decided to head for Veracruz, and go straight for Becky's finca, which, she insisted, contained the final clue to the fulfillment of my purpose: to learn the why-fore of my name. She had left instructions with her caretaker to present me with a document she'd procured for me before I'd arrived in Mexico. In it I would find the reason why I was named.

All the same, I had arrived as the climate deteriorated. Tourists fled the ports as a Hurricane roared its way through the Gulf, but many slum dwellers in Orizaba, the town where-from my mother's maternal ancestors hailed, worried about looting, and refused to give-up their imperiled shanties. The damned storm would be a Category 4 hurricane with winds near 145 mph (230 kph), and would rake this region of humid jungly topography fringed with picturesque beaches and fishing villages by nightfall.

Police, firefighters and navy personnel drove through shantytowns trying to persuade some 10,000 people in the Orizaba area to evacuate their primitive shacks. Fortunately, I didn't have to worry about such accommodations. Nonetheless, For my safety and of families all along the coast, we had to board a vehicle and head to the nearest shelter. The same advisory was bellowed over a loudspeaker by a fire-fighter as his fire-truck wound its way through the sandy streets of a slum built along a stream bed that regularly springs to life when a hurricane hits.

While the storm's eye was forecast to pass west and north of the city, another 20,000 were expected to evacuate elsewhere along the coast.

I stayed in the shelter for a few hours, but the danger alert was called down long enough for me to head for the Ange-Ingel family finca near Puerto Alvarado. The Mexican government went on to declare a state of emergency for the lower states of Tabasco and Campeche, and many ports were closed. Rescue workers from the Mexican military and the Red Cross prepared for post-hurricane disaster relief. Two Mexican Army Hercules aircraft loaded with medical supplies arrived, dropping them within the boundaries of the finca itself. Children on the property ran through strong gusts of wind waving pieces of paper and trash bags under bands of intermittent rain as they received me. They expected a foot of rain, but already the dry stream beds had turned into gushing torrents.

The finca caretaker, an older man named Hilario, snapped photos outside the mansion, enjoying the driving winds before welcoming me inside. "The waves have been great," Hilario gushed. "I think we're going to be out of harm's way as far as major damage. We're in a very good structure here."

Well, that was reassuring enough for me.

Most of Hilario's family lived in the nearby shantytown of Chuburna, where they maintained a brick-making operation. After conversing with me about Becky's poignant departure months before, he warily eyed a growing stream that rushed past the great eastern gate. "We are here with our nerves on edge," he said. "If this hits, many of the workers quarters are not going to hold. Other storms have passed but not this strong."

Hilario then recalled the hurricane that killed several people and caused millions in damages in September 2001 was the most frightening one in the storm-prone state's history. This storm had already made a raging 12-day trip through Mexico and the southern United States. Many tourists left Mexico even though Christmas festivities were under way. I would stay and take my chances.

After twelve hours the storm moved on, and I could leave for the American border the following day.

In the meantime, Hilario led me to the foyer where the old document Becky found was awaiting me. On it was genealogical information which showed tables of family history extending back to the early 17th Century. At the bottom was an addendum with a prophecy which stated that the last Lord of Lagos would return after the generation which had fought in the Revolution was consumed. My father had told me that the demise of the last Lord of Lagos, a rogue if ever there was one, spelled the end of the family fortunes after four centuries in the New World, but I didn't believe him. Legend said that the family fortunes would rise again when a descendant would be named for him.

Well, here I was. Here I was waiting to make sense of my purpose in life. Here I rendezvoused with mystery, with fulfillment, and with the end of my journey. Only the future now; only an emptiness so vast in which I would plunge my imagination, and never return to this place of reckoning ... never return to the same old complacency, and conventionality, and hypocrisy.

So, I was named for a rogue? I was named in expectation of the resurrection of a dynasty virtually extinct by the time I'd made it down here? I was left numb. I was left disillusioned. I was left ... elated! All that I could think of from there-on was that the time had come to leave Mexico.

THE REASON WHY I WAS NAMED WHAT I WAS NAMED

At last I had come to the point of my quest: to find out who I am! While I was growing up, no one would tell me why I was named Federico since neither my immediate ancestors nor my uncles were named with this not very common name. I was the anomaly, the oddball, and no one would tell me why. By the time I arrived back in Chihuahua I had learned enough, and was ready to say my goodbyes to Billy, to Becky, to Corazon, to Nena, to everyone. Nonetheless, I had no room left in my conscience to mourn for nostalgia.

In fact, I spent my last hours in Mexico studying the document, reflecting on the life of a man I was led to believe was mythical, but it turned out he had been real enough. He was a legendary character my father mentioned once, an unmourned Jalisco ancestor of his who had first defended the honor of Porfirio Diaz just before the outbreak of the Revolution. He had switched sides and committed rapine, pillage and murder on behalf of Emiliano Zapata. Afterwards, once the latter's forces had captured the capital in 1914, he offered his services to Pancho Villa, all the while touting that he lived to serve the cause of Christ and his Church, the true masters, in the fanatical opinion of others like him, of all Mexico. His insurrectionist activities and devotion to a Christian cause presaged *La Cristiada*, or the Cristero War, that was fought between the socialist government and Roman Catholic fascist-rebels after 1926.

His full name was Federico de Martin-Lopez de la Cruz y Vivar, and he was celebrated by my grandfather Ismael, who had reputedly known him, as the most learned and virtuous gentleman of his crowd; but such virtue, and such learning, contributed neither to the perfection of the person, nor to the happiness of his beloved. He was a slave of the most abject superstition. He was surrounded by visible and invisible enemies, in the streets where he'd provoked many a duel, or in his nightmares; nor were the fires of Hell less dreadful to his whims. Yet, he insisted that he sacrificed all for the well-being and security of his siblings and descendants. In a letter to his children, dated one day before his death in 1924, which coincided with the transfer of power from Alvaro Obregon' to Plutarco Elias-Calles, his two remaining and most powerful nemeses, he wrote:

"My treasures, they shall be consecrated to the common cause; and happy would be my demise, could I deserve and procure the laurel of martyrdom. Words cannot express the ardour with which I pray for the joining of the scattered members of Christ. If my death could avail, I would gladly present my pistol and ask them to point it at my heart. If the spiritual phoenix could arise from my ashes, I would build the pyre, and kindle the conflagration with my bare hands."

... Unfortunately for him and his convictions, the clergy, from whom he took his actual orders, were greedy and fanatic monks; and their vices and venality, their knowledge or ignorance, were equally mischievous or contemptible.

Fortunately for me, it was revealed in the document that the next one to inherit the name would succeed where Federico had failed.

The qualities of this character assuredly explain why my present relatives turned out the way they are ... the way I am. I suppose they are traits, good or bad, that were shared by the entire clan. There was plenty of hypocrisy and piety to be had, much cruelty or clemency to dish out, wanderlust or isolation that impelled the fancy. There was so much religious intolerance putrefying the family atmosphere that it suffocated some to the point of resorting to atheism for some peace of mind, but that the sinner should swallow the last dregs of the cup of penance, it was an option of last resort. Such was his pretense of Christian rectitude that the foolish tale was propagated of his punishing a sacrilegious donkey that had tasted the greens of a monastic garden.

Many rebels fighting on Federico's side were not safe from his wrath. In fact, some were shot on evidence provided by him to the Obregon' loyalists, frequently in their houses, or in front of their wives and children. Particularly horrific to Catholics, after a verbal truce had been betrayed, was the government's insistence on a complete state monopoly on education. They began by suppressing all Catholic indoctrination and introducing "socialist education" ("atheistic brainwashing" to Catholics) in its place, which really became widespread after Calles, his one-time battle-field nemesis in 1915, had taken office in 1924. Worried that he was losing his grip on his purpose and posterity, he told his followers: "We must enter and take possession of the mind of childhood, the mind of youth. Otherwise, my friends, we have lost possession of the future."

Their future, however, was already in the past. The persecution continued for many years as Calles, who had succeeded Obregon', consolidated power and expanded the anti-clerical legislation, maintaining control under his *Maximato* (behind the scenes dictatorship) and did not relent until 1940 when President Manuel Avila Camacho, a believing Catholic, took office ~ long after my ancestor had perished.

Federico's treachery caught up with him however, and he tried to involve his family. He assured them that he did everything for their spiritual salvation, but they refused to uphold his lies. Consequently, he trembled on the brink of the abyss, which his own dishonesty had dug under his feet. He had counted himself among the truly faithful. He had viewed himself as the shepherd of his family and town and had vowed to lead them down the path of Christ, but by the time Zapata, Villa, and Venustiano Carranza had all been killed, they no longer trusted, nor would defend, him in the face of adversity.

Untamed by disgrace and hardened by solitude, this shepherd of rebellious souls was inexecrably odious to the flock, and his enemies contrived a singularly successful mode of revenge; Federico was painted with a bridle in his mouth, and a caricature of the Archbishop of Mexico leading the tractable beast to the feet of Christ. The awful mural provoked moral outrage amongst the local yokels, and led to a public ostracism with rotten vegetables.

Federico's motives may have been selfish; his ends always legitimate. He had conspired with the Church, and rebelled without any views of interest. The violence which he inflicted or suffered is celebrated as the spontaneous effect of reason mixed with rascality. The faults of his character became still more conspicuous to those whom had trusted him with their own souls as well as safety.

After 1920, according to my grandfather, he saw the proverbial writing on the wall. The intemperance of his libertine youth had accelerated the infirmities of age, and he cried that he had failed the revolution. Upon learning of Carranza's assassination, he led his men against a brigade loyal to Obregon'. The latter's forces were repeatedly baffled by what they perceived as a rebel's challenge, whom they pursued with seeming contempt and implacable resentment. At the head of sixteen hundred horse, Federico entered Sonora, home state of Obregon'. He might have ravaged the open country, occupied the defenseless pueblos, re-opened the boarded-up churches and took possession of abandoned provisions and materiel, and punished with death his adult and obstinate captives, but the conquests of the rag-tag band were confined to the petty fortress of San Juan De La Cruz.

The federal garrison, invincible to his arms, was oppressed by the paltry artifice of ideals and the superstitious scruple of illiterates. Federico retired with shame and loss from the walls of San Juan and retreated to Guaymas, a port in Sonora, where-from many of his followers came. The march, the siege, the retreat were all harassed by an vexatious, and almost invisible, adversary; and the disappointment of San Juan De La Cruz might have embittered, perhaps shortened, his last days, but he didn't know it yet. In the fullness of his rise to power, Obregon' still felt at his bosom this domestic thorn; his lieutenants were permitted to negotiate a truce, but their adversary was reduced to a shadow of his former self. Without disparagement to his fame, they might have owned that Federico and his loyal men were finally oppressed by the admission of their own defeat. In his extreme danger he applied to other rebel groups associated with Carranza, to Pancho Villa, and to Zapatista guerrilleros for a refuge from the judgment awaiting him. His resources, regrettably, were almost exhausted, leaving him as a fugitive in Sonora,. His intended flight to Durango was impeded by the demoralization and vocal disgust of his men. He was consequently delivered with all of his men to the firing-squad of justice, the vengeance of the people, and the sodomitic intentions of Satan. His fortunes were confiscated, and his aged father, who had fought on the side of the Diaz, then Huerta, reactionaries, was cast into prison. All of his past services were buried in accusations, and his surviving supporters were driven by injustice to perpetrate the crimes of which he was accused.

Upon learning of his fate, a monk entered his cell and prayed with him, repeating an old monastic rule that he thought might help him in his final hours: "shut thy door, and seat thyself in a corner; raise thy mind above all things vain and transitory; recline thy beard and chin on thy breast; turn thy eyes and thy thoughts toward the middle of thy belly, the region of the navel; and search the place of the heart, the seat of the soul. At first, all will be dark and comfortless; but if you persevere day and night, you will feel an ineffable joy; and no sooner has the soul discovered the place of the heart, than it is involved in a mystic and ethereal light."

Well, the latter might be good for a monk, but it certainly left Federico baffled. Despite the self righteous calling that drove him to take up arms on behalf of his Christ, this light the monk was describing was little more than the production of a distempered fancy, the animal of a growling belly and a vacant brain, like all monastic epiphanies are, and no amount of monkish meditation was going to turn him into a saint over-night. He was nonetheless adored by his comrades-in-arms as the pure and perfect essence of Christ himself, or a Mexican proto-Christ at least, for having suffered on their behalf.

For his part, Federico actually questioned what good prayer had produced during that whole time. He even ridiculed his confessor by remarking that as long as the folly was confined to monasteries, no one cared. Furthermore, the simple solitaries were not inquisitive about how the divine essence could be a material substance in any case, or how an immaterial substance could be perceived by the eyes of the body. Federico was not of a mind, and repudiated his Christ during those very hours before his execution.

Writing to his brother, and sending his last will and testament, he stipulated: "Since the death of my mother and the imprisonment of our father, who alone advised me without interest or passion, I am robbed of the Mexico I have so loved, and am instead surrounded by men whom I can love no longer, nor trust, nor esteem. The Federal agents are swayed by their personal or factious views, and how can I consult the monks on questions of amnesty or legal clemency? My commands have ceased to carry weight with my comrades, and my jailers laughed when I asked them to consider that if I am thus perpetually absent from my family, my wife may be tempted either to seek the arms of another man, or to abandon herself to a convent."

After laughing at his apprehensions, the colonel in charge of his imprisonment gravely consoled him by the less-than pleasing assurance that the payment of his debts (his execution) should be his last service to the Mexico he "so loved."

From the outset he had pledged himself to divide with his followers the sweets and the bitters of life, and now they had preceded him to the grave, thus there was nothing left to struggle for or against. The sphere of his attraction had been magnified by the ruin of the proud and the submission of the prudent, thus it was incumbent upon him to accept an early demise, and allow the dead to bury their dead. At the appointed hour, perhaps 12pm, on December 1, 1924, protesting his innocence and accusing his fortune, he was led out to the "field of woe" along with three others, blind-folded and tied to an old tree-stump. His last words were fated, ironically, to be repeated as the lyrics to the battle hymn of the future Cristeros:

> *The Virgin Mary is our protector*
> *and defender when there is something to fear,*
> *She will defeat the demons crying "Long live Christ the King!"*
> *She will defeat the demons crying "Long live Christ the King!"*
> *Soldiers of Christ let us follow the flag*
> *that the Cross shows the army of God!*

He was then shot dead at the age of 45 (as I wrote this, I suddenly remembered that I am 44, and none too certain about the immediate future). His mortal remains were left to the crows and buzzards to dispose of as they saw fit. By the Vespertine hour, his mourners had meekly picked up what was left of his skeleton, and they buried it close to his family home.

Thus ended the legend of Federico de Martin-Lopez de la Cruz y Vivar.

The introduction of barbarians and savages into the contests of civilized nations is a measure fraught with grief and cynicism (so explained the librarian who had allowed me to examine the genealogical archives while I was traveling through Jalisco a couple of months before), and the revolution was a contest between shame and mischief; the governmental barbarians on the winning side had the interest of the moment to compel them and do good for the republic, but the shame of their fancy was reprobated by the worst principles of cruelty and reason. The rebel savages on the losing side employed mischief to grasp at their moment of interest, but itself was reprobated by the best principles of humanity and madness. Grief and cynicism was had, therefore, on both sides before the smoke of retribution had cleared. It was the practice of both sides to accuse their enemies of the guilt of the first alliances. Those who had failed in their negotiations were loudest in their censure of the other's example of order, discipline, and ruthless purpose, which they envied and would gladly imitate.

Federico envied and imitated well.

Thus was the life that inspired my name. Thus was the life of one who gave everything to his faith, his family, and the history of his country. He was not remembered by posterity, at least the way he should have been. He could have inspired a great epic, but even one so knowledgeable of his country's mythology like Fulgencio San Roman somehow missed out and never learned of his existence. This is strange, even mysterious, but my ancestor had more than his fair share of enemies, and they possessed the power of the pen. His memory was therefore ignored by the learned, and those who had actually known and admired him died illiterate, hence failing to honor his name even by an oral tradition.

All that had existed was this very document Becky had discovered while doing some genealogical research for me, and I was not permitted to take it home with me.

Damn!

His memory, nevertheless, just might survive through me.

FORWARD BACK TO AMERICA

Time had run out on this most unforgettable (for all the wrong reasons) and turbulent journey. The time had come to *reverse* my course, and I looked forward to a most welcome end. It was time to back track to the border, and the memory of my ill-remembered ancestor haunted me in the final days of this Mexican sally. He fought for what others believed in, yet clung to a few convictions of his own. He knew, and he certainly understood that everything for which Mexico had torn itself apart had been in vain and could have come about in more peaceful ways. The swashbuckler inside of him, however, just had to glory in the blood-letting and terror. Mexico had triumphed, had overcome the forces of intolerance and stagnation to reinvent itself, and, by the time Lazaro Cardenas assumed the presidency, the victory of the people over tyranny had been declared. And yet, the philosophic strain in his blood was not ashamed to confess that the ruin of his cherished country might be the consequence of a second and similar victory. So much has happened since Federico's death in 1924 that this unrepentant wetback writing this story is paying no mind to what others fear may come in 2012. Actually, many people here, the descendants of the ancient Mayas in particular, think that their world will explode not in 2012, as the Mayas foretold, but by the time they celebrate the Bicentennial of their Independence, and the Centennial of the Revolution, in the fall of 2010.

So, what if the sky falls sooner than later? More of that "who gives a damn" attitude will see them through the worst of it. Mexican history has a strange way of rectifying itself by the mistakes of her people who care not for the lessons of history. The Revolution of 1910 witnessed the onset of ten years of bloody civil war, which ended the lives of over a million wretches, mostly peasants, in a cataclysm of murder, betrayal, rapine, destruction, and tequila binging. And that very cataclysm occurred just over one-hundred years after Miguel Hidalgo gave his "*grito de independencia*" in 1810, which then led to the ten years of bloody murder, arson, destruction, and drunkenness that is known as "Guerra de la Independencia" (War of Independence).

Everyone is now asking themselves: "I wonder what the next ten years have in store for us?"

In Mexico, things do tend to repeat themselves, blindly *and* purposely. Wagging tongues have spread the anxiety that terrible things are oncoming. Narco-traffickers are the new oppressors, the government is as corrupt and inefficient as it has always been ... actually, the last time it was really efficient was during the very dictatorship of Porfirio Diaz. Armed rebel groups are again gathering strength, and, many believe, shall erupt in a bloody reaction against Mexican Society by the time Christmas, 2010 rolls around.

There is really no reason for concern, according to the average Mexican. Things may have been worse back in 1809, before Independence, or in 1909, before the Revolution, but grievances abound at all times. Mexico has known bloody war many times in her history ~ before and after the arrival of the Spaniards with Cortez, and the land does not reject new corpses, which shall fertilize the neglected fields. The peasants may no longer be exploited by the landed gentry, and people exercise their right to vote as never before, but the modern descendants of the sainted *Soldaderas* are brutalized still by the most cruel criminal violence and social repression in its history, and reeling from one of the most miserable economic recessions. An intellectual from the University of Mexico, in Mexico City complained that "We are very near a social crisis ...The conditions are there."

Mexican mutinies have coincided with significant dates, and many people know it, yet laugh at the suggestion that history does repeat itself. In any case, Zapatista guerrillas did in fact unleash an insurrection in the poor, underdeveloped state of Chiapas on the 1st of January, 1994, the very day that the new NAFTA, or North American Trade Agreement, took effect. Was this a coincidence? Or did the Zapatistas feel that Yankee Doodle was again invading their sacred land to turn it into one big *maquiladora*, or sweat-shoppe, for the over-fed Gringoes?

A festering fear bites at the ears of ordinary citizens, that the seemingly all-powerful drug cartels, which have cold-bloodedly murdered about 15,000 hapless suckers during a period of ten years, are trading their armaments and materiel to the restless guerrillas. They are ready to pounce on the imagination of Mexicans willing to trade the inertia of their circumstances for the thrill of seeing their country blown apart by the accumulated anger of the most desperate, and the resurgent barbarity of the worst, of their compatriots.

Whatever the fears of the average folk, it appears that the plan of the malcontents may be to spread Bicentennial terror, have ordinary Mexicans betray their allegiance to President Felipe Calderon' and his successors, and repudiate his drug-war offensive. The seizure of immense weapons arsenals over the course of the present administration, allegedly transferred from the Zetas, a savage drug gang, to Jose' Enrique Hernandez, a notorious head-buster of the rebel group called the Popular Revolutionary Army (EPR), has not stemmed the tide of resentment. The EPR in recent years has boasted of its terrorist reprisals against government officials, and assaults on the Mexican oil infrastructure, including the destruction of six pipelines in the last few years. Although Hernandez repudiated the charges, many Mexicans, from what I have gathered during my illegal stay, have actually cheered him on.

Meanwhile, I've noticed that political pundits regularly express their worry that provincial governments, like that of Michoacan, which have had more than their fair share of terrorist attacks and related government corruption, and where weapons caches have been discovered, are using the fear of a 2010 apocalypse as an excuse for reactionary social reprisals. "They're drawing questionable parallels between those who fight for the poor and the self-serving armed terrorists," a journalist friend of mine warned me, and added that there is no sign that Hernandez has anything to do with the EPR despite claims to the contrary. So, what is the ordinary fool supposed to believe? The drug cartels are ready as ever to exploit popular national holidays as excuses for narco-terror. Last year, for example, during Independence Day festivities in drug-infested Michoacan, narcos brutally murdered seven innocent bystanders with fragmentation-grenade explosions. Mexicans were shaken again in September when bombs exploded at three Mexico City banks, and another near an old 16th Century church. No one, from what I gathered, was hurt, but to many *chilangos*, or capital residents, the blasts appeared to be an omen of things to come.

Apart from over-reported guerrilla and drug-cartel violence, another specter is the unrest surging like some swamp creature from Mexico's besieged economy. Given its enormous reliance on the production of oil for income, and its slavery to the American market, and not to mention remittances from Mexican wetbacks, legal or illegal, living and thriving there, which tumbled unexpectedly following the loss of their jobs, the global recession has hit Mexico where it really hurts. Unemployment has exacerbated Mexico's chronic poverty as well, while nearly 30 million people face hunger every day. A report I'd recently read by the Colegio de Mexico, one of the country's top universities, warned, "A national social explosion is knocking at the door."

Then, the head Roman Catholic Bishop, Gustavo Rodriguez, cried on television that, "We cannot separate the economic crisis from the violence and criminal crisis that we live day by day."

So much for looking forward to salvation from above!

While many are afraid the Bicentennial observances could aggravate the fermenting discontent, most notably with the symbolic parallels surrounding 1810 and 1910, the president, along with his ministers, insists that Mexico will break free from horrors that menace its very existence, and the awful historical cycle will come to an inevitable end. In fact, many believe 2010 will be a time of peaceful transformation, and to have that happen requires only the positive affirmation of the natives. Furthermore, just in the last couple of months I've heard many say that they believe Mexico to be on a different course, inching toward reform, the restoration of peace, and lasting financial recovery. And yet, the voice of democracy has been strangely silent given threats that entrenched political groups conspire to remove constraints on re-election for Mexican office-holders, which they call "major political reforms." It would be a change, they insist, that will give the voters more power, though they may lose their freedom of choice. They obviously count on the old historical adage that for evil to triumph, good need only do nothing to stop it. The move is significant, moreover, because, on the eve of the Bicentennial, many recall that the present ban on re-election was a pillar of the Revolution of 1910.

Before anyone, including the president, can use the Bicentennial as a means by which to effect the much heralded change, notwithstanding, something, anything, must happen to jar the ever-whining majority out of its smug intransigence. The economic crisis has forced chronic delays for most of the projects the government, along with private groups, had in the offing. Fortunately for Mexicans, their "me vale madre" attitude has spared them much grief with respect to the imminent doom forecast for 2010. On the contrary, they seem to be, according to my correspondents, sick and tired of the warmed-over economic crap flung at them by the financial power-brokers, and are ever-willing to turn on their leaders for serving it to them cold. The Bicentennial year might not offer the fireworks of a revolution, but, unless Mexico can escape its overall miasma of trouble, perennially hanging over the ever-deferred promise of prosperity, the year shall witness a melancholy and dispiriting cultural and political devolution.

Many in this exasperating country still want to blame America for ALL of its ills, but this incurable jealousy and resentment still rankle in the hearts of the inexorably bonded nations, which have despised each other, the one as a wilderness of barbarians, and the other as an extensive plantation of slaves ever since Davy Crockett called it quits at the Alamo. Ignorance is the ground of suspicion, the wise have said, and suspicion has been inflamed into daily provocations since that moment they signed the NAFTA agreement. And, if not caused by the leaders, certainly their respective citizenry have causes to gripe: prejudice is blind, hunger is deaf; and Mexico (if taken as a metaphor for its leadership) is accused, even by her own dissidents, of a design to starve its people out of their pride, sense of purpose, and national dignity.

I have tried to read as much of Mexico's classic literature while I could, and in some 19th Century folk-tale there is a fable of a *campesino* (peasant), who was ruined by the answer to his own prayers: he had prayed for water; the Rio Bravo was turned into his grounds, and his flock and cottage were swept away by the inundation. Such was the fate deserved by, or at least it was the belief of, the commons in praying for the unattainable since it leads to divine punishment for conceit and presumption, hence the recurring reason for all of Mexico's woes.

They esteem themselves, nevertheless, as the first of the North American nations; but this foolish arrogance has been humbled by the unfortunate events of their social, narco-trafficking, and guerrilla wars against their elected governments, not to mention the very inhabitants they pretend to defend and protect.

Fortune has left Mexico little to lose, except its identity; with all the hate, murder, and narco-trafficking going around, Mexicans seem to have lost their respect for life, and to despise life is the first qualification of a rebel ~ a label many Mexicans gleefully embrace. Regarding the narco-traffickers and their despicable ways, assassination has been their recourse in view of the government crackdown as of late, yet they do not seem to know that assassination is the last resource of cowards ~ an insulting charge your average Mexican will not deign to forgive.

Whether or not Mexicans really care for their future or the sanctity of their national identity, they are still distinguished by the subtlety and sublimity of their understandings, and they are the first ones to boast of it; but these qualities, unless dignified by liberty and illuminated by contemplation, will decay into a base and boorish cleverness (at least that is what historians write). It is a proverbial saying of the persecuted descendants of Moctezuma, "From the Spanish caballeros who oppress our bodies, the monks who torment our souls, and the hacendados who starve us into humiliation, Good Lord deliver us!"

The *Gachupines* (Spanish) and Criollo *hacendados*, or wealthy cattle-ranchers, always walked with supine disdain among the glorious ruins of Aztec and Maya antiquity; and such was the destitution of their character, that they seemed incapable of admiring the genius of the people from whom they stole this country.

In the great revolutionary struggle for reform, restoration of rights, and restitution of ancestral lands, the vigor of opposition was succeeded by the lassitude of despair, and the common folk ended up no better economically than they had been before the ouster of Diaz, except that now they were nominally in control.

Yes, it is true that some lasting gains were made, democracy proceeded along a difficult and dangerous course, and freedom, in all of its political forms, is the first step to curiosity and knowledge. The latter did not exactly flourish, but they slowly re-awakened in the consciousness of Mexicans, and the pleasing reign of poetry and fanciful fiction was succeeded by the light of speculative and empirical philosophy, and today Mexicans are as literate as the citizens of advanced industrialized nations. Genius may anticipate the season of maturity, say the wise men, but in the instruction of a people, as in that of any person, the memory must be massaged before the powers of reason and imagination can be expanded. The artist may not hope to equal or surpass, till he has learned to emulate, the works of his predecessors ~ and what predecessors Mexicans have had!

This portrait of Mexico was transcribed from the diaries of an historian of the revolutionary period; but the adulation of a servile and superstitious people has been lavished on the worst of tyrants, incompetents, the corrupt and the frivolous. The virtues of demagogues and political charlatans are often the vices most useful to their ambitions, or most agreeable to those who voted for them. A nation ignorant of the equal benefits of liberty and law, as Mexico was during the Porfiriato, must be awed by the flashes of arbitrary power. The cruelty of despots, like Huerta or Calles, or the corruption of most of the PRI (Partido Revolucionario Institucional) leaders after World War II, assumed the character of justice; their profusion, of liberality; their obstinacy, of firmness. If the most rational pretext be denied, few acts of obedience will be found impossible. Thus, guilt must tremble where innocence is threatened, and conviction takes cover where doubt lurks about.

Heaven and earth must rejoice in the perdition of miscreants, but Mexico laments losers more than she lauds the virtuous and brave.

As for my now sainted, departed ancestor, Fulgencio San Roman, I learned that the more you try to chase life down, the more you are renounced to it when comes the awakening to vanity and the vexation that carnal pursuits bring. Ambition, he would say, is a weed of quick and early vegetation in the vineyard of dreams. But, there is also inconstancy to be had in the swamp of superstitions, and his art, his imagination depended on all those ugly and inconstant creatures that inhabit this swamp of the subconscious.

He held his metaphorical mirror to life, and it reflected images of his people he would have preferred not to behold. He admired and at once deplored the currents of thought running below the facade of conventionality. Such powerful motives should have firmly attached the voluntary and pious obedience of the Mexican people to their spiritual and temporal attachments. But, the machinations of partiality and of interest are often upset by the sallies of undisciplined passion.

The Indian who fells the tree that he may gather the fruit, and the Mestizo who plunders the trains of commerce, are actuated by the same impulse of savage nature, which overlooks the future in the present, and renounces for momentary rapine the long and secure advantage of the most important blessings. And, it was thus that the country was profaned by the thoughtless revolutionaries and so-called reformers. They pillaged the offerings and wounded the faithful without computing the number and value of similar commerce, which they prevented by their inhospitable terrorism. Even the influence of superstition is fluctuating and precarious, and the Cristeros and other defenders of the Church's prerogatives in Mexico were no better; and the slave, whose reason is chained to the pillar of fear, will often be delivered by his avarice or pride. Mexicans have somehow managed to conciliate ambition and avarice since those terrible days during and following the Cristero War. The generations who went though all that are dying off, and the newer ones are screwing things up again for their own gain.

A credulous devotion for the fables, supernatural visions and oracles of the Catholic priesthood most powerfully acts on the mind of a Mexican; yet such a mind is the least capable of preferring imagination to sense, of sacrificing to a distant motive the appetites and interests of the present world. It sacrifices to an invisible object, perhaps an improbable ideal. In the vigor of health and youth, Fulgencio's practice would perpetually contradict his beliefs till the pressures of age, sickness, and calamities awakened his terrors, and compelled him to satisfy the double debt of piety and remorse. Under the reign of superstition, he had much to hope from the ignorance, and much to fear from the violence, of his fellow Mexicans.

Of the vanity and arrogance of Mexicans, what can I say? A nation nursed in sedition, intractable and scorning to obey, unless they are too feeble to resist. They have been feeble for too long not to have noticed what became of their precious revolution of a hundred years ago. When they promised to serve, they aspired to prosper; if they swore allegiance, they watched the opportunity of revolt. Yet, they vented their discontent in loud clamors. Yet, their doors, and their counsels, were shut against them. Dexterous in mischief, they have never learned the science of doing good in good conscience; such displays of do-gooding were only viable as public pronouncements of piety and Christian humility. *Odious to earth and heaven, impious to God, seditious among themselves, jealous of their neighbors*, as Fulgencio once wrote, and inhuman to strangers (who have no money, as I observed), they love no one, by no fellow Mexican are they beloved; and while they wish to inspire fear amongst themselves, they live in base and continual apprehension of the outside world, especially of the colossus directly to the north.

Thus wrote Fulgencio just before passing away: "Lofty in promise, poor in execution; adulation and calumny, perfidy and treason, are the familiar traits of their collective character.

They will not submit. They know not how to govern. Faithless to their betters, intolerable to their equals, ungrateful to their benefactors, and alike impudent in their demands and their refusals, they are my people. They are my blood!"

And with that, no more excuses would matter.

A Wetback in Reverse

EPILOGUE

The last feeling has departed from the heart of charity. I would broker no more bullshit, no more prejudice and intolerance. There wasn't much to reflect upon, only the end of an extraordinary, tedious, scary year-long journey. I departed with an indictment of Mexico for lauding itself a failed state whereby I ended up whispering to myself, "Me vale madre!"

My friend Billy's words would resonate in my head, round and round, during my final hours in Mexico: *Free your mind, and your ass will follow*!

Well, my mind was free. I had now to get the old butt in gear to head North once more. No more tacos, no more beans, only introspection.

... Thus I left old Mexico ~ as magical, musical, mystical, muddle-headed, and certainly as malodorous as I had entered it!

THE END

www.ingramcontent.com/pod-product-compliance
Lightning Source LLC
Chambersburg PA
CBHW022048160426
43198CB00008B/160